REVOLUTIONARY ENGLAND AND THE NATIONAL COVENANT

STATE OATHS, PROTESTANTISM AND THE POLITICAL NATION, 1553–1682

This book studies the oaths and covenants taken during the late sixteenth to the late seventeenth century, a time of great religious and political upheaval, assessing their effect and importance. From the reign of Mary I to the Exclusion crisis, Protestant writers argued that England was a nation in covenant with God and urged that the country should renew its contract with the Lord through taking solemn oaths. In so doing, they radically modified understandings of monarchy, political allegiance and the royal succession. During the civil war, the tendering of oaths of allegiance, the Protestation of 1641 and the Vow and Covenant and Solemn League and Covenant of 1643 (all described as embodiments of England's national covenant) also extended the boundaries of the political nation. The poor and illiterate, women as well as men, all subscribed to these tests of loyalty, which were presented as social contracts between the Parliament and the people. The Solemn League and Covenant in particular continued to provoke political controversy after 1649, and even into the 1690s many English Presbyterians still viewed themselves as bound by its terms; the author argues that these covenants had a significant, and until now unrecognised, influence on 'politics-out-of-doors' in the eighteenth century.

Edward Vallance is lecturer in early modern British history at the University of Liverpool. He is currently writing a new history of the Glorious Revolution.

REVOLUTIONARY ENGLAND AND THE NATIONAL COVENANT

State Oaths, Protestantism and the
Political Nation, 1553–1682

Edward Vallance

THE BOYDELL PRESS

First published 2005
The Boydell Press, Woodbridge

ISBN 1 84383 118 X

The Boydell Press is an imprint of Boydell & Brewer Ltd
PO Box 9, Woodbridge, Suffolk IP12 3DF, UK
and of Boydell & Brewer Inc.
668 Mount Hope Avenue, Rochester, NY 14620, USA
website: www.boydellandbrewer.com

A CIP catalogue record for this book is available from the British Library

Library of Congress Cataloging-in-Publication Data
Vallance, Edward, 1975–
Revolutionary England and the national covenant : state oaths, Protestantism, and
the political nation, 1553–1682 / Edward Vallance.
p. cm.
Includes bibliographical references and index.
ISBN 1-84383-118-X (alk. paper)
1. Great Britain—Politics and government—1603–1714. 2. Church and
state—Great Britain—History—17th century. 3. Church and state—Great Britain—
History—16th century. 4. Great Britain—Politics and government—1485–1603.
5. Great Britain—Politics and government—1642–1660. 6. Protestantism—
England—History—17th century. 7. Protestantism—England—History—16th
century. 8. Oaths—Great Britain—History—17th century. 9. Oaths—Great
Britain—History—16th century. 10. Reformation—England. I. Title.

DA375.V35 2005
942.06—dc22
2004019947

This publication is printed on acid-free paper
Typeset by Keystroke, Jacaranda Lodge, Wolverhampton
Printed in Great Britain at
the University Press, Cambridge

Contents

Acknowledgements	vii
Abbreviations and conventions	viii
Introduction: the idea of a national covenant	1
1 The origins of the idea of a national covenant in England	6

PART I THE LONG PARLIAMENT AND THE NATIONAL
COVENANT

2 Protestation, Vow and Covenant	51
3 Covenants and allegiance, 1641–1646	61
4 Secular contracts or religious covenants?	82
5 Protestation, Vow and Covenant: the public response	102

PART II THE SOLEMN LEAGUE AND COVENANT, 1644–1682

6 'A Covenant for Liberty of Conscience': the Levellers, the Diggers and the national covenant	133
7 The Covenant, the execution of Charles I and the English republic	157
8 Covenants, oaths and the Restoration settlement	179
Epilogue: 'For the Preservation of Our Happy Constitution in Church and State': Protestant associations in the eighteenth century	200
Conclusion	217
Select bibliography	223
Index	245

Acknowledgements

This book has been a very long time in gestation and the longer it has gone on, the more debts, intellectual, emotional and pecuniary, I have accumulated. My Oxford D.Phil. thesis from which this book has sprung (or more accurately emerged) was ably guided by Dr Robert Beddard and Dr Jonathan Powis. Dr John Spurr was very generous in sharing his own research on oath taking. The British Academy paid the bills. My external examiners Professor John Morrill and Dr Mark Goldie gave me some very good pointers as to where to take the project next. The Faculty of Arts at the University of Sheffield did me the great service of appointing me De Velling Willis Post-Doctoral Faculty Research Fellow, a job title almost as long as the term of appointment, during which incarnation most of the additional research for the book was completed. Sheffield was a great place to start my academic career and I will always look back on my two years there fondly. Various people at various times have looked at and commented on my work. In particular I would like to thank Profs Mike Braddick, Mark Greengrass, Steven Pincus and J. C. Davis, and Dr Mark Knights. As ever, what doesn't slavishly follow their suggestions is my own work. Portions of this book have also been delivered at seminars and conferences in Hull, Sheffield, Cambridge, Oxford, Reading and, less glamorously, Chicago and I thank those that attended for their questions and comments. I have also been lucky at first Sheffield and then the University of Manchester to teach enthusiastic and intelligent students on my civil war courses who kept me on my toes. Other bits of this book have appeared in journals, including *EHR*, *Historical Journal*, *Historical Research*, *Albion*, *Huntington Library Quarterly* and *The Seventeenth Century*. I appreciate these journals' consent in reproducing extracts from my articles and for their help in developing my arguments. Especial thanks of course go to Peter Sowden at Boydell & Brewer for agreeing to take the book on, and to John Walter, both for his support for the project and for his insightful criticism of those chapters that came his way. Thanks as ever go to my Mum and Dad for supporting my rather bizarre career choice and for always taking an interest in my work. Finally, I dedicate this book to my wife Linnie, without whom none of this would have been possible. Linnie, you don't have to read it all the way through, but this one's for you.

Abbreviations and conventions

Unless otherwise stated, the place of publication for works printed before 1800 is London. The first letters of principal words in the titles of books and articles have been capitalised. The original capitalisation and spelling have been retained in quotations from primary sources. As a number of oaths are seen as embodying a national covenant with God, they have been distinguished from each other in the following way: the Commons Protestation of 1641 is referred to as the Protestation, the Vow and Covenant of 1643 as the Vow, and the Solemn League and Covenant of the same year as the Covenant. For allusions to covenant theology or to a generic national covenant the lower case 'covenant' is preferred.

The following abbreviations are used in this book:

BL	British Library
Bodl.	Bodleian Library
CJ	*Journals of the House of Commons*
Cobbett, *Parl. Deb.*	*Parliamentary Debates*, ed. W. Cobbett (London, 1812–)
CSPD	*Calendar of State Papers Domestic Series*
CSPV	*Calendar of State Papers Venetian Series*
ERO	Essex Record Office
HLRO	House of Lords Record Office.
LJ	*Journals of the House of Lords*
PRO	Public Record Office, Kew
Rel. Bax.	*Reliquiae Baxterianae, or Mr Richard Baxter's Narrative of the Most Memorable Passages of His Life and Times Faithfully Publish'd from His Own Original Manuscript by Matthew Sylvester* (1696)
SR	*The Statutes of the Realm* (9 vols, London, 1805–22)

Introduction

The idea of a national covenant

> But remark, at least, how natural to any agitated Nation, which has Faith,
> this business of Covenanting is.
>
> Thomas Carlyle[1]

This book is a study of the significance of the idea of an English national
covenant from the middle of the sixteenth to the late seventeenth century,
but focusing in particular on the civil war. Here the term national covenant
is used to describe the notion of a nation or nations in a covenanted relationship with God, in which the faithfulness of the people in keeping their
covenant (by defending the gospel, praying, fasting, supporting good ministers
and their co-religionists abroad) corresponds to the nation's temporal success,
and the fortunes (earthly and spiritual) of individuals within the covenant.
This idea was incorporated into actual political practices, namely the making
and taking of oaths and associations. It is a concept which has important ramifications for our understanding of the nature of political thought, contemporary
attitudes towards the early modern English polity and questions of political
allegiance. It is not an examination, more broadly, of the term 'covenant' in
this period. Historians, including Perry Miller, Christopher Hill, Michael
Walzer and David Zaret, have linked the discussion of covenants in theological
discourse to legal changes in forms of land ownership and to what they see as
an increasingly commercially orientated society.[2] Certainly, many instances
occur in which preachers used economic analogies in discussing the covenants
between God, man and the nation (although it is not clear whether this
represents much more than godly ministers' preference for a 'plain style' of
preaching, using comparisons that would be familiar to an unlearned audience

---

[1] T. Carlyle, *The French Revolution: A History* (3 vols., London, 1898), ii, 42.
[2] P. Miller, *The New England Mind: Part One the Seventeenth Century* (Cambridge, Mass.,
1954 edn.), pp. 412–15. Elsewhere Miller describes the idea of a national covenant as a
'downright commercial' bargain between God and the nation, ibid., p. 485; C. Hill, *The
English Bible and the Seventeenth Century Revolution* (London, 1993), pp. 271–84; M. Walzer,
The Revolution of the Saints: A Study in the Origins of Radical Politics (London, 1966), p. 168:
D. R. Zaret, 'An Analysis of the Development and Content of the Covenant Theology of
Pre-Revolutionary Puritanism' (Oxford Univ. D.Phil., 1977), pp. 95–179; *idem*, *The
Heavenly Contract: Ideology and Organisation in Pre-Revolutionary Puritanism* (Chicago, 1985).

to open up Biblical texts).[3] However, a wider investigation of the covenant idea in early modern England would clearly have merited at least another book-sized study on its own (and probably one considerably larger than this present work).

This book grew out of a doctoral thesis on oaths of loyalty in England, concentrating on the period from 1640 to 1702.[4] That thesis was concerned with whether the power of the oath as a means to bind individuals to truthfulness and fidelity was in decline in this period. As a means of approaching this question, it looked at the ways in which individuals resolved moral dilemmas raised by taking oaths through applying the methods of casuistry. In so doing, the thesis addressed many of the themes at the heart of work on oaths by historians such as John Spurr, Christopher Hill and David Martin Jones.[5] However, the thesis departed from the approach of these historians in two important ways. First, unlike much historical work on oath taking in early modern England, in particular David Martin Jones's book-length study, the thesis exploited existing records of public subscription to oaths of allegiance as a way of uncovering the public's response to these demands for their loyalty. Secondly, the thesis also uncovered the ways in which many oaths of allegiance were also described as national covenants.

It is the reinterpretation of oaths in this way, as constituting sworn contracts with God involved as a party, rather than as merely a witness, which is the central concern of this study. During the civil war the Long Parliament's main oaths of loyalty, the Protestation of 1641 and the Vow and Covenant and Solemn League and Covenant of 1643, were all described as reaffirmations or renewals of England's national covenant. Yet, whereas the theological, social, cultural and political underpinnings of the Scottish National Covenant of 1638 have been examined in great detail, the English use of the term 'national covenant' has gone almost unnoticed.[6] Indeed, some historians (without, it

---

[3] Is it any more significant, for example, than the use of proverbial wisdom by ministers? On which see now A. Fox, *Oral and Literate Culture in England, 1500–1800* (Oxford, 2001).
[4] E. Vallance, 'State Oaths and Political Casuistry in England, 1640–1702' (Oxford University D. Phil. thesis, 2000).
[5] J. Spurr, 'Perjury, Profanity and Politics', *The Seventeenth Century*, viii (1993), 29–50; *idem*, 'A Profane History of Early Modern Oaths', *TRHS*, 11 (2001), 37–63; *idem*, '"The Strongest Bond of Conscience": Oaths and the Limits of Tolerance in Early Modern England', in *Contexts of Conscience in Early Modern Europe 1500–1700*, eds. H. Braun and E. Vallance (Basingstoke, 2004); D. M. Jones, *Conscience and Allegiance in Seventeenth Century England: The Political Significance of Oaths and Engagements* (Woodbridge, 1999); C. Hill, 'From Oaths to Interest', in his *Society and Puritanism in Pre-Revolutionary England* (London, 1964), ch. 11; C. Robbins, 'Selden's Pills: State Oaths in England, 1558–1714', *Huntington Library Quarterly*, 35 (1972), 303–21.
[6] D. Stevenson, *The Scottish Revolution 1637–44: The Triumph of the Covenanters* (Newton Abbot, 1973); A. I. MacInnes, *Charles I and the Making of the Covenanting Movement 1625–1641* (Edinburgh, 1991); *The Scottish National Covenant in its British Context*, ed. J. S. Morrill (Edinburgh, 1990).

should be noted, much supporting evidence) have argued that the concept never took hold in an English context. Others, namely Michael McGiffert, have suggested that though a politically charged notion of a national covenant was evident in Elizabethan England, it effectively disappeared with the failure of the classical Presbyterian movement in the 1580s.[7] (Indeed, I followed this line of argument in one of my own articles, in which I contended that the notion had to be reintroduced by the Scots into England in the late 1630s.)[8] As this study demonstrates, though, the idea of a national covenant for reformation had been a part of English political discourse going back to the reign of Mary, it was integral to Elizabethan plans for an 'association' to defend the Protestant succession and was still being publicly discussed in the reign of James.

However, this book is meant to do rather more than just 'fill a gap' in our knowledge of seventeenth-century England by showing us that there was indeed an English discussion of the idea of a national covenant. The reinterpretation of oaths of loyalty as national covenants had important ramifications. It redefined loyalty in primarily religious terms, making the monarch essentially a vehicle for defending Protestantism from attack and furthering the process of reformation. As the public discussion and tendering of oaths of association demonstrated, the covenant idea could provide justifications for overriding the hereditary line of descent in order to ensure a Protestant succession. Further-more, viewed in this way, the king or queen could be deemed a covenanted monarch, owed loyalty by his or her subjects only so far as s/he fulfilled his/her contracted duties to defend the faith. A reigning monarch who neglected these duties, or worse was deemed an active opponent of Protestantism, could be resisted on religious grounds. As we will see, this introduces some qualifications into the general consensus amongst historians that Parliamentarian writers largely advanced secular arguments for resisting the king's forces in the early 1640s.

This is also a study of the impact of the idea of a national covenant upon early modern understandings of the political nation. To a considerable extent, this book is concerned with the pamphlet discussion of the national covenant idea and this printed debate was largely the preserve of puritan ministers. Yet, as a concept incorporated into oaths of allegiance, such as the Protestation, and tendered to adult males (and often women as well) across the country, these devices had an impact upon a far broader segment of the population than just rival writers or the literate readers of pamphlets. As we will see, the response of many subscribers to these covenants was hostile and some with Royalist/

---

[7] Miller and McGiffert's approaches to the idea of a national covenant are discussed in greater detail below, pp. 28–30.

[8] E. Vallance, '"An Holy and Sacramentall Paction": Federal Theology and the Solemn League and Covenant in England', *English Historical Review*, 116 (2001), 50–75. This article reappears here in revised form as Chapter 4.

Anglican sympathies rejected them outright. Others refused for fear of forswearing themselves in taking conflicting oaths of loyalty, seemingly unconvinced of or oblivious to the arguments of ministers that these were all renewals or reaffirmations of one national covenant.

Yet, it is argued that in three main ways the public subscription to these covenants was highly significant. First, these covenants, for strategic as well as religious reasons, were intended to force subscribers to reject local allegiances in favour of national loyalties. There has been a massive growth in recent years in historical works on English and British nationalism and concepts of national identity in the early modern period, sparked off by Benedict Anderson's notion of nations as intellectual constructs, the publication of Linda Colley's superb *Britons* and the ruminations on Britishness that devolution has provoked.[9] Previously seen as a phenomenon of the post-1789 world, discussions of English national consciousness have now been tracked as far back as the writings of the Venerable Bede.[10] Religion has been seen as a prime factor in shaping national identity in this period, and Patrick Collinson has linked these discussions of nationalism before the French Revolution to the concept of a national covenant. In their use of the 'Israelite paradigm', comparing sixteenth and seventeenth-century England to the Old Testament Jewish kingdoms as being alike God's most favoured people, St Paul's Cross and fast sermon preachers regularly appealed to the idea of the elect nation. This was a nuanced form of national identity. As Collinson points out, although this rhetoric often took on a jingoistic tone, ministers usually referred to England as an elect nation, not as the definitive article. Equally, as this study will demonstrate, the idea of national covenant could often be applied to a federal covenant between Protestant nations, either in terms of a British union or a pan-European association of reformed countries.[11] That said, Alexandra Walsham is right to question to what extent the audiences listening to these sermons were able to pick up on this distinction or whether they simply took in John Aylmer's soundbite that 'God is English'.[12]

Subscription to these covenants also involved a broadening of the boundaries of the political nation. Individuals whose wealth or sex excluded

---

[9] Benedict Anderson, *Imagined Communities: Reflections on the Origin and Spread of Nationalism* (London, 1983); L. Colley, *Britons: Forging the Nation 1707–1837* (London, 1992); for an example of the kind of vapid navel gazing on Britishness that became popular in the 1990s see M. Leonard, *Britain TM: Renewing Our Identity* (Demos, 1997).

[10] P. Wormald, 'The Venerable Bede and the "Church of the English"', in *The English Religious Tradition and the Genius of Anglicanism*, ed. G. Rowell (Wantage, 1992); P. Wormald, J. Gillingham and C. Richmond, 'Elton and the English: A Discussion', *TRHS*, 7 (1997), 317–36.

[11] P. Collinson, 'Biblical Rhetoric: The English Nation and National Sentiment in the Prophetic Mode', in *Religion and Culture in Renaissance England*, eds. C. McEachern and D. Shuger (Cambridge, 1997), ch. 2.

[12] A. Walsham, *Providence in Early Modern England* (Oxford, 1999), p. 289.

them from participating in elections were brought into the political process through swearing to these covenants. Although failure to subscribe was often punished, the extent to which these were devices signed under duress was undercut by the rhetoric of Parliamentarian ministers who stressed the secular as well as religious benefits of subscribing. The subscriber was presented as being not only personally involved in the process of religious reformation (leading some, as we will see, to take this as giving sanction to the use of direct action against perceived idolatrous images and places of worship) but also as being involved in a secular contract, in which the Parliament promised to defend the subjects' rights and liberties in return for their allegiance. Groups such as the Levellers and Diggers, influenced by this Parliamentarian rhetoric and, in Gerrard Winstanley's case, by the actual experience of subscribing to the Solemn League and Covenant, used these covenants as models for their proto-constitutions, the Agreements of the People and the Law of Freedom in a Platform.

Finally, although the restoration of the Stuart monarchy saw all civic and ecclesiastical office-holders required to repudiate the Solemn League and Covenant on pain of deprivation, these covenants continued to have an important impact on politics 'out-of-doors' well into the eighteenth century. Protestant associations, which had been interlinked with the concept of a national covenant since the Elizabethan era, remained a vital weapon for securing the Protestant succession and were revived in 1696, 1715 and 1745. However, their connection to the Long Parliament's covenants was severed in the public memory, through a fear both of radical Whigs hijacking these associations to pursue reformist agendas and of Jacobite opponents conversely accusing the Whig leadership of being old Parliamentarians in sheep's clothing.

What follows is an attempt to remove this lacuna in our understanding of the idea of a national covenant and delineate the significance of its application in an English context. To provide a background to the discussion of the national covenant in the period of the civil war, the book begins by examining the emergence of the idea in English political discourse from the reign of Mary Tudor to the end of Charles I's personal rule.

1

The origins of the idea of a national covenant in England

This introductory chapter deals in broadly chronological fashion with the discussion of the idea of a national covenant in England from the 1550s to the opening of the Long Parliament. It begins by looking at the role of the concept in English political thought from the reign of Mary to the 1580s. It then discusses the relationship between the device of an oath of association, binding English Protestants together in a union to defend the monarch, and the national covenant idea. It moves on to trace the subsequent impact of federal theology upon the notion of a nation in covenant with God, examining the arguments of Perry Miller, Michael McGiffert and T. D. Bozeman concerning the connection (or lack of) between the individual covenant of grace and corporate covenants. Concurring with Bozeman, it is argued that in England, the nation's entrance into covenant with God was seen as conferring both secular and spiritual benefits. However, the chapter contends that federal theology, unlike the political and religious circumstances of Mary's reign, did not represent a formative influence upon the idea of a national covenant. In the light of this historiographical analysis, the chapter looks at the importance of the idea of England as a covenanted nation to sermon jeremiads and public fasts. It finishes by examining the most controversial of these jeremiads, those delivered against the backdrop of the Thirty Years War which called for the abandonment of James I's pacific foreign policy. It contrasts the suppression of these arguments in England with the renewed importance of the idea of a national covenant in Scotland. The chapter suggests, however, that attempting to determine which nation exerted the greatest influence overall in this understanding of a national covenant, Scotland or England, is pointless given the degree to which it was part of a shared Anglo-Scottish Protestant culture.

Political thought

The sermons Hugh Latimer delivered at the court of Edward VI compared the young king to the biblical monarch Josiah. The comparison was based not only on their equivalent age but also the fact that Josiah had presided over the providential discovery of the law by the priest and its reinstatement as the governing principle according to which Judah was ruled. Latimer set the king's office in the conditional terms of Deuteronomy 17, demanding that

Edward should set his face against mere political counsel and instead follow the promptings of the word. Like Josiah, the king should complete his reforms by symbolically renewing the nation's covenant with God.[1] Presciently, Latimer warned of the dire consequences that would befall England if the next in line to the throne should marry a foreign prince, presenting such a match as the likely outcome if the nation failed to suppress covetousness and vice. 'God', Latimer said, had given England 'a deliverer, a natural king; let us seek no stranger of another nation.'[2] The accession of Mary to the throne, her marriage to Philip of Spain, and the return of Catholicism fulfilled Latimer's prophecy, and it presented those divines that fled into exile on the continent with a number of quandaries. How could they deal with England's apostasy from the reformed faith and how were they to reconcile their earlier preaching up of obedience and the royal supremacy with the policies their divinely appointed monarch was now pursuing?

The response of a significant number of reformers was to continue to stick to the doctrines of passive obedience and the evil of rebellion that had been earlier promulgated by Thomas Cranmer before the Devonshire rebels in 1549. Edwin Sandys refused to be liberated from jail by Wyatt's army or to sanction their rebellion, falling back on divine providence, stating that 'if this rising be of God, it will take place; if not, it will fall.' Others submitted to a martyr's fate rather than resist or take flight.[3] Yet, amongst those exiles that gravitated to Geneva after the disputes amongst the English ministers at Frankfurt, theories of resistance emerged which were far more radical, especially in their sanctioning of tyrannicide by private individuals, than anything previously produced by Protestant theologians either within or outside England. It is in these works of resistance theory that we find the first explicit discussion of the idea of a national covenant in English.

Certainly, not all of the Genevan exiles adopted the covenant idea as the basis for their resistance theory. John Ponet's important *A Short Treatise of Politike Power* (1556) made no real use of the idea of a national covenant.[4]

---

[1] C. Davies, '"Poor Persecuted Flock" or "Commonwealth of Christians": Edwardian Protestant Concepts of the Church', in *Protestantism and the National Church in Sixteenth-Century England*, eds. P. Lake and Maria Dowling (London, 1987), pp. 78–102, at p. 88.

[2] *Sermons by Hugh Latimer*, ed. Rev. G. E. Gorrie (Cambridge, Parker Society, 1844), pp. 91–2.

[3] G. Bowler, 'Marian Protestants and the Idea of Violent Resistance to Tyranny', in *Protestantism and the National Church*, eds. Lake and Dowling, pp. 124–43.

[4] [J. Ponet], A Short Treatise of Politike Power (1556). For Ponet see, C. H. Garrett, *The Marian Exiles 1553–1559* (Cambridge, 1938), pp. 254–8; B. Peardon, 'The Politics of Polemic: John Ponet's *Short Treatise of Politike Power* and Contemporary Circumstance, 1553–1556', *Journal of British Studies*, 22 (1982), 35–50; G. Redworth, 'Bishop Ponet, John Stow, and Wyatt's Rebellion of 1554', *Bodleian Library Record*, 16 (1999), 508–12. As we will see, Ponet's work was a significant influence on Parliamentarian writers. The text was reprinted in 1639 and 1642, Garrett, *Marian Exiles*, p. 258.

However, as Jane Dawson and Joy Shakespeare have shown, the idea of England as a covenanted nation was particularly appealing to the Marian exiles. It allowed them to accommodate the Edwardian experience, whilst explaining why England had turned its back on the Protestant faith at the accession of Mary. The Edwardian reformation had been England's entry point into a covenanted relationship with God, but the English people, in particular the Protestant nobility, had rejected these divine blessings and, in return, God had sent the Marian persecution both to punish the ungodly and to set a rod for the backs of the godly. The material hardships of mid-century Tudor England, rampant inflation, poor harvests, famine and plague, were further grist to the mill of the exiled ministers who readily adopted the role of Old Testament prophets, calling on Israel to repent. The idea of a national covenant with God had the added benefit of circumventing the legal establishment of Catholicism in England and the constitutional propriety of Mary's accession. Within this concept of national blame for England's fate, and the need for national repentance to reverse it, divines incorporated the notion of the saving remnant, particularly apt for the exiled community, whose writing and preaching might avert further catastrophe (although they often did not distinguish between the nation and the elect).[5] For exiled divines like John Bradford and Anthony Gilby, this 'implied Covenant between God and the English', as Shakespeare puts it, was an integral part of their thought.[6]

For John Knox and Christopher Goodman, the idea of a national covenant was more than an implicit assumption, structuring their thinking. Both saw England, and in Knox's case, Scotland, as nations bound by their explicit covenant with God to resist idolatry and overthrow Marian tyranny. Christopher Goodman, a close friend of Knox and Lady Margaret Professor of Divinity at Oxford from 1548 to 1554, viewed England's relationship with God as identical to that between God, Moses and the Israelites.[7] As the Jews had promised obedience to Moses so Christians promised loyalty to Christ through their baptismal vows.[8] Goodman stated that it was a duty to obey magistrates that uphold God's law, even if they were 'rough and forward' in their application of civil laws, or, like Saul, were personally reprobate.[9] Resisting magistrates was only justified on religious grounds, but such resistance was not only legitimate, it was required of the people on pain of dire penalties should they neglect this duty.

---

[5] J. E. A. Dawson, 'Revolutionary Conclusions: The Case of the Marian Exiles', *History of Political Thought*, 11 (1990), 257–72; *idem*, 'The Apocalyptic Thinking of the Marian Exiles', *Studies in Church History, Subsidia 10*, ed. M. Wilks (Oxford, 1994); Joy Shakespeare, 'Plague and Punishment', in *Protestantism and the National Church*, eds. Lake and Dowling, pp. 103–23.

[6] Ibid., p. 121.

[7] Garrett, *Marian Exiles*, pp. 162–4.

[8] C. Goodman, *How Superior Powers Ought to be Obeyed* (Geneva, 1558), pp. 164–6.

[9] Ibid., pp. 115–18.

For this cause [God's] have you promised obedience to your Superiors, that they might herein helpe you: and for the same intent have they taken it upon them. If they will so do, and keepe promisse with you according to their office, then do you own unto them all humble obedience: if not, you are discharged, and no obedience belongeth to them: because they are not obedient to God, nor be his ministers to punishe the evell and to defend the good.[10]

Although Goodman did make use of more familiar arguments from Lutheran resistance theory based on the natural right of self-defence, overall his theory of resistance was grounded on the vision of a Protestant crusade against the forces of Popish idolatry.[11] Goodman cited the biblical examples of the slaughter of the Benjaminites and the Israelites' attack on the tribes of Ruben, Gad and Manasseh as positive examples of the use of force against idolaters or suspected idolaters.[12] (The same example was later employed by the author of the radical Huguenot resistance tract, *Vindiciae Contra Tryannos* (1579).[13] No mercy was to be shown to the 'Massemongers and false preachers' who must be 'punished with deathe'.[14] From the text of Deuteronomy 13: 17, 18, Goodman insisted that the duty to carry out this judgement rested on everyone and that these penalties were to be carried out without respect to persons:

Yf thine owne naturall brother, sonne, daughter, or the wyffe of thine owne bosome, or thy neyghboure whom thou lovest as thine owne liffe, secretly provoke thee to idolatrie, to serve stra[n]ge Gods . . . nether shalt thou pardo[n] him, but shalt utterly slay him.

Goodman used the idea of resistance being carried out by inferior magistrates, but his lack of trust in the nobility (a feature of the writings of the Genevan exiles as a whole) led him to confer the role of leadership upon figures as lowly as aldermen, constables and JPs.[15] However, like Ponet, he also cited in positive terms the example of divinely appointed assassins such as Phineas.[16] He also seemed to move close to advocating mass popular resistance, stating that if the magistrates failed to offer leadership, then 'God giveth the sworde in to the peoples hande'. He urged the people in such a situation to associate

---

[10] Ibid., p. 190.
[11] Ibid., p. 185; *John Knox and the British Reformations*, ed. R. A. Mason (Aldershot, 1998), p. 151.
[12] Goodman, *Superior Powers*, pp. 186, 188.
[13] *Vindiciae Contra Tyrannos, or, Concerning the Legitimate Power of a Prince Over the People and of the People Over a Prince*, ed. G. Garnett (Cambridge, 1994), pp. 36–7.
[14] Goodman, *Superior Powers*, p. 196.
[15] Ibid., p. 215.
[16] Ibid., p. 196.

themselves together and appoint a leader, portraying Wyatt's rebellion as just such a popular religious crusade.[17]

Like other Marian exiles, Goodman viewed the nation's apostasy from the Protestant religion and the rule of a Catholic woman in place of a godly prince as a divine judgement from God for England's backsliding. God, he said, had placed an 'infidel woman over us, to returne us to our olde vomite'.[18] Adopting, like other preachers, the role of the prophet, Goodman insisted that God would impose further plagues on England still, perhaps effective rule by the Spanish if the country was not reformed and idolatry destroyed: 'Repent, repent you miserable men: for your synnes be at the highest, your cupp of iniquitie is full, and the houre of your hevy visitation is come.'[19]

Like Goodman, Knox was also influenced by continental writers, such as Jacques Almann and Theodore Beza, who had advocated resistance by inferior magistrates. Added to this was a Scottish influence in the form of the conciliarism of John Major, who may have tutored Knox at St Andrews, and the secular practice of establishing bands of manrent and maintenance.[20] Yet Knox was also convinced, like his close associate Goodman, that the biblical covenants applied to Christian as well as Jewish societies: 'The Gentiles (I mean everie citie, realme, province or nation amongest the Gentiles, embrasing Christ Jesus and his true religion) be bound to the same leage and covenant that God made with his people Israel.'[21] For Knox, it was England, through the Edwardian reformation, which had first entered into covenant with God. In Knox's *Godly Letter* (1554) he warned his English congregation of the dangers not only of going to mass, but of tolerating its practice and, like Goodman, applauded the example of the Benjaminites who had been punished, not because they were adulterers, but because they permitted adultery to go unchecked.[22] A *Faithful Admonition* of the same year called for a Phineaus, Elijah or Jehu to overthrow the Catholic regime in England. Knox did not, like Goodman, though, move on to advocate explicitly popular resistance of idolatry, although in his *Appellation to the Nobility* (1558) he made many arguments that had resonances with those voiced in *How Superior Powers Ought to be Obeyed*. He urged that the nobility were not placed in authority merely

---

[17] Ibid., pp. 185, 201–2; Dawson, 'Revolutionary Conclusions', p. 258. Goodman was himself implicated in plots against Mary's government, see Garrett, *Marian Exiles*, p. 163.

[18] Goodman, *Superior Powers*, p. 57.

[19] Ibid., p. 94.

[20] On these influences upon Knox, see W. Stanford Reid, 'John Knox's Theology of Political Government', *The Sixteenth Century Journal*, 19 (1988), 529–40. The historiography on Knox is vast. I have been greatly aided by the bibliography offered in J. T. Kirk's, 'Knox and the Historians', in *Knox and the British Reformations*, ed. Mason, pp. 7–29.

[21] From the *Appellation to the Nobility* (1558), quoted in *Knox*, ed. Mason, p. 140.

[22] In *The Works*, ed. D. Laing (6 vols., Edinburgh, 1846–64), V, 157–217; R. Kyle, 'John Knox and the Purification of Religion: The Intellectual Aspects of his Crusade Against Idolatry', *Archiv für Reformationsgeschichte*, 77 (1986), 265–80.

to 'flatter your king in his folly and blind rage' but were 'bound to correct and repress whatsoever ye know him to attempt expressedly repugning to God's word, honor and glory'. If they failed in this duty, they would bring divine judgement down upon themselves for 'Pharaoh was not drowned alone, but his captaines, chariots, and great army drank the same cup with him.'[23] Like Goodman, he affirmed that the punishment of idolatry was to be carried out with utmost severity and without respect to persons, a practice he grounded in the precedent of Asa's 'solemn oath and covenant' that 'whoseover should not seek the Lord God of Israel should be killed, were he great or were he small.'[24] As with Goodman, Knox stated that the duty to carry out this punishment rested on everyone, though he introduced the caveat that this should be according to their vocation 'and according to that possibility and occasion which God doth minister to revenge the injury'.[25] Again, the actions of Joshua and the Israelites against the tribes of Reuben, Gad and Manasseh were chosen as positive examples.[26] The radical potential of Knox's ideas is indicated by his unpublished outline for *The Second Blast*, written in 1558 but rendered obsolete by Mary's death. Here he urged that monarchs should be chosen on the basis of their fitness to defend the faith, over and above any hereditary claims. If the people were mistakenly to elect an idolater or persecutor of the godly, those electors might 'depose and punish him'.[27] As we shall see, the idea of a covenanted monarch would acquire considerable significance under Elizabeth I. Following Mary's death, Knox reaffirmed his belief that England was a covenanted nation, but in A *Brief Exhortation* (1559) warned of the plagues that would be visited upon the country if she again repudiated God's divine favour. In order to avoid this fate the English people, their rulers and prince must by 'solemned othe renue the convenant betwixt God & you'. The substance of this covenant must be the same as Asa's, that those that will not seek the Lord God of Israel should be put to death.[28]

Without doubt, Knox and Goodman had offered innovative and radical justifications of tyrannicide based on the idea that England was bound in the same kind of covenanted relationship with God as Old Testament Israel. However, the overall influence of the exile community on subsequent events has been challenged since Garrett's assertion that they essentially constituted a political party which fought the passage of the Supremacy Bill through the Commons in 1559. The exiles were forced to make public recantations of their resistance theories. Their attacks on feminine rule, now that a Protestant queen had restored the reformed faith, also became an embarrassment, and had to

---

[23] In *The Political Writings of John Knox*, ed. M. A. Breslow (London, 1985), pp. 125–7.
[24] Ibid., pp. 28–9.
[25] Ibid., p. 130.
[26] Ibid., p. 134.
[27] Ibid., pp. 159–60.
[28] In *Works*, ed. Laing, V, 505–17.

be repudiated. Although Goodman remained active in Elizabethan puritan circles his work was never reprinted, and Ponet's writings only resurfaced in the seventeenth century.[29]

It might be argued that the resistance theory expounded by the Genevan exiles was an aberration which even its authors came to see as an embarrassment out of its original context. Indeed, many historians have claimed that the accession of Elizabeth to the throne saw the disappearance of any public voicing of resistance theory.[30] Yet we do not need to accept the idea that the exiles were in the political ascendancy after 1559 to see that their political ideas resurfaced in very public forums during Elizabeth's reign.[31] The political ideas of the Marian exiles were widely disseminated through the explanatory marginalia attached to the Geneva Bible of 1560. According to Dan G. Danner, the compilers of the bible, William Whittingham, Anthony Gilby and Thomas Sampson, shared Knox and Goodman's belief that England was a nation in a covenanted relationship with God. In their preface to the queen, they urged the need for the 'utter abolishing of idolatrie' and the advancing of the true religion if the kingdom was to prosper. They warned that if other nations and their leaders could not escape divine judgement, 'that we vile wormes can not looke to escape punishment for ours'.[32] Danner sees their bible as being dominated by an 'anti-tyrant motif'.[33] Numerous kings, Pharaoh, Saul and Ahab are described as tyrants. The notes clearly associate idolatry with tyranny and urge the death of Jezebel as a 'spectacle and example of God's judgements to all tyrants'. They showed approval of Jehu's action in killing her, as a divinely appointed assassin, and of Daniel's disobedience to the king Darius. The compilers' broad attitude on the issue of political obedience was made clear by their commentary on the key text of Romans 13, arguing that subjects were to offer obedience as 'far as lawfully we may: for if unlawful things be commanded, we must answer as Peter teacheth us, it is better to obey God than men.'[34] Like Knox and Goodman, they stated that the public were not absolved from responsibility for wicked acts committed at the behest of their superiors, but the notes stopped short of condoning popular resistance, at most

[29] For Goodman's later career see D. G. Danner, 'Christopher Goodman and the English Protestant Tradition of Civil Disobedience', Sixteenth Century Journal, 8 (1977), 61–73.

[30] R. L. Greaves, 'Concepts of Political Obedience in England: Conflicting Perspectives', Journal of British Studies, 22 (1982), 23–34; D. R. Kelley, 'Elizabethan Political Thought', in The Varieties of British Political Thought, ed. J. G. A. Pocock (Cambridge, 1993), ch. 2.

[31] The exiles' declaration of loyalty to Elizabeth was itself deeply ambiguous, G. Bowler, 'English Protestants and Resistance Writings' (University of London Ph.D., 1981), p. 286. See also Goodman's equivocal recantation in Danner, 'Goodman', p. 65.

[32] D. G. Danner, 'The Contribution of the Geneva Bible of 1560 to the English Protestant Tradition', Sixteenth Century Journal, 12 (1981), 5–19.

[33] Ibid., p. 13.

[34] C. Hill, The English Bible and the Seventeenth-Century Revolution (London, 1993), pp. 56–66.

emphasising the role of lesser magistrates in checking ungodly rulers.[35] Between 1560 and 1603 ninety editions of the Geneva Bible were produced, and even though after 1616 editions had to be smuggled in from the Netherlands, from 1611 to 1715 a further eight editions of the authorised version of the bible were printed with the Geneva notes.[36] Not only the Geneva Bible but also the Bishops Bible of 1568 contained similarly politically sensitive marginal notes.[37]

In Scotland, the idea of a covenanted nation structured Knox's *History of the Reformation*. Unlike John Foxe, Knox made no attempt to construct much of a Protestant history for Scotland prior to the climatic year of 1560, the point at which he believed the nation had entered into covenant with God. Beyond wanting to see Scotland governed as covenanted nation, punishing the practising of idolatry with death, Knox urged a Protestant union of England and Scotland. Writing to William Cecil in 1559, he talked of forming a 'confederacy, amity and league' between the two realms which would be quite unlike 'the pactions made by worldly men for worldly profit'.[38] He expressed similar sentiments in his sermon of 1560 given at St Giles Kirk Edinburgh in thanks for the victory over the Guises:

> And seeing that nothing is more odious in Thy presence O Lord, than is ingratitude and violation of a covenant made in Thy name: and seeing that Thou has made our confederates of England the instruments by whom we are now set at liberty, to whom we in Thy name have promised mutual faith again; let us never fall to that unkindness O Lord, that either we declare ourselves unthankful to them or profaners of Thy holy name. Confound Thou the counsels of them that go about to break that godly league contract in Thy name and retain thou us so firmly together by the power of Thy Holy Spirit.[39]

According to Stephen Alford, Cecil himself was amenable to the idea of a religious union of the kingdoms and in the diplomatic instructions of 26 May 1560 had proposed that a league should be formed to preserve Scottish autonomy and the Protestant religion.[40] Similar pleas for a covenanted union with England had been made by the Lords of the Congregation in 1559.

---

[35] R. L. Greaves, 'The Nature and Intellectual Milieu of the Political Principles in the Geneva Bible Marginalia', *Journal of Church and State*, 22 (1980), 233–51.

[36] Hill, *English Bible*, pp. 58, 66.

[37] G. Bowler, '"An Axe or an Acte"? The Parliament of 1572 and Resistance Theory in Early Elizabethan England', *Canadian Journal of History*, 19 (1984), 349–61, at p. 357.

[38] R. A. Mason, 'Usable Pasts: History and Identity in Reformation Scotland', *Scottish Historical Review*, 76 (1997), 54–68.

[39] J. Knox, *The History of the Reformation of Religion with the Realm of Scotland*, ed. C. J. Guthrie (London, 1898), pp. 225–6.

[40] S. Alford, *The Early Elizabethan Polity: William Cecil and the British Succession Crisis, 1558–1569* (Cambridge, 1998), pp. 59–62, 80–1.

Proposals for a British covenant were supported by the biblical example of the covenants between Israel and Judah, an example which was later much favoured by advocates of the Solemn League and Covenant in 1643.[41] As Jane Dawson has shown, these proposals for a religious union of the kingdoms were based upon a shared printed language, shared religious texts like the Geneva Bible and close personal contacts between English and Scottish Protestants. The idea of a covenanted union between the nations was encouraged by the conviction that Britain's island status was a sign of special providential favour, sharpened by a developing belief in an international Catholic conspiracy, against which Britain alone could offer refuge and resistance. Such ideas fed into proposals that the queen marry a Scotsman; indeed some Scots believed that the earlier failure of the 'rough wooing' was a providential sign of God's displeasure with Scotland's then apostasy.[42]

Resistance theory was not limited just to lurking in the margins of Scottish or English bibles, awaiting the attention of a particularly selective reader. As Gerald Bowler has shown, political ideas with clear parallels in the thought of Knox and Goodman were being publicly voiced in Elizabethan England, in Parliament, in sermons at court and in university disputations. The idea that the monarch herself was in some covenanted relationship with God, with harsh penalties if she failed to keep its terms, which had earlier been hinted at by Latimer was more forcefully expressed in Edward Dering's sermon before the queen on 25 February 1570. Dering presented Elizabeth as a Davidic monarch, lifted up by God to act as his instrument, with the implication that God could just as easily cast her down if she failed to do her duty. The sermon was hardly uncritical of the queen's government, referring to offences against the godly and the evils within the church that needed reform, including the removal of ignorant and/or corrupt clergy and the buying and selling of benefices. He urged the queen not to be 'cruel unto God's anointed and do his Prophets no harme'. He reminded her that God's mercies to England were only a consequence of the covenant he had made with the nation:[43] 'God delt favorably with Sion, that is, wyth the children of Israel, not because of their obedience, for they

---

[41] A. H. Williamson, *Scottish National Consciousness in the Age of James VI: The Apocalypse, the Union and the Shaping of Scotland's Public Culture* (Edinburgh, 1979), pp. 14–15.

[42] J. E. A. Dawson, 'Anglo-Scottish Protestant Culture and Integration in Sixteenth-Century Britain', in *Conquest and Union: Forging a Multi-National British State*, eds. S. Ellis and S. Barber (London, 1995), pp. 87–114.

[43] M. McGiffert, 'Covenant, Crown and Commons in Elizabethan Puritanism', *Journal of British Studies*, 20 (1980), 39. For a late Elizabethan work on the idea of a covenanted prince see Anon., *The Reformation of Religion by Josiah: A Commendable Example for All Princes Professinge the Gospell to Follow* (1590), p. 8. Similar ideas were expressed in Dudley Fenner's *Sacra Theologica* (1585) in which he described a 'double covenant' binding the rulers of the kingdom, see D. Wootton, 'From Rebellion to Revolution: The Crisis of the Winter of 1642/3 and the Origins of Civil War Radicalism', *English Historical Review*, cv (1990), 654–69, at 661.

were a rebellious nation: but because hee remembred his oth wych he swore unto their forefathers.'[44] Although this performance, unsurprisingly, finished Dering's career at court, according to Patrick Collinson it was reprinted more times than any other Elizabethan sermon.

The debates which broke out in Parliament in 1572 in the wake of the Ridolfi plot also saw the uttering of arguments which bore a great deal of similarity to those produced by the Genevan exiles. In response to the situation two bills were proposed against Mary Stuart. The first would have stripped her of any claim to the English crown, made it treason for her to advance such a claim and made her subject to the death penalty, whilst the second would only have disqualified her from the throne. In the Commons there was a clear preference for the first option, but Elizabeth refused to give it her sanction, permitting instead the passage of the latter bill. This passed the Lords and Commons, but was never given the royal assent.[45]

The petition presented by the bishops during this debate warned of the likelihood of divine punishment falling upon the queen if she did not fulfil her duty in executing wrongdoers. God, they said, was no respecter of persons and they enumerated the examples of biblical kings who had suffered for failing to punish malignants. In particular, there was an especial duty to punish idolaters 'even by death . . . for that offence God hath alwaies most greevously punished as committed against the first table, Deut. 13'. Echoing Goodman, they stated that we were not to spare them even if they were our parents, wives or children. There was a danger that if the queen did not stamp out these Catholic plots and insurrections, the violence would widen out and more people would suffer. In such a case, they said, 'God will require there blood at the prince's hande'.[46] Thomas Digges and Thomas Dannet used the same threat of the likely punishments that would follow if the queen did not fulfil her duty to punish wrongdoers in the debates on 31 May 1572, this time in reference to the execution of the Duke of Norfolk. If, they said, 'her Majesties hart shold still be hardened' against taking such action 'we are enforced with great terror to feare that horrible judgement of the prophet pronounced upon Achab for neglecting of iustice, "Thy life for his life" '.[47]

The idea that the monarch's authority was conditional fitted in with another aspect of early Elizabethan political culture, the prevalence of notions of the realm as a mixed-monarchy or 'monarchical republic'. John Guy has argued that there was a division between the political ideas that were dominant in

[44] P. Collinson, 'A Mirror of Elizabethan Puritanism: The Life and Letters of "Godly Master Dering"', Friends of Dr Williams Library Seventeenth Lecture (1963), pp. 16–17; E. Dering, A Sermon Preached Before the Queene Majestie (1572) (unpaginated).

[45] Bowler, 'An Axe or an Acte', pp. 349–50.

[46] Proceedings in the Parliaments of Elizabeth I, vol. 1 1558–1581, ed. Hartley (Leicester, 1981), pp. 275–82.

[47] Ibid., p. 295.

the years prior to the Armada, which supported beliefs in the necessity and authority of political counsel to the monarch and the limited nature of the monarch's powers, and those voiced after 1588 which offered an exulted vision of the queen's absolute sovereignty.[48] Writers like John Aylmer and Thomas Smith discussed England in terms of a mixed-monarchy, and their discussions had an influence on political reality. Cecil took on board these ideas as a means of dealing with the problem of the royal succession, developing schemes for interim republican governments which involved a named council sitting in the event of the queen's death.[49] Such proposals were even aired in Parliament. Gerald Bowler suggested that Thomas Dannet had hinted that Elizabeth might be deposed if she would not take action herself to secure the succession. Yet his comment that, if the queen continued to be 'unmindeful' of her own life, 'her true and faithfull subjects despeiring of safetie by her meanes shalbe forced to seke protection ellshwere, to the end they be not alltogether destitute of defense' suggests rather that measures for a provisional government would have to be put in place, without the queen's consent if necessary, to safeguard the nation.[50] The affinity between such schemes, and the notion that the English monarch existed in a covenanted relationship with God, is clear.[51] In both formulations, the monarch was essentially a vehicle for stabilising the nation and defending the church. They could be held accountable, punished, and if need be, done away with.

The Marian exiles, John Knox and Christopher Goodman, had offered a resistance theory based on the notion that England was a covenanted nation, and that allegiance was first and foremost owed to God, not the monarch. Their ideas did not simply go underground in 1559, but resurfaced in debates in Parliament, in the marginalia of bibles and in sermons offered at court. The idea that the monarch and the people existed in a covenanted relationship with God, in which allegiance was based on their success or failure in keeping to the terms of the covenant by defending the faith keyed in with a no less important belief that England was a mixed-polity and that the queen's counsellors had a prime role in advising and guiding the monarch, and even in times of crisis of taking hold of the reins of power themselves. In the mind of a privy counsellor who was also keen to advance the Protestant reformation in England, William Cecil, we can see the effects of these two strands of thought coalescing.

---

[48] J. Guy, 'Introduction, The 1590s: The Second Reign of Elizabeth I', in *The Reign of Elizabeth I: Court and Culture in the Last Decade*, ed. J. Guy (Cambridge, 1995), pp. 1–20, at pp. 13–15.

[49] Alford, *Early Elizabethan Polity*, pp. 34–8, 109–11.

[50] Bowler, "An Axe or an Acte", p. 353.

[51] On the connections see P. Lake, 'Presbyterianism, the Idea of a National Church and the Argument from Divine Right', *Protestantism and the National Church*, pp. 193–224.

Oaths of association

Plans for a provisional government in the event of the monarch's death often incorporated the device of an oath of association. As we will see, the instrument of an association had close affinities with the concept of a national covenant. In the seventeenth century, these connections would become more overt as the term 'oath of association' effectively became a synonym for 'national covenant'. English discussions of the idea of a national covenant did not always mention public subscription to a solemn oath. As will be demonstrated below, writers often saw the formal acceptance of Protestantism as the national religion, as in the Edwardian reformation or Elizabethan church settlement, as the point of entry into covenant with God. At an individual level, baptismal vows were seen as the beginnings of a person's covenanted relationship with God. Nonetheless, ministers did often call for the taking of solemn oaths as a way of reaffirming and renewing the nation's covenant with God. Here they were keying in with a political trend in the sixteenth century, which saw successive Tudor monarchs resort with increasing frequency to nationally subscribed oaths as a means of testing the religious and political loyalties of their subjects. This process in turn prompted forces opposed to the Tudors' assumption of ecclesiastical supremacy to develop their own counter-oaths. By the end of the sixteenth century, England had turned into a nation in which mass oath taking was an almost customary part of political life and in which even the lowliest members of society were aware of the penalties for swearing falsely.

An oath can be defined as a religious affirmation in which the swearer, by bringing God to witness his testimony, imprecates divine vengeance if it should prove false. It was the threat of eternal damnation, even more than the temporal penalties that attended oath breaking, which gave the oath its power. The gravity of the sins of perjury and scandal warned of the dangers of breaking promises before God. Before the Norman Conquest, according to John Selden, perjury was punishable by banishment, cutting out of the tongue, loss of the hand, denial of Christian burial, forfeiture of goods and sometimes death.[52] Earthly punishments for perjury in the early modern period were mild by comparison. It had only become an offence before the royal courts in 1563 and in common law courts around 1613. Those convicted of perjury were liable to fines and/or imprisonment and the pillory.[53] Consequently, the homilies stressed the heavy spiritual censures in the next life, rather than the immediate punishments in this life, incurred by breaking oaths. By their sin, the homilies declared, the perjured had utterly forsaken 'Gods mercy, goodnesse and trueth'

---

[52] J. E. Tyler, *Oaths: Their Origins, Nature and History* (London, 1834), p. 227.
[53] J. Spurr, 'Perjury, Profanity and Politics', *The Seventeenth Century*, viii (1993), 29–50, 31.

and would be condemned at the day of judgement to 'everlasting shame and death'.[54]

During the sixteenth century, clear rules for swearing lawfully were set down and promulgated to the public. The thirty-ninth article of religion and the homily against rash swearing and perjury, attacking the flat refusal of some radical Protestant groups to swear at all, reaffirmed that it was lawful to make oaths. The thirty-ninth article stated that 'a man may swear when the magistrate requireth, in a cause of faith and charity'. In keeping with the use of oaths in early modern society, the homily listed oaths before judges, oaths of office and oaths of allegiance as sworn statements that it was lawful for Christians to make. Both stressed that these types of oaths still had to be taken 'according to the Prophet's teaching in justice, judgement and truth', citing Jer. 4: 2.[55] English casuists who dealt with cases of conscience thrown up by the demand to take oaths of loyalty, followed this biblical rule. They were agreed that oaths should normally be taken in the imposer's sense and that the use of mental reservations in swearing was unlawful. Neither, said William Ames, was it enough to swear to the 'primary intention of the tenderer'. To take an oath in judgement the swearer must be eligible to swear to the matter of it. The oaths of madmen and children were not obliging, neither was the oath of an inferior to the prejudice of a superior's right effective. Oaths should not be taken rashly without due consideration of their contents and the circumstances in which they were to be made. An oath could not be taken in justice if the matter sworn to was unlawful. English divines were agreed that an oath to an unlawful thing should not be kept. It was better to sin once in breaking an evil oath than to sin twice by keeping it.[56] These Protestant casuists were also in agreement that there were a number of tacit conditions to lawful oaths. Oaths were conditional on the matter sworn to remaining the same, that it was not impossible to be performed and that they were permitted by the superior power. Both the 'puritan' Ames and the conformist Robert Sanderson made clear that a subsequent oath could not make a former obligation void.[57]

---

[54] *Certaine Sermons or Homilies Appointed to be Read in Churches in the Time of Queen Elizabeth I*, eds. M. E. Rickey and T. B. Stroup (Gainsville, 1968), p. 50.

[55] *Certain Sermons Appointed by the Queen's Majesty to be Declared and Read*, ed. G. E. Corrie (Cambridge, 1850), p. 617; *Certain Sermons and Homilies*, eds. Rickey and Stroup, pp. 45–6.

[56] W. Ames, *Conscience with the Power and Cases Thereof* (Leiden, 1639), book four, pp. 48–59; R. Sanderson, *De Juramento: Seven Lectures Concerning the Obligation of Promissory Oaths*, trans. Charles I ? (1655), pp. 47–8; see also J. Hall, *Resolutions and Decisions of Divers Practicall Cases of Conscience* (1649), pp. 73–81.

[57] Ames, *Conscience with the Power*, pp. 54–5; Sanderson, *De Juramento*, pp. 55–8. These rules seem to have been understood at a popular level, M. Ingram, *Church Courts, Sex and Marriage in England, 1570–1640* (Cambridge, 1987), pp. 97–8; J. Spurr, 'A Profane History of Early Modern Oaths', *TRHS*, 11 (2001) pp. 52, 56.

The importance of sworn statements to early modern society cannot be overestimated. In a postlapsarian world oaths were seen as the only means of assuring truthfulness in human affairs. Sanderson, then Regius Professor of Divinity at Oxford, stated that the oath had been instituted by God himself as a 'remedy of humane defects' to be 'the last moral refuge for the defence of verity'.[58] Oaths in early modern England were used to underpin almost every element of church and state relations. In the fifteenth and sixteenth centuries oaths fulfilled three basic roles: they bound those invested with public or spiritual office to carry out their obligations faithfully; they gave the assurance of truthfulness to statements given in court; and they tied subjects to giving obedience to their rulers.

The lowliest of public occupations could carry an oath of office, binding the swearer to fulfil their duties. Midwives, forest rangers and ale tasters, along with lord lieutenants and judges, swore to faithfully serve the crown or the parish. A compendium printed in 1689 listed over two hundred oaths of this type.[59] The number of occupations that carried an oath of office made these compendia equally commonplace.[60] The fact that, by the sixteenth century, the royal coronation ceremony now only represented the acclamation of the new monarch, not their election, did not prevent some seventeenth century Englishmen from suggesting that the king, like an ale taster or forest ranger, could be held liable for the breach of his oath of office.[61] As will be shown later, even those who saw the coronation oath as sacramental and non-reciprocal took the obligations to defend the church and protect the people, as promises made before God, very seriously. Others, though, claimed that the king was not merely accountable to God. They suggested that the coronation was a mutual contract embodying the monarch's duty of protection and the subject's corresponding obligation of obedience, and that the bonds of allegiance between the two might be dissolved by the king's failure to keep his oath. Oaths were also essential for the administration of justice. In Anglo-Saxon jurisprudence, the oath of the accused or the accuser alone was frequently not deemed adequate and had to be attested to by compurgators or 'oath-helpers'.[62] Although compurgation itself had gone out of use in common law courts by

---

[58] Sanderson, De Juramento, p. 45.
[59] The Book of Oaths and the Several Forms Thereof (2nd edn., 1689); Bodl. MS Clarendon 73, f. 2–3, 6, 378; Bodl. MS Clarendon 92, f. 202.
[60] C. Robbins, 'Selden's Pills: State Oaths in England, 1558–1714', Huntington Library Quarterly, XXXV (1972), 308.
[61] On the history of the coronation in England see G. Garnett, 'Coronation', in The Blackwell Encyclopedia of Anglo-Saxon England, eds. M. Lapidge, J. Blair, S. Keynes and D. Scragg (Oxford, 1999), pp. 122–4; P. E. Schramm, A History of the English Coronation, trans. L. G. W. Legg (Oxford, 1937); Regicide and Revolution: Speeches at the Trial of Louis XVI, ed. M. Walzer (2nd edn., New York, 1992).
[62] F. W. Maitland, The Constitutional History of England (Cambridge, 1909), pp. 115–19.

the end of the twelfth century, in ecclesiastical courts, the procedure continued to be employed under the Tudors and Stuarts.[63]

However, it is the use of oaths to test political and religious loyalties that has the most significance for the development of the idea of a national covenant in England. Both Henry IV and Henry VI used the medieval oath of allegiance to bind the lords to obey them and it was still being employed in the seventeenth century to test the loyalty of subjects.[64] With the Tudors' assumption of ecclesiastical supremacy loyalty came increasingly to be defined in political and religious terms. Subjects were for the first time asked to swear to a set of beliefs. The 1534 Oath of Succession was tendered to all men over the age of 14. By requiring the swearer to assert that the progeny of Henry and Anne were the heirs to the throne it effectively required subscribers to side with Thomas Cromwell and the king against the Pope and Catherine.[65] The priors of King's Langley and Dunstable, who, when asked to swear this oath, also promised to be loyal to any wife whom Henry might marry after Anne's death, were clearly very far-sighted.[66] Barely two years later, the trial of Anne for treason and Henry's subsequent marriage to Jane Seymour necessitated a new oath of allegiance, leaving the succession to Henry's will. The new oath made it treasonable for any to protest 'upon any interrogatories that shall be objected to them for or conc[er]ning this Acte as any thing therin contayned, that they be not bound to declare their thought and consciens'.[67] Henry made it clear that, along with the church, the individual's conscience also fell within royal jurisdiction. The same year an oath was passed through Parliament confirming the king's ecclesiastical supremacy, extended in 1543 to be tendered to all public officers, ministers, schoolmasters and students studying for degrees.[68] The wider political impact of this increasing resort to oaths as a means of testing the loyalty of his subjects can be seen in the fact that the rebel armies of the Pilgrimage of Grace were combined by oaths modelled on the Henrician oath of supremacy.[69] More explicitly still, the 1559 Elizabethan Oath of Supremacy required all ministers and public officers to declare that the queen was the 'only supreme governor in this realm . . . as well in all

[63] Ingram, *Church Courts*, pp. 331–4. C. Hill, *ociety and Puritanism in Pre-Revolutionary England* (London, 1964), p. 265.
[64] R. W. Perceval and P. D. G. Hayter, 'The Oath of Allegiance', *The Table: The Journal of the Society of Clerks-at-the-Table in Commonwealth Parliaments*, xxxiii (1964), 85–90; 86; Robbins, 'Selden's Pills', 308; *CSPD*, 1640–1, p. 574.
[65] D. Cressy, *Literacy and the Social Order: Reading and Writing in Tudor and Stuart England* (Cambridge, 1980), p. 64; *SR*, iii, 474, 493.
[66] C. Russell, *The Crisis of Parliaments: English History 1509–1660* (Oxford, 1971), p. 98.
[67] *SR*, iii, 661.
[68] Ibid., iii, 665, 956–7.
[69] M. Bush, *The Pilgrimage of Grace* (Manchester, 1996), esp. pp. 28–30, 113–15. See also S. Alford, 'Politics and Political History in the Tudor Century', *The Historical Journal*, 42 (1999), 535–49.

spiritual or ecclesiastical things or causes as temporal'. The Supremacy of the Crown Act of 1562 obliged all new members of Parliament (except for the temporal lords) to take the Oath of Supremacy.[70]

Under the Elizabethan regime it was not just ministers and public servants that were required to express their loyalty to the monarch. In 1584, the Dutch leader, William of Orange, having survived one Catholic assassination attempt, had been murdered that year and an English conspiracy, the Throckmorton plot, had recently been uncovered. Parliament was not in session and there was a clear danger of a political vacuum should Elizabeth be killed.[71] To deal with this situation, in October Walsingham and Burghley, seemingly without the queen's knowledge, set about drawing up an 'Instrument of Association'.[72] In its final form the association bound those taking it to give their 'lyves, landes and goodes in her defence' and promise that they would 'revenge, all maner of persons of what estate soever they shalbe and their abettors, that shall attempte by any acte counsell or consent to any thinge that shall tende to the harme of her Maties royall person.' They would pursue such persons and 'their comforters, ayders and abettors' to the 'uttermost extermination of them'. Should any pretender (namely Mary Queen of Scots), in the event of the queen's untimely death, advance a claim to the throne, they promised to view that person as 'unworthy of all government in any Christian realme of cyvill societie'.[73] The association was quickly made public and dispersed throughout England and Wales representing what David Cressy describes as an 'ideological mustering' to the queen (and, implicitly, to the Protestant state).[74] Leading nobles and magnates gathered subscriptions which were then returned to the Privy Council.[75]

Patrick Collinson has shown how the Association in defence of Elizabeth made in 1584 fitted in with schemes for an interim republic to ensure that the crown passed to a Protestant successor in the event of the queen's death.[76] However, this was not the only time that an oath of association was promoted as a device to secure both Protestantism and the monarch's safety, with the

---

[70] G. R. Elton, *The Tudor Constitution* (2nd edn., Cambridge, 1982), p. 375; Perceval and Hayter, 'The Oath of Allegiance', 87.

[71] D. Cressy, 'Binding the Nation: The Bonds of Association, 1584 and 1696', in *Tudor Rule and Revolution, Essays for G. R. Elton from his American Friends*, eds. D. J. Guth and J. W. McKenna (Cambridge, 1982), pp. 217–37; at p. 217.

[72] *Proceedings in the Parliaments of Elizabeth I, vol. 3*, ed. T. E. Hartley (London, 1995), p. 252. Elizabeth claimed that the association was made 'before I ever heard [of] it, or [litle] ever thought of such matter, till a thousand handes with many obligacions were shewed mee at Hampton Court'.

[73] *The Egerton Papers*, ed. J. P. Collier (Camden Soc., xii, 1840), 108–11.

[74] Cressy, *Literacy and the Social Order*, p. 62.

[75] P. Collinson, 'The Monarchial Republic of Queen Elizabeth I', *Bulletin of the John Rylands Library*, lxix (1986–7), 394–424, at 414.

[76] Collinson, 'Monarchial Republic'; *idem*, 'The Elizabethan Exclusion Crisis and the Elizabethan Polity', *Proceedings of the British Academy*, lxxxiv (1994), 51–93.

idea being mooted as early as the 1560s. These oaths of association shared a number of basic characteristics: they were imposed at times of particular Protestant crisis; they often accepted the possibility of the death of the reigning monarch; and they often attempted to deal with this eventuality by making provision for a temporary republican government. In particular, the notion of an oath of association shared similarities with the idea of a national cove-nant. As will be made clear, these connections carry with them important implications for political allegiance, defining loyalty in confessional terms and making obedience to the monarch conditional on his or her readiness to defend the faith. Under Elizabeth, the consequences of this redefinition of allegiance were muted. However, as will be shown later, under a more religiously suspect ruler like Charles I, or an outright papist like James II, the king's apparent inability or unwillingness to defend the faith could offer not only grounds for resisting him, but also for deposing him.

The research of Stephen Alford has shown that the 1584 Bond of Association had a considerable pre-history. Plans were considered as early as 1563 for safe-guarding the Protestant succession, prompted by the queen's serious ill health. These included the possibility of a named council governing in the event of Elizabeth's death.[77] During the Parliamentary session of 1563, firm calls were made for the queen to establish 'some certen limitacion of th'imperiall crowne of your realme'.[78] The previous year the Prince of Condé's 'treaty of association', in support of Charles IX and religious liberty, had been printed in an English translation, offering William Cecil a European model for his 'Bond'.[79] Another possible influence came from the Scottish practice of banding, in which these documents were often referred to as associations.[80] Neither was the resort to 'lynch law' in the 1584 Association a novelty. The crisis of 1569 led to Cecil drawing up plans for an association which contained many of the features of the later bond, the use of an oath, the call to association, the term 'instrument' and the idea of subscription by shire. He called for the inclusion of people of

---

[77] Alford, *Early Elizabethan Polity*, pp. 109–11.

[78] *Proceedings in the Parliaments of Elizabeth I*, vol. 1, ed. Hartley, p. 90; pp. 61–2.

[79] See, *The Treaty of Thassociation [sic.] made by the Prince of Condee* (1562); M. K. Zabrowski, 'The Corruption of Politics and the Dignity of Human Nature: The Critical and Conservative Radicalism of James Burgh', *Enlightenment and Dissent*, 10 (1991), 78–104, at 92; D. R. Kelley, *The Beginnings of Ideology* (Cambridge, 1981), ch. 7. Like the Elizabethan associations, Condé's pact was not restricted to social elites but was to be taken by members of 'all estates'.

[80] S. A. Burrell, 'The Covenant Idea as a Revolutionary Symbol, 1596–1637', *Church History*, 27 (1958), 338–50. In a French context, it appears to have been Catholics who first forged religious associations for common defence, J. Bossy, 'Leagues and Associations in Sixteenth-Century French Catholicism', *Voluntary Religion* (Studies in Church History, 23, 1986), 171–89; Offering an interesting parallel with the rhetoric of Marian exiles, Bossy notes that Catholic leagues often portrayed Protestantism as a plague which had been visited on France for its faithlessness, p. 180.

lower status than nobles, bishops and leading gentry to subscribe and envisaged this association as being taken by farmers, householders and others as well. Subscription would be accompanied by the raising of money for arms. Those that refused the association would be deemed recusants, as would those that would take the 'instrument' but refuse to contribute money.[81] During the 1570s Elizabethan puritans toyed with the idea of forming covenanted groups of armed godly to defend the nation from the threat of popery.[82] In discussions of the draft bill against Mary Queen of Scots in the Commons one member called for the taking of a 'generall oth' by the public to the justice of the proceedings against Mary.[83] On 25 June 1572, it was urged that it should be made lawful for 'all persons . . . to maintaine, sett forth and defend to the utmost of their powers' everything contained in this act.[84] A petition offered on the same day went even further demanding that

> if any person or persons shall attempt to despatche and destroy her [Mary Stewart], for whom and by whom such tumult was reysd, that then the said partie so attempting or committing shall [not] be any kinde of wayes troubled or impeached for the same, but to be clearly quitt by the vertue and authorities of this acte.[85]

As Frances Alford complained, this would mean that any man 'were he never so mean a subiect' might lay his hands on her.[86]

Despite these misgivings about the extra-legal nature of the device, an Association in defence of Elizabeth was tendered in 1584. Patrick Collinson has described the Instrument of Association of 1584 as in form 'a covenant'. The text of the association revealed the way in which it redefined allegiance in confessional terms. God, the association said, had instituted kings, queens and princes, to preserve their subjects 'in profession and observation of the true Christian religion, accordinge to his holy worde and commandementes'. So, 'in like sorte' subjects should love, fear and obey their sovereigns. Here, the association hinted at an implicit relationship between the sovereign's defence of the faith and the subject's duty of obedience. Although, unlike later associations, the bond was mainly administered by the gentry and nobility, not via county machinery, there were no distinctions of rank as to the role of those within the association.[87] The tendering of the association was also accompanied with much solemnity. The gentlemen of Lancashire came to Wigan to see the Earl of Derby take the oath, bareheaded and on his knees

---

[81] Alford, *Early Elizabethan Polity*, pp. 196–8.
[82] P. Collinson, *The Elizabethan Puritan Movement* (3rd edn., Oxford, 1990), p. 145.
[83] *Proceedings in Parliament*, vol. 1, ed. Hartley, p. 392.
[84] Ibid., p. 309.
[85] Ibid., p. 314.
[86] Ibid., p. 315.
[87] Collinson, 'Monarchial Republic', p. 416.

before the Bishop of Chester.[88] Burghley reported that preachers were also active in encouraging the public to take the association, noting that a 'great multitude of people both of gentlemen and merchants and vulgar people, especially in good towns, where they be taught by discreet preachers, very zealous towards God' were 'thereby earnestly bent to all services for her Majesties safety'.[89] Some expressed the hope that the association would be employed as a shibboleth, not only to discover Catholics, but also to distinguish the zealous Protestants from the lukewarm. Writing to Lord Cobham in December 1584, Sir Thomas Scott and Sir James Hales asked for the names of subscribers to aid the prosecution of 'every backslider, faithless and, by attestation, perjured person' that had not persevered in the association.[90]

However, almost as soon as the association had been sent out, some were expressing misgivings about its possible implications. Thomas Digges, the mathematician and administrator, believed that the oath's lack of social distinctions could provoke anarchic rebellion. More than this, the association's resort to lynch law meant that there was no definition of what actions against the queen were punishable by death; moreover it made Mary Stuart liable for the actions of persons that she might not even have knowledge of.[91] Some attempt at limiting the consequences of the association was made by its incorporation into the bill for the queen's safety produced in December 1584. By this law, claimants to the throne implicated in any rebellion would, after investigation by a Parliamentary committee, lose any title to the throne, not only for themselves but also for their heirs. The element of lynch law from the original oath remained, although James VI would now be exempted from any revenge. It was made clear that the Bond of Association was to be interpreted in terms of the act.[92] Members who complained that they were now forsworn, either on the grounds of the Bond of Association or the terms of the oath of allegiance swearing to be true to the queen and her lawful successors, were told to consider the 'equity' rather than the letter of the 'Instrument'.[93] However, making the association law did not clear up what would happen if an assassination attempt were successful. It was for this reason that both Digges and Burghley drew up proposals for a republican government which would fill the political void created by the monarch's death. A bill providing for an interregnum was actually introduced into Parliament in January 1585.[94] These proposals were not successful, and we can question how realistic they

[88] Ibid., 414.

[89] Collinson, 'Elizabethan Exclusion Crisis', 64n.

[90] HMC, *Salisbury MSS*, iii (1889), p. 77.

[91] BL Lansdowne MS 113, f. 156–8.

[92] Sir J. Neile, *Elizabeth I and Her Parliaments 1584–1601* (London, 1957), pp. 33–5, 52–3.

[93] *Proceedings in Parliament, vol. 3*, ed. Hartley, pp. 151–2. For the objections voiced, see ibid., pp. 149–50.

[94] BL Add. MS 48099 (Yelverton MS 108), f. 6–21; Collinson, 'Monarchial Republic', 419–21.

were, but they highlight the extent to which the purpose of measures to safeguard the queen's person was really to protect the Protestant state. They also show the readiness with which Burghley, a key government minister, was prepared to turn England from a hereditary monarchy into an elective one, like Poland.

This was not the last instance in Elizabeth's reign that proposals were made for an oath of association. The so-called 'Appellant Controversy' between English secular priests and Jesuits, generated by the appointment of George Blackwell as archpriest in 1598, provided the context for a pamphlet titled *Humble Motives for Association to Maintain Religion Established*.[95] The book was printed in 1601 but it contains a tract by Thomas Digges, written some time between 1584 and his death in 1595.[96] In this tract, Digges argued that the only way to extinguish Catholic hopes of overthrowing Elizabeth was for her to 'establish a firme continuance and perpetuation of the substance and sinceritie of doctrine now professed in this realme'. This, he urged, could only be done by 'generall lawes, by generall league, and by generall oth [sic]'. All magistrates, gentlemen and freeholders would take the oath of association whilst the oath of supremacy would be administered to all men aged 16 and older. Any that refused to take these oaths would be disabled from taking public office.[97] Digges felt sure that these measures would convert the 'Papists of estate' (those whose religious affiliation stemmed only from a belief that Protestantism would be short-lived in England) to the reformed religion.[98] Digges ended his treatise in apocalyptic terms, paraphrasing the text of Rev. 3: 15–16. If the queen would accept these proposals, he said, her enemies would find that 'the sword of the Lord shalbe upon them in the mountains of Israel'. However, a lack of zeal in this regard would be costly for 'If we be neither hott, nor cold, but luke warme, and so rather frozen than fervent, when the Lord shall taste us in to his judgement, he will voyd us out of the mouth of his maiestie.' However, if England would be a 'mountayn of Israell' by making an oath of association, God would rain fire and brimstone down upon her enemies.[99] The postscript to this treatise, written (in all probability) by the puritan William Bradshaw, warned against granting toleration to those secular priests

---

[95] On the Appellant Controversy see J. Bossy, *The English Catholic Community, 1570–1850* (London, 1975), ch. 2; D. Lunn, *The English Benedictines, 1540–1688* (London, 1980), pp. 11–14; P. Milward, *Religious Controversies of the Elizabethan Age* (London, 1977), pp. 116–25.
[96] See commonplace book of Gilbert Frevile, bishop of Middleham, Co. Durham, e.g. MS 2877 f. 90–90v, 'A peticon pferred to Qi Elizabeth for association in religion, about the end of her highnes raign.' This treatise seems to have been heavily circulated, BL Add. MS 38823, f. 13–16; BL Lansdowne MS 98, f. 14–18.
[97] [W. Bradshaw and T. Digges], *Humble Motives for Association to Maintain Religion Established* (1601), pp. 6–7.
[98] Ibid., pp. 14–15.
[99] Ibid., pp. 20–1.

that offered allegiance to the queen, as the Pope would let them make any declarations of loyalty they wanted provided they were still ready to strike when the time was right.[100]

After the accession of James to the throne, allegiance was almost exclusively defined by the terms of a sworn oath. The new oath passed in 1606 had been provoked by the panic following the discovery of the Gunpowder Plot in the following year. It was also the first oath of loyalty to take into account Catholics' use of tactics of equivocation and mental reservation to avoid the spiritual and temporal penalties for refusing these oaths.[101] The oath prescribed by *An Act for the Better Discovering and Repressing of Popish Recusants* was to be taken by all persons over the age of 18 who were convicted or indicted for recusancy. In it, the deponent was asked to declare that James was 'lawful and rightful king of this realm and of all other his Majesty's dominions and countries', and that he did 'abhor, detest and abjure as impious and heretical' the doctrine 'that princes which be excommunicated and deprived by the Pope may be deposed or murdered by their subjects or any other whatsoever.' As the title of the act and the requirement to abjure the papal deposing power made clear, the oath was essentially targeted at the king's Catholic subjects. It was not intended to be a test of allegiance to be taken by the populace as a whole. Despite James's statement that his main hope had been that the new oath would separate his moderate Catholic subjects, who respected their 'natural duty to their sovereign', from the radicals, Michael Questier has characterised it as 'possibly the most lethal measure against Romish dissent ever to reach the statute book'.[102] In Parliament the Jacobean Oath of Allegiance supplanted the feudal oath of allegiance as the test of loyalty required from MPs and peers. In 1609 the provisions of the act were extended so that both the spiritual and temporal lords were obliged to take the oath. In February 1626 it was ordered that the Lords should take the new Oath of Allegiance at the beginning of each Parliament.[103]

However, the tendering of a new oath of allegiance in 1606 specifically designed to counter the threat from seditious papists did not satisfy those that wanted a new Protestant association. One anonymous manuscript treatise written some time after 1606 called for all the 'youth of the Realm' to take an oath of association. The seminary priests and Jesuits, the author argued, were already teaching English Catholics to combine against the state, and loyal Protestants must put in an opposing condition of readiness. Gentry that refused

---

[100] Ibid., p. 30.
[101] For a discussion of the debate on equivocation and mental reservation in England see below, pp. 103–7.
[102] J. P. Kenyon, *The Stuart Constitution* (Cambridge, 1966), pp. 458–9; M. C. Questier, 'Loyalty, Religion and State Power in Early Modern England: English Romanism and the Jacobean Oath of Allegiance', *Historical Journal*, xl (1997), 311–29, at 313.
[103] Perceval and Hayter, 'The Oath of Allegiance', 87–8.

the oath would be imprisoned and those of 'base quality' banished.[104] This treatise reinforces the point that, as with the Elizabethan association, these oaths were not merely meant to uncover Catholics but also to strengthen and unite Protestants.

Further proposals for a new oath of association were made in the 1621 Parliament. In one of his first recorded speeches, on 27 November John Pym urged the passing of a new oath of association. The session took place against the background of the deteriorating fortunes of Protestantism in Europe. First, he urged that English arms would do little good for Protestants in Germany. To undertake a military expedition there was dangerous and expensive and the chances of success were slim. Secondly, it would, for this reason, be better to take measures against Roman Catholics at home to ensure internal security. Finally, the Commons should give up a session to the question of granting the king supply, in return for which he would end his lenient policy towards papists and approve a new oath of association. The king, Pym urged, should not presume he was safe because he had a Protestant heir. Again, an association was proposed on the grounds that Catholics were already combining themselves via confederations like the Catholic League.[105]

By the end of the reign of James I, a clear concept of an oath of association, distinct from oaths of allegiance, like that imposed in 1606, had emerged. In contrast to the Jacobean Oath of Allegiance, oaths of association were devices which explicitly linked political loyalty to confessional identity. Nor were they predominantly anti-Catholic measures, but were aimed at testing the zeal of Protestants.[106] Far more than other oaths of loyalty, they demanded military as well as political support from subscribers and carried the threat of violence to those that opposed, or were unwilling to swear to, these associations. As we shall see, like national covenants, they removed distinctions of rank within the association and the subscription to them was accompanied by preaching and great public solemnity. Although some contemporaries may have seen these devices as simply new oaths of loyalty to the monarch, occasioned by particular national emergencies, it is not surprising that some members of the Long Parliament would later see the Elizabethan association as a forerunner of documents like the Protestation, Vow and Covenant and Solemn League and Covenant.

---

[104] BL Add. MS 25277, f. 101–2v. I am dating this treatise on the basis of references to James I and 'the Oath of Alledgeance now sett downe'.

[105] W. M. Macdonald, *The Making of an English Revolutionary: The Early Parliamentary Career of John Pym* (London, 1982), pp. 49–53; J. S. Morrill, 'The Unweariableness of Mr Pym: Influence and Eloquence in the Long Parliament', in *Political Culture and Cultural Politics in Early Modern England: Essays Presented to David Underdown*, eds. S. D. Amussen and M. A. Kinshlansky (Manchester, 1995), pp. 19–55, at p. 23; *Commons Debates 1621*, eds. W. Notestein, F. H. Relf, H. Simpson (7 vols., London, 1935), ii, 453, 461–3.

[106] Although there were allegations that Catholics had taken the 1584 association, *Proceedings in Parliament, vol. 3*, ed. Hartley, p. 123.

Federal theology

It is a key claim of this book that, aside from the influence of political thought and the tradition of swearing oaths of allegiance, there was also a close relationship between reformed theology and the idea of a national covenant. Yet, contrary to the opinion of some historians who have treated this question, this was not a relatively straightforward process by which social or political covenants were simply extrapolated from religious ones. For one thing, such an argument faces the obstacle that well-developed resistance theories based on the idea of a national covenant had emerged before either the idea of a covenanted congregation or the soteriological concept of a covenant-based theology had surfaced.[107]

In his history of the emergence of federal theology, David Weir makes an important distinction between the 'covenant idea', inferences drawn from the many covenant forms found in scripture, 'covenant theology', an outgrowth from this in which the notion of covenant is the governing concept, and 'federal theology' which he defines as 'a specific type of covenant theology, in that the covenant holds together every detail of the theological system'. Around the middle of the sixteenth century, the word covenant, instead of being used to refer to a unilateral 'testament', took on an increasingly conditional sense. Weir finds a general consensus amongst historians that the idea of a prelapsarian covenant did not enter into theological discourse until the 1560s, probably first originating in the works of Zacharius Ursinius. It was not until the late sixteenth century that federal theology proper emerged, incorporating a 'prelapsarian and postlapsarian schema centred around the first Adam and the Second Adam, who is Jesus Christ'. God's covenant with Adam was simple: obey him and receive life, disobey him and receive death. Besides this, Adam was also bound by the natural law which God had implanted in his heart. This covenant was binding upon all men in all times and places, both before and after the fall. After the fall, degenerate man was no longer capable of fulfilling this covenant and required God's grace to be restored to his original state of perfection and happiness. Through Christ God offered man this second covenant of grace. However, as the Westminster Confession of Faith made clear, these were not really two distinct covenants: 'There are not therefore

---

[107] D. A. Weir, *The Origins of the Federal Theology in Sixteenth-Century Reformation Thought* (Oxford, 1990), p. 34. For a sense of the scale of the historiography, see the bibliography in Weir, *Origins*, pp. 160–95. Aside from his work, I have made use of J. W. Baker, *Heinrich Bullinger and the Covenant: The Other Reformed Tradition* (Ohio, 1980); E. Brooks Holifield, *The Covenant Sealed: The Development of Puritan Sacramental Theology in Old and New England, 1570–1720* (New Haven, 1974); R. L. Greaves, 'John Knox and the Covenant Tradition', *Journal of Ecclesiastical History*, 24 (1973), 23–32; M. McGiffert, 'From Moses to Adam: The Making of the Covenant of Works', *The Sixteenth Century Journal*, 19 (1988), 131–55; *idem*, 'Grace and Work: The Rise and Division of Covenant Divinity in Elizabethan Puritanism', *Harvard Theological Review*, 75 (1982), 463–502.

two Covenants of Grace differing in Substance, but one and the same under various Dispensations.' The postlapsarian covenant of grace was really therefore the prelapsarian covenant of works in disguise, although now a new Adam (Christ) was needed to keep the covenant which God had established with man. The idea that the covenant of works was still in place had important ramifications. It provided preachers with a justification for demanding that the state enforce the moral law and provided Protestant states with a social ethic, making up for the loss of the sacraments as the test of those included under grace.[108]

Discussions of the idea of a national covenant have largely situated it in the context of this late sixteenth and early seventeenth century development of federal theology, long after Knox and Goodman had used the concept in their resistance theories. The first, and most influential, exploration of the concept was made by Perry Miller in his book *The New England Mind* and his article 'The Marrow of Puritan Divinity'.[109] For Miller, the idea of national covenant was essentially a seventeenth century phenomenon and one that was only really of importance in the context of New England. As far as the history of the mother country was concerned, the idea was an irrelevance:

> Try as they would, Puritans could never convince themselves, let alone others, that the English people were united in a single public engagement, as were the Scots; with the miscarriage of the Solemn League and Covenant the idea of the nation bound as one personality in covenant with God, liable to physical punishment should it violate the bond and assured of material blessings for observing it, died a natural death.[110]

Miller contentiously viewed the growth of covenant theology as a whole as a response to the psychological pressures exerted by the Calvinist creed of predestination. In order to alleviate the enormous burden of anxiety and despair that doubts about assurance of election produced, ministers tempered God's sovereignty with the conditionality of the covenant idea.[111] The didactic value of this for ministers was that it reasserted the importance of human agency and allowed them to impose and defend a strict moral orthodoxy.[112] Miller noted that divines frequently made analogies between the personal covenant between God and man and the social covenant between ruler and ruled, but he made a clear distinction between the covenant of grace and the idea of

---

[108] Weir, 'Origins', pp. 3–8.
[109] P. Miller, *The New England Mind: Part One the Seventeenth Century* (Harvard, 1954), esp. ch. 16; *idem*, 'The Marrow of Puritan Divinity' in his *Errand into the Wilderness* (New York, 1956), ch. 3.
[110] Miller, *New England Mind*, p. 476.
[111] Miller, 'Marrow of Puritan Divinity', pp. 54–5.
[112] Ibid., pp. 82–9.

national covenant.[113] Whereas the personal covenant of grace was predicated on the offer of salvation for faith, under the national covenant God returned only temporal blessings for the commonwealth's faithfulness and dished out earthly punishments when it strayed from the path.[114] The communal covenant 'ceased very soon to be a mere adjunct of the doctrine of the Covenant of Grace, but commenced to thrive as a self-sufficient principle, and became before the end of the century a dominant idea in the minds of social leaders in Massachusetts and Connecticut.'[115]

Michael McGiffert has followed Miller's distinction between the covenant of grace and the idea of a national covenant, but contends that England was viewed as a covenanted nation.[116] For McGiffert, the concept of a national covenant is essentially an extension of the covenant of works. Following the failure of the classical Elizabethan Presbyterian movement in the 1580s, the covenant of works achieved a heightened importance as a means by which to promote personal piety and public morality. The godly saw two covenants in operation in England, the church covenants of 'saints' in a state of grace and the covenant of works upon the common people as a yoke of obedience.[117] Whilst acknowledging that the covenant idea had had political ramifications, as evidenced in the works of the Genevan exiles and Elizabethan puritans like Dudley Fenner and Edward Dering, McGiffert argues that there was little role given in these discussions for the ordinary people. Its radical implications came in the form of the suggestion that the monarch was in a covenanted and conditional relationship with God and could be deposed if he or she did not fulfil their duties, but not in any affirmation of popular sovereignty. Resistance was largely placed under the direction of inferior magistrates.[118] These political elements to the idea had largely vanished by the beginning of the seventeenth century when the concept of a national covenant was essentially being used as a means to control the moral conduct of the laity.[119]

As we shall see, Miller and McGiffert's conclusions have heavily coloured historians' approaches to the idea of a national covenant in England. They have tended either to dismiss its relevance altogether, or with McGiffert, restricted its application to the realms of personal and public morality. However, T. D. Bozeman has challenged the separation made by both Miller and McGiffert between the personal covenant of grace and corporate or national covenants.[120] He points out in the first place that pre-Marian figures in the

---

[113] Ibid., p. 91.
[114] Miller, *New England Mind*, pp. 479–82.
[115] Ibid., p. 478.
[116] McGiffert, 'Covenant, Crown and Commons', 32–52.
[117] Ibid., p. 33.
[118] Ibid., pp. 36–42.
[119] Ibid., pp. 45–6.
[120] T. D. Bozeman, 'Covenant Theology and "National Covenant": A Study in Elizabethan

English church, Thomas Becon, Myles Coverdale and William Tyndale, had all expounded federal ideas and understood their nation as a 'modern Israel standing under divine favour and wrath'.[121] Tyndale had already explicitly extended the covenant concept to the political realm:

> And if the people come again [to the covenant] let the priest or bishop, after the example of the prophets and high priests of the Israelites, take an oath in God's stead, of the kings and lords. And let the king and lords receive an oath of the people.[122]

Bozeman has noted the ways in which Elizabethan Presbyterians like Thomas Cartwright and John Knewstub slipped from discussing the covenant of grace into talking about the nation's corporate covenant with God. In what he describes as the concept of 'deuteronomic punishment' there was an organic connection between the self and society. The sins of the individual, as much as those committed by a community, could incur divine wrath.[123] The failure of ministers in this discussion of the national covenant to distinguish the elect from the reprobate was a consequence of their acceptance that 'a national church embracing more tares than wheat yet remained an authentic church'.[124] It was this belief which underwrote the proliferation of fasts and days of humiliation and thanksgiving.[125] To be sure, the concept of a national covenant retained a didactic function, with the sermon jeremiad warning England of the dangers that would befall her if she would not reform. Yet the cycle of rewards and punishments that Miller identified as an integral part of the preachers' message in New England was not restricted to the temporal realm but was part of the process of sanctification for God's saints. Punishments were a rod for their backs to chary them to keep to the straight and narrow path to salvation.[126] The offer of a national covenant was, then, a sign of God's mercy, offering the opportunity to avoid punishment via repentance and amendment. God's covenant with the Jews was part of the same 'continuum of redemptive history defined first and finally with Abraham'.[127] Bozeman finds that Presbyterian preachers did not distinguish between the elect and the reprobate in discussing this covenant leading him to argue that they knew 'nothing of

Presbyterian Thought' (unpublished conference paper, I am grateful to Professor Bozeman for letting me see a copy of his paper); a shortened version of this was published as 'Federal Theology and the "National Covenant": An Elizabethan Presbyterian Case Study', *Church History*, 61 (1992), 394–407.

[121] Bozeman, 'Covenant Theology', p. 3.
[122] Quoted in Greaves, 'Knox and the Covenant Tradition', p. 39.
[123] Bozeman, 'Covenant Theology', pp. 5–6.
[124] Ibid., p. 9; *idem*, 'Federal Theology', p. 401.
[125] Bozeman, 'Covenant Theology', p. 18; *idem*, 'Federal Theology', p. 402.
[126] Bozeman, 'Covenant Theology', p. 19.
[127] Ibid., p. 24.

separate national and gracious covenants' but were instead 'exponents of a single "league" in which individual and corporate, evangelical and temporal elements were integrated'.[128]

Patrick Collinson has supported Bozeman's interpretation of Elizabethan writings on the idea of a national covenant, seeing the concept as crucial to the logic of the St Paul's Cross sermons, with ministers often describing baptism as the entrance into this covenant.[129] However, he notes that preachers' rhetoric in St Paul's Cross sermons, whilst being imbued with this notion of 'deuteronomic punishment', incorporated the belief that 'God's covenant would be honoured not by the whole nation, but only by a remnant, a remnant which might for a time redeem and preserve the nation, but which would also survive the temporal ruin of the nation.'[130] In a broader context, Alexandra Walsham has seen the sermon tradition of the jeremiad as informed by an implicit covenanted relationship between God and the nation.[131]

Jeremiads and fasts

The treatment of the idea of a national covenant offered in this book follows Bozeman in seeing it as incorporating both personal and corporate elements and offering both spiritual and temporal punishments and rewards. Like the Elizabethan Presbyterians, the godly of seventeenth century England also found it easy to move seamlessly from discussing covenants of grace between man and God to talk about the covenants which bound the nation of Israel to the Lord. Like Cartwright and Knewstub, they did not distinguish between the elect and the reprobate in their sermons, but talked in inclusive terms about the duties attendant on entering into covenant with God (though they did incorporate the idea of a 'saving remnant' into their discourse). Moreover, they saw this covenant as having political as well as religious implications, implications which could render allegiance to the monarch conditional, urge the alteration of the course of foreign policy, legitimise war and even sanction the use of violence against fellow Protestants.

Part I of this book will examine in detail the lengthy discussion of the idea of a national covenant by the Long Parliament's fast sermon ministers. However, these sermons, with their warnings about the dangers facing England and the imminent threat of divine vengeance were, as Alexandra Walsham

---

[128] Ibid., p. 11.

[129] Collinson, 'Biblical Rhetoric: The English Nation and National Sentiment in the Prophetic Mode', in *Religion and Culture in Renaissance England*, eds. C. McEachem and D. Shuger (Cambridge, 1977), pp. 27–8.

[130] Ibid., p. 20.

[131] Walsham, '"England's Warning by Israel": Paul's Cross Prophecy', in her *Providence in Early Modern England* (Oxford, 1999), ch. 6 esp. p. 306.

and Patrick Collinson have shown, only following the tradition of the Paul's Cross jeremiads which had resounded from the pulpit since 1534. Crucial to the message of these preachers had been what Michael McGiffert has dubbed the 'Israelite paradigm', the idea that England was really a new Israel, and that the Old Testament provided examples of what would happen if the nation did not remedy her flaws and imperfections.[132] They stressed the blessings that God had granted the nation, in particular the special privilege of the gift of the word and the country's salvation from the threat of Catholic insurrection and foreign invasion. In return for the mercy and favour that God had shown England, the preachers stressed that the people in turn owed him a special debt of gratitude, suggesting an implicit covenanted relationship.[133] According to Collinson, the message of Paul's Cross ministers concerning the nation was 'always the same: most favoured, most obligated, most negligent'.[134] Their preaching 'offered to unite a nation in the renewal of its national, covenanted relationship with God'.[135] Walsham argues that this implicit covenant relationship was 'intrinsically seditious' in that it suggested that magistrates who winked at sin were as guilty (and liable to punishment) as the sinners themselves. During the 1620s and 1630s, these radical implications came to fruition as 'Calvinists became convinced that the Caroline government was not merely conniving at popery and profanation of the Lord's Day but actively enjoining these abominations'.[136]

Walsham and Collinson both see the idea of a national covenant as integral to the Paul's Cross sermons. Recently, however, Mary Morrissey has offered a blunt rebuttal of their arguments, stating that 'the prophetic sermons preached at Paul's Cross do not presuppose a "national covenant" or any kind of special relationship between God and England.'[137] According to Morrissey, Walsham and Collinson have made a crucial mistake in blurring the distinction between the identification of Israel as a type of true church and Israel as an example of a sinful nation. She argues that it was only as a type of invisible church, or communion of saints, that Israel was covenanted to God on Sinai.[138] Preachers saw an analogy between Israel and England *as nations*, on the basis of Israel's sinfulness, not her status as most favoured by God.[139]

---

[132] M. McGiffert, 'God's Controversy with Jacobean England', *American Historical Review*, 88 (1983), 1151–74.

[133] Walsham, *Providence in Early Modern England*, ch. 6.

[134] Collinson, 'Biblical Rhetoric', p. 28.

[135] Ibid., p. 20.

[136] Walsham, *Providence in Early Modern England*, pp. 291–2.

[137] M. Morrissey, 'Elect Nations and Prophetic Preaching: Types and Examples in the Paul's Cross Jeremiad', *The English Sermon Revised, Religion, Literature and History 1600–1750*, eds. L. A. Ferrell and Peter McCullough (Manchester, 2000) pp. 43–58.

[138] Ibid., pp. 48–9.

[139] Ibid., p. 52.

The use of the simple analogy between Israel and England as nations was certainly commonplace. Richard Jefferay's *The Sonne of God's Entertainment by the Sonnes of Men* (1605) offers just one example: 'if we examine our estate of Israel and England, by the rule of Prophets and Apostles; is it not with England as it was the little land of Goshen, which had the light of God, when all Egypt was darke?'[140] Likewise Stephen Denison, who stated that by 'the house of Israel in this place, is meant the Church of God both among the Iewes and among the Gentiles. For the name Israel is given to both peoples.' The name of Israel can be applied to 'all Gods people, because they are a generation that can wrestle with God in prayer, and also prevail'.[141] However, some ministers clearly saw the connection between the two nations as being that both were in covenant with God. George Carleton's *A Remembrance* (1624) explicitly compared England and Israel as covenanted nations.[142] The examples of divine punishment against Israel also concerned England because both enjoyed a covenanted relationship with God.

Divine punishments and rewards alone were though no indication of covenanted status because God also lifted up heathen or idolatrous nations to prosperity.[143] However, as Thomas Jackson pointed out in 1622, England might even fare worse than idolatrous nations under its covenant with God because

> small sinnes, of such a people as have entred into league and covenant with God, and have received the knowledge of his truth, and make profession of his feare, are more grievous and displeasing unto God, than great rebellions of professed Atheists and Idolators.[144]

This was why England and Israel had suffered so, because they had received the word but in time neglected it.

Elizabethan and Jacobean preachers not only referred to an 'implicit covenant relationship' in describing a history of divine rewards and punishments, but also described an explicit national covenant that bound England. The anonymous author of *The Reformation of Religion by Josiah* (1590) said that the 'Lord tyed himselfe to this whole nation, that wee might bee his people' but asked whether 'wee on our behalfe again kept covenant with the Lord, in taking him to bee our god, to know and cleave unto him in all our wayes?'[145]

---

[140] p. 25. For eulogies to England alone see Thomas Clarke, *The Popes Deadly Wound* (1621), 'To the Christian Reader', 'The Kingdom of England is Gods . . . God hath made speciall choyce of England above all Nations in the World, to effect some notable and extraordinary worke.'

[141] S. Denison, *The New Creature* (1622), pp. 8–9.

[142] pp. 216–17.

[143] Morrissey, 'Elect Nations', p. 52.

[144] T. Jackson, *Judah Must Into Captivitie* (London, 1622), p. 101.

[145] 'To the Christian Reader'.

He called on the queen to bring the godly people and ministers together and make a covenant with the Lord by which he would increase England's blessings.[146] Nehemiah Rogers told his congregation that if they wondered why England was afflicted with plagues and punishments, it was because they had 'taken of that execrable thing, and broken the Covenant of the Lord'.[147] How terrible it was, he went on, that 'civill honesty' would make men have 'some conscience of keeping promise made with man', but that they would 'willingly and wilfully breake covenant with God'.[148] John Brinsley urged England to follow the example of Judah in renewing their vowes under Hezekiah and then Josiah, 'even to a generall renewing of the Covenant amongst all the people'.[149] Theodore Herring stated that God had 'entred into a covenant with us, striken a firme league: Hee hath taken us for his people; we challenge him for our God.'[150] John Preston preached before Charles I that God had made a covenant with England. Citing Leviticus 26: 25 – 'I will send a sword upon you, which shall avenge the quarrell of my covenant' – Preston glossed it as 'if he should say, there is a covenant, and you have broke that covenant, and therefore I have a quarrel, and I will send my sword to avenge my quarrell.'[151]

At times there are suggestions that preachers are only talking about the 'invisible' church of saints when they refer to those that are in covenant with God. Jackson talked of 'all the true members' of the church as 'the people that God hath redeemed with his bloud, entred into a perpetuall league and covenant with him'.[152] Certainly we can see in these sermons the concept of the 'saving remnant', used earlier by the Marian exiles, coming back into play. Here the godly minority have a special role to play in interceding with God to stave off judgement provoked by the majority's faithlessness and backsliding. The godly's prayers were, said Jackson, 'bands to tie his hands, and as a wall against him, that he cannot execute his anger'.[153] John Brinsley concurred, urging that only those 'in a true League and Covenant with God' had the power to 'turne the plot devised agaynst Gods people to their joyfullest day'.[154] However, the idea of a national covenant presented by these ministers is more complex than simply a covenant of grace which bound only the elect. Brinsley, whilst making use of the idea of the 'saving remnant' was keen to state that

---

[146] Ibid., p. 12.

[147] N. Rogers, A Strange Vineyard in Palaestina (1623), p. 188.

[148] Ibid., p. 198.

[149] J. Brinsley, The Fourth Part of the True Watch: Containing Prayers and Teares for the Churches (1624), p. 41.

[150] T. Herring, The Triumph of the Church (1624), p. 9.

[151] J. Preston, 'A Sensible Demonstration of the Deitie', in Sermons Preached Before His Majestie (1630), pp. 61–93, p. 83.

[152] Jackson, Judah Must Into Captivitie, p. 31.

[153] Ibid., p. 50.

[154] Brinsley, Fourth Part, pp. 157, 161.

all his congregation should strive to be part of this happy few.[155] Moreover, these preachers often alluded to the individual's entrance into this national covenant being through their baptismal vows.[156] Brinsley urged his readers to 'remember our Baptisme vow in a speciall manner, to fight manfully under his [God's] banner, and to stand for him for ourselves and for our brethren'.[157]

If the covenant was applied nationally, via baptism, the blessings that accom-panied keeping it, and curses that followed breaking it, were also described in national terms. These ministers rehearsed the great mercies that God had shown to England, as in 1588 and 1605, and the spiritual debt that this good fortune had incurred.[158] They warned that England's neglect of the word and ingratitude for the gifts God had bestowed on the country would bring down dire punishment upon the nation. However, as a covenanted deity, God did not deal out his judgements peremptorily but warned when he was about to strike, giving the nation an opportunity to repent. Through storms and tempests, dearth, plague and famine, God warned of even worse to come.[159] Preston believed that people must learn to read nature for signs of the workings of God's providence. God's will was not seen because ungrateful man had lost sight of the miracle of creation. In taking heed of these warnings, ministers occupied a crucial role as 'watchmen' and 'must give warning, that we may deliver our owne soules, lest your bloud be required at our hands'.[160] He stated that God's 'promises are as his threatenings, to bee understood with a con-dition'. It was good for the nation 'to compound with the Lord, and to take up this suite before it come to execution and judgement'.[161] Thomas Jackson laid out the elements of this providential, covenanted relationship: God gives warning of his judgements, God's people make efforts to pacify him when they see these signs; God's servants hold great sway with the Lord and their prayers and supplications can turn away his wrath; sometimes, however, the sins are so great that God will not hear their prayers. As examples of the sins that could lead God to turn his back on a nation, Jackson included idolatry and atheism, corrupt clergy, blasphemy, hypocrisy, prophaning the sabbath, criminality, usury, drunkenness and thanklessness.[162]

Set against the backdrop of the Thirty Years War, the jeremiads of the 1620s took the misfortunes of continental Protestantism as a dire warning to England. Jackson claimed that godly ministers in Europe had tried, as he was now, to

---

[155] Ibid., p. 3.
[156] Rogers, *Strange Vineyard*, p. 198.
[157] Brinsley, *Fourth Part*, 'The Epistle' and p. 39. The same allusion was made by John Lawrence, *A Golden Trumpet to Rowse up a Drowsie Magistrate* (1624), p. 21.
[158] Brinsley, *Fourth Part*, p. 34; Herring, *Triumph of the Church*, p. 26; T. Taylor, *A Mappe of Rome* (1620), p. 94.
[159] Rogers, *Strange Vineyard*, pp. 209, 214.
[160] Preston, *Sermons*, pp. 81–3.
[161] Preston, 'Sensible Demonstration of the Deitie', pp. 85–6.
[162] Jackson, *Judah Must Into Captivitie*, pp. 1, 89–93.

alert their congregations to the consequences of their sinfulness but they had been deaf to these pleas. The fruits of their obstinacy were now plain.[163] Thomas Gataker urged his audience not to be complacent about events in far off lands:

> Neither let any man say; what is their affliction to us? What are those part to these? What is France to Germanie or to England? For what was Jerusalem to Antioch? Or what was Judea to Macedonia and Achaia?[164]

He warned that if England withheld help to her co-religionists, the curse of Meroz would be upon her.[165] Other divines, without calling for intervention in Europe, warned of the curse that would fall on England if she remained lukewarm in her faith.[166] War in Europe also prompted these divines to extend the idea of a national covenant to incorporate the notion of a union of Protestant states. Thomas Scott remarked that it was 'a shame whilst Heathens and Idolators bynde themselves in strict leagues, that Abraham, and Lot, should not helpe each other'.[167] Preston warned that the enemies of Christendom were 'not only stirred up, but united together, and we dis-joyned to resist them'.[168] Brinsley talked of the 'wished and happy union amongst thy churches and servants, and the cutting off the long wished hopes of the enemies of thy church'.[169]

As the penalties attached to breaking this covenant were national in effect, so the proposed means of assuaging God's anger or averting the execution of divine wrath were corporate and public. Although the works of Preston, Scott and Gataker clearly had a subversive potential and a more belligerent bent, the main remedies proposed to England and Europe's maladies were spiritual not carnal. Heavy stress was laid on the need for regular public fasting and prayers.[170] Special prayers and masses were well established in England prior to the reformation but were encouraged under Thomas Cranmer's influence until the Edwardian articles and injunctions ended processions and put a note of caution into discussions of fasting. The Book of Common Prayer furnished

---

[163] Ibid., p. 25.

[164] T. Gataker, *A Sparke Toward the Kindling of Sorrow for Sion* (1621), p. 33.

[165] Ibid., p. 37. The curse of Meroz is mentioned in the song of Deborah and Barak in the Book of Judges, v. 23, 'Curse ye Meroz, said the Angel of the Lord/Curse ye bitterly the inhabitants thereof/because they came not to the help of the Lord/to the help of the Lord against the mighty.'

[166] Brinsley, *Fourth Part*, p. 3; T. Beard, *Antichrist the Pope of Rome* (1625), title page; Preston, *Sermons*, p. 50; Jackson, *Judah Must Into Captivitie*, p. 60.

[167] [T. Scott], *Vox Dei* (1624), pp. 45–6. Scott blamed the failure to forge such alliances on the advice of evil counsellors.

[168] Preston, *Sermons*, p. 84.

[169] Brinsley, *Fourth Part*, p. 400.

[170] Rogers, *Strange Vineyard*, pp. 266, 298; Brinsley, *Fourth Part*, p. 37; Preston, *Sermons*, pp. 91–2; Jackson, *Judah Must Into Captivitie*, pp. 41–3; R. Wakeman, *Jonah's Sermon and Ninevehs Repentance* (1606), p. 74.

prayers for death, famine, war and plague. These were quickly supplemented by additional special prayers, both of supplication and thanksgiving, tailored to specific emergencies. Prayers were usually accompanied by calls for fasting and almsgiving and reinforced by sermons and homilies as in the case of the homily against disobedience and wilful rebellion (1571) and after the 1580 earthquake. The initiative for compiling these prayers often came from the secular authorities, the monarch, secretary of state or Privy Council. The concept of keeping a particular day each year in thanksgiving for a certain event was introduced in 1576 to celebrate the queen's accession.[171]

Non-state sponsored fasts flourished in puritan areas like Southam in Warwickshire. Sometimes these occasions were used not to raise money for the local poor but to get financial aid for Protestants in France and Germany. However, the 1604 canons banned all unauthorised fasting and in the first two decades of James I's reign there were few fasts except for the commemoration of the Gunpowder Plot on 5 November and Elizabeth I's accession day on 17 November. Charles I established a regular fast day in July 1625 on Wednesday each week to ward off the plague and agreed to requests for several more public fasts. Yet, the godly remained at the forefront of this activity, with John White, 'The Patriarch of Dorchester', holding weekly fasts in the 1620s. The Harleys of Brampton Bryan held fasts deliberately timed to coincide with important debates in Parliament. Although Laud continued to concede the need for solemn public fasting, as during the plague visitation of 1636, he looked upon private fasts, like other aspects of puritan voluntary religion, as inherently seditious, and placed clear restrictions on the administration of that fast. The ruling that there were to be no sermons in areas badly affected by the plague and no sermons longer than an hour in areas outside the infected zone led to the fasts being derided as 'Popish dumb Pageants' by Daniel Rogers.[172]

Although physical privation remained a part of the godly fast, the emphasis was on preaching and moral self-examination, rather than bodily mortification.[173] These fasts keyed in with the idea of a saving remnant who could stave off divine retribution. Thomas Hooker stated in 1626 that however 'wicked men will be persuaded and humbled, yet if there be a competent

[171] CJ Kitching, 'Prayers Fit for the Time': Fasting and Prayer in Response to National Crises in the Reign of Elizabeth I', in *Monks, Hermits and the Ascetic Tradition* (Ecclesiastical History Society, 1985), pp. 241–51.

[172] T. Webster, *Godly Clergy in Early Stuart England* (Cambridge, 1997), ch. 3; C. Durston, '"For the Better Humiliation of the People": Public Days of Fasting and Thanksgiving During the English Revolution', *The Seventeenth Century*, 7 (1992), 129–49; S. Hindle, 'Dearth, Fasting and Alms: The Campaign for General Hospitality in Late Elizabethan England', *Past and Present*, 172 (2001), 44–86; H. Bartle, 'The Story of Public Fast Days in England', *Anglican Theological Review*, 37 (1955), 190–200.

[173] Durston, '"For the Better Humiliation"', p. 135; but see also Webster, *Godly Clergy*, p. 73.

number, if there be so many as will make an army of fasting and prayer to grapple with God [note again the idea of binding God], they may prevail with God for mercy for a kingdom.'[174] The texts of the prayers used on fast days sometimes explicitly refer to the nation's covenanted relationship with God. A prayer of 1563 issued in response to the plague stated that the 'people of Israel' had often offended God and he had 'most justly afflicted them, but as oft as they returned to thee, thou didst receive them to mercy'. God had made 'the same covenant' with England 'or rather a covenant of more excellency and efficacy' enriched with Christ's grace. The supplicants flew to the terms of this covenant to seek defence from God's just wrath.[175] Other prayers made in response to the plague visitation of 1563 used the same idea that God had sent this afflic-tion to chastise, not destroy England, for 'though he make a wound, he giveth a plaster'.[176] We can even find hints in these prayers of the idea of Elizabeth as a covenanted monarch. A prayer issued in 1568 for the recovery of the queen from her sickness, suggested in its original form that Elizabeth had suffered because she had 'not in dede soo well as she ought to have done remem-bered and acknowledged' that she was God's 'subiect and handmayden'.[177]

By the time of the Armada public prayers accompanying days of fasting and thanksgiving were strident in their belief in England's 'special relationship' with the Almighty:

We the people of England are thy people, O Lord, and thou are our God: we are thy flocke, and thou art our shepheard: we are thy children, and thou art our Father, Be merciful unto us thy children: tender us thy flock, and defend us thy English nation. Turne thy wrath upon the nations that have not known thee, and that doe not call upon thy name.[178]

As a more interventionist foreign policy was pursued in the last decade of the queen's reign, prayers referred, as would the jeremiads of the 1620s, to the dangers that came from the enemies of God associating together, as in the French Holy League, and called on God to 'associate unto him such as may aid him to maintain his right, and be zealous of thy glory'.[179] Some ministers later saw the regular recourse to public prayers and fasting in the Elizabethan period as frequent renewals of the nation's covenant with God. John Brinsley stated that 'hereunto we have so oft, and so solemnly bound ourselves every-one, at least by those in our places, I meane by our Magistrates and Ministers, as namely we did in those . . . solemne fasts by commandment in the yeare

---

[174] Ibid., p. 64.
[175] *Liturgies and Occasional Forms of Prayer, Set Forth in the Reign of Queen Elizabeth*, ed. W. K. Clay (Cambridge, 1847), pp. 483–5; apparently based on Knox's Book of Common Order.
[176] Ibid., p. 494.
[177] Ibid., pp. 516–17.
[178] Ibid., p. 609.
[179] Ibid., pp. 630, 647–8, 653.

[fifteen] eighty-eight.' Then, Brinsley said, God had shown that he was willing to fight for England.[180]

Contrary to Morrissey's claims, the idea of national covenant was integral to the sermon jeremiad and public prayers and fasting. The allusion between Old Testament Israel and England as God's most favoured nations was a nuanced one, and could incorporate the idea of a 'saving remnant', or the idea of a covenanted union of reformed nations, but remained potent despite these complexities. Preachers saw England as a new Israel, not merely because both nations were at times sinful, and deserving of divine punishment, but because they were both in a covenanted relationship with God. If both nations were at times cast down it was because they had been neglectful of the great gifts that God had bestowed upon them. The remedy for the nation's woes was public and national, as well as private and personal, reformation and repentance. Divines did not refuse to distinguish between the elect and the reprobate within the covenant for purely 'hortatory' reasons, as Morrissey suggests, but, like John Brinsley, they simply did not know who was within the 'saving remnant' and who was not. As the scale of reformed practical divinity suggests, the question of assurance of salvation, and God's sovereignty over all events, exercised godly consciences greatly. The failure to divide goats from sheep was not a didactic ploy to harness all to the task of moral reformation, but recognition of the fact that making such a distinction was fraught with difficulties and dangers.

Holy war and covenanted rebellion

Many of the sermons cited above were delivered against the background of confessional warfare in Europe. However, though these divines might use the examples of the fate of reformed nations on the continent to show what would happen if England did not repent, they did not all argue for the abandonment of James I's pacific foreign policy. Nehemiah Rogers, though his work reflected a belief in the imminence of the apocalypse, believed that England's peace was one of its covenanted blessings and he attacked divines that cried for war.[181] In a recent article, Ben Lowe has argued that historians like J. R. Hale and Timothy George have over-exaggerated the belligerence of late Elizabethan and early Stuart preachers, and that there was in fact significant discourse in praise of peace maintained by preachers like Jewel, Pilkington and Sandys. He contends that many of the pro-war divines of the 1610s and 1620s were really talking about spiritual, rather than carnal warfare.[182]

---

[180] Brinsley, *Fourth Part*, p. 36.
[181] Rogers, *Strange Vineyard*, pp. 262–3.
[182] B. Lowe, 'Religious Wars and the "Common Peace": Anglican Anti-War Sentiment in Elizabethan England', *Albion*, 28 (1996), 415–35. J. R. Hale, 'Incitement to Violence? English Divines on the Theme of War, 1578–1631', in *Renaissance War Studies* (London, 1983), ch. 18.

Certainly, when many of these divines warned of the curse of Meroz, they were mostly talking about the need to abandon religious, rather than military, neutrality. Equally, even a minister like John Preston, who warned of the likely divine punishments that would follow the failure to aid the Protestant cause in Europe, and has been identified as one of the most politically engaged of the godly ministers of early Stuart England, did not explicitly advocate a pro-war stance in his court sermons.[183] There remained, none the less, a small number of divines, William Gouge, Richard Bernard, Thomas Barnes, Alexander Leighton and Samuel Bachiler, who clearly legitimated war on religious grounds. In the case of Leighton and Bachiler their advocacy of a confessional foreign policy clearly incorporated the idea of a national covenant.

Religiously grounded arguments for the use of force were not solely the preserve of godly ministers, as J. R. Hale suggested.[184] Indeed, as the research of Timothy George and Peter Lake has shown, religious war arguments formed an important part of mainstream theological discourse in the 1620s and 1630s, urging a more interventionist, pro-Protestant foreign policy. From 1588 onwards English Protestant writers began to suggest that it would be carnal, not spiritual weapons that would overthrow the papal Antichrist. In the work of Alexander Leighton, Thomas Barnes, William Gouge and Richard Bernard, George has seen a shift from the moderation in fighting urged by William Ames (which included a condemnation of the slaughter of the children of Benjamin by the Israelites as a wanton act of violence – Bernard and Gouge both saw the slaughter of the Benjaminites as giving a positive sanction to holy wars against other Protestants) to the assertion that God himself was a 'man of war'.[185] Barnes went as far as to suggest that military service could actually lead to religious conversion, whilst Gouge was already considering the possibility of a holy war against Protestants themselves.[186]

None the less, it was possible for the holy war idea to cohabit with the theory of just war given some basic shared assumptions between the two strands of

---

[183] C. Hill, 'The Political Sermons of John Preston', in his *Puritanism and Revolution* (Panther edn., London, 1968), ch. 8. (Preston did refer to the judgement of God against the house of Eli, who lived in peace and became soft, *Sermons*, p. 84.)

[184] Hale, 'Incitement to Violence', pp. 503–5.

[185] R. Bernard, *The Bible-Battels, or the Sacred Art Military* (1629), p. 42; W. Gouge, *Gods Three Arrows* (1631), p. 213.

[186] T. George, 'War and Peace in the Puritan Tradition', *Church History*, 53 (1984), 492–503; P. Lake, 'The Moderate and Irenic Case for Religious War: Joseph Hall's *Via Media* in Context', in *Political Culture and Cultural Politics in England: Essays Presented to David Underdown*, eds. S. D. Amussen and M. A. Kishlansky (Manchester, 1995), pp. 55–84. For the political background to these sermons, see S. Adams, 'Foreign Policy and the Parliaments of 1621 and 1624', in *Faction and Parliament*, ed. K. Sharpe (Oxford, 1978), pp. 139–73; *idem*, 'Spain or the Netherlands? The Dilemmas of Early Stuart Foreign Policy', in *Before the English Civil War*, ed. H. Tomlinson (Basingstoke, 1983), pp. 79–103; T. Cogswell, *The Blessed Revolution: English Politics and the Coming of War, 1621–4* (Cambridge, 1989).

thought: that there should be rules for governing the conduct of war and that war must be authorised by a higher authority. As J. R. Hale showed, some of these authors like Bernard essentially wanted to show that the bible was just as valuable a source of military information as the popular classical texts of Vegetius, Frontinus and Caesar.[187] Writers like Gouge and Sutcliffe justified war on the grounds of natural and international, as well as divine law, incorporating into their works the ideas of European theorists on 'just war'.[188] They were also careful to establish limits to the use of violence in God's cause. The soldiers of Christ should take no joy in killing. Old men, women and children were not to be treated harshly, and mercy was, in most cases, to be shown to the conquered.[189] However, holy writ was occasionally used to extend the types of conduct permitted in war, beyond the scope of the just war concept, allowing ministers to justify tactics such as attacking a neutral country if it hinders an army from crossing its territory.[190]

Although authors like Gouge and Bernard were keen to stress the religious preparations, prayers and humiliation needed before going into battle, their works did not amount to calls for 'holy wars' or crusades, but offered biblical justifications for the use of force in a variety of contexts. The same was still true of those authors that incorporated the idea of a national covenant into their defences of violence. Alexander Leighton's *Speculum Belli Sacri*, published in Amsterdam in 1624, called on the Parliament to 'strike your Covenant then with the Lord, and your warre shall surely prosper'.[191] Wars, Leighton said, were lawful when they were based upon the 'Law of Nature and Nations' or when they were called for by the absolute command of God.[192] He called on the king to see in Germany 'how the Lord hath met with tolerators of false religion'.[193] Here, though, we should note an important difference between Leighton's rhetoric and that used by advocates of holy war in the 1640s. He did not use the religious justification for the use of force to remove the usual restraints urged on military conduct. The conquered were to be treated humanely, there was to be no revelling in bloodshed, and in siege warfare, restraint was to be shown when taking a town by force rather than negotiation.[194] Samuel Bachiler's *Miles Christianus, or the Campe Royal*, published in Amsterdam in 1629, also urged the need to ensure that the cause of the war

---

[187] Hale, 'Incitement to Violence', p. 499.
[188] B. Donagan, 'Codes and Conduct in the English Civil War', *Past and Present*, 188 (1988), 65–95, at 76; Gouge, *Gods Three Arrows*, pp. 215–16; Bernard, *Bible-Battells*, ch. 5.
[189] [A. Leighton], *Speculum Belli Sacri, or the Looking Glasse of the Holy War* (Amsterdam, 1624), pp. 247–8; Gouge, *Gods Three Arrows*, p. 295; Bernard, *Bible-Battells*, pp. 250–1.
[190] Hale, 'Incitement to Violence', pp. 496–7.
[191] [Leighton], *Speculum Belli Sacri*, 'To Parliament'.
[192] Ibid., p. 6.
[193] Ibid., p. 240.
[194] Ibid., pp. 162, 247–8.

was just. No Christian conflict could be fought without provocation, Christians must not be the aggressors, and equally war that was undertaken for booty or fame was illegitimate.[195] However, like John Preston, but in a far more obviously martial context, Bachiler also used the text of Leviticus, stating that 'God will make his people revenge the quarrell of his Covenant upon them.'[196] God would desert the cause of a sinful people, so it was vital that the military leadership eradicate immoral behaviour from the camp and from their soldiers. Holiness would serve, far more than uniforms or insignia, to distinguish the forces of God from his enemies.[197]

Leighton's *Sion's Plea*, published the same year, repeated the covenant-based arguments for war but, after the short-lived alliance of Buckingham with godly ministers during the 'Blessed Revolution' of 1624 had disintegrated, adopted a far more politically threatening tone. Afflictions and plagues continued to be visited upon England because of its attachment to prelacy and the toleration of the twin heresies of separatism and Arminianism.[198] Worse than this, England had neglected the signs of God's divine providence evinced in the failure of the Spanish Match, and instead married her prince to 'the Daughter of Heth', Henrietta Maria.[199] Leighton praised John Felton, Buckingham's assassin, as a divine emissary, a projection aided by Felton's own belief that, like Ehud or Phineas, he was an agent of the Lord's vengeance.[200] As if this attack on the queen and the duke was not controversial enough, Leighton also stated that the king would be counted an enemy of God if he continued to follow the advice of prelates.[201] There was no time to wait for Charles or the Parliament to begin the work of reformation in earnest but instead 'Gods people, with all, must labour to be of one minde, and of one heart, and by entering covenant with God, against those his enimies, all that is enmitie to God, resolve to hould them at staves end, till God give the victorie.'[202] Leighton paid severely for his remarks. In 1630 Star Chamber fined him £10,000, imprisoned him for life, ordered his nose to be slit, his ears trimmed and his forehead branded with S. S. for 'sower of sedition'.[203] Leighton's imprisonment in the Fleet was never 'close' and within two years of this punishment being

---

[195] S. Bachiler, *Miles Christianus, or the Campe Royal* (Amsterdam, 1629), pp. 12–13.

[196] Ibid., p. 37.

[197] Ibid., pp. 38–40.

[198] A. Leighton, *An Appeal to the Parliament; or Sion's Plea against the Prelacie* (Amsterdam, 1629), pp. 79–83.

[199] Ibid., p. 172.

[200] S. Foster, *Notes from the Caroline Underground: Alexander Leighton, the Puritan Triumvirate, and the Laudian Reaction to Nonconformity* (Connecticut, 1978), pp. 28–32.

[201] Leighton, *Sion's Plea*, p. 271.

[202] Ibid., p. 333.

[203] V. T. Wells, 'The Origins of Covenanting Thought and Resistance: c. 1580–1638' (Stirling Ph.D., 1997), p. 141. Leighton apparently gloried in his mutilation, Foster, *Notes from the Caroline Underground*, p. 34.

carried out, he was again keeping conventicles, where he preached before future Parliamentary fast sermon ministers, Stephen Marshall, Edmund Calamy and Cornelius Burgess. Leighton's works influenced William Prynne and in 1635 John Bastwick would openly defend the contents of *Sion's Plea* before the Court of High Commission.[204] Although sporadic attempts were made to revive the idea of a confessional foreign policy in the 1630s, conformist divines increasingly disassociated themselves from this Protestant internationalist outlook and dealings with foreign reformed churches were viewed with growing suspicion during the Personal Rule.[205] What had been a discourse open to bishops like Joseph Hall, had now become identified with a dangerous puritan anti-episcopal alliance.

With the possibility of a pro-Protestant foreign policy stalled and the Laudian repression of dissenting voices like Leighton's, discussions of a national covenant in England were scarce.[206] In Scotland, however, the idea of a national covenant would form the basis for a successful resistance movement opposed to the political and religious policies of Charles I. There has been a great deal of debate concerning the origins of the Scottish National Covenant in 1638. Some have stressed religious influences from the reformed theology of Robert Rollock.[207] Others have pointed to the importance of legal traditions in Scotland and the legacy of cultural practices like banding.[208] For Margaret Steele 'what became known as the National Covenant was largely a piece of political brinkmanship born of accommodation and political expediency.'[209] She argues that the precedents offered by bands of manrent were incomparable with a movement that acquired signatures to the covenant in the tens of thousands. For this reason she defines the Scottish covenanting movement as essentially a petitioning campaign.[210] David Mullan has argued that prior

[204] Wells, 'Origins of Covenanting Thought', pp. 143–8, 161.

[205] A. Milton, *Catholic and Reformed: The Roman and Protestant Churches in English Protestant Thought: 1600–1640* (Cambridge, 1995), esp. chs. 2 & 9.

[206] Although see the importance of the covenant idea to Henry Burton's anti-popery sermons of the 1630s, below, pp. 80, 139–41.

[207] M. Steele, '"The Politick Christian": The Theological Background to the National Covenant', in *Scottish National Covenant*, ed. J. S. Morrill, pp. 31–68. J. D. Ford, 'Conformity in Conscience: The Structure of the Perth Articles Debate in Scotland, 1618–38', *Journal of Ecclesiastical History*, 46 (1995), 256–77; *idem*, 'The Lawful Bonds of Scottish Society: The Five Articles of Perth, the Negative Confession and the National Covenant', *Historical Journal*, 37 (1994), pp. 45–64.

[208] S. A. Burrell, 'The Apocalyptic Vision of the Early Covenanters', *Scottish Historical Review*, 43 (1964), 1–24; *idem*, 'The Covenant Idea as a Revolutionary Symbol, 1596–1637', *Church History*, 27 (1958), 338–50. E. J. Cowan, 'The Making of the National Covenant', in *Scottish National Covenant*, ed. Morrill, pp. 68–90.

[209] M. Steele, 'Covenanting Political Propaganda, 1638–89' (Glasgow University Ph.D., 1995), p. 48. My thanks to Dr Steele for granting me permission to read her thesis.

[210] Ibid., pp. 74–5.

to the National Covenant, 'no Scottish divine advocated rebellion in the immediate national context, not even as a result of a broken contract'.[211] Overall, Mullan argues that the Jacobean period saw a retreat from the political radicalism of men like Knox and Goodman.[212]

V. T. Wells has complained that the work of Steele and others which concentrates on social or political explanations for the development of the National Covenant, whilst perhaps increasing our understanding of how the mechanisms for tendering these documents were established, leaves us with the problem of where the idea of the covenant itself originated.[213] Here, there are similarities with the discussions of the idea of a national covenant in an English context. As in England there has been an attempt to link too closely the development of federal theology with the idea of a national covenant. As in England, the chronology is wrong, with clear evidence of the idea of a national covenant emerging in a Scottish context by the mid-sixteenth century. Equally, as in England, it is hard to see how a theological system, federal theology, whose energies were largely channelled into practical divinity and the cure of souls, offered a ready springboard for developing an idea with such obvious political ramifications as that of a national covenant. Indeed, Arthur Williamson has argued that the work of the leading Scottish exponent of federal theology, Robert Rollock, was largely apolitical, and that his work on the prophecies of Daniel and St John was uncontroversial and lacking an apocalyptic edge.[214] This is not to say that federal theology did not have an important influence on the national covenant idea once the concept had already emerged. As will be made clear in Chapter 4, in both England and Scotland, it had the effect of enriching the discussion of the benefits and obligations placed on individuals that were within the covenant. It was not, though, a formative influence.

Wells, like Jane Dawson, stresses the close contacts between Scottish Presbyterians and opponents of episcopacy in England, and the exchange of ideas between these groups. This interaction was encouraged by schemes for a 'holy league' between England and Scotland, as had earlier been promoted by Knox. The notion was taken up in the 1620s by John Davenport and the irenicist John Dury. Davenport wrote in 1624, 'How much better would it beseeme us to combine together in an holy league against the common [Catholic] adversary.'[215] It was also the case that looking back from the seventeenth century, covenanters described many of the kirk's confessions of faith as national covenants. Archibald Johnston of Wariston, the main author

---

[211] D. G. Mullan, *Scottish Puritanism, 1590–1638* (Oxford, 2000), p. 254.

[212] Ibid., p. 257.

[213] Wells, 'The Origins of Covenanting Thought', p. 13.

[214] Williamson, *Scottish National Consciousness*, pp. 77–8. According to Williamson, Rollock located the fourth earthly monarchy of Rome firmly in the past.

[215] Wells, 'Origins of Covenanting Thought', pp. 149–51.

of the National Covenant of 1638, already believed Scotland to be a covenanted nation, bound by the Short Confession of 1580 and the Negative
Confession of 1581.[216]

As in England, it appears that the practice of taking oaths of loyalty acted
to promote the idea of a national covenant. Williamson suggests that the
idea of combining this covenant with subscription to an oath was inspired by
the question of the binding force of subscription to the Black Acts of 1584,
which bound those subscribing to them to support *juro humano* episcopacy.
Presbyterians like James Carmichael argued that it was a contravention of
a prior engagement, in this case a pre-existing covenant. Here Carmichael
probably had in mind the anti-papal oath of 1581 or the King's Confession
which abjured the 'Roman Antichrist', 'his worldly monarchie and wicked
hierarchy' and was first signed by members of the court but later subscribed by
the whole country.[217] The King's Confession was renewed in 1589/90 by the
General Assembly during Maitland's period of ascendancy, an era characterised by a vigorous programme of public banding. According to Williamson,
by the time of the renewal of the covenant in April 1596 the idea of a national
covenant 'was now firmly fixed in Scottish thinking as a feature of popular
piety'. Although the important Scottish Presbyterian thinkers John Davidson
and Andrew Melville were heavily involved in this effort to renew Scotland's
covenant with God, Williamson argues that their ideas 'almost certainly
sprang from the political needs of Scottish society rather than any elaborated
covenant theology'. When Melville discussed the renewal of Scotland's covenant, he thought first of the controversy over subscribing the Black Acts, not
of the covenant of grace or covenant of redemption.[218]

This is not to say that there was no subsequent influence from federal
theology upon the idea of a national covenant, only that it did not immediately
emerge directly from it. By the early seventeenth century, federal theology
had become an integral part of clerical education in Scotland. The Scottish
theologians John Forbes, Robert Howie and Robert Rollock ensured, through
their positions in the universities of Aberdeen and Edinburgh, that works of
federal theology like the Heidelburg Catechism were made required reading
for students of divinity. Margaret Steele has argued that these ideas permeated
the laity. As the only verification of faith, laymen often renewed their covenant
with God on a personal basis. Covenanting diaries, like that of Sir Archibald
Johnston of Wariston, recorded the process of moral self-examination by
which the laity attested their faith.[219] Covenanter propaganda described the
National Covenant as infinite and perpetual, and pamphleteers described
the covenant made by God with Israel as analogous with that made with his

---

[216] Williamson, *Scottish National Consciousness*, pp. 211–13.
[217] Ibid., pp. 67–8.
[218] Ibid., pp. 73–4.
[219] Steele, '"The Politick Christian"', pp. 46–9.

latter-day Scottish Israelites. They employed the idea that those that joined in the covenant gained special privileges, whilst those outside it were deemed amoral, irreligious and unpatriotic and urged that God would easily defeat those outside the covenant.[220]

The response of the king to the creation of the Scottish National Covenant was to tender a covenant of his own in an attempt to draw off support from the covenanter movement whilst appeasing Scottish grievances. The King's Covenant incorporated the 1581 Negative Confession but removed the politically controversial elements of the band in the National Covenant, thereby continuing the process of tendering oath and then counter-oath.[221] The covenanters, as well as feeding into the tradition of Knox in seeing the need for a covenanted union of the two kingdoms, believed that a solution to their grievances could only be reached by influencing events in England. Likewise, the covenanters' English supporters were sympathetic to the idea of a national covenant, and pamphlets printed in 1640 called on gentlemen, apprentices and others to 'resolve to do anything for religion' and mentioned 'a secret oath . . . so that if anyone individually suffered all should suffer, or else all should be relieved'.[222] The suspicion that some of his leading subjects were secretly in cahoots with rebels north of the border led Charles to impose another oath at a special meeting of the king's councillors at York. Lords Saye and Sele and Brooke refused to take the oath and were placed in custody, whilst Samuel Hartlib, who was suspected of acting as a go-between, was also arrested. The oath itself owed much to the Jacobean oath of allegiance, although it did not include its theological positions. Those who refused to swear questioned how far they were obliged to commit themselves against the Scots and whether the oath obliged them to an invasion of Scotland as well as the defence of England. Pointedly, they asked why the king could not have administered the 1606 oath if he had wanted to test the loyalty of his subjects, and queried the dubious novelty of an oath of allegiance directed not against Catholics, but against fellow Protestants.[223] The king nonetheless continued to resort to the use of oaths to uncover English sympathisers with the Scottish covenanters. The infamous 'etcetera' oath included in the sixth clause of the canons of 1640 has been described as Charles's answer to the National Covenant. Ironically though, as the research of Tom Webster has shown, it

---

[220] Steele, 'Covenanting Political Propaganda', pp. 217–23.

[221] P. Donald, *An Uncounselled King: Charles I and the Scottish Troubles, 1637–41* (Cambridge, 1990), pp. 89–94.

[222] Ibid., pp. 246–51. Evidence of popular sympathy in England for the Scottish covenanters' grievances is discussed by Dagmar Freist, 'The King's Crown is the Whore of Babylon: Politics, Gender and Communication in Mid-Seventeenth Century England', *Gender and History*, 7 (1995), 457–81. Pro-covenanter propaganda circulated widely in England at the time, see J. Black, 'Pikes and Protestations: Scottish Texts in England, 1639–40', *Publishing History*, XLII (1997), 1–19.

[223] C. Hibbard, *Charles I and the Popish Plot* (Chapel Hill, 1983), pp. 118–20.

actually acted to build connections between godly ministers as they joined in opposition to the device.[224]

Conclusion

In this chapter we have seen how the idea of a national covenant first fully emerged in the thought of the Marian exiles, John Knox and Christopher Goodman. It developed less as an offshoot of reformed covenant theology and more as a response to the political circumstances of Mary's reign. Ideas similar to the exiles' radical resistance theories resurfaced throughout Elizabeth's reign, in debates in Parliament, the marginalia of the Geneva Bible and the sermons of Edward Dering and Dudley Fenner. Uncertainty about the royal succession encouraged discussion of Elizabeth as a covenanted monarch and prompted proposals for an interim government that included the device of an oath of association, analogous to a sworn national covenant. This was not a case, though, of a few radical blips in an Elizabethan political picture otherwise characterised by harmony and consensus. The idea of a national covenant offered the fundamental structure for the cycle of divine punishments and rewards in Jacobean jeremiads and explained the recourse to public fasts and days of thanksgiving or humiliation. The idea that England was a covenanted nation was also a feature of the pro-war works of Alexander Leighton and Samuel Bachiler published in the 1620s. Neither was this simply a case of the importing of political ideas from Scotland or Europe into England. It is as hard to find the clear predecessors to Knox and Goodman's theories is it is to ascertain whom, out of the two, influenced the other most. Instead, we should, with Jane Dawson and V. T. Wells, see this as a reciprocal process in which English and Scottish ideas on a national covenant were readily exchanged as part of a shared Protestant culture. Just as it had been the Edwardian reformation which had first encouraged Knox to write of a nation in covenant with God, so the example of the Scottish covenanters would show the critics of Charles I exactly what a people covenanted to God through a publicly subscribed oath could achieve.

---

[224] J. Eales, 'A Road to Revolution: The Continuity of Puritanism, 1559–1642', in *The Culture of English Puritanism 1560–1700*, eds. C. Durston and J. Eales (1996), ch. 6; Webster, *Godly Clergy*, pp. 231–2, 288, 320.

Part I

The Long Parliament and the national covenant

2

Protestation, Vow and Covenant

Between May 1641 and September 1643 the Long Parliament imposed three main oaths of loyalty, the Protestation, the Vow and Covenant, and the Solemn League and Covenant. During the controversy over the sixth of the 1640 canons, some had questioned the wisdom of imposing oaths at all. Thomas Warmstry, clerk of the diocese of Worcester, argued that matters had not yet come to such a crisis in the church as to warrant the imposing of a new test upon the clergy, 'an Oath being like to sleeping or opiating Medicines, not to be administered but upon urgent exigencies'. John Ley, later president of Sion College, felt that the oath would only be a barrier to the conscientious,

> for they [Catholics] will easily bee persuaded to flight this oath, as they doe the oath of Allegiance, whereof some of them shew how the cautions against equivocation, mentall reservation, and Papall dispensation may bee eluded, and say, that the Oath, as unjust . . . is presently nullified ipso facto.[1]

Despite these cautions, less than six months later the Long Parliament produced the first of its oaths of loyalty, the Protestation in defence of the Church of England.

The Protestation

The Protestation was introduced into the Commons on 3 May 1641.[2] It was largely intended as a measure to help accelerate the process of the Earl of Strafford's attainder and stampede the bill through the Lords. The revelation of the first army plot helped to give weight to the Protestation's claim that England was now under threat from a papal conspiracy. This included a suggestion that the king's evil councillors intended to use the English army to subdue Parliament. Like the oath in the sixth canon, however, the Protestation

---

[1] T. Warmstry, *A Convocation Speech . . . Against Images, Altar Crosses, the New Canons and the Oath* (1641), p. 21; J. Ley, *Defensive Doubts, Hopes, and Reasons for Refusall of the Oath, Imposed by the Sixth Canon of the Late Synod* (1641), p. 4.
[2] *CJ*, ii, 132.

was ostensibly made in defence of the Church of England. The swearer promised to defend 'the true reformed religion expressed in the doctrine of the Church of England, against all Popery and popish innovation within this realm'.[3] Yet the original version of the oath only protected an ill-defined 'true reformed Protestant religion' with no mention of the Anglican Church.[4] Moreover, following petitions from the London clergy for guidance about parts of the Protestation, the clause later had to be explained by the Commons as only defending the public doctrine of the Church of England, 'so far as it is opposite to Popery, and popish innovations'. It was not to be extended to maintaining 'any form of worship, discipline, or government; nor any rites or ceremonies of the said Church of England'.[5]

Aside from protecting the church, the text of the Protestation also bound those that took it to defend the monarchy. The swearer promised that according to his 'duty of allegiance' he would 'maintain and defend His Majesty's royal person and estate, as also the power and privilege of Parliaments, the lawful rights and liberties of the subject, and every person that shall make this Protestation'.[6] Although, as will be demonstrated later, many made allusions to the Protestation being a kind of national covenant,[7] some of its supporters portrayed it as a traditional oath of loyalty for the defence of the monarch. It was compared to the 1584 Association, George Peard, MP for Barnstaple, citing the association as being the same in substance as the Protestation.[8] Denzil Holles used the same analogy, describing the MPs as having entered into 'an Association among themselves' by taking the oath.[9]

Yet, in spite of the Protestation's apparently moderate aims of defending the church and the king, it was clear that some wished to use it as a test of the loyalty of MPs and the general public to the cause of further reform. Referring to Judges 12: 5–6, John Pym described the Protestation as a 'shibboleth to establish a true Israelite'.[10] Pym's use of the book of Judges, detailing the descent of the Israelites into idol worship after their deliverance from Egypt, indicated the extent to which he believed England had only exchanged the tyranny of the papacy for the arbitrary rule of Laudian prelacy. The exact citation recalled the use of the word 'shibboleth' as a means of distinguishing the godly Gileadites from the idolatrous Ephraimites, a way of discriminating between the faithful and the unfaithful amongst the Israelites themselves. The

---

[3] Kenyon, *Stuart Constitution*, pp. 222–3.
[4] *Verney's Notes of the Proceedings of the Long Parliament*, ed. J. Bruce (Camden, xxxi, 1855), pp. 66–71, pp. 67–8.
[5] Kenyon, *Stuart Constitution*, p. 258; *CJ*, ii, 134.
[6] Kenyon, *Stuart Constitution*, p. 258.
[7] See below, Chapter 4.
[8] S. R. Gardiner, *The Fall of the Monarchy of Charles I, 1637–1649* (2 vols., London, 1882), ii, 159.
[9] *Speeches and Passages of this Great and Happy Parliament* (1641), p. 236.
[10] HMC, *5th Report* (London, 1876), p. 3.

militancy of this text, with the use of extreme violence against those that could not take the shibboleth, was drawn out in subsequent discussions of the Protestation.[11] On 5 May 1641 every shire was sent copies of the Protestation, but subscription was not enforced. It was not until January 1642 as a result, according to the Commons, of 'the Remissness of some of those that had the care of recommending it to others' that it was impressed upon the whole country.[12]

However, despite greater enforcement, the hope that the oath might act as a shibboleth was largely thwarted. The subscription returns for the Protestation revealed that it was not even a very effective means of distinguishing Catholics from Protestants. In West Sussex, some Catholics were allowed to take the oath whilst making reservations concerning their religion. Others who had previously appeared on recusancy lists reappeared on the oath rolls as having taken the Protestation wholesale. In the upper house, the Catholic peers John Paulet, marquis of Winchester, James Touchet, earl of Castlehaven and Earl Rivers were allowed to take the Protestation omitting the clause relating to the defence of the Protestant religion.[13] As a whole, the Lords queried the use of the Protestation as a political test and raised the question as to what would become of those that refused to take it.[14]

Oaths of association 1642–1643

Although, as will be demonstrated later, the tendering of the Protestation to the nation in early 1642 provoked equivocal replies from many subscribers concerned about its political intent, it was not the exacting shibboleth that Pym had hoped for. Its failure to act as a discriminating test led those committed to continuing the war against Charles to press for more radical oaths of loyalty. William Montagu wrote to his father in June 1642 that it was 'whispered . . . that there is a Covenant and an oath of association a-drawing like those of Scotland'.[15] (Note here the way that Montagu was already using the terms association and covenant interchangeably.) In response to the king's proclamation against the forces raised by the Earl of Essex, the Commons ordered the drawing up of a covenant to be taken by Parliament.[16] On 27

[11] Those that could not say 'shibboleth' had their throats cut.
[12] CJ, ii, 135, 389.
[13] See T. J. McCann, 'Midhurst Catholics and the Protestation Returns of 1642', *Recusant History*, xvi (1983), 319–23; LJ, vi, 242; *West Sussex Protestation Returns*, ed. R. G. Rice (Sussex Record Society, v, 1906), p. 75.
[14] LJ, iv, 338–9; HLRO, Hist. Coll. 114; Braye MS 21, f. 18v. See also G. Williams, *The Discovery of Mysteries* (Oxford, 1643), p. 38.
[15] HMC, *Buccleuch-Whitehall MSS*, i (London, 1899), p. 303. See also p. 291.
[16] CJ, ii, 715; *Stuart Royal Proclamations Volume II: Royal Proclamations of King Charles I 1625–46*, ed. J. F. Larkin (Oxford, 1983), p. 791.

August 1642 the members acceded to a covenant to assist the earl's forces 'with Life and Fortune, in the Defence of the true Protestant Religion, the King's person, the laws of the Land, the Liberties and Property of the Subject'. John Adamson has described this device as a baronial oath of fealty to the earl, but it is better understood as another one of the abortive efforts to impose a nationally subscribed covenant upon the country.[17] Not all MPs were prepared to take it. Two members with Royalist sympathies, Sir John Evelyn, the MP for Bletchingley, and Edmund Waller, the poet, were forced to take the covenant and lend £100 and £150 respectively to the Parliamentary war effort to keep their seats. In the midst of proceedings disabling him from sitting in the house for refusing the covenant, Sir Sidney Mountague produced one of the king's declarations, which pronounced all signatories to it traitors.[18]

The covenant to the earl seems largely to have been intended as a test of MPs' and soldiers' loyalty to the Parliament. However, Pym proposed the imposition of a new nationwide oath of loyalty to the Commons in October 1642, referring to it as a 'new Covenant or association'.[19] On 20 October Pym reported a conference with the Lords in which they had agreed that it was necessary 'that the Kingdom should be quickened and thoroughly awakened'.[20] The words of this association bound subjects to assist one another in defending the Protestant religion, the privileges of Parliament and the liberty and property of the subject, but not the person of the king.[21] On the 22nd a declaration of both houses was produced urging the necessity of an association for the defence of the kingdom. The king, the declaration stated, was now so embroiled with the popish party that 'all hopes of Peace and Protection were excluded'. In employing these popish councillors the king had gone against the terms of his coronation oath 'whereby His Majesty Bound Himself to maintain the Protestant Religion and the Law of the Land'. (As will be shown in the next chapter, the idea that the coronation oath formed a political contract between king and people formed an important part of Parliamentarian resistance theory.) For these reasons, the Parliament had resolved to enter into a 'solemn Oath and Covenant with God' and they expressed the hope that Scotland would join them in this association.[22] Despite protestations of loyalty to Charles, this was clearly an association in defence of God's cause, not the king's life.

This particular proposal seems to have foundered on renewed peace negotiations in the winter of 1642 but Pym did not give up on this project. In

[17] J. S. A. Adamson, 'The Baronial Context of the English Civil War', *TRHS*, 40 (1990), 93–120, p. 106.
[18] *CJ*, ii, 740, 822, 827, 874.
[19] S. R. Gardiner, *The History of the Great Civil War* (4 vols., London, 1987), i, 39–40.
[20] *CJ*, ii, 821.
[21] *LJ*, v, 412–13.
[22] Ibid., v, 418 .

December 1642 he managed to get a similar oath included into the legislation setting up the Eastern Association. This could be seen as merely a pragmatic measure, binding the counties to mutual defence. However, Clive Holmes states that for 'Pym and his allies the ideal association would parallel the Scottish National Covenant.'[23] Perhaps unsurprisingly given the ideological commitment now required, local committees appeared reluctant to tender the oath. Calls for a more efficient means to uncover the Parliament's enemies (and the unfaithful within the Parliamentarian cause itself) continued in spite of this. The author of *Plain-English* (printed in January 1643), possibly Edward Bowles, chaplain to the Earl of Manchester, demanded a new national association 'more particular than the Protestation, which like the net in the Gospel brought up fishes good and bad'. Instead this association should 'be wisely laid so as to give us to know our friends and our enemies'.[24] In these proposals for an association we do not find, as in 1584, plans for an interregnum. At this stage, the deposition or execution of Charles I was too extreme a solution for even members of the 'War Party' to fully contemplate.[25] However, the radical potential of the covenant idea was demonstrated by the suggestion that it could be an extra-parliamentary association, in case the two houses should betray the people by making a soft peace with the king.[26] The threat of an impending Royalist attack in February 1643 also led to the oath which Pym had incorporated into the Eastern Association finally being tendered in Suffolk.[27] In March 1643 there were calls from radical groups in the city that the oath of association should be applied there.[28] On 10 April 1643 the Commons named a committee to 'consider the desires of the citizens, concerning a covenant, and an Oath of Association; and to bring it into the House'.[29] That same month the Venetian secretary reported that Parliamentary commissioners had already begun 'to apply the oath of association in the country, considering those who refuse to take it as royalists'.[30]

[23] C. Holmes, *The Eastern Association in the English Civil War* (Cambridge, 1974), pp. 62–6.

[24] *Plaine-English or, a Discourse Concerning the Accomodation, the Armie, the Association* (1643), p. 27.

[25] Though a plan was hatched in 1644 to depose Charles I and replace him with Charles Louis, elector of the Palatinate, C. Hibbard, *Charles I and the Popish Plot* (Chapel Hill, 1983), pp. 151, 177, 207–8.

[26] Wootton, 'Rebellion to Revolution' , 664. The possibility of an extra-parliamentary association was even explored in the otherwise moderate *Scripture and Reasons Pleaded for Defensive Armes* (1643), p. 44; for references to an association in this tract see p. 1. See also H. Woodward, *The King's Chronicle* (1643), part I, *passim*.

[27] Bodl. MS Tanner 284 f. 42–7. The lieutenants and deputy lieutenants of Essex, Cambridge and Huntingdonshire also took the oath; Bodl. MS Tanner 114 f. 98.

[28] *CSPV*, 1642–3, p. 255.

[29] *CJ*, iii, 37.

[30] *CSPV*, 1642–3, p. 265.

Vow and Covenant

Although the oath of association incorporated into the structure of the county associations was being tendered more frequently, this was still not the nation-wide shibboleth that Pym hoped for. However, the discovery of Waller's plot to seize control of London for the king allowed Pym to pass the new oath, the Vow and Covenant, through the Commons with almost no opposition. On 6 June 1643 the Commons resolved to draw up a covenant 'for Discovery of such Designs as these . . . and to distinguish the good and well-affected Party from the bad; and to unite the good Party faster among themselves'.[31] The same day the Vow and Covenant was presented to the house. Subscribers were to 'covenant' rather than swear to its contents. The covenant required the swearer to state that he was convinced that 'the Forces raised by the Two Houses of Parliament' were 'raised and continued for their just defence and for the defence of the true Protestant Religion, and Libertie of the Subject, against the Forces raised by the King'.[32] Again, this covenant was also referred to as an oath of association, the Venetian secretary writing on 26 June that the Commons had passed 'the oath for the Covenant or Association'.[33]

The oath broke with the conventional rhetoric of the Long Parliament by failing to make any claim that it was made for the defence of the king's person and authority. Denzil Holles believed the oath had been designed to test the extent of allegiance in London, the army and Parliamentary controlled areas and force MPs and peers to choose between king and Parliament.[34] Pym undoubtedly hoped this harsher tone would help separate the zealous from the lukewarm within the Parliamentarian cause. The Lords, however, attempted to ameliorate the language of the oath. On 9 June 1643 a committee was drawn up including Lord Saye and Sele and the Earls of Manchester and Pembroke to produce a declaration of their loyalty to 'the King's Person, and His Crown and Dignity'. On 16 June 1643 Algernon Percy, the earl of Northumberland, reported the committee's declaration. Having entered into an oath and covenant, the Lords and Commons declared that their intentions had 'been, and still are, to our Power, to maintain, preserve, and defend His Majesty's Person, and just Rights of the Crown, together with the Persons of His Royal Issue; and that we shall use our uttermost Endeavours in Pursuance of the same'.[35] This was to be communicated to the Commons, but no record

---

[31] CJ, iii, 117–18.

[32] Gardiner, History, i, 149; A Sacred Vow and Covenant Taken by the Lords and Commons Assembled in Parliament (1643).

[33] CSPV, 1642–3, p. 289.

[34] Jones, Conscience and Allegiance, p. 120.

[35] LJ, vi, 87, 97; HLRO, Original Journals, HL, 27, f. 158–61, 215–16. Pembroke and Northumberland were implicated in the plot and there was an attempt to have the latter imprisoned, P. Crawford, Denzil Holles 1598–1680: A Study of His Political Career (London, 1979), pp. 90–1.

exists in the journal, indicating that it was suppressed. However, a printed pamphlet of that year referred to 'a trick your Lordships have found out, to save you harmlesse from any obligation by this Oath, a Salvo to all your other Oathes Lawfully taken'. It suggests that some of the Lords took the Vow and Covenant with the kinds of reservations included in the declaration of loyalty.[36] The manuscript minutes refer to some of the Lords 'having made explanations touching [?] the said Protestation [meaning the Vow and Covenant]' before the house took it.[37] The oath also represented a new departure in that it produced an opposing Royalist oath of allegiance to be taken by all loyal subjects.[38] On 24 June 1643, three days after issuing a proclamation condemning the Vow and Covenant, Charles produced his own Sacred Oath or Covenant. By taking the oath, the swearer promised to defend the king's person *and prerogative*. Yet the oath also kept within the rhetoric of the mixed constitution by declaring that neither the king nor Parliament had sole legislative power.[39] For the first time, subjects were presented with two conflicting demands for allegiance, neither of which bore relation to earlier tests of loyalty.

The Solemn League and Covenant

As a political test the Vow and Covenant's life was short-lived. It was undoubtedly too divisive, acting as a catalyst to the Kentish Rebellion. Following Parliament's military reversals at Chalgrove Field, Lansdowne and Bristol, the oath ceased to be tendered.[40] The defeats suffered by the Parliament's forces during the summer of 1643 did not dampen the enthusiasm of many, in particular Presbyterians, for a new Parliamentary covenant. Indeed, as early as June 1643, some had been calling for a new device which would join England and Scotland together. The Parliamentarian lawyer Sir Cheney Culpeper wrote to Samuel Hartlib on the 16th of that month referring 'to the Couenante lately made for the unitinge of ourselues & to another which I hope shortly to see for the stronger union of the 2: [Kingdoms] in theire [Common] intereste of Religion & liberty'. This covenant would need to incorporate a confession of faith which would 'beget a better union & correspondency between all the

---

[36] A Letter to a Noble Lord at London from a Friend at Oxford, upon Occasion of the Late Covenant Taken by Both Houses (n. pl., 1643), p. 2.

[37] HLRO, Manuscript Minutes, HL, 10, 9 June 1643.

[38] Stuart Royal Proclamations, ii, ed. Larkin, pp. 918–20.

[39] A Sacred Oath or Covenant to be Taken by All His Majesty's Loyal Subjects (Oxford, 1643).

[40] A. Everitt, The Community of Kent and the Great Rebellion 1640–60 (Leicester, 1973), ch. 6; The Knyvett Letters, ed. B. Schofield (Norfolk Historical Society, xx, 1949), p. 119; The Diary of Ralph Josselin 1616–1683, ed. A. Macfarlane (British Academy, 1976), p. 13; however, on 29 January 1645 the Commons ordered that all members that had not already taken the Vow and Covenant were to swear to it, CJ, iv, 35.

reformed Churches & States'.[41] On the 21st he wrote again to Hartlib that a 'Couenante personall between the 2: nations will ere longe be as necessary; that soe the well affected in bothe nations beinge united by Couenante first with themselues & then with one another; our strength & our enimies may be fully knowen.'[42]

Instead, military failure necessitated a treaty with Scotland, which drove the English Parliament to accept a new covenant as a means to cement the alliance. The Solemn League and Covenant was the product of these negotiations. Like the Protestation and the Vow and Covenant, its contents were sworn to by an oath, but the preamble explicitly declared that it was 'a mutual and solemn league and covenant'. The religious intent of the Solemn League and Covenant was clearly expressed in the hope 'that the Lord may be one, and His name one in the three kingdoms'. It bound the parties sworn to the defence of the Church of Scotland and the reformation of the Church of England 'according to the example of the reformed Churches' so that the churches in both kingdoms could be brought into 'the nearest conjunction and uniformity in religion'. Henry Vane the younger managed to secure the inclusion of the phrase 'according to the word of God' in the clause relating to the reform of the Church of England to ease the taking of the oath by Independents (an alteration that assumed prime importance in debates over liberty of conscience between 1644 and 1646). Its second clause swore the covenanters to 'endeavour the extirpation of Popery, prelacy (that is, Church government by archbishops, bishops, their chancellors and commissaries . . .), superstition, heresy, schism, profaneness, and whatsoever shall be found contrary to sound doctrine and the power of godliness'. The Solemn League and Covenant returned to the more orthodox Parliamentarian position of arguing that the war was continued for the king's defence. The third clause required the swearer to promise to defend 'the King's Majesty's person and authority, in the preservation and defence of the true religion and liberties of the kingdoms'. The apparent equivocation in this declaration of loyalty would form the central issue in the debate over how the Covenant affected the individual's duty of allegiance. Again, in the text of the Solemn League and Covenant we find the terms 'association' and 'covenant' used as equivalents of each other. The sixth clause of the Covenant expressed the hope that other Christian churches would 'join in the same or like association'.[43] Similarly, the irenicist John Dury wrote several letters in which he referred to the Covenant

[41] 'The Letters of Sir Cheney Culpeper (1641–1657)', eds. M. J. Braddick and M. Greengrass, Camden Miscellany, 33 (Camden Fifth Series, 7, 1996), pp. 105–403, at p. 176. Similar allusions were made to a covenanted union between England and Scotland by preachers promoting the 1641 Protestation, see below p. 86.

[42] Ibid., p. 177.

[43] Gardiner, History, i, 226–36; Kenyon, Stuart Constitution, pp. 263–6.

as an association for reformation of religion.[44] Following the breakdown of the Uxbridge peace negotiations in early 1645, Parliament strengthened the Covenant with the creation of the Negative Oath. This was intended to draw off Royalist support by offering indemnity to those who would swear that they would not 'directly or indirectly adhere unto or willingly assist the King in this war'.[45]

On 26 August 1643 the Covenant between England and Scotland was read in the Commons and a copy sent to the Assembly of Divines to debate the 'Lawfulness of taking it, and entering into it, in point of Conscience'.[46] The divines dealt with the Solemn League and Covenant as a grand case of conscience. Not all of its members were satisfied that it could be taken. Cornelius Burgess, Thomas Gataker and 'abundance more' refused to take the Covenant in its original form. Burgess, Gataker and Robert Rich, earl of Essex, did not want the word 'prelacy' to be interpreted as including 'ancient moderate Episcopacy'.[47] Nevertheless, depending on the acceptance of their interpretations of the phrases 'word of God' and 'prelacy', the Assembly declared the Covenant lawful. With these alterations, and the inclusion of the Church of Ireland into the Covenant's provisions, the oath passed the two houses.[48] Though the Parliament took the oath in September 1643 it was not until January 1644 that it was imposed nationally.[49] Like the Vow and Covenant, the Solemn League and Covenant divided the zealous in Parliament from MPs and peers less committed to the war against the king.[50]

As we will see in the rest of Part I, the Protestation, Vow and Covenant and Solemn League and Covenant were all seen as embodiments and renewals of one national covenant. Incorporating ideas from federal theology, covenanting divines presented these documents as binding subscribers to endeavour both personal and national reformation. In also tying subscribers to the Parliamentarian war effort, those advocating these covenants employed not only the stock arguments based on mixed-government or private law theory, but also justifications of resistance drawn from the religious duty to punish idolatry. Seen as the perfection of these attempts to forge a national covenant, the Solemn League and Covenant would, unlike the Protestation and Vow and

---

[44] Sheffield University, Hartlib Papers, electronic version, Disc I 29/9/1A, 67/19/1A–2B. See also W. Kaye, *Satisfaction for all such as Oppose Reformation* (2nd edn., York, 1647), p. 3, where the author refers to the 'blessed union, association, or covenant' that the people had entered into.

[45] S. R. Gardiner, *Constitutional Documents of the Puritan Revolution, 1625–1660* (3rd edn., Oxford, 1906), pp. xliii, 289.

[46] *CJ*, iii, 219–20.

[47] *Rel. Bax.*, part one, p. 48.

[48] *CJ*, iii, 223, 229, 242.

[49] Ibid., iii, 382.

[50] Ibid., iii, 249, 297, 299, 302; *LJ*, vi, 293; Jones, *Conscience and Allegiance*, p. 127.

Covenant, beget no successors. Instead, as will be demonstrated in Part II, it would stand at the centre of the major political and religious controversies of the seventeenth century from 1644 to the Exclusion Crisis.

3

Covenants and allegiance, 1641–1646

The 1641 Protestation was frequently compared to the 1584 Bond of Association. The idea of an association in defence of the monarch and the Protestant religion carried radical overtones. In the 1640s the term 'association' came to be seen by some as synonymous with the concept of a national covenant. None the less, it would be wrong to claim that this was the only meaning attached to the word. Doubtless many of those that subscribed to the Elizabethan Association felt that they were doing nothing more than expressing their loyalty to their queen. Similarly, some of those that made allusions between the bond of 1584 and the Protestation, may have wished to imply nothing more than that both devices were made to secure the person of the monarch.

Viewed in this way, the Protestation could be rendered compatible with the argument that allegiance was a natural and indivisible bond to the person of the king, an argument that, ironically, went against the Tudors and Stuarts' increasing reliance on statutory oaths to define obedience. According to the church homilies obedience was 'the principall vertue of all vertues, and indeed the very root of all vertues and the cause of all felicitie'. Conversely, the first author of vice was the sin of rebellion. The homilies argued that the political order was a parallel of that which God had ordained in nature. It was Adam's rebellion against his place in this natural scheme that precipitated the fall of man. Any rebellion against this divine order would be punishable, according to St Paul, with damnation. St Peter reminded subjects that their obedience was not only due to good kings but also to the cruel and 'froward' as well.[1] In conjunction with the homilies, the judges' decision in Calvin's Case 1608 formed the basis for later Royalist arguments in favour of giving the king unqualified allegiance. In his report on the case, Sir Edward Coke argued that the subject and the king were bound together by mutual obligations of obedience and protection 'for as the subject oweth to the king his true and faithful ligeance and obedience, so the sovereign is to govern and protect his subjects'. Allegiance did not begin in the courts of leet because many subjects who owed a natural duty of obedience had never sworn in the courts. It was, Coke said, ridiculous to suppose that allegiance could be given to an invisible

---

[1] *Certaine Sermons or Homilies*, eds. Rickey and Stroup, pp. 69–76, 275–307.

entity like the political capacity of the king.[2] Lord Chancellor Ellesmere concurred that allegiance must be tied to the person of the king. 'An oath', he said, 'must be sworne to by a naturall bodie: homage and fealty must be done by a naturall bodie, a politick bodie cannot doe it.'[3]

This chapter will look at the impact of the Long Parliament's covenants on theories of political allegiance. In doing so, it will challenge some of the prevailing historical opinions concerning political thought during the civil wars. The idea that civil war represents either the seed-bed of radical ideas for resisting oppression, or that it is a glorious and climactic chapter in the foundation of liberal and democratic values has now largely been swept aside by revisionist historiography.[4] Even those that argue for significant ideological divisions before 1640 dispute that they were a major factor between the opening of the Long Parliament and the outbreak of civil war.[5] After the fighting had begun, the paper war was as tentative as the first stages of the physical conflict, preferring to deal with the issue of allegiance as a case of conscience, rather than as a battle between competing ideologies.[6] As we will see, some of the arguments used to defend the Parliaments' covenants fit into this picture, urging these documents as a means to protect the king from his evil counsellors or on the basis of the natural right to self-defence. Even when more radical theories did emerge – the Parliamentary absolutism of Henry Parker and William Prynne's borrowings from *Vindiciae Contra Tyrannos* – their radicalism lay less in theoretical innovation and more in the potential of these ideas to sanction drastic action.[7] Moreover, Parliamentarian thought as a whole has

---

[2] *A Complete Collection of State Trials and Proceedings for High Treason and Other Crimes and Misdemeanors*, ed. T. B. Howell (21 vols., London, 1816), ii, 607–30.

[3] Ibid., ii, 577–602, 690–2.

[4] I have benefited greatly in writing this summary of the state of play in the historiography of political thought in the English civil war from reading J. C. Davis's chapter on 'Political Thought During the English Revolution', *A Companion to Stuart Britain*, ed. B. Coward (Oxford, 2003), ch. 19. I am very grateful to Professor Davis for letting me see a draft of this prior to publication. The revisionist case has been most convincingly made by G. Burgess, *The Politics of the Ancient Constitution* (London, 1992); *idem, Absolute Monarchy and the Stuart Constitution* (London, 1996). See also C. Russell, 'Rule of Law, Whose Slogan?' in *The Causes of the English Civil War* (Oxford, 1991), ch. 6; J. S. Morrill, 'Charles I, Tyranny and the English Civil War', in *The Nature of the English Revolution* (London, 1993), ch. 15.

[5] J. H. Sommerville, 'Ideology, Property and the Constitution', in *Conflict in Early Stuart England: Studies in Religion and Politics 1603–1642*, eds. R. Cust and A. Hughes (Harlow, 1989), ch. 2, p. 65. The role of ideological disagreement is also played down in recent Marxist interpretations, E. M. Wood and N. Wood, *A Trumpet of Sedition, Political Theory and the Rise of Capitalism, 1509–1688* (London, 1997), pp. 71–3.

[6] B. Donagan, 'Casuistry and Allegiance in the English Civil War', in *Writing and Political Engagement in Seventeenth-Century England*, eds. Derek Hirst and Richard Strier (Cambridge, 1999), pp. 89–111; and see also my '"The Kingdome's Case": The Use of Casuistry as a Political Language 1640–1692', *Albion*, 34 (2003), 557–83.

[7] See for Parker, M. Mendle, *Henry Parker and the English Civil War: The Political Thought*

been characterised as shying away from religious justifications for the use of force. Michael Walzer, who has argued forcefully for the reality of revolutionary puritanism, states that most of the early arguments were constitutional.[8] His comments have recently been backed up by an analysis of Parliamentarian resistance tracts by Glenn Burgess.[9] Whilst a real war against idolatry was undoubtedly taking place in the parishes, it has been very hard to link the support of iconoclasts for Parliament with any explicit, religiously based resistance theory.[10]

Without engaging in a discussion of Parliamentarian resistance tracts (roughly defined) which I have undertaken elsewhere, I want here to challenge what now amounts to pretty much a consensus on the role of ideas in the civil wars.[11] We will see that in defending the imposition of these Parliamentary covenants, many pamphleteers and divines used the idea of the ruler as a covenanted monarch to legitimise resisting, perhaps even deposing, Charles I. Like Alexander Leighton in the 1620s, some of these writers also incorporated the idea of national covenant into 'holy war' arguments for the use of force. Royalists responded to these arguments by showing the ways in which the Parliament's covenant failed to meet the criteria established by casuists for lawful oaths, and by utilising Calvin's Case, the homilies and other sources to show the ways in which these covenants interfered with the natural, indivisible bond of allegiance between king and subject.

The Protestation was the least controversial of the three Parliamentary covenants discussed in this Part. Yet, mass subscription to the Protestation across the country and its avowed support for the political and religious status quo did not prevent the oath from prompting misgivings about its implications for political obedience. The 'Marginal Notes and Interpretations' added by the Royalist heads of houses at Oxford to the text of the Protestation denied any right to resistance by force and demanded that the exact rights and liberties

---

of the Public's Privado (Cambridge, 1995); for Prynne see D. Wootton, 'Rebellion to Revolution'; J. R. Greenberg, *The Radical Face of the English Constitution: St. Edward's "Laws" in Early Modern Political Thought* (Cambridge, 2001). John Sanderson makes a strong case for the development of two distinct ideological positions, Royalist and Parliamentarian, post-1642, *'But the People's Creatures': The Philosophical Basis of the English Civil War* (Manchester, 1989); *idem*, 'Conrad Russell's Ideas', *History of Political Thought*, 14 (1993), 85–102.

[8] Walzer, *Revolution of the Saints*, p. 293.

[9] G. Burgess, 'Was the Civil War a War of Religion?', *Huntington Library Quarterly*, 61 (2000), 173–203.

[10] I am grateful to John Walter for his comments on this point, see his 'Confessional Politics in Pre-Civil War Essex: Prayer Books, Profanations, and Petitions', *The Historical Journal*, 44 (2001), 677–701.

[11] See my 'Preaching to the Converted: Religious Justifications for the English Civil War', *Huntington Library Quarterly*, 65 (2002), 395–420.

of the subscriber ought to be clearly defined by the imposing party.[12] The addition of qualifying equivocations to the text of the Protestation seems to have been a commonplace tactic. An annotated copy of the oath kept by Gerard Langbaine, the provost of Queen's College, expanded the clause promising to defend 'His Majesties Royall Person, Honour and Estate' adding 'ag[ains]t whom no subject of this K[ing]dome may, w[i]th safe conscience take up armes offensive or defensive'.[13] Robert Arnold, minister of Melcomb Bingham in Dorset, resolved only to take the Protestation so far as 'it may stand with Gods word, the standing lawes of the kingdome, the oath of aleagiance and oath of supremacie'.[14] The author of *Queries of Some Tender Conscienced Christians* (1642), one of the first of a long line of Royalist pamphlets opposing the Long Parliament's oaths of loyalty, reminded would-be subscribers that the oath had not received the royal assent. Moreover, he pointed out that many of the complaints levelled by John Ley against the 'etcetera' oath could also be made against the Protestation. It too was ambiguously worded, failed to define what it meant by the doctrine of the Church of England and, in requiring the swearer never to relinquish it, was as much a '*Median and Persian*' oath 'that cannot be altered' as that contained in the sixth canon.[15]

In response, some authors with Parliamentarian sympathies tried to show that the Protestation was consonant with previous oaths of loyalty. The Presbyterian John Geree claimed that the king's sufferance, and the fact that the king's printer produced the Protestation, were evidence enough of the sovereign's consent.[16] Parliamentarian authors writing in the early 1640s also justified taking arms against Charles's forces by claiming that resistance was compatible with the Oaths of Allegiance and Supremacy. Henry Parker stated that giving support to the forces raised by the Lords and Commons was no breach of these oaths as the supremacy of the king as *singularis major* remained unchallenged as long as Parliament resisted, not the king's person, but the evil counsellors about him.[17] Charles Herle argued that the Oath of Allegiance was sworn to the king's lawful, and not his wilful commands, and that the Oath of Supremacy had been specifically directed at papal usurpation, not at the reforming efforts of Parliament.[18] Similar arguments would be used to defend subsequent oaths of loyalty imposed by the Long Parliament.

---

[12] *Oxfordshire and North Berkshire Protestation Returns and Tax Assessments: 1641–42*, ed. J. S. W. Gibson (Oxfordshire Record Society, lix, 1994), pp. 149–72.

[13] Oxford University Archives, WPψ 26/1.

[14] *Dorset Protestation Returns Preserved in the House of Lords, 1641 to 1642*, eds. E. A. and G. S. Fry (Dorset Record Society, xxiv, 1911), p. 52.

[15] *Queries of Some Tender Conscienced Christians, About the Late Protestation* (n. pl., 1642), pp. 1, 4, 7.

[16] J. Geree, *Judah's Joy at the Oath* (1641), [c].

[17] H. Parker, *Observations upon Some of His Majesties Late Answers and Expresses* (1642), p. 44.

[18] C. Herle, *An Answer to Mis-led Doctor Fearne According to His Own Method* (1642), pp. 14, 26–7.

However, moderate interpretations of the Protestation of the kind made by John Geree were being undermined, on the one hand, by the works of religious radicals like the Independent Henry Burton and, on the other, by the idea that Charles could be held accountable for breaking this oath. Burton saw the obligation to defend the reformed religion 'against all Popery and Popish Innovations' as extending to withdrawing from communion with the Church whilst these popish elements remained in place.[19] George Lawrence shared this expansive view of the oath:

> the Tearme, *All Popery*, hath a large periphery and circumference, which as it doth reach out to that Popery, which was discovered at the time when the Protestation was composed, so also (yet with submission bee it spoken) may it bee extended to all those severall graines, which lay under the Turffe, and should hereafter budforth, and appeare to bee superstition, and Idolatrie in after times.[20]

Indeed, Thomas Robinson took the Protestation as a call to direct action to begin the process of removing 'all the Altars and Images' and casting 'away all vain Ceremonies out of the Service of God throughout the Land. For these must be removed before our oaths can be fulfilled, or God truly worshipped.'[21] He made the political ramifications of this interpretation clear:

> The Law of the Land therefore is not to be taken principally for the bounds and limits of our Oath, but the Law of God; and lawfully may we oppose the law of man so far forth as it opposeth the Law of God.[22]

The research of John Walter has demonstrated that in Suffolk and Essex, the Protestation was used to justify 'popular interventions in the political process', interventions that, by 1642 at least, the preaching of puritan ministers encouraged.[23] Both Keith Lindley and John Walter have found that the taking of the Protestation was the catalyst to violent acts of iconoclasm. Catholics who refused to take the oath were marked out as targets for crowd violence.[24] Griffith Williams, bishop of Ossory, from a Royalist perspective claimed that the oath had been framed to provoke Catholics into rebellion via 'their large expression of what religion they protested to defend, not the Protestant religion, as it is established by Law and expressed in the 39 articles of the

---

[19] H. Burton, *The Protestation Protested: or a Short Remonstrance* (1641), A3.

[20] G. Lawrence, *Laurentius Lutherizans* (1642) [unpaginated, p. 7].

[21] T. Robinson, *The Petitioners Vindication* (1642), p. 5. Robinson explicitly describes the Protestation as a covenant with God.

[22] Ibid., p. 16.

[23] J. Walter, *Understanding Popular Violence in the English Revolution* (Cambridge, 1999), pp. 292–6.

[24] Ibid., pp. 295–65, 304; K. Lindley, *Popular Politics and Religion in Civil War London* (Aldershot, 1997), pp. 38–40.

Church of England; but as it is repugnant to popery, and taught perhaps by [Henry] Burton, [Cornelius] Burges [sic], [John] Goodwin and [Jeremiah] Burrowes [sic], or the like.'[25] Presbyterians like Thomas Edwards and John Geree criticised these radical interpretations of the Protestation on similar grounds.[26] As the heads of house at Oxford had noted, the oath also seemed to attack the idea that allegiance to the monarch was unconditional and natural. Although the oath contained a promise to defend the king's person and authority, Conrad Russell has detected a 'more than implicit' threat to use force in the Protestation. The oath seemed to make allegiance to the king conditional on his defence of religion and the laws. Like the Scottish National Covenant of 1638, Russell argues, the Protestation 'identified loyalty with a cause, rather than with a person'.[27]

In contrast with the largely secular case for resistance put forward by Parliamentarian authors, Scottish covenanters developed an essentially religious justification for rebellion. For the covenanters, both the people and the king were bound in a covenant with God to defend the true faith. Alexander Henderson, the minister of Leuchers, Fife, who, with Archibald Johnston of Wariston, drafted the Scottish National Covenant, made clear that the king was just as accountable as the people were for any breaches of the covenant. The 'people and Magistrates' were, Henderson said, 'joyntly bound in Covenant with God' and, therefore, the 'fault of the king would not excuse the people if they resist not his violence pressing them against the Covenant of God'.[28] Samuel Rutherford, whose Lex Rex (1644) crystallised Scottish covenanting thought, stressed that the covenant between king, people and God was not peculiar to Scotland, but was a feature of all Christian societies. Indeed, for Rutherford, the specific constitutional arrangements of a country were only a means to the end of fulfilling the covenant. Consequently, if certain political structures proved an obstruction to the defence of the faith, they should be altered, or, in the final resort, done away with.[29]

Following the conclusions of Michael McGiffert and Perry Miller, some historians have argued that in England the covenant with God was viewed essentially in spiritual and personal terms.[30] I have already demonstrated in Chapter 1 some of the problems with Miller and McGiffert's interpretation of the national covenant idea. Moreover, as we will see in the next chapter,

---

[25] G. Williams, *The Discovery of Mysteries* (Oxford, 1643), pp. 37–8.

[26] D. Cressy, 'The Protestation Protested, 1641 and 1642', *The Historical Journal*, 45 (2002), 251–79, at 265.

[27] C. Russell, *The Fall of the British Monarchies, 1637–1642* (Oxford, 1991), p. 295.

[28] Quoted in I. M. Smart, 'The Political Ideas of the Scottish Covenanters: 1638–88', *History of Political Thought*, i (1980), 167–93, at 169.

[29] Ibid., 176–180; J. Coffey, *Politics, Religion and the British Revolutions: The Mind of Samuel Rutherford* (Cambridge, 1997), ch. 6; G. Burgess, 'Was the Civil War a War of Religion?', *Huntington Library Quarterly*, lxi (2000), 173–203, at 193–5.

[30] Ibid., 187; Jones, *Conscience and Allegiance*, p. 134.

as with Scottish advocates of the National Covenant of 1638, divines promoting the Parliament's covenants saw them as devices for both private and public moral renewal with political as well as spiritual ramifications. English divines such as Herbert Palmer were adamant that subscribing to these covenants brought with it public obligations. Speaking of the Vow and Covenant (1643), he said that:

> If any shall offer to say, they meant nothing in this clause of the Covenant, but in reference onley to their personall carriage, and not any way concerning matters of publike reformation; I would onley put this dilemma to him. Either he hath done well or ill as a Parliament-man, and toward reformation hitherto. If he have done well, doubtlesse he that promises to amend in other things . . . cannot but even thereby be engaged to persevere in *all good for reformation*, and to *proceed further* in it, *as farre as is necessary* [my emphasis].[31]

Even in the case of the Protestation of 1641, at face value the least controversial of the Parliament's covenants, we can find it used to support the notion that Charles I, like Elizabeth I, was a covenanted monarch. It is clear that, as early as 1642, some English pamphleteers, in line with Scottish covenanting thought, were suggesting that the king could be held accountable for breaking his covenant. The author of *Annotations upon the Late Protestation* (1642) stated that, by making this oath, 'his Majesty and the Parliament hath tyed themselves each to [the] other in an Abraham-like Covenant, not to passe the limits of their own bounds', so that if the king should forget this 'so serious Protestation, vow and profession, this were deplorable'. It was, the author said, an abomination for kings not 'to hold and keepe Covenants, vowes and Protestations'.[32]

Equally, other writers could incorporate the Protestation into holy war arguments. Jeremiah Burroughes's sermon, *The Glorious Name of God, the Lord of Hosts* (1643) which preceded his reply to Henry Ferne's *The Resolving of Conscience* (1642) contained 'private law' (meaning based on the natural right of self-defence) arguments for resistance. However, in the same sermon Burroughes also stated that there was 'no war to be undertaken but for God and according to God's will' and described the soldiers who fought for God's cause as 'his sanctified ones'.[33] Burroughes said that once God had drawn his

---

[31] H. Palmer, *The Necessity and Encouragement, of Utmost Venturing for the Churches Help: Together with the Sin, Folly and Mischief of Self-Idolizing* (1643), p. 55 [sermon delivered on 28 June 1643].

[32] L. T., *Annotations upon the Late Protestation: or a True Character of an Affectionate Minde to King and Parliament* (1642), pp. 2, 5, 6, 11. Professor Cressy mistakenly reads this pamphlet as a plea for accommodation between king and Parliament, 'Protestation Protested', p. 269. The emphasis is clearly on the obligations the Protestation places upon the king, not upon Parliament.

[33] J. Burroughes, *The Glorious Names of God, the Lord of Hosts* (1643), pp. 26, 92.

sword 'he many times will not put it up again, untill it bee bathed, filled, satiated, drunke with blood'.[34] Within the reply to Ferne itself, Burroughes argued that by 'our solemn vow and Protestation' the Parliament had 'endeavoured to deliver our Kingdom and Parliament from the rage of the ungodly'.[35] He expressed the belief that the time was at hand 'for the pulling down of antichrist'. 'Let Babylon Fall, let the Church prosper', he urged, 'it is enough, our lives are not much worth.'[36]

Yet the Protestation, though it had been taken with qualifications by some future Royalists, did not flagrantly contradict the Oaths of Allegiance and Supremacy. Some presented the oath as an English national covenant, but many others viewed it simply as a traditional device to bind the nation to the defence of the monarchy and the Protestant religion. In fact, after the fighting had begun, a number of Royalist writers argued that the Protestation bound those that had taken it not to raise arms against the king. Edward Fisher preached from the text of Ecclesiastes 8: 1–2 – 'And who dare sin so far against his owne soule, as to breake this oath of God by disobedience and rebellion?' – stating that this scriptural warning included those that had 'taken the oathes of supremacy and allegiance unto the King, and hast so solemnly vowed to keep the late Protestation, which includes them both'.[37] William Ingoldsby, the rector of Watton in Hertfordshire, added the texts of the Oaths of Supremacy and Allegiance with the Protestation to his printed sermon 'against Disobedience and wilfull Rebellion', implying that all three oaths committed subjects not to resist their king.[38] Similar Anglican–Royalist interpretations of the Protestation were made in petitions to Parliament.[39] The Parliamentarian governor of Scarborough, Sir Hugh Cholmeley, claimed that he switched sides in 1643 as a result of 'the oaths of alleagiance and protestacion, both obligiing protection to the King's person' which, he said, weighed heavily upon his conscience.[40]

---

[34] J. Burroughes, A Briefe Answer to Dr. Fernes Booke, Tending to Resolve the Conscience (1643), p. 12.
[35] Ibid., p. 15.
[36] Ibid., p. 16.
[37] E. Fisher, An Appeale to Thy Conscience: as Thou Wilt Answere it at the Great and Dreadfull Day of Christ Jesus (n. pl., 1644 [really 1643]), pp. 4, 18, 30.
[38] G. I. [W. Ingoldsby], The Doctrine of the Church of England, Established by Parliament Against Disobedience and Wilfull Rebellion (1642); G. J. [idem], England's Oaths. Taken by All Men of Quality in the Church and Commonwealth (1642); A. G. Matthews, Walker Revised: Being a Revision of John Walker's Sufferings of the Clergy During the Grand Rebellion (reprint, Oxford, 1988), p. 200 and for more on Ingoldsby see below p. 112.
[39] Cressy, 'Protestation Protested', 268–9.
[40] C. H. Firth, ed., 'Sir Hugh Cholmeley's Narrative of the Siege of Scarborough, 1644–5', Eng. Hist. Rev., 32 (1917), 570.

An abrupt shift in Parliamentarian rhetoric came with the passage of the Vow and Covenant in June 1643. The absence of any mention of the king's person in the Vow precluded making a Royalist interpretation of the document and Royalist writers attacked it on the basis that it was a clear violation of the Oaths of Allegiance and Supremacy. A Letter to a Noble Lord (1643) spoke of the Vow and Covenant as being 'poynt blank' against these oaths.[41] The author of Observations upon the Instructions for the Taking [of] the Vow and Covenant (1643) recognised the new harshness of tone in this covenant. Previous Parliamentary ordinances had only angled at the loyal supporters of the king but 'by this order they intend to catch us all in a net and to gather us together as in a drag'.[42] The tendering of the Vow was in itself, the author said, evidence of the growing arbitrary power of Parliament. The oath was being administered by new county committees, which would oppress the subjects' liberties and impinge upon their consciences in the same way as the 1640 etcetera oath. The author of the Observations also complained that the age limit for the Vow was set too low at 15 years of age. In contrast, the Oath of Allegiance had not been required of any subjects under the age of 18.[43] Another Royalist pamphleteer noted that the oath contained a combination to stick to the other subscribers which 'is a thing never done in a lawfull warre, but in conspiracies, and confederacyes'. This showed that the Parliament's model in making the Vow and Covenant was the Scottish National Covenant. Compared with the king's covenant, the Vow and Covenant was also against the nature of biblical covenants in being forced.[44]

Against the accusation that they were at one and the same time breaking the Oaths of Allegiance and Supremacy and setting up an arbitrary power to govern England, some Parliamentarian writers again used the tactic of stressing the consonance of the Vow and Covenant with earlier oaths of loyalty. The author of The Harmony of Our Oathes (1643) insisted that 'the scope of our Protestation and Covenant, thwart not the oathes of Allegeance and Supremacy, but concurre with them.' Provision for the defence of the king's person had already been made in the Protestation and there was no need for subjects to swear again to this matter.[45] The stock answer given by these Parliamentary writers was that the Vow and Covenant was not opposed to the Oath of Allegiance, as by this subjects were only bound to obey the lawful

---

[41] A Letter to a Noble Lord, p. 2.

[42] Observations upon the Instructions for the Taking the Vow and Covenant Throughout England (Oxford, 1643), p. 12.

[43] Ibid., pp. 3, 5.

[44] Certaine Observations upon the Two Contrary Covenants Lately Published (Oxford, 1643), p. 5.

[45] The Harmony of Our Oathes. Shewing an Agreement Betwixt the Oathes of Supremacie, Allegeance, the Freemans Oath, Protestation and Covenant (1643), p. 2; The Un-deceiver (1643), p. 9.

commands of the king and not his personal will. Only the king in council constituted the supreme authority, not the king *in camera*, much less *in campo*.[46]

Arguments such as these were largely in keeping with the Parliamentarian claim that the war was being fought for the king's safety. However, there were again signs that some supporters of the Vow were adopting theories remarkably similar to those employed by Scottish covenanters. The author of *The Late Covenant Asserted* (1643) argued that Charles and Henrietta Maria were themselves guilty of breaking the Oaths of Allegiance and Supremacy, he for failing to defend the church and she for bringing in foreign powers. As a result the Parliament had a warrant to take up arms even against the king's person. The king's Sacred Oath or Covenant was, the author said, a covenant with the devil and the author warned his readers that any protestations that Charles might make in defence of the Protestant religion were worthless. He reminded his readers that Queen Mary had made a similar plea to the men of Suffolk in order to gain England for the Pope.[47] Advocating resistance on religious grounds alone, the author argued that it did not even have to be proved that Protestantism was under threat. He compared the Parliament's case with that of the children of Israel who declared war against the children of Reuben, Gad and Manasseh (Joshua 22: 10) on the mere suspicion that they had committed idolatry.[48] (The same biblical justification for the pre-emptive use of force had earlier been employed by Christopher Goodman, in his *How Superior Powers Ought to be Obeyed*, and by the author of *Vindiciae Contra Tyrannos*.)[49] He urged covenanters to do their duty and 'make good our Vow, Not to lay downe Armes, till the wicked be destroyed, and evill put away'.[50] The Presbyterian minister Samuel Clarke argued from the theory of the king's two capacities that Charles had sanctioned resistance to the unlawful commands of a tyrant himself in giving aid to the Rochellais against Louis XIII.[51] The clear implication was that Charles had now turned tyrant as well.

Compared with the Vow, the Solemn League and Covenant appeared to be a far less radical document. The text of the Solemn League and Covenant returned to the more orthodox Parliamentarian position that the war was being fought on the king's behalf, yet it generated a far greater number of Royalist replies than its predecessor. After the Protestation, the Solemn League and

---

[46] *The Late Covenant Asserted* (n. pl. [London], 1643), p. 10; *Un-deceiver*, p. 7; *Harmony*, p. 3.
[47] *Late*, pp. 5, 9, 20.
[48] Ibid., pp. 13–14.
[49] *Vindiciae Contra Tyrannos or, Concerning the Legitimate Power of a Prince Over the People and of the People Over a Prince*, ed. G. Garnett (Cambridge, 1994), pp. 36–7. C. Goodman, *How Superior Powers Ought to be Obeyed* (1558), p. 188.
[50] Ibid., p. 17.
[51] S. Clarke, *England's Covenant Proved Lawfull and Necessary Also at this Time, Both by Scripture and Reason* (1643), p. 15.

Covenant was the most widely impressed of the Long Parliament's oaths of loyalty.[52] However, the controversy it provoked was not simply a matter of the greater number of people to whom the oath was tendered, but also a consequence of the areas in which the Covenant was imposed. In particular, the tendering of the oath to Cambridge University in 1644, and the expectation that it would be imposed on Oxford University during the Parliamentary visitation begun there in 1647, prompted these Royalist propaganda centres into producing some of the finest responses to the Covenant. The pamphlet war was also drawn out as a result of Parliament making swearing to the Covenant part of the process by which Royalists compounded for their estates.[53]

Royalist propaganda was exhaustive in detailing the unlawfulness of the Covenant. Royalists urged that the Covenant did not meet the criteria for lawful oaths agreed upon by earlier casuists. Robert Sanderson stated explicitly that the Solemn League and Covenant, in being tendered upon certain penalties for refusal, was contrary to the nature of a covenant. Sanderson defined a covenant as a reciprocal contract, which had the 'voluntary mutuall consent of the Contractors' in making it.[54] Daniel Featley stated that such a forced oath was 'a heavy yoke laid upon the Conscience, inconsistent with our Christian liberty'. Such an oath was not likely to secure the Lord's blessings for the nation, as some of its promoters alleged, but rather would 'pull down the vials of Gods vengeance upon it'.[55] Another Royalist writer argued that the absence of the king's assent to the Covenant, indeed his public approbation of it, was another sign that this was not a lawfully imposed oath. This was against the biblical examples of the Jewish covenants in which the whole nation covenanted with the prince's or supreme magistrate's consent.[56] The author of A Briefe Discourse (1643) claimed that making a national covenant without the king's consent was unnatural as well as unlawful, for in the body politic orderly motion could only come from the head.[57] Moreover, the oath could not be taken in truth, as the articles of the Covenant were often vague and contradictory. The clause referring to the word of God and the example of the best-reformed churches would clearly elicit different interpretations from Independents and Presbyterians.[58] One author suggested that this ambiguity had been intentional, the authors of it having dealt so subtly 'as to put it into such generall terms, that there might be no bogling or starting aside, but that each side might take it, though intending severall senses'.[59]

---

[52] See below, pp. 119–28.

[53] CJ, iv, 327.

[54] Reasons of the Present Judgement of the University of Oxford (1647), p. 2.

[55] D. Featley, The League Illegal (1661) [reprint of letters written in 1643], p. 26.

[56] Certain Observations upon the New League or Covenant (Bristol, 1643), p. 11.

[57] A Briefe Discourse Declaring the Impiety and Unlawfulnesse of the New Covenant with the Scots (n. pl., 1643), p. 8.

[58] Ibid., p. 11.

[59] Certain Observations, p. 9.

Now that the public had been pressed to swear several differing oaths of loyalty to the Long Parliament, the Royalists also employed the tactic of comparing the Solemn League and Covenant with the Protestation and pointing to inconsistencies between the two that would leave subjects forsworn. Many authors pointed out that in the Protestation subjects had promised to defend the doctrine of the Church of England, which in the Thirty-Nine Articles included a defence of episcopacy and that they would be perjured if they attempted to endeavour the destruction of it.[60] One writer extended this use of the Protestation to deny the Parliament's claim that resisting the king's forces was lawful. The doctrine of the Church of England, which, it was pointed out, the oath had defended, included in article thirty-seven recognition of the king's ecclesiastical supremacy and forbade rebellion in one of its homilies.[61] In the Protestation, it was noted, the defence of the king's person and authority had been unqualified. Now, in the Covenant, it was dependent on his defence of the true religion and the liberties of the kingdom.[62]

Royalist writers attacked the third clause of the Covenant, as equivocating with the subject's duty of allegiance to the king. The author of *The Anti-confederacie* (1644) questioned why the clause protecting the king's person and authority was hedged in with the phrase 'in the preservation and defence of the true Religion'. It seemed that 'here the Jesuite (the Covenanters best friend) hath put in his foot'. The king would be supported only so long as he endeavoured to support the 'true religion' as defined by the Parliament's friends. To make our bond of allegiance in this way was 'to forsweare a great part of our duty and Allegiance towards him [the king]'. Subjects were bound 'by our Bond of Allegiance and Obedience, to preserve and defend the Kings Person and Authority, though he were a Persecutor or Tyrant'.[63] Another Royalist pamphleteer suggested that the covenanters' practice of raising their right hands at the swearing of the Covenant was a sign that their real intention was to raise their hands against the Lord's anointed. The same author noted that the liberties of the subject and the privileges of Parliament were to be defended unequivocally by the Covenant but the king's person and authority only when in the defence of the true religion and the liberties of the kingdom. No mention was made in this clause of the law so 'that every errour in a Sectary may upon the point bring a Religious Kings life into question'.[64] One anti-Covenant author used Calvin's Case and the Jacobean Oath of Allegiance to remind those considering swearing to the Covenant that their allegiance was

---

[60] *The Anti-confederacie: or an Extract of Certaine Quaeres, Concerning the Solemne League and Covenant* (Oxford, 1644), p. 17; *Reasons*, p. 6.

[61] *Examinations or a Discovery of Some Dangerous Positions Delivered in a Sermon . . . [with] New Quaeres of Conscience Touching the Late Oath* (London [really Oxford], 1643), pp. 4–5.

[62] *An Examination of Such Particulars in the Solemne League and Covenant, as Concerne the Law* (1644), p. 30.

[63] *Anti-confederacie*, pp. 18–19.

[64] *A Briefe Discourse*, pp. 9, 15.

due to Charles 'by Nature and Birth-Right' and could not be qualified in any way.[65] Sanderson felt that the third clause of the Covenant left the 'duty of the subject at so much loosenesse, and the safety of the King at so great uncertainty; that whensoever the People shall have a mind to go withdraw their obedience, they cannot want a pretence from the same for so doing'.[66]

Those writers who defended the Solemn League and Covenant did not attempt to refute the charge that they had made the subject's allegiance to the king equivocal. They often explicitly stated that the people's loyalty was conditional on the king's continued defence of the Protestant religion and the kingdom's liberties. Here they were following the rationale of the Scottish National Covenant of 1638 by which the subscribers promised to 'stand to the defence of our dread Soveraigne, the Kings majesty, his Person and Authority, in the defence and preservation of the foresaid true Religion, Liberties and Lawes of the Kingdome'.[67] The English Presbyterian Richard Ward defined the allegiance to be given the king under the Solemn League and Covenant in similar terms. The subscribers had, Ward said, promised to defend the king's person and estate 'so long as he really endeavours the preservation, and defence of the true religion, and Liberties of the Kingdom'.[68] The Covenanters Catechisme (1644) reversed the wording of the clause to show that the king would be defended by the preservation of religion.[69] However, the author also stated that the Solemn League was equivalent to the Scottish National Covenant, 'and we of the same relation to the King'.[70] The Presbyterian Thomas Case echoed this sentiment, stating that religion and the kingdom's liberties were the bulwarks of monarchy. Those, he said, who would dispense with these to gain power would quickly dispense with monarchy in turn.[71] In a late entry into the pamphlet controversy over the Solemn League and Covenant, John Robinson stated that actions based upon the first principle of the public safety required no legal precedent. He followed Scots covenanters in discussing constitutional arrangements as temporary and subservient to the wider aims of the Covenant. In this way, Robinson said, monarchy was but a means to the end of securing the public safety.[72]

---

[65] An Examination, pp. 20–2.

[66] Reasons, p. 15.

[67] Quoted in J. S. Morrill, The Nature of the English Revolution (Harlow, 1993), p. 104.

[68] R. Ward, The Analysis, Explication and Application of the Sacred and Solemne League and Covenant (1643), p. 2.

[69] The Covenanters Catechisme: or, a Brief and Familiar Analysis and Exposition of the Covenant (1644), pp. 25–6.

[70] Ibid., p. 16.

[71] T. Case, The Quarrell of the Covenant, with the Pacification of the Quarrell, Delivered in Three Sermons (1644), p. 54.

[72] [J. Robinson], The People's Plea: Fully Vindicating the Power and the Proceedings of the Parliament Occasioned by the Defence of the Covenant (1646), pp. 6, 8.

Most pro-Covenant authors, though, continued to use arguments based on the notion of a mixed-constitution and Parliamentary sovereignty to justify giving only qualified allegiance to the king. Thomas Mocket, formerly chaplain to the 1st Earl of Bridgewater, used William Prynne's *The Soveraigne Power of Parliaments* (1643) to show that covenants could be made without Charles's consent as the Parliament was the supreme sovereign power. The king's wilful commands could carry no weight compared to the authoritative commands of the two houses. Mocket argued that historically covenants had been used to fight the king's evil counsellors on a number of occasions. This was the case, he said, with the Scottish Covenant, and in 1215 in England when the barons, prelates and commons took a solemn oath to maintain the laws even against the king.[73] The army preacher John Shawe also argued that the Covenant was consonant with the Oaths of Allegiance and Supremacy. Shawe claimed that a distinction had to be made between the king's lawful commands made with the two houses and expressions of his personal will which the subject was not obliged to follow. Shawe also stated that Parliament had the power to make the Covenant as the king's legal power was in his courts, whether he was present in person or not, and the supreme court of the country resided in Parliament.[74]

One argument in defence of the qualified allegiance given in the Covenant that is deserving of special mention, if only for its sheer argumentative audacity rather than its actual influence, is Robert Austine's *Allegiance Not Impeached* (1644). Austine actually used the judges' decision in Calvin's Case to support the tendering of the Covenant. He acknowledged the judges' verdict that allegiance was due to the king's natural capacity and not to his public person but he also noted Coke's statements about the reciprocal relationship between protection and obedience. As a result, Austine concluded that this natural allegiance was 'of as great extent and latitude as the royall power and proteection of the King'.[75] If our allegiance was a natural duty, Austine reasoned that that same obedience must be governed by natural law. He then noted that 'the chief politicall principle in nature' was, '*Salus populi suprema lex* . . . therefore there must be a power in the whole to preserve itself against any part that shall rise against it'. Austine believed that the power to secure the public safety was vested in the laws and privileges of the land. His incredibly circular argument took him from the statement that allegiance was due to the king's natural capacity to the conclusion that allegiance must be regulated by the laws of the land. The best judges of what actions were beneficial to the public safety were, of course, the two houses.[76]

---

[73] T. Mocket, A *View of the Solemn League and Covenant* (1644), pp. 12–13, 17–23.

[74] J. Shawe, *Brittains Remembrencer, or the Nationall Covenant* (York, 1644), pp. 6–7.

[75] R. Austine, *Allegiance Not Impeached: Viz by the Parliaments Taking Up of Arms* (1644), pp. 2–4, 8.

[76] Ibid., pp. 5, 8, 19, 21. A later pamphlet in support of the Negative Oath made similar use of the judgement in Calvin's Case: [E. Buckler], *Certaine Queries Concerning the Lawfullness of Imposing and Taking of the Negative Oath* (1647).

Although the notion of a covenanted monarch and 'holy war' justifications for the use of force were employed in promoting Parliament's oaths and covenants, the arguments deployed by English pamphleteers were not identical to those advanced by Scottish covenanters. Beyond the continued resort to private law and mixed-government theory (which was also a feature of Rutherford's work) one crucial difference lies in the importance of the coronation oath in Scottish covenanting thought.[77] The notion that the king, either implicitly or expressly, entered into a covenant with the people on assuming the throne was central to Samuel Rutherford's political beliefs. In his *Lex Rex*, Rutherford stated that there was 'an oath betwixt the King and his people, laying on, by reciprocation of bands, mutuall civil obligations upon the King to the people and the people to the King'. This contract, which he saw as being embodied in the king's coronation oath, was additional to the religious covenant between God, king and people. The contract made 'betwixt him and his people at his Coronation oath' was the proof that the king was accountable to law.[78]

The idea that the coronation oath was a social contract had been employed by the monarchomachi of sixteenth century Europe. Of the sixteenth century theorists, George Buchanan, tutor to the young James VI, advanced the idea that kings born after the first inauguration of monarchy owed their position to the same conditional election as the first king. In his history of Scotland, Buchanan spoke of 'the ceremonies used at the inauguration of our kings' that 'have an express reference to this law; from all which it is that government is nothing more than a mutual compact between the people and their kings.'[79] However, the idea that the king's oath was contractual was hardly new. The charges ranged against Edward II in 1323 included the accusation that he had broken his coronation oath by failing to observe law and custom. The remonstrances produced by the Long Parliament tended to make more use of these precedents from medieval English history than of Scottish resistance theories.[80]

Parliament initially used the king's oath as evidence that the monarch had not been granted a negative voice concerning bills for the public safety (i.e., the control of the militia). On 21 May 1642 the Commons ordered a committee to 'examine the King's Oath, with the Record, that it may be inserted into that Declaration'. Two days later the committee brought in the oath with the record and it was ordered that 'the Clause of His Majesty's Answer to the Commons Claim, in the Statute of 25. E. III. of Provisors shall be inserted

---

[77] Coffey, *Rutherford*, p. 183.

[78] S. Rutherford, *Lex Rex: The Law and the Prince* (1644), pp. 96, 232.

[79] J. W. Gough, *The Social Contract: A Critical Study of its Development* (2nd edn., Oxford, 1957), pp. 55–65.

[80] J. Greenberg, 'The Confessor's Laws and the Radical Face of the Ancient Constitution', *English Historical Review*, civ (1989), 611–37, at 618; see also *idem*, *The Radical Face of the Ancient Constitution*.

in the Declaration.'[81] This was included in a remonstrance of the Lords and Commons printed on 26 May 1642. The Statute of Provisors of Benefices 25. Edw. III. contained the Latin form of the coronation oath. According to Parliament, the key clause, *quas vulgus elegerit*, showed that the king was thereby bound to pass all laws necessary to remedy any mischiefs and damages that might happen to the kingdom. This applied to new laws as well as old. In deciding what would be necessary to this end 'they [the Parliament]' were 'the most proper Judges who are sent from the whole Kingdome for that very purpose'. Their evidence came from the customary reply to bills which have passed both houses, *le roy savisera*, which the remonstrance claimed signified 'rather a suspension then a refusal of the Royal Assent'.[82]

Charles replied to the remonstrance, stating that, as it appeared in the statute 25 Edw. III., the king's oath was only a confirmation of already existing laws. The references to customs made clear that the clause referred to the laws the commonality *had* chosen. It could not be imagined that the king would be obliged by his oath to assent to the taking away of the power to protect his subjects. Moreover, the form used at Charles's coronation had omitted the word chosen altogether so that he had assented only to observe such laws as the commonality have.[83] The Commons appointed another committee on 20 June 1642 to deal with Charles's reply. The committee, which included Sir Symonds D'Ewes, was to 'search the Records in the Exchequer, and elsewhere, to see what Oath his Majesty took at his Coronation; and what Oathes other Kings, his Majesty's Predecessors, took'.[84] The committee's efforts did not become public until the publishing of another remonstrance on 2 November 1642. The Parliament excused the delay as being a result of more pressing business. They also complained that they had not been able to use the English form of the coronation oath taken by James and Charles as these had been kept in Archbishop Laud's collections. They did not allege that the king was required by his oath to pass all bills presented to him by the two houses. The effective resigning of the king's negative voice was only required to those bills which were essential for the good of the whole kingdom. The implication was that Parliament (meaning the Lords and Commons) would be the arbiter of what was conducive to the public good. The form of coronation oath taken by King James and his son was in any case, the remonstrance argued, exceptional. English kings had previously always assented to govern by the laws that the commonality had chosen or would choose. However, the interpretation of the phrase *quas vulgus elegerit* was not, they said, fundamental to the meaning

---

[81] CJ, ii, 582–3.

[82] A Remonstrance of the Declaration of the Lords and Commons, Now Assembled in Parliament, 26 May, 1642 (1642), pp. 7–8.

[83] His Majesties Answer to the Declaration of the Lords and Commons Now Assembled in Parliament, May 26. 1642 (1642), pp. 14–15.

[84] CJ, ii, 634.

of the oath. The memorandum on the coronation oath of Richard II made clear that it referred to laws 'as a thing future and not passed'. This was later confirmed in Henry VIII's annotations on the form of the coronation oath. Other evidence was found to support the view that the king had no negative voice on public bills. Justice Hutton's verdict in Hampden's case was that the king never bluntly refused the laws presented to him by the two houses but only gave the answer *le roy savisera*.[85]

Parliamentarian theorists made similar denials of the king's negative voice. Henry Parker stated that though the king's oath took greater care with 'Canonicall Priviledges, and of Bishops and Clergymen (as having been penned by Popish Bishops) then of the Commonalty, yet it confirmes all Lawes and rightfull customes, amongst which we most highly esteeme Parliamentary Priviledges'. Irrespective of the tense of the word *elegerit* the king was 'bound to consent to new Lawes if they be necessary, as well as defend old'.[86] William Prynne concluded from the phrase *quas vulgus elegerit* that the king's assent was not what created law. The coronation oath demonstrated that if the Commons 'are to chuse Lawes, and the King by his Oath bound to grant, strengthen, maintain and defend them when chosen by them, then doubtlesse they [the Commons] are the chief legislators and not the King'.[87]

However, the coronation oath was not only used to demonstrate the legislative supremacy of Parliament and deny the king's negative voice. Parliament and its apologists also presented the king's oath as a social contract, implying that the monarch's authority was in some way derived from the people. Parliament suggested that the king's levying of arms was a violation of his mutual contract with the people enshrined in the coronation oath. On 20 May 1642 the Lords resolved that 'Whensoever the King maketh War upon the Parliament, it is a Breach of the Trust reposed in Him by His People, contrary to His Oath, and tending to the Dissolution of this Government.'[88] John Morrill and John Adamson have noted that in the Nineteen Propositions of June 1642 the office of lord high constable was included amongst the list of royal officials the two houses were to approve. The inclusion of this office was remarkable for two reasons. First, the office of constable had been vacant since 1521 and, second, it had been held by many antiquaries to carry the authority, in extreme cases, to arrest the king for breach of his coronation oath. Morrill and Adamson have argued that, as a whole, the claims over the appointment of royal counsellors in the Nineteen Propositions reveal the extent to which

---

[85] *A Remonstrance of the Lords and Commons Assembled in Parliament, or the Reply of Both Houses, to a Printed Book, Under His Majesties Name* (1642), pp. 1, 25–7; C. C. Weston and J. K. Greenberg, *Subjects and Sovereigns: The Grand Controversy over Legal Sovereignty in Stuart England* (Cambridge, 1981), p. 36.

[86] Parker, *Observations*, pp. 4–5.

[87] W. Prynne, *The Soveraigne Power of Parliaments and Kingdomes: Divided into Foure Parts* (1643), part one, pp. 47–9.

[88] *LJ*, v, 76.

the civil war 'began as an aristocratic coup'.[89] In fact, the unusual reference to the office of constable seems to provide further evidence that Parliament viewed the coronation oath as contractual. The position of lord high constable had earlier been used by John Ponet in his *A Short Treatise of Politike Power* (1556) to offer evidence for the legality of deposing tyrants. Ponet's work was reprinted (and, it seems, avidly read) in 1639 and 1642.[90]

Parliamentarian writers made clear that, as with all mutual contracts, the obligations of one party could be forfeited by the non-performance of the other. In the case of severe breach of faith, the contract might be dissolved altogether. To Charles Herle, the evidence that England was a mixed-monarchy of co-ordinate powers lay in 'the mutuall Oathes the King and people are to take to maintaine the Laws that have so constituted it'. The king's oath was not, as the court divines insisted, only to God. This was because a vow is to God but 'an Oath is by God, wherein there are three parties still, who, by whom and to whom; belike then, if he sweare to God, the people are the party by whom he sweares.' Harking back to the feudal origins of the coronation oath, Herle stated that 'the king is our liege lord, as well as we his liege people, that is (as the word signifies) mutually bounden to each other.'[91] William Bridge, who had spent the 1630s in exile in the Dutch Republic, saw the coronation oath as a 'mutuall covenant betwixt the King and the people', which 'binds the king, to the people, as well as the people to the king'. This was the best type of government where 'the King and the people strike a Covenant at his Coronation, which covenant the King is bound to observe.'[92] Prynne viewed the oath as the main evidence that the kingdom was above the king. He argued that even those kings that came to the crown by hereditary descent were not deemed kings until they had submitted to the people's consent at the coronation.[93]

These authors were unanimous in viewing the coronation oath as a mutual and conditional covenant between king and people. They were more equivocal in stating how far breaches of this contract would free the subjects from their duty of obedience. Some of the earlier theorists, William Bridge and Jeremiah Burroughs in particular, were very reluctant to explain what might be forfeited by the king violating his public trust. Burroughs said that he did not think 'every breach of promise, and not performance of covenant in everything makes

---

[89] Adamson, 'Baronial Context', p. 100; Morrill, *Nature of the English Revolution*, pp. 12, 299–300; Kenyon, *Stuart Constitution*, pp. 244–7.

[90] Ponet, *Short Treatise*, p. 106; Garrett, *Marian Exiles*, pp. 254–8. These ideas seem to have penetrated down to a popular level. John Troutbeck was tried at Knaresborough Assizes in 1641 for claiming the king could be deposed for breach of his coronation oath, see A. J. Hopper, '"The Readiness of the People": The Formation and Emergence of the Army of the Fairfaxes, 1642–3', *Borthwick Papers*, 92 (1997), 9.

[91] C. Herle, *A Fuller Answer to a Treatise Written by Doctor Ferne* (1642), pp. 3–5.

[92] W. Bridge, *The Wounded Conscience Cured, the Weak One Strengthened, and the Doubting Satisfied* (1642), pp. 43, 51.

[93] Prynne, *Soveraigne Power*, part one, pp. 51, 78.

a forfeiture'. This would be, he said, 'a dangerous consequent'. Burroughs evaded the question of whether any breach of the covenant might dissolve the contract between king and people, confessing that he was 'not willing to dispute this too far'.[94] Bridge was also reluctant to 'presse the forfeiture of the Kings power upon non-performance of covenant'. However, he was less non-committal than Burroughs in stating that, if the king should neglect the public safety, 'the state will be free to act on their own to supply that deficiency'.[95] Yet the punishment for breach of covenant was still not made explicit.

William Prynne's *The Soveraigne Power of Parliaments* was far more overt in enumerating the consequences of a king breaking his covenant with the people. David Wootton has shown that the fourth part of this work contained large extracts from the radical Huguenot resistance tract, *Vindiciae Contra Tyrannos* (1579), not published in full English translation until 1648.[96] Yet the most pregnant remarks about the consequences of a royal violation of the coronation oath came earlier, in the third part of Prynne's book and appear to have been of his own invention. Here the barrister began a redefinition of the idea of treason. To Prynne, the wording of the treason laws made it clear that the crime included not simply attempts on the king's person or authority but attacks 'against the realm'. He used Coke's description of the king as liege lord in Calvin's Case to claim a reciprocal bond in the coronation oath. If the king should attack his subjects Prynne believed he would cease to be their king *de jure* and the people would be free to defend themselves against him. For a king to levy war against his subjects, except in instances of dire necessity (which, according to Prynne, was not presently the case), would be to go against the wording of the coronation oath, which obliged the king to keep the peace. Indeed, if the king should wage war on his subjects, the people were obliged by the original compact to array and arm themselves against the enemies of the kingdom. Prynne had reinterpreted the breach of the king's coronation oath as treason.[97]

Yet, although the coronation oath formed an important part of the armoury of Parliamentarian resistance theorists in the 1640s, discussions of the king's oath are almost entirely absent from pamphlets generated by the imposition of the Protestation, Vow and Covenant and Solemn League and Covenant (although the coronation oath was discussed as political contract in the

---

[94] J. Burroughs, *A Briefe Answer to Dr. Fernes Booke, Tending to Resolve the Conscience* (1643), p. 10.

[95] Bridge, *Wounded Conscience*, p. 44.

[96] Wootton, 'Rebellion to Revolution', p. 661.

[97] Prynne, *Soveraigne Power*, part three, pp. 8–9, 13; Greenberg, 'The Confessor's Laws', 621–2. Prynne used his redefinition of treason as the prosecuting counsel in the trial of William Laud. W. Prynne, *Canterburies Doome or the First Part of a Compleat History of the Commitment, Charge, Tryall, Condemnation, Execution of William Laud* (1646), pp. 38–41, 69–70; *State Trials*, iv, 462–4.

Commons' proclamation promoting a national association).[98] In the 1620s and the 1630s, Henry Burton, as will be shown later, was an advocate of a publicly subscribed national covenant. He combined this vision of England as a covenanted nation, like Scottish covenanters, with a reinterpretation of the coronation oath as a religious and political contract. In his sermons *For God and the King*, published in 1636, he described the king's coronation oath as a 'mutuall stipulation or covenant'. The king, according to Burton, 'bindes himself, by a double oath to the observation of the fundamentall Lawes of the Kingdome: Tacitly, as being a King, and so bound as well to protect the People, as the Lawes of his Kingdome: and expresly, by his Oath at His coronation.' Burton compared the king's coronation oath with the covenant God had made with Noah.[99] In an earlier work, *The Seven Vials* (1628), Burton had hinted at the consequences of a king who failed to observe his coronation 'covenant': 'a king, governing in a settled Kingdome, leaves to be a King, and degenerates into a Tyrant, as soon as he leaves off to rule according to his Lawes.'[100]

However, Burton's work appears to be exceptional amongst English writers in combining the idea of a national covenant with the reinterpretation of the coronation oath as a social contract. The reasons for this difference between English and Scottish covenanting thought are not obvious, but they may lie in the tendency of English divines to locate the national covenant in the larger historical act of the reformation, whether identified as beginning in Edward or Elizabeth's reign, rather than in specific oaths or covenants.[101] As will be demonstrated in the next chapter, documents like the Solemn League and Covenant were often presented as only renewals and reaffirmations of England's covenant with God. There may be something too in the argument put forward by Arthur Williamson that in Scotland the covenant idea was a means of binding a nation that was only partially under the effective rule of law. The covenant idea in Scotland took on a more legalistic character, whereas in England, there was more reliance on scriptural examples.

Following the brief experimentation with an oath of loyalty that did not take account of the safety of the king in the Vow and Covenant, the Long Parliament and its supporters largely returned to the theories of allegiance used to defend their taking up of arms in 1642. Nevertheless, some advocates of the Solemn League and Covenant did not see this as a flinching away, as J.C. Davis has described it, from more radical resistance theories.[102] In a number

---

[98] See below, pp. 139–41.
[99] H, Burton, *For God and the King* (1636), pp. 14, 144–5. For more on Burton's belief that England was a covenanted nation see below, pp. 139–41.
[100] H. Burton, *The Seven Vials* (1628), The Epistle. See also *idem, Israel's Fast* (1628), A3.
[101] See for example John Cotton's belief that the Elizabethan church settlement constituted England's covenant with God, D.D. Hall, 'John Cotton's Letter to Samuel Skelton', *William and Mary Quarterly*, 22 (1965), 478–85.
[102] Davis, 'Political Thought', p. 377.

of pamphlets written in support of the Protestation, Vow and Covenant and Solemn League and Covenant writers had referred to these oaths as embodiments of a religious covenant between God, king and people. They had argued that Charles had forfeited the subject's duty of allegiance by failing to keep this covenant. This presented subscribers with a purely religious justification for resistance. Royalist writers condemned these arguments as equivocating with the allegiance that was due to the king. Yet, as in Scotland, these theories never developed into arguments for regicide (although the notion that the coronation oath was a political contract was used to justify Charles I's execution).[103] Indeed, as we will see, many English Presbyterians would oppose the trial and execution of the king as violations of the Covenant, including William Prynne, whose *Soveraigne Power of Parliaments* would ironically supply so much of the ideological ammunition necessary to justify killing the king.

---

[103] For a fuller discussion of the use of the coronation oath in arguments and apologetics for Charles I's execution see my 'State Oaths and Political Casuistry in England, 1640–1702', (unpublished Oxford University D.Phil. thesis, 2000), pp. 107–11.

4

Secular contracts or religious covenants?

In discussing the existence of a social contract between the prince and his subjects, writers often described the bond as a covenant. Given the parallels that have been seen between the notion of a 'double covenant' in *Vindiciae Contra Tyrannos* and elements of Scottish covenanting thought, it seems likely that the covenant idea informed Parliamentarian interpretations of the coronation oath.[1] Any connection must remain speculative, however, given the lack of reference to the king's oath in tracts in support of the Protestation, Vow and Covenant and Solemn League and Covenant. Historians have also argued that religious covenants binding congregations of believers together provided the foundation for conceptions of mutual social contracts. Christopher Hill suggested religious covenants themselves reflected a more market-driven society. Changes in contract law giving Englishmen 'a new freedom to regulate their business affairs', Hill argued, were paralleled by changes in attitudes towards the biblical covenant. This covenant became 'an agreement between equals, which established rights for both parties'. By covenanting with God, the people, the church and the nation could put themselves on an equal footing with him.[2] Covenants were often discussed as mutual contracts that were conditional on all parties fulfilling their obligations. The term covenant was often used to describe reciprocal agreements. However, mutuality was only one facet of the covenant idea. In a religious context, the importance of the covenant of grace to covenant theology and the idea that these documents were national obligations qualified their contractual elements.

The Solemn League and Covenant of 1643 and the oaths of loyalty that preceded it, the Protestation and Vow and Covenant, have received relatively little attention in comparison to their Scottish counterpart, the National Covenant of 1638.[3] The Protestation has mainly been tackled as a source of

---

[1] Smart, 'Political Ideas of the Scottish Covenanters', 170; Coffey, *Rutherford*, p. 165.

[2] Hill, *English Bible*, p. 278; Gough, *Social Contract*, p. 85.

[3] For good, but brief, treatments of the Solemn League and Covenant see Hill, *English Bible*, pp. 271–84; J. H. Wilson, 'Puritan Piety for a Covenanted Nation' in his *Pulpit in Parliament: Puritanism During the English Civil Wars, 1640–1648* (Princeton, 1969), pp. 166–96; D. G. Mullan, '"Uniformity in Religion": The Solemn League and Covenant (1643) and the Presbyterian Vision', in *Later Calvinism: International Perspectives* ed. W. F. Graham

evidence for levels of literacy, the Vow and Covenant has largely been ignored and the Solemn League and Covenant has been treated as, for the English, essentially a political 'marriage of convenience', securing Scottish military aid for Parliament.[4] These oaths have essentially been seen as tests of political loyalty, with scant notice being paid to the arguments used to promote them. However, as we will see, the advocates of the Solemn League and Covenant in England frequently presented it as a religious covenant binding all three kingdoms to national and personal reformation.

The Protestation, Vow and Covenant and Solemn League and Covenant were all described not as oaths, but as national covenants. This interpretation was informed by the now fully developed federal theology that had taken root in England, Scotland and the American colonies. The elements of federal theology that reappeared in arguments for the Solemn League and Covenant will be explored in detail using the extensive pamphlet literature devoted to the Covenant. Federal theology emphasised that the sacraments of baptism and the Lord's Supper were renewals of the covenant of grace. The idea of a repeatedly renewed covenant with God was a fundamental part of the work of Johannes Koch (Cocceus, 1603–1669), the theologian usually credited with perfecting reformed federal thought.[5] It will be demonstrated that the advocates of the Solemn League and Covenant often claimed that it was no more than the renewal of a national covenant previously embodied in the Protestation and Vow and Covenant. The personal elements of the covenant idea will be traced through the belief that the Protestation, Vow and Covenant and Solemn League and Covenant could inspire the moral reformation of individual sub-scribers. Equally, the national aspects of covenant theology will be explored through the conviction that joining in a religious covenant would spiritually purify both the church and the commonwealth. Here the distinction between the covenant of grace as understood in a broad and narrow sense is an impor-tant one. In a narrow sense the covenant of grace is only made with the elect. However, in terms of the administration of the covenant of grace, the covenant must be said or thought to be with all the baptised, since only God knows who is elect. The baptised, or those that have made some credible confession of faith, those who are broadly within the covenant, do enjoy some benefits

(Kirksville, Mo., 1994), pp. 249–66; E. J. Cowan, 'The Solemn League and Covenant', in *Scotland and England: 1286–1815*, ed. R. A. Mason (Edinburgh, 1987), pp. 182–203; J. L. Kim's recent thesis is exceptional for treating both Scottish and English perceptions of the Solemn League and Covenant: 'The Debate on the Relations Between the Churches of Scotland and England During the British Revolution (1633–1647)' (Cambridge Univ. Ph.D. thesis, 1997), ch. 7.

[4] D. Cressy, *Literacy and the Social Order*, pp. 62–103, 191–201, 215–21; idem, 'Vow, Covenant and Protestation, Sources for the History of Population and Literacy in the Seventeenth Century', *Local Historian*, xiv (1980), 134–41.

[5] See Derk Visser, 'Covenant', in the *Oxford Encyclopedia of the Reformation*, ed. H. J. Hillerbrand (4 vols., Oxford, 1996).

of it, but unlike the elect, they do not enjoy the full or 'double' benefit of it: justification and sanctification. Hence the advocates of the Parliament's covenants placed considerable emphasis upon an analogy with the sacrament of baptism and upon external, visual signs, such as the raising of the right hand, which denoted entrance into a covenant with God.

As we will see in Chapter 6, differences over what this 'covenanted religion' would entail would soon destroy the broad base of support for the Solemn League and Covenant that had existed at its inception. However, as the next part of the book will demonstrate, divisions between the religious parties after 1644 did not render the Solemn League and Covenant a dead letter. Describing these documents as covenants rather than oaths changed their perceived obligation. In an oath God was only involved as a witness, judging human testimony and threatening his wrath if it should prove false. In a religious covenant, God was involved as an active party in a contract containing mutual obligations. To some, the Solemn League and Covenant embodied fundamental duties to God that could not be revoked by any temporal authority. It will be argued that it was the belief that these obligations to God were indissoluble and perpetual which, in part, led many Presbyterians to oppose the republican Engagement in 1649, and refuse the declarations abjuring the Solemn League and Covenant in 1661–2.

By the early seventeenth century, both England and Scotland could boast ministers such as William Ames, William Perkins, Robert Rollock and Robert Howie offering sophisticated treatments of federal theology. In both countries, but especially in Scotland, the covenant motif took on political dimensions. The Scottish National Covenant of 1638 clearly bound the covenanter to a particular form of government, in Margaret Steele's words to a 'limited monarchy co-existing in a theocratic state'.[6] Subscribers were obliged to defend 'the Kings' Majesties person and authoritie' but only in 'preservation' of 'religion, laws and liberties'.[7] By claiming the unimpeachable nature of the 1581 Negative Confession, the National Covenant reasserted the kirk's independence from the subsequent acts of Parliament and the General Assembly.[8] This theocratic emphasis in Scotland contrasted with the development of the covenant idea in the New England colonies. Here the church and the state were under the control of the same individuals and there was no equivalent antagonism between kirk and crown. In the place of a national Presbyterian church there was a system of regional uniformity. The elect of each local church would choose their own ministers and decide upon their own practices.

---

[6] Steele, 'Politick Christian', p. 56.
[7] Russell, *Fall*, p. 51. See also E. J. Cowan, 'The Making of the National Covenant', in *Scottish National Covenant*, ed. Morrill, pp. 68–90.
[8] J. S. Morrill, 'The National Covenant in its British Context', in *Scottish National Covenant*, ed. Morrill, pp. 1–31, at p. 12.

From the community a small group of the godly would be chosen to form the pillars of the new church. They would prepare and swear to a church covenant, effectively a way of testing the faith of members. This group would form the nucleus that would vote on whether to admit new members to the covenant. By its nature the church covenant was an instrument of exclusion, limiting access to the sacraments to those that were truly faithful. This model of the covenant ideal was nevertheless influential. The New England colonists intended their churches to be a guiding light to the church back in England. Colonial clergy spent much of their literary efforts in the 1640s in attempting to convince the English of the benefits of the Congregational way. New England ministers like John Cotton retained strong contacts with religious exiles in the Netherlands, including Philip Nye and William Bridge, and with remaining Congregationalists in England.[9]

Contacts between the English and Scottish opponents of Charles I, and later the presence of Scots ministers in England, made the Scottish interpretation of the covenant idea an influential one. However, a powerful alternative to this vision of the national covenant gained support through the works of New England divines printed in England, the clerical contacts between Congregationalists in the Netherlands, the colonies and England, and the political leadership of Independents in the House of Commons. The existence of these different interpretations of federal theology would later create divisions over the nature and purpose of the Solemn League and Covenant (discussed below). Nevertheless, common to all these formulations was the idea that the covenant was, unlike an oath, a mutual contract, albeit one in which the duties falling to man could only be fulfilled as a result of the efficacious grace of God.

Elements of both the national and personal covenant ideals appeared in pamphlets advocating the Protestation, Vow and Covenant and Solemn League and Covenant. The use of outward signs, the emphasis on the continuity and renewal of the covenant and the vision of a nation in mutual covenant with God were evident in works promoting the Protestation and the two subsequent Parliamentary covenants. *The Covenanters Catechisme* explained that there were several circumstances in which it was appropriate for nations to make a covenant with God: when a nation or a people had been guilty of sin; when God had threatened or visited his people with terrible judgements; or when a nation wished to offer thanks for mercies received.[10] However, the

[9] F. J. Bremer, *Shaping New Englands: Puritan Clergymen in Seventeenth Century England and New England* (New York, 1994), pp. 9–11, 60; *idem, Congregational Communion: Clerical Friendship in the Anglo-American Puritan Community, 1610–1692* (Boston, 1994); E. B. Holifield, *The Covenant Sealed: The Development of Puritan Sacramental Theology in Old and New England, 1570–1720* (New Haven, 1974), pp. 152–8; M. McGiffert, 'American Puritan Studies in the 1960s', *William and Mary Quarterly*, 3rd series, xxvii (1970), 36–67.
[10] *The Covenanters Catechisme*, p. 3.

role of human agency in making these covenants was strictly limited. The author of *The Un-deceiver* (1643) stated that the Vow and Covenant was a covenant of grace; 'and therefore we do not enter into this Covenant, presuming upon our own, but trusting upon the free and effectual Grace of God.'[11] Yet the content of these Parliamentary covenants was not purely religious. Rather, they were mixed covenants containing civil and spiritual elements.[12] Consequently, the roles assigned to them were many and varied. It was expected that a covenant made with God would further both national and personal reformation. As a chosen nation of covenanted people, England would fulfil its special providential destiny, regaining its place in divine favour and waging war against the conspiracies of Antichrist.

The Protestation, Vow and Covenant and Solemn League and Covenant were all promoted as national covenants. The research of Peter Donald and Conrad Russell has shown that there were significant links between the covenanter leaders in Scotland and outspoken critics of Charles in England, notably Lord Brooke, Viscount Say and Sele and his son Nathaniel Fiennes.[13] Pro-Scots MPs, Sir John Wray, Sir Robert Harley and George Peard, proposed the Protestation. It was clear that some of them viewed the oath as an English national covenant.[14] On 3 May 1641, during the Commons debate on the Protestation, Wray argued that to complete the task of spiritual reformation members should 'endeavour to be loyal Covenanters with God and the King' by 'first binding ourselves by a Parliamentary and National Oath, (not a Straffordian nor a Prelatical one)'.[15] Others also saw the oath in this light. Edward Hyde, later earl of Clarendon, reported that a preacher in Bury St Edmund's had used the text Jeremiah 31: 31, 'Behold the dayes come, saith the Lord, that I will make a new covenant with the house of Israel, and with the house of Judah', to press subscription to the Protestation.[16] Thomas Mocket, in a sermon to the Commons in August 1642, discussed national covenants as being 'when a whole Nation, at least the generality, do thus engage themselves to the Lord', and such, he said, was 'the Protestation lately taken'.[17]

---

[11] *The Un-deceiver*, p. 7; see also J. Brinsley, *The Saints Solemne Covenant with Their God* (1644), pp. 28–9.

[12] G. S., *The Three Kingdoms Healing-Plaister, or the Solemne League and Covenant* (1643), p. 3.

[13] P. Donald, *An Uncounselled King: Charles I and the Scottish Troubles, 1637–41* (Cambridge, 1990), pp. 135–6, 184–5, 244–7; *idem*, 'New Light on the Anglo-Scottish Contacts of 1640', *Historical Research*, lxii (1989), 221–9; Russell, *Fall*, pp. 60–4, 68–70, 151–3, 165–71.

[14] Ibid., pp. 176–7.

[15] Cobbett, *Parl. Deb.*, ii, 778; *Letters and Journals of Robert Baillie*, ed. D. Laing (3 vols., Edinburgh, 1841), i, 351.

[16] Bodl. MS Clarendon 31, f. 30–30v. (note here the allusion already being made to a covenanted union between kingdoms).

[17] T. Mocket, *The Nationall Covenant; or a Sermon on the Covenant* (1642), p. 3.

Following the tenets of federal theology, great importance was given to renewing covenants made with God. The English Presbyterian John Geree noted the Scots' 'joy at the renovation' of their covenant and chided his countrymen for their slowness in following this example.[18] In the same way that the Scots had harked back to the Negative Confession of 1581 to justify the making of the National Covenant of 1638, MPs and ministers used the Elizabethan Association of 1584 as evidence of an earlier Parliamentary 'covenant'. Thomas Mocket clearly had the Association in mind when he spoke of the Protestation as 'the renewing of our Nationall Covenant'.[19] The Vow and Covenant and Solemn League and Covenant were also described as associations and it seems likely that John Pym and others used the terms association and covenant interchangeably because they felt they were synonymous with each other. The parallel was also made between taking these Parliamentary covenants and the renewal of the covenant of baptism through the taking of communion. Thomas Case reminded those who scrupled at subscribing to the Protestation that, 'every day of humiliation, and every approach to God's table, is a solemn renewing of thy vow and covenant with God.' The timorous should, therefore, be equally afraid to take communion as to take the Protestation.[20]

The emphasis on the importance of renewing covenants helped explain the imposition of new and seemingly conflicting oaths of loyalty. Ministers justified the subsequent tendering of the Solemn League and Covenant by pointing both to the shortcomings of preceding covenants (meaning the Protestation and Vow and Covenant) and to the need to renew them to remedy any breaches. The Independent Philip Nye's exhortation to the two houses to take the Solemn League and Covenant argued its necessity on the basis of the 'sinfull neglect' of the Protestation, which had opened the floodgates to pour calamities upon the nation.[21] Hezekiah Woodward, a divine who gravitated from Presbyterianism to Independency in the later 1640s, listed the deficiencies of the Protestation and the Vow and Covenant which had made imposing the Solemn League and Covenant necessary. The Protestation, whilst joining God to the Parliament's cause had made the enemy strive harder and they had hatched a plot against the 'Mother City of Israel', London. The people had entered a covenant against this design (the Vow and Covenant) but they had not come up 'fully unto that Work'. The Vow and Covenant had been too driven by self-interest, being over-occupied with the subject's rights and

---

[18] Geree, *Judah's Joy*, p. 16.

[19] Mocket, *Nationall Covenant*, p. 1.

[20] T. Case, *Two Sermons Lately Preached at Westminster* (2nd edn., 1642), pp. 34–5. The sacramental aspect of the Solemn League and Covenant has been noted by Stephen Baskerville, 'Blood Guilt in the English Revolution', *The Seventeenth Century*, 8 (1993), 181–202, at p. 198.

[21] *An Ordinance of the Lords and Commons Assembled in Parliament; with Instructions for the Taking of the League and Covenant* (1643), p. 2.

privileges. 'There was not', Woodward said, 'that spiritually [sic] in that business, as God requires.' This had only been achieved with the creation of the Solemn League and Covenant.[22] By arguing that these Parliamentary covenants were merely public acclamations and renewals of the original covenant between God and man, ministers were able to reconcile seemingly antithetical oaths of loyalty whilst retaining a powerful framework of theological censure.

Subscription, like baptism, was only the seal of entering into covenant with God. Having emphasised that the power to enter into these covenants was only a consequence of the covenant of grace, ministers nevertheless stressed the efforts that had to be made by both the nation and the individual swearer so that these covenants were kept. Basil Feilding, the earl of Denbigh, having ordered his troops to take the Solemn League and Covenant, gave further instructions on how the newly covenanted soldiers were to conduct themselves. He demanded that they regularly and strictly observe public fasts and days of humiliation. The troops had at all times to refrain from drinking and swearing. They were to behave in a civil and orderly way and make a general promise to conduct themselves with 'good carriage'.[23] The importance of keeping to the terms of the Protestation and Covenant was also stressed in soldiers' catechisms.[24] Humiliation and repentance for sins both national and personal, public and private were essential to covenant making. John Ellis, in a fast sermon preached before Parliament, complained that one of the deficiencies of the Protestation was that it did not make any confession of the nation's sins.[25] The Vow and Covenant and the Solemn League and Covenant made amends for this. In the former, the deponent declared his sorrow for his own sins, 'and the sins of this nation, which have deserved the Calamities and Judgements that now lie upon it'. In the latter the swearer stated that the kingdoms were 'guilty of many sins and provocations against God and his son Jesus Christ'. They did therefore 'profess and declare before God and the world our unfeigned desire to be humbled for our own sins and for the sins of these kingdoms'.

The repentance and reformation of the individual subscriber were equally as important as the humiliation of the nation in making and keeping these covenants. Paul Seaver has argued that the 'examined life' was 'the veriest commonplace among lay and clerical Puritans in the 1620s and 1630s'. Godly diarists and letter writers like Nehemiah Wallington, Roger Lowe, William Kiffin and Lady Brilliana Harley spent most of their literary efforts in recording

---

[22] H. [sometimes listed as Ezekiah] Woodward, *Three Kingdoms Made One, by Entering Covenant with One God* (1643), pp. 3–4.

[23] HMC, *4th Report* (London, 1874), p. 263. (Despite these exhortations, accusations of misconduct were later made against Denbigh's troops, ibid., pp. 265, 267, 270.)

[24] [R. Ram], *The Souldiers Catechisme* (1644), pp. 10, 13, 17; for these catechisms see I. M. Green, *The Christian's ABC: Catechisms and Catechising in England c. 1530–1740* (Oxford, 1996), pt. III 'A Finding List of English Catechisms', pp. 575–752.

[25] J. Ellis, *The Sole Path to a Sound Peace* (1643), p. 48.

this rigorous process of self-examination.[26] Similarly, the covenanters of the 1640s were expected to search their souls for any signs of their uncleanness and unworthiness before subscribing. Joseph Caryl stated that, before taking the Solemn League and Covenant, the swearer must first examine himself and make sure that he was not still tied to the carnal covenant with sin.[27] One tract from the civil war era was made up entirely of the author's diary of his endeavours to keep his Covenant.[28] Nehemiah Wallington saw both the Protestation and the Solemn League and Covenant as spiritual yokes, binding the people to a stringent moral discipline.[29] The three sermons contained in Thomas Case's *The Quarrell of the Covenant* (1644) reveal the process by which the ministers were supposed to make ready their parishioners to take the Solemn League and Covenant. Case's first sermon dealt with the grave dangers and divine punishments that would accompany covenant breaking or covenant refusal. This was followed by a sermon immediately prior to taking the Covenant that removed common scruples over it. After the parish had sworn the oath, another sermon was given reminding them of their duties in keeping faith with the Covenant. The instructions for the nationwide tendering of the Solemn League and Covenant prescribed these kinds of preparations, with the ministers in each parish offering a sermon to prepare their flocks for taking the Covenant. This would be followed on the next Lord's day with an exhortation to take the Covenant, after which the whole parish would subscribe.[30]

The process of internal examination was accompanied by external preparations for taking the Solemn League and Covenant. In line with covenant theology, covenanting ministers placed great importance on the outward signs that were used in subscribing.[31] These were contained in the practice of raising the right hand in assent to the Covenant and reading the text of the oath aloud.[32] Hezekiah Woodward claimed that the absence of such solemnities had been one reason for the failure of the Vow and Covenant. The subscriber, Woodward said, 'at such a time as this . . . must not creep into a corner. In these cases, and at such Solemnities, he must confess his god before Men, else he knows what follows.'[33] Even Royalists accepted that visual signs increased the obligation of sworn statements.[34] It was not only suggested that they be

[26] P. S. Seaver, *Wallington's World: A Puritan Artisan in Seventeenth Century London* (London, 1985), p. 184.
[27] J. Caryl, *The Nature, Solemnity, Grounds, Property and Benefits of a Sacred Covenant* (1643), p. 10.
[28] B. W., *To the Faithfull and True-Hearted Covenanters* (1644).
[29] Seaver, *Wallington's World*, p. 147.
[30] *CJ*, iii, 382.
[31] On this aspect of covenant theology, see Visser, 'Covenant', in Hillerbrand.
[32] Mocket, *National Covenant*, p. 2; Brinsley, *Saints Solemne Covenant*, p. 9.
[33] H. Woodward, *The Solemne League and Covenant of the Three Kingdomes* (1643), p. 14.
[34] Sanderson, *De Juramento*, p. 184.

employed in the act of swearing. Both Thomas Mocket, referring to the Protestation, and Thomas Case, with reference to the Solemn League and Covenant, recommended that subscribers place a copy in their homes to remind themselves of their duties.[35] David Cressy has described the Protestation as an 'instantly recognizable textual totem' which supporters of the Parliament would proudly brandish on 'poles and pikes, muskets and swords, coats and hats' (see Figure 4.1). He has found that in several parishes, fair copies of the Protestation were framed for displaying in church.[36] Editions of the Covenant were produced with accompanying prints, illustrating each of its clauses.[37] When the Solemn League and Covenant was briefly reimposed by Parliament in March 1660 a copy was set up in the Commons as 'a constant monitor to their activities'.[38]

As well as effecting a personal reformation amongst its subscribers, it was anticipated that nationally the Covenant would purify and revive both the church and the commonwealth. In the very first fast sermon of the Long Parliament, Cornelius Burgess, looking back on what he saw as the spiritual apostasy of the past decade, called on the members to enter 'anew into a solemn and strict covenant with God' to assure England's deliverance from popery.[39] Observing God's good faith in keeping his part of the Solemn League and Covenant, Wallington cited the execution of Laud and the sweeping away of the 'trash and rubbish' of prelacy as evidence of its spiritual effectiveness.[40] Reformation 'according to the Word of God', as sworn to in the Solemn League and Covenant, drew forth the support of churchmen of varied theological backgrounds. The irenicist John Dury hesitantly accepted the Covenant, provided that it was taken as being a call to universal reformation.[41] Specifically, he hoped to see a common confession of faith and directory of worship for the three kingdoms.[42] New Englanders also offered their support for the Solemn League and Covenant. The Reverend John White of Dorchester, a member of the Massachusetts Bay Company, preached for over an hour to prepare the Assembly of Divines for taking the Covenant.[43] As late as 1646 the New

---

[35] Mocket, *National Covenant*, p. 23; Case, *Quarrell of the Covenant*, p. 88.

[36] Cressy, 'Protestation Protested', pp. 267, 271.

[37] See BL Thomason Tract E. 253 [8] which features engraved editions of the Protestation, Vow and Covenant and Solemn League and Covenant bound together, presumably as some sort of commemorative edition.

[38] *CJ*, vii, 862; Timoricus, *The Covenanters Plea*, p. 70.

[39] Hill, *English Bible*, pp. 79–109, 84–5.

[40] Seaver, *Wallington's World*, p. 171.

[41] J. Dury, 'The Vow which J. D. hath made, and the Covenant which he doth enter into with God, in reference to the Nationall Covenant of the Kingdoms', in *A Case of Conscience Resolved: Concerning Ministers Medling with State-Matters* (1649), pp. 23–8.

[42] Ibid., p. 25.

[43] On White 'the Patriarch of Dorchester' see D. Underdown, *Fire from Heaven* (London, 1993), esp. pp. 203–4.

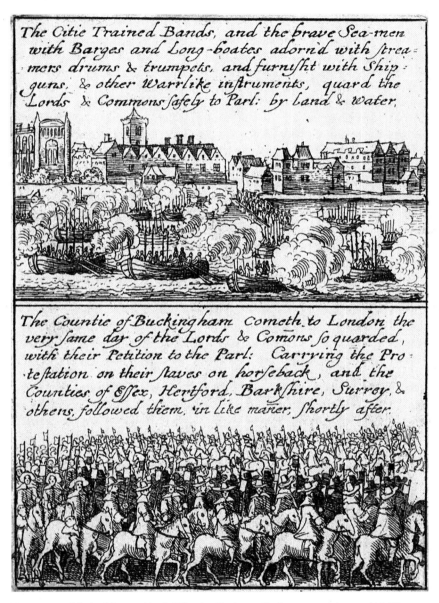

Figure 4.1 All the Memorable & Wonder Strikinge Parlamentary Mercies (1642). (By permission of the British Library (E116(4)).)

England minister Richard Bulkeley was applauding 'that holy and gracious practice begun by our renowned Parliament, going before the body of the Kingdome, in entring into an holy Covenant with the God of heaven, to become the Lord's people'.[44]

Despite this support, the precise form reformation of the church might take had raised misgivings even before the Solemn League and Covenant was passed through Parliament. Amongst those sent to negotiate with the Scots commissioners in August 1643 were many that had closer links with New England Congregationalism than with Scottish Presbyterianism. Sir Henry Vane was a former governor of Massachusetts, Sir Henry Darley an original member of the Massachusetts Bay Company, and Sir William Armine, MP for Lincoln, a friend of the leading Congregationalist divine John Cotton. New Englanders stated their general approval of the Solemn League and Covenant but reminded Parliament that the crucial point was not 'that it was made with the Scottish, but that tis made by them and you with the Great God of Heaven'.[45] Both Philip Nye, who had spent the 1630s in exile in the Netherlands and had close links with New Englanders, and the Presbyterian Thomas Case were keen to state that the Scottish kirk would not automatically be the model for reformation in England.[46] For the advocates of the Covenant, the word church could also have a variety of meanings. The army chaplain John Saltmarsh viewed it as a 'company of godly gathered by his [Christ's] own spirit, having their Lord and Saviour in the midst, confederated by an holy and sacramentall paction'.[47] However, for the Presbyterian John Brinsley the church meant something more concrete than just the body of believers. Discussing the word 'saints' Brinsley stated that this meant neither a select band of true worshippers nor hypocrites who only looked to external signs, 'but the whole body of the Jewish church'.[48] For Brinsley, reformation involved not just the extirpation of prelacy, but also the establishment of presbytery and the eradication of heresy.[49] These later conflicts have obscured the extent to which, at its conception, the Covenant's main goal of national reformation had attracted broad support from Puritan churchmen.

These covenants bound subscribers to furthering the reformation in the commonwealth as well as in the church. Joining in a national covenant brought forth not only spiritual benefits but also temporal blessings with its

---

[44] M. McGiffert, 'The Problem of the Covenant in Puritan Thought: Peter Bulkeley's Gospel-Covenant', *The New England Historical and Genealogical Register*, cxxx (1976), 107–29, at 109.

[45] Bremer, *Congregational Communion*, pp. 129–30, 144.

[46] A Henderson and P. Nye, *The Covenant with a Narrative of the Proceedings and Solemn Manner of Taking it* (1643), p. 14; Case, *Quarrell of the Covenant*, pp. 41–5; Kim, 'Relations Between the Churches', pp. 186–8.

[47] J. Saltmarsh, *A Solemn Discourse upon the Grand Covenant* (1643), pp. 31–2.

[48] Brinsley, *Saints Solemne Covenant*, p. 4.

[49] Ibid., p. 32.

divine lustre.[50] The covenant ideal linked with the perception of England as an elect nation. According to John Saltmarsh, God granted the covenanted country special privileges, 'setting it higher then other nations'.[51] For Thomas Coleman, making a national covenant granted the people the right to 'be his [God's] peculiar people, the people of his own proper profession, joyned so high, united so neer'.[52] The day that the Solemn League and Covenant was taken by the two houses, Coleman claimed, was 'the very birth-day of this Kingdome, borne anew to comfort and successe'.[53] These material benefits were often interpreted in the form of the political programme of the Long Parliament. Thomas Case, preaching in support of the Protestation, reminded the Commons that the reformation must be universal, touching the common-wealth as well as the church. He listed Ship Money and other illegal taxes amongst the public crimes that the nation must humiliate itself for.[54] John Saltmarsh noted the excellence of the Solemn League and Covenant's political maxims, which attempted to keep the mixture of estates within the government even.[55] Henry Burton, an early advocate of Independency, also applauded the way that it had defended the privileges of Parliament and the liberties of the subject, whilst at the same time implicitly suggesting that these were now under threat from an oppressive Presbyterian faction.[56] The benefits to be accrued from the union of England and Scotland were also promoted. Hezekiah Woodward stated that given the fractious history of Anglo-Scottish relations over the past three hundred years, the union forged in the Covenant between the two nations was nothing short of miraculous.[57] Coleman exhorted the Scots to enter the Solemn League and Covenant 'so that England and Scotland after this religious Union in one Covenant, may for ever be one people in this Island of great Britaine'.[58] With the exception of the Vow and Covenant, these covenants (the Protestation and the Solemn League and Covenant) continued to proclaim the Parliament's loyalty to the king. Thomas Coleman argued from scripture that covenants were a traditional means of restoring a king usurped from his right to the throne of thrones.[59] However, it now seemed that the Covenant, and not the godly prince, had revived national fortunes.

When advocating the role of national covenants in reviving the fortunes of God's chosen nation, or nations, writers and preachers harked back to the

---

[50] Saltmarsh, *Solemn Discourse*, p. 18.

[51] Ibid., p. 34.

[52] T. Coleman, *The Hearts Ingagement: a Sermon Preached at St. Margaret's, Westminster, at the Publique Entering into the Covenant* (1643), p. 10.

[53] Ibid., p. 18.

[54] Case, *Two Sermons*, p. 33.

[55] Saltmarsh, *Solemn Discourse*, p. 54.

[56] Burton, *Peace Maker*, p. 6.

[57] Woodward, *Three Kingdoms Made One*, p. 15.

[58] Coleman, *Hearts Ingagement*, pp. 29–30.

[59] Ibid., p. 33.

Old Testament covenants, in particular to the example of biblical Israel that had proved so fruitful for Elizabethan Presbyterians. Thomas Mocket spoke of the Protestation as 'our Nationall Covenant, to bring back again all *Israel* to worship the Lord their God in *Jerusalem*'.[60] The union of England and Scotland in the Solemn League and Covenant also offered biblical parallels. Thomas Case argued that the union between the two countries was like that between Israel and Judah, as these two nations had also emerged from an 'Antichristian Babylon' of 'Papal Tyranny'.[61] Thomas Coleman noted the closeness of this analogy. Like Israel and Judah, England and Scotland had the same king and were part of the same land. Emulating Israel and Judah's example, England and Scotland were also working towards having the same ministry and religion.[62] Scripture also helped to justify the Parliament's practice of pressing these covenants without the king's consent. John Geree used the examples of Ezra and Nehemiah's covenants (which had been made without the sovereign's approval) to legitimise the tendering of the Protestation without the royal assent.[63]

National covenants were an essential part of the armoury of reformed nations against the combined threat of an expansive Counter-Reformation Catholicism abroad and an alleged treacherous fifth column of crypto-papists at home. The plethora of Old Testament examples of national covenants contrasted sharply with their total absence from the New Testament. Thomas Case explained this deficiency by claiming that 'in a Gospel sense' the word covenant was 'to be applyed to the Churches of Jesus Christ in the latter dayes'. The 'literal' covenants of the Old Testament had been followed by the 'evangelical' one of Luther's times when the true churches had turned away from superstition and idolatry back to the path of righteousness. This second age would be followed by the 'universal day' when all nations would join in a holy covenant with Christ to overcome Satan.[64] Recent European history was ransacked to provide examples of Christ's covenants against the papal Antichrist. The United Provinces had joined together in a covenant and actively rebelled against their Catholic sovereign. The English monarchy had set its seal of approval on this through Queen Elizabeth's military aid to the Netherlands in the 1590s. King James and his son had both contributed forces to the continental struggle against the papacy. Above all, the Scots had shown what a people covenanted to God could achieve against the encroachments of popery.[65] John Geree applauded their success and urged the Protestation as

---

[60] Mocket, *Nationall Covenant*, p. 1.

[61] Case, *Quarrell of the Covenant*, pp. 31–2.

[62] Coleman, *Hearts Ingagement*, p. 23.

[63] Geree, *Judah's Joy*, p. 10.

[64] Case, *Quarrell of the Covenant*, pp. 29–31.

[65] *Instructions for the Taking of the League and Covenant*, p. 5; [R. Hollingworth], *An Answer to a Certain Writing, Entitled, Certain Doubts and Quaeres upon Occasion of the Late Oath and Covenant* (1643), p. 9.

a means to imitate their achievements. 'Hath not', he said, 'the Scotch nation in this given us a brave example? Shall we be behind them in duties, whom God hath made to outstrip in outward mercies?'[66] Thomas Case saw the Scots' experience as evidence of the benefits that could be gained from a national covenant to extirpate prelacy. In Scotland the 'Dagon of the Bishops Service-Book' had broken 'its neck before this Arke of the Covenant'.[67]

Confederations of reformed nations, like the Solemn League and Covenant, offered the greatest defence against 'satanic' conspiracies such as the Holy League of sixteenth century France, the Confederacy of Kilkenny and the 'Oxford Covenant' of 1643.[68] It was the sense that Protestantism internationally was once again under siege that made the comparison between the Protestation and the 1584 Association (also made at a time of Protestant crisis) so appealing. The text of the Protestation itself spoke of a Catholic plot 'to subvert the fundamental laws of England' and undermine 'the true reformed religion'.[69] Denzil Holles, in his speech to the Commons in support of the Protestation, pleaded its necessity to ensure that the enemies of popery were unified against its threat. The argument that the Protestants were divided was, he said, 'one main engine by which our enemies work their mischief'.[70] The members of the Westminster Assembly believed that the Solemn League and Covenant could similarly be used to unify European Protestantism against the Catholic threat. The preamble to the Solemn League and Covenant also reminded the swearer of 'the treacherous and bloody plots, conspiracies, attempts and practises of the enemies of God against the true religion'.[71] On 30 November 1643 the Assembly sent a letter to the reformed churches including a copy of the Solemn League and Covenant. The divines begged other Protestant churches to view the Parliament's case as their 'own common cause' and asked for their favourable judgement and sympathy for the Covenant.[72] As a further example of its perceived international purpose, the Covenant was translated into Latin, French and Dutch.[73] Joseph Caryl stated that one of the great benefits of the Solemn League and Covenant was that it would unite those who kept it because a 'few united are stronger than a scattered

---

[66] Geree, *Judah's Joy*, p. 19.
[67] Case, *Quarrell of the Covenant*, p. 66.
[68] *Late Covenant*, p. 9. The 'Oxford Covenant' refers to the Royalist loyalty oath that was issued in response to the Parliament's Vow and Covenant.
[69] Kenyon, *Stuart Constitution*, p. 262.
[70] Cobbett, *Parl. Deb.*, ii, 779.
[71] Kenyon, *Stuart Constitution*, p. 263.
[72] S. Orr, *Alexander Henderson, Churchman and Statesman* (London, 1919), pp. 250–1.
[73] *Foedus Pactum[que] Solenne pro Reformatione et Propugnatione Religionis*, trans. J. Arrowsmith (1644); *Convenant [sic] & Alliance Saincte pour la Reformation & Defense de la Religion* (1643); *Het Verbont, of Naerder Unie Van Dedrie Koninckrijcken, Engelant, Schotlandt en Yerlandt* (n.pl., 1643).

multitude'.[74] Hezekiah Woodward recalled that the making of a covenant had secured Judah against the attack of 'a thousand thousand Ethiopians'.[75]

As we have already seen, these covenants would not only act to bind the swearers closer together against their common foe, but would also operate as tests to discover enemies or neutrals. Not all divines were happy with this. The moderate Presbyterian, Richard Vines, complained that the Solemn League and Covenant had become 'a mere Shibboleth of distinction betweene party and party'. He lamented that far too many were now ready to swear only 'to such a Reformation as may serve selfe interests, or politicke respects, makeing their owne ends the standard of Reformation, not the word or glory of God'.[76] However (to use Pym's idiom), divines were often more interested in the Covenant as a shibboleth to separate the 'Israelites' from the unfaithful 'Ishmaelites' than simply as a means to distinguish Royalists from Parliamentarians. Like Pym, John Geree believed that the Protestation would uncover those who were not zealous for the cause of the reformed church, those, he said, 'that be in *word with us*, in *heart* with *Rome*'. He fully expected these crypto-papists to be able to take the oath, 'so that [it] cannot di[s]cover them', but their lukewarmness would be their undoing. Recalling the text of Judges 12: 5–6 ('Then said they unto him, say nowe Shibboleth and he said Sibboleth for he could not so pronounce, then they took him, and slew him at the passage of Iorden'), Geree said that the equivocator would not be able to promote the oath but would 'lispe, he will not speake out cordially, rejoycing at the Oath and so is layd open'.[77] Anticipating a Royalist attack on Dorchester, John White, William Benn and Hugh Thompson had convinced their parishioners to take the Vow and Covenant, which the ministers swore they would seal with their blood.[78] Another pamphleteer used the text from the book of Judges in relation to the Solemn League and Covenant, declaring it 'Great Britaines Shibboleth'. The author made his militant stance clear, stating that whosoever could not or would not 'pronounce it [meaning the Covenant]' was 'an Ephraimite, and must looke for his reward'.[79] For Joseph Caryl, the Solemn League and Covenant was an even 'Finer Sieve' than the Protestation, admitting only those that sincerely promised to endeavour the preservation of the reformed religion.[80] Caryl noted that some had thought the Covenant impolitic, as it would make more enemies than friends.[81] He made clear that

---

[74] Caryl, *The Nature*, p. 24.
[75] Woodward, *Three Kingdoms Made One*, p. 14.
[76] R. Vines, *The Posture of David's Spirit* (1644), p. 15.
[77] Geree, *Judah's Joy*, pp. 15–16.
[78] Underdown, *Fire from Heaven*, p. 203. The ministers' courage proved fleeting, as after the fall of Bristol, Benn and White scurried off to London.
[79] *Covenanters Catechisme*, p. 23.
[80] Caryl, *The Nature*, p. 4.
[81] Ibid., pp. 22–3.

the purpose of the Covenant was to 'distinguish Ephraimites from Gileadites, Judges 12: 6'.[82]

Promoters of the Solemn League and Covenant demanded the execution of harsh punishments against 'malignants'. The Covenant contained a 'discovery clause' by which subscribers swore to uncover 'all such as have been or shall be incendiaries, malignants, or evil instruments'.[83] Royalists complained that this clause would subvert the natural, patriarchal order by urging sons to turn against fathers and wives against husbands.[84] Hezekiah Woodward did not deny that this might happen, but he said that though the person suspected of malignancy might be 'my friend, perhaps my Childe . . . he is an enemy of God', and should be proceeded against without mercy.[85] In a sermon largely devoted to stressing the need for personal reformation before taking the Solemn League and Covenant, Herbert Palmer diverged from this more pacific approach to beseech his congregation to 'look upon your covenant . . . and doe Justice upon Delinquents'. The staying of the hand of justice was, Palmer said, one reason why God was maintaining the 'quarrell of the warre'.[86] The Souldiers Catechisme (1644), which stressed the importance of the Solemn League and Covenant to the success of the Parliament's war effort, urged troops 'not now to look at our enemies as Country-men, or Kinsmen; or fellow Protestants, but as enemies of God and our Religion, and siders with Antichrist, and so our eye is not to pitie them, nor our sword to spare them'.[87] Woodward's The King's Chronicle (1643) argued that the way to deliver the nation from evil was not 'by commanding the sword to be still (for it is the Lord's Sword, and out of your command)' but 'by striking at the root, Idolatrous persons and things'.[88]

---

[82] Ibid., p. 22. The Covenant was tendered to prisoners of war, see The Journal of Thomas Juxon 1644–1647, eds. K. Lindley and D. Scott (Camden Soc. 5th series, 13, 1999), p. 44.
[83] Kenyon, Stuart Constitution, p. 264.
[84] The Anti-confederacie: or an Extract of Certaine Quaeres, Concerning the Solemne League and Covenant (Oxford, 1644), p. 20; [J. Barwick and others], Certain Disquisitions and Considerations (Oxford, 1644), p. 26; D. Featley, The League Illegal (1661) [reprint of letters written in 1643], p. 42. The use of informants was common in the early modern period, see D. R. Lidington, 'Parliament and the Enforcement of Penal Statutes', Parliamentary History, 8 (1989), 309–28; idem, 'Mesne Process in Penal Actions at the Elizabethan Exchequer', Journal of Legal History, 5 (1984), 33–8; W. Epstein, 'The Committee for Examination of Parliamentary Justice: 1642–47', Journal of Legal History, 7 (1986), 3–22; the theme of the subversion of the rule of law by warfare was also familiar, Donagan, 'Codes and Conduct', at 70–3; J. R. Hale, 'Sixteenth-Century Explanations of War and Violence', Renaissance War Studies (London, 1983), pp. 341–2; I. Roy, 'The English Civil War and English Society', in War and Society, eds. B. Bond and I. Roy (London, 1975), p. 33.
[85] Woodward, Solemne League and Covenant, p. 11.
[86] H. Palmer, The Glasse of Gods Providence Towards His Faithfull Ones Held Forth in a Sermon (London, 1644), p. 48.
[87] p. 14.
[88] First Section [A3].

Covenanting divines presented the civil war as a conflict fought at God's command which should be pursued not only without mercy to their ungodly opponents but also without conceding ground to those that wanted to parley and plead terms with the king. Palmer stressed the importance of venturing human life for God's cause and stated that 'God called this Parliament for his Churches sake; and for his Churches sake it is that he hath so establisht and continued it.'[89] The Parliament's oaths and covenants were seen as solemn commitments to continuing the war against the king's forces. Palmer was adamant that no peace could be made with the Cavaliers that compromised the terms of the Protestation and Vow and Covenant.[90] Hezekiah Woodward, in a sermon promoting the Solemn League and Covenant, brushed aside the pleas of moderates for a negotiated peace. 'Let them', he said, 'talk what they will of their Peace, God has sworn and his people too, that he will have war with them, avenge upon them the Blood of his servants, cast them down, and lay them lower than the earth.'[91] Elsewhere he stated that the takers of the Covenant had 'vowed to stand up against this Generation of Vipers, till they are so subdued that they shall no longer sting'.[92] Thomas Coleman, in his sermon given at the taking of the Covenant by MPs, stated that 'His [Gods] sword hath not eaten flesh enough.'[93]

J. L. Kim has claimed that the 'English vision of British religious uniformity and pan-Protestantism' was not 'derived from any apocalyptic vision', yet many ministers saw these covenants as divine weapons in the final struggle with Antichrist.[94] Having discussed the three stages of God's covenant, Thomas Case suggested that his parishioners were now witnessing the dawning of the final 'universal' day.[95] Stephen Marshall, the most renowned of the Parliamentarian preachers, also believed that the making of these covenants, specifically the Vow and Covenant, was a sign that the world had entered the last days. He stated that it was 'generally accepted' that England was now witnessing the outpouring of one of the phials of Christ's wrath against Antichrist.[96] Whilst many ministers had been keen to ground the practice of covenant making in historical and biblical precedent, Philip Nye and the army preacher John Shawe spoke of it as a thing unwitnessed in the history of the world. The Solemn League and Covenant was, said Nye, 'such an oath as

---

[89] Palmer, *Necessity*, p. 9.

[90] Ibid., p. 69.

[91] H. Woodward, *The Solemne League and Covenant of the Three Kingdomes* (1643), p. 1.

[92] H. Woodward, *Three Kingdoms Made One, by Entring Covenant with One God* (1643), pp. 17–18. See also [E. Bowles], *The Mysterie of Iniquitie* (1643), pp. 46–7.

[93] Quoted in R. Bainton, 'Congregationalism and the Puritan Revolution from the Just War to the Crusade', in his *Studies on the Reformation* (London, 1964), pp. 248–75, at p. 272.

[94] Kim, 'Debate Between the Churches', p. 46.

[95] Case, *Quarrell of the Covenant*, p. 31.

[96] S. Marshall, *The Song of Moses* (1643), pp. 11, 44.

for matter, persons, and other circumstances, the like hath not been in any age'.[97] Here the historical, biblical and apocalyptic visions merged. These Parliamentary covenants represented the final fulfilment of a providential design begun in Israel, revived by Luther and now to be concluded in England.

By incorporating the covenant into a providential plan, the nation's good or ill fortune was directly linked to its faithfulness in keeping these promises to God. In fast sermons to Parliament, the violation or neglect of covenants was often seen as the primary cause of the tribulations afflicting the nation. For one Suffolk minister the sin of covenant breaking was 'the worme that lies gnawing at the root of that gourd that hath heretofore overshadowed England'. The land itself bore evidence to this in the failure of the local harvest, the 'unnatural showers of blood' that fell from the heavens and the 'strange diseases' afflicting the cattle.[98] As J. H. Wilson pointed out, ministers usually maintained that this kind of divine judgement had a 'double effect' or function which simultaneously worked good for those in covenant whilst still chastising a nation that, as a whole, remained in a state of apostasy.[99] However, Nehemiah Wallington, though blaming 'our sinful and wicked armies' and 'London's pride, security, and hypocrisy', also pointed at divisions among the godly as violations of the nation's covenant with God.[100]

Just as these covenants were personal as well as national in effect, so it was expected that God would visit his own particular judgement upon each breaker or refuser of his covenant. One Presbyterian author, John Vicars, specialised in works detailing the gruesome divine punishments meted out to covenant breakers.[101] Moreover, all of these Parliamentary covenants were enforced by the addition of oaths. The power of an oath came mostly from the invocation of divine witness. It threatened the false swearer with divine punishment for committing perjury. However, breaking the oaths in these covenants only aggravated the sin incurred. The bond of a covenant was made substantially different from that of an oath by the involvement of God as a party and not just as a witness. Thomas Mocket stated that until God was satisfied that his conditions had been fulfilled, 'no law of man, or power of any worldly Prince or Potentate whatsoever' could absolve the swearer from the obligations of the covenant. If man would not perform his part, God would perform his and wreak divine wrath upon him.[102] Given that degenerate mankind was only able to enter this covenant through the free grace of God, the Presbyterian Edmund Calamy argued that to reject or break a covenant was effectively to

---

[97] *The Covenant, with a Narrative of the Proceedings* (1643), p. 12; Shawe, *Brittains Remembrancer*, pp. 1–2.

[98] *Breach of Covenant a Ruinating Sinne* (1648), pp. 19–20.

[99] Wilson, *Pulpit in Parliament*, p. 181.

[100] Seaver, *Wallington's World*, p. 171.

[101] For these works see below, pp. 159, 163.

[102] Mocket, *Nationall Covenant*, pp. 20, 22.

reject God's love for man.[103] This would be to scorn God's mercy. Breach of covenant was thereby an act of sacrilege, a sin worse than breaking one of God's commandments. According to Calamy, there was no greater mark of the reprobate than that they were covenant breakers.[104]

The belief that the Solemn League and Covenant was an indissoluble contract with God, coupled with fears about the severity of divine judgement, helps explain the scale of Presbyterian opposition to both the Engagement to the Commonwealth and the declarations in the Corporation Act of 1661 and the Act of Uniformity of 1662. As we will see, the imposition of a nationwide Engagement of loyalty to the Commonwealth established 'without a King and Lords' provoked a vigorous pamphlet debate. Some refused the Engagement, feeling it in conflict with the clause of the Covenant which required subscribers to defend the king's person. Others, however, exploited the license offered by some of the Rump's spokesmen and took the Engagement as a mere submission to the Commonwealth, containing no sanction of the act of regicide or the setting up of a republic. The Cavalier Parliament tried to prevent Presbyterians from using equivocations of this kind by requiring a frank admission that the Covenant was an 'unlawful oath' and demanding that the swearer admit there was no obligation upon himself or anyone else from it.

In the minds of many Presbyterians, the Protestation, Vow and Covenant and Solemn League and Covenant were not a disparate collection of occasionally imposed oaths of loyalty. Instead, they constituted renewals of God's original covenant with man and with his chosen nation, England. Initiatives at a Parliamentary level keyed in with a desire amongst lay and clerical puritans for a spiritual instrument that would bring their lives into obedience with divine law and allow them to impose a strict moral code on the ungodly. In the end, these efforts were often more divisive than unifying. Particularly during the negotiations over the Solemn League and Covenant, different conceptions of the Covenant created conflict over the purpose of the document. The Scots' broad vision of a nation in covenant with God clashed with the narrow covenant of the godly familiar to New Englanders. Divisions over the exact form of covenanted religion rapidly destroyed the religious peace negotiated between Congregationalists and Presbyterians. The combined religious and political aims of the Solemn League and Covenant divided loyalties with the imposition of the Engagement in 1650. Some viewed it as primarily a religious obligation that could be observed under any human government. For others, fulfilment of the Covenant involved a commitment to the confessional state and a mixed-constitution of king, Lords and Commons.

Paradoxically, it was the presence of both religious and political elements in the Solemn League and Covenant that granted it an afterlife in the

---

[103] E. Calamy, *The Great Danger of Covenant-refusing and Covenant-breaking* (1646), p. 8.
[104] Ibid., pp. 18, 20.

1660s. Instead of being seen as a commitment to a limited monarchy and a Presbyterian church, Presbyterians could claim retrospectively that the Solemn League and Covenant was no more than a reminder to every Christian of their fundamental duties. Stressing these personal elements to the Covenant was not simply a convenient rhetorical ploy. In the 1640s advocates of the Solemn League and Covenant, New Englanders and Scots alike, had emphasised that it could only be kept through the efforts of the individual covenanters to lead a pious and penitent life.

5

Protestation, Vow and Covenant: the public response

The last three chapters have concentrated on describing the content of these Parliamentary covenants, their impact upon concepts of political allegiance and the influence of federal theology upon them. This discussion has so far been limited largely to analysing the printed material generated by the imposition of the Protestation, Vow and Covenant. Clearly, such material can tell us relatively little about how far the intended audience for most of these works (those that were being required to subscribe to these covenants) was receptive to their theological and political arguments. Here letters, manuscript treatises and, most importantly, oath subscription returns will be used to afford us an opportunity to see how individuals at a local level responded to the demand to subscribe to these covenants.

Long before the civil war, certain ways of taking oaths had been publicly condemned by both Protestant and Catholic authors. The harshest and most bi-partisan censure, which came in the wake of the Gunpowder Plot, was reserved for the doctrine of mental reservation. However, as we will see, English casuists still permitted certain other types of equivocation. The pamphlets provoked by the tendering of oaths of loyalty during the civil war were equally concerned that subscribers should take oaths in certain approved ways. During the 1640s the pronouncements of Parliamentarian and Royalist writers on how to swear lawfully were largely in keeping with the advice offered by earlier casuists. Yet, the increasingly heavy penalties attached to refusing these covenants eventually led some pamphleteers to sanction the use of declared limitations in swearing.

Oath returns will be used to examine how far subscribers followed the guidance offered in these pamphlets in taking these covenants. However, the information that can be gleaned from oath returns is often inadequate. In many cases returns for a specific oath exist for only a tiny fraction of parishes. Even when they are in greater abundance, the way in which the returns are organised often hampers uncovering the different ways in which individuals subscribed. Nonetheless, there is enough evidence to show that individuals were well aware of the political and religious ramifications of these covenants but that they often equivocated with or refused them, not only in some cases because they were anathema to them, but also because they were seemingly in conflict with previous sworn obligations.

The theological background[1]

The range of responses that English casuists and pamphleteers considered were legitimate in swearing was limited. Those most heavily inveighed against were the tactics of mental reservation and equivocation, developed by Catholic casuists and later used by English seminary priests as a means to avoid detection by the Protestant authorities. Mental reservation allowed that there were two kinds of statements, those that were given orally and those that were assented to only mentally. In certain circumstances, Catholics might be allowed to give a full answer only in this mentally cogitated statement. Equivocation involved using internal ambiguities within an oath to loosen its binding power. Alternatively, the addition of qualifying remarks in swearing, such as 'as far as lawfully I may', could be used to effect the same purpose.

The use of mental reservations by Catholics first gained notoriety in England during the trial of the Jesuit poet Robert Southwell in 1595.[2] However, the heaviest attack on these tactics came in the wake of the Gunpowder Plot. Henry Garnet's A Treatise of Equivocation, which he restyled as A Treatise Against Lying and Fraudulent Dissimulation, was found in manuscript in the rooms of one of the conspirators, Francis Tresham. It was later found that Tresham had used mental reservations during his trial to deny that he had met Garnet before.[3] In his treatise Garnet had stated that oaths to answer truthfully all questions must be understood as being taken with a tacit condition that 'I will do or say so farr as I may lawfully do or say'. So if a person's examiners, having made him take such an oath, 'come to unjust questions, I am not bound to answere, although I thought not expressly of that condition when I swore'.[4] The revelations produced several fierce Anglican attacks with the future Bishop of Durham, Thomas Morton, the foremost critic. Morton, like his Catholic opponents, accepted Augustine's definition of a lie as a statement that was not in agreement with the mind of its speaker. However, he felt that the 'amphibologies' used by Garnet and others contained such a great contradiction between speech and thought that these statements were not 'hidden truths' but 'grosse lies'.[5] Rather than being practices with a long and distinguished pedigree as they claimed, the Jesuits' equivocation was but a 'new-bred Hydra'.[6] Another Anglican polemicist, Henry Mason, who called it the 'new-found Arte of Equivocation' and a 'novell, new designed and upstart

---

[1] This is a condensed version of the discussion given in my 'State Oaths and Political Casuistry', pp. 188–200.

[2] P. Zagorin, 'England and the Controversy over Mental Reservation', in Ways of Lying: Dissimulation, Persecution and Conformity in Early Modern Europe (London, 1990), ch. 9, pp. 190–8.

[3] Ibid., p. 196.

[4] H. Garnet, A Treatise of Equivocation, ed. D. Jardine (London, 1851), p. 78.

[5] T. Morton, A Full Satisfaction Concerning a Double Romish Iniquitie (1606), p. 49.

[6] Ibid., p. 47.

fancie', also asserted that mental reservation as practised by English Jesuits was unprecedented.[7] Mason portrayed mental reservation as a kind of verbal rebellion, destructive to society at large in the way that it distorted the accepted meanings of words and undermined the natural expectation that what others say to us is true.[8]

Undoubtedly, English Jesuits were instructed in the use of tactics of equivocation and mental reservation. Casuistry formed an essential part of the education of missionary priests sent to England during the reign of Elizabeth I.[9] However, priests at Douai were instructed not to use these tactics in front of uneducated Catholics for fear of causing scandal. Henry Garnet and Robert Parsons, both authors on equivocation, stated that mental reservation could only be employed in extreme circumstances and that Catholic thinkers only permitted and did not recommend the use of these tactics.[10] The Douai–Rheims cases themselves generally avoided the use of mixed speech, instead encouraging priests to turn questions back on their interrogators, or simply refuse to answer them. If asked if he thought the queen was a heretic, it was suggested that the priest ask why the questioner thought she was. There was no way that sophistry could be used in matters of faith, which ought to be defended even when a person was interrogated unjustly. Priests could not, therefore, deny their profession if examined by 'the highest royal officials or their pursuivants' and they would 'sin mortally if they are silent or equivocate'. However, it was not unlawful to equivocate about one's profession with toll collectors or customs men, as their primary aim was not to persecute the faithful but to get money. Equally, there was no need to feel obliged to confess one's true identity in the course of common conversation.[11] This hierarchy of disclosure was mitigated by the cases later drawn up by William Allen and Robert Parsons, which stated that interrogations by the ministers of the queen were never lawful 'because a heretic queen is not a legitimate Queen'.[12]

Given the actual content of the cases taught at Douai–Rheims, it is questionable how far the Protestant (and Catholic secular) attacks on Jesuit casuistry were justified. This casts doubt on whether the 'Anglican horror at popish dishonesty' was as genuine as authors like Morton and Mason made out.[13] Doubtless, some of this propaganda was simply a hysterical knee-jerk

[7] H. Mason, *The New Art of Lying* (1624), pp. 2, 25.

[8] Ibid., pp. 95–6.

[9] A. R. Jonsen and S. Toulmin, *The Abuse of Casuistry: A History of Moral Reasoning* (Berkeley, 1988), pp. 200–1.

[10] Zagorin, *Ways of Lying*, p. 186; *Elizabethan Casuistry*, ed. P. J. Holmes (Catholic Record Society, 1981); J. P. Sommerville, 'The New Art of Lying: Equivocation, Mental Reservation and Casuistry', in *Conscience and Casuistry in Early Modern Europe*, ed. E. Leites (Cambridge, 1988), pp. 159–85, at p. 178.

[11] *Elizabethan Casuistry*, pp. 52–5.

[12] Ibid., p. 65.

[13] E. Rose, *Cases of Conscience: Alternatives Open to Recusants and Puritans Under Elizabeth I and James I* (Cambridge, 1975), p. 93.

reaction to the Gunpowder Plot. There seems, though, to have been an ulterior motive behind the Protestant pamphleteers' concentration on equivocation and mental reservation. By suggesting that Jesuits (and Catholics in general) were dishonest, Protestant authors were able to cast doubt on the authority of the judgements and doctrines of the Catholic Church as a whole. Whilst claiming with Morton that 'Jesuitical' equivocation was a new Machiavellian art, Henry Mason wanted to make it clear that its development had been fully authorised by the Catholic Church. Mason stated that it had been the papal censor who had struck out the cautions against making equivocations in the work of Emmanuel Sa. The 'arte' of equivocation had, he said, 'received its life from the State and See of Rome'. For this reason, Mason said, we 'may not beleeve them [Catholic writers] when they tell of great wonders and miracles, For they professe to equivocate when it may bee some good to themselves'.[14] The same conclusion was implicit in the work of Thomas Morton. His *Exact Discoverie of Romish Doctrine* (1605) included equivocation in an attack on Catholic principles in general. If the everyday speech of Catholics was unreliable then so too were their professed principles and beliefs.[15] The assault on the reliability of Catholic testimony extended into drama, satire and popular literature. Weasel words and double talk became part of the archetype of the treacherous papist.[16] All seventeenth century penal legislation against Catholics included clauses against the use of mental reservations and equivocations.[17]

Yet the attitude of Protestant casuists to the use of equivocations was more complex than the rhetoric of Elizabethan and Jacobean polemics against mental reservation suggested. Although their attacks were ferocious, neither Henry Mason nor Thomas Morton condemned all equivocation. Both writers made a distinction between exploiting the ambiguous meanings of words and phrases, described by Mason as 'verbal' or 'logicall' equivocation, and the practice of reserving part of a statement in the mind, or 'Jesuitical' equivocation, as Mason styled it.[18] He stated that verbal equivocation was acceptable because it was supported by scripture and because it was an unavoidable part of common discourse. It was therefore 'not unlawful' for some 'further good' to make use of 'ambigious [sic] speeches' in 'the lesse knowne and common significance, and in another meaning than it is likely the hearers will understand them for the present'.[19] English Protestant casuists used the same distinction between

---

[14] Mason, *Art of Lying*, pp. 34–5, 104.

[15] See also W. Crashaw, *Romish Forgeries and Falsifications: Together with Catholike Resitutions* (1606).

[16] Zagorin, *Ways of Lying*, pp. 201–2. For examples see: J. Donne, *Ignatius His Conclave* (1634), p. 32; *The Parricide Papist* (1606), p. 14; T. James, *The Iesuits Downefall* (1612), pp. 17–18.

[17] Kenyon, *Stuart Constitution*, pp. 459, 460–1, 465–6.

[18] Mason, *Art of Lying*, pp. 3–4; Morton, *A Full Satisfaction*, pp. 49, 54.

[19] Mason, *Art of Lying*, pp. 7–12.

lawful and unlawful equivocation. William Perkins and his pupil William Ames both seem to have permitted employing 'verbal' equivocations. Perkins used the example of Paul's pretence to be a Pharisee before Ananias to claim a distinction between lying and 'simulation'. According to Perkins, a lie was something against the truth, whilst 'simulation' was an act or statement 'not contrary to, but beside or divers unto that which we think'.[20] Ames also appears to have sanctioned the use of this kind of equivocation. He stated that it was 'even lawful on occasion, saving the truth, to use such words as will probably lead the hearers to understand what is not true'.[21]

Nevertheless, Protestant casuists did not extend the circumstances in which it was lawful to use equivocations to include swearing. Ames condemned the use of both limitations and mental reservations in taking oaths.[22] Robert Sanderson was equally circumspect in his lectures on the obligation of promissory oaths. He quoted Morton and Mason as to the unlawfulness of using mental reservations and reminded those that swore with private limitations that they were still obliged in conscience to the imposer's interpretation. Sanderson urged caution even when the imposer seemed to have left it to the individual subscriber to choose in what sense to take an oath. He feared that ambiguous oaths were generally designed as snares to entrap those that swore to them.[23]

However, there is clear evidence that Protestants were using equivocations, even in making sworn statements, well before the civil war. Early English reformers like Edward Crome survived the theological fluctuations of Henry VIII's reign through equivocal recantations of their Protestantism.[24] Elizabethan Puritan clergy appear to have used their own reservations to avoid taking Whitgift's three articles in full. Phrases like 'as far as the law requireth' were added to their subscriptions. Evidence for the use of these equivocations comes from the Millenary Petition of 1603, which referred to subscriptions being made 'uppon protestation, some upon expositions given them, some with Conditions'.[25] Tom Webster has shown that godly ministers were using equivocations and perhaps even mental reservation to avoid persecution by the ecclesiastical authorities in the 1630s.[26]

It seems that the Church authorities were beginning to anticipate the use of these equivocations by Protestants. The infamous 'etcetera oath' included

---

[20] Zagorin, *Ways of Lying*, p. 238; W. Perkins, 'The Whole Treatise of Cases of Conscience', in *William Perkins, 1558–1602, English Puritanist*, ed. T. F. Merrill (Nieuwkoop, 1966), pp. 171–2.

[21] Ames, *Conscience with the Power*, book five, pp. 271–5; Jonsen and Toulmin, *Abuse of Casuistry*, p. 202.

[22] Ames, *Conscience with the Power*, book four, pp. 51–3.

[23] Sanderson, *De Juramento*, pp. 194–211.

[24] S. Waduba, 'Equivocation and Recantation During the English Reformation: The "Subtle Shadows" of Dr. Edward Crome', *Journal of Ecclesiastical History*, 44 (1993), 224–42.

[25] Kenyon, *Stuart Constitution*, p. 132; Zagorin, *Ways of Lying*, pp. 227–8.

[26] Webster, *Godly Clergy*, pp. 245–7.

in the 1640 canons contained a clause demanding that it should be taken according to the exact sense of the words.[27] Martin Blake, vicar of Barum in Devon, wrote to his brother in November 1640 concerning his scruples over the oath. Blake felt that if his superiors would allow him to take the oath simply as a reaffirmation of the oath of canonical obedience 'our scruples might have received good satisfaction'. Thinking that a clarification of the oath's meaning might receive favour from his diocesan Blake set himself 'awork, and proceeded a great way in the framing of such an explication, according to these Rules, with an intent to have presented them to our good Bishop'. However, Blake soon realised that his efforts were in vain as he was 'by this clause so tyed to the very letter, that an explication either from the giver or Receiveer of it may not be allowed: and yet without an explication, who can take it?'[28]

The Protestation

The pamphlets devoted to the Protestation, Vow and Covenant and Solemn League and Covenant also offered guidelines on lawful swearing. This advice generally remained in line with that offered by Protestant casuists, prohibiting the use of equivocations and reservations in swearing. Royalist writers in particular affirmed the need to refuse oaths that the swearer suspected were unlawful. The effectiveness of their injunctions was undermined by the increasingly heavy penalties for non-subscription, in particular, the linking of taking the Covenant with the process by which Royalists compounded for their estates. As a result, Royalist writers began to permit the use of declared limitations in swearing, as a means to avoid both breaking previous oaths and suffering the consequences for refusal.

Through an analysis of oath returns, we can see just how far individual subscribers followed the advice offered in the pamphlet literature. Records of individual subscriptions are extant, but they are rarely complete. Some, in the case of the Protestation returns, are kept in central depositories whilst others are scattered in parish registers and churchwardens' accounts. Returns kept mainly in local record offices, including those for the Solemn League and Covenant and Vow and Covenant, are frequently out of sequence in the parish records they are contained in, or pasted on the reverse of other items in the same volume.[29] With these returns, the problem is not merely that they are dispersed in many separate local archives, or that they are poorly catalogued.

---

[27] Kenyon, *Stuart Constitution*, p. 169.

[28] Bodl. MS Tanner 65, f. 199; J. F. Chanter, *The Life and Times of Martin Blake B. D.* (Edinburgh, 1909), p. 27.

[29] For these records see *The Protestation Returns 1641–42 and Other Contemporary Listings*, eds. J. S. W. Gibson and A. Dell (Family History Society Publications, 1995) and Cressy, *Literacy and the Social Order*, pp. 62–103, 191–201, 215–21.

There is much evidence that after 1660 the records of the more politically sensitive oaths of the civil war period were destroyed, either in belated acts of vengeance or in an attempt to cover up any collaboration with the Parliamentarian regimes. The Cavalier Parliament ordered that all records of the Solemn League and Covenant should be removed.[30] Some registers were scratched through, like that for the Solemn League and Covenant at Hadleigh in Essex.[31] Other returns were altered by Royalist wits. At Woodchurch in Cheshire, the preamble to the same Covenant was changed to read 'a Solemn League and Covenant for [de]formation and [pret]ence of Religion, the [dis]-honour and [un]happiness of the King, and the [extirpation] of the peace and safety of the three kingdomes'.[32] At Dengie in Essex, the list of subscribers to the Vow and Covenant ended with the added comment 'Rebellion is as the sin of witchcraft.'[33] The minister of the parish of Long Sutton in Hampshire appears to have cut out the return for the Solemn League and Covenant at the Restoration to avoid incriminating himself as a subscriber.[34]

Unfortunately, the oath for which most returns remain in existence, the 1641 Protestation, was also the one which occasioned least comment as to how it should be subscribed. Before Speaker Lenthall's letter of January 1642 demanding nationwide subscription to the oath, there seems to have been an impression that the Protestation could be taken in whatever sense the subscriber thought fit. Writing to Sir Robert Harley in March 1642, Wallop Brabazon, Sir William Croft and other Hertfordshire JPs, who later formed the core of the Royalist party in the county, said that they had advised 'those who had any scruple in their not understanding the power of Parliament and the lawfulness of making any new oath, that, as it was a voluntary act, they had the power of interpretation in themselves, and might make it without danger'. Brabazon noted that now the Protestation came under the recommendation of the speaker's letter it seemed 'not to be so voluntary as that anyone can be admitted to their own interpretation'. The JPs felt this freedom of interpretation was 'most needful, especially in the matter of priviledge of Parliaments' whereof the justices felt ill-qualified to speak 'as it has raised questions between the King and both Houses, and the Houses themselves'.[35]

Although, as will be demonstrated below, the Protestation raised misgivings amongst subscribers about its religious and political purpose, many others viewed it as an uncontroversial oath of loyalty in defence of the church and king. Many local officials saw it as simply a new test for recusancy and in a

---

[30] CJ, viii, 258.
[31] D. Cressy, 'Vow, Covenant and Protestation', 134–41; Essex Record Office T/R 138/1.
[32] 'The Solemn League and Covenant in Wirral', Wirral N & Q, i (1892), 58.
[33] R. E. Fanshawe, 'An Intruded Minister at Dengie', Essex Review, xxxii (1923), 34–5.
[34] C. R. S. Elvin, 'Some Notes on the Solemn League and Covenant in England', Papers and Proceedings of the Hampshire Field Club, viii (1919), 271–6, at 275.
[35] HMC, Portland MSS, iii, p. 85; J. Eales, Puritans and Roundheads: The Harleys of Brampton Bryan and the Outbreak of the English Civil War (Cambridge, 1990), ch. 6, pp. 132–3.

number of parishes the names of refusers of the oath are headed 'recusant'.[36] As has been shown in Chapter 3, even by early 1642, Royalist writers preferred to offer their own gloss upon the Protestation rather than state categorically that it should be refused. Neither side wished to appear to lack zeal in defending the Protestant religion. Moreover, the text of the oath itself was fairly equivocal, being carefully hedged in with several 'as far as lawfully I may's'.

Returns for the Protestation exist for all counties in England except for Gloucestershire, Herefordshire, Rutland, and the east riding of Yorkshire. No returns exist for Wales except for the county of Denbighshire. Some counties, for instance Cornwall and Devon, have near complete coverage but some, like Essex and Hampshire, have only a few isolated returns.[37] The Protestation was passed by the Commons on 5 May 1641 and declared 'fit to be made by everyone'.[38] However, only a few parishes subscribed at this stage. Several parishes in London took the oath in May and June of 1641.[39] Apart from London, parishioners at Barnston in Essex (under the godly minister John Beadle), Aylestone and Bitteswell in Leicestershire, Brampton, Wigmore and Leintwardine in Herefordshire (where the puritan Harleys were influential), and in the city of Exeter took the Protestation that year.[40] The majority of returns, however, were collected between February and March 1642 following the speaker's letter.

Returns were organised by hundred, or in the northeast by wapentake. Ministers, churchwardens and other parish officers were to take the Protestation before justices of the peace at the local market town. The officials were then to supervise the taking of the Protestation by their parishioners. The returns for individual parishes vary greatly in character. Some of the London returns provide an insight into the way that the oath was taken by parishioners. At St Catherine Kree the minister read out the full text of the Protestation 'because it woold take up more time and indeed was impossible for every one to express the same wordes'. For greater brevity the people simply swore after the 'leading p[er]son' that they did 'in the p[re]sense of Allmighty God freely and heartily

---

[36] *West Sussex Protestation Returns*, ed. Rice, p. xi.
[37] Gibson, *Protestation Returns*, p. 6.
[38] HMC, *5th Report*, p. 3.
[39] Guildhall Library MS 1196/1, f. 30–4, St Catherine Kree, 5 May 1641?; 4835/1 (unfoliated), Holy Trinity the Less, 30 May 1641; 5019/1, f. 71–3, St Pancras, Soper Lane, 30 May 1641; 3579, f. 339–41, St Mathew, Friday Street, 3 June 1641; 2597, f. 58v–59, St Mary Magdalen, Milk Street, 30 May 1641; 959/1, f. 400v–1, St Martin, Orgar, 30 May 1641.
[40] A. Clarke, 'Barnston Notes 1641–9', *Essex Review*, xxv (1916), 55–70, at 55–64. For Beadle see A. G. Matthews, *Calamy Revised* (Oxford, 1934), p. 41; *Leicestershire Parish Registers*, v, eds. W. P. W. Phillimore and T. M. Blagg (London, 1911), pp. 143–51; Jones, *Conscience and Allegiance*, p. 118; Eales, *Puritans and Roundheads*, p. 114; T. J. Falla and M. M. Rowe, 'The Population of Two Exeter Parishes in 1641–2', *Devon and Cornwall N & Q*, xxxv (1983), 89–95.

p[ro]mise and protest the same'. The same method was used at Holy Trinity the Less, and as we shall see, seems to have been a fairly common practice used in subscribing to oaths.[41] In Lincolnshire, the Commons' claim that the Protestation was fit to be subscribed by everyone seems to have been taken rather literally. Dutch and Flemish workers assisting Cornelius Vermuyden in drainage schemes on the Isle of Axholme were also tendered the oath and gave their promise to defend the 'true reformed religion'. Parish officials do not seem to have bothered to ask whether they thought this was contained in the doctrine of the Church of England.[42] The view of the Protestation as essentially an asservation of faith in the Protestant church, rather than a political test, may explain the inclusions of women as subscribers in some parishes. At Whitchurch in Buckinghamshire all women in the parish took the Protestation 'excepting recusants, and those that are diseas'd, and in Childberth'. However, 'seeing that they doe not take it in other parishes', the people of Whitchurch did not wish to appear 'singular' and had not recorded the women's names.[43] At Croston in Lancashire not only the names of women were recorded. The parish officers here also made a note by each name of the subscriber's occupation and marital status.[44] Although it was widely viewed as a new test for recusancy, in some parishes Catholics appear either to have taken the oath wholesale, or are recorded as subscribing to it saving the part relating to religion. At Abbots Aston in Buckinghamshire, William James and his wife replied that they would give their 'life, power and estate' in defence of the king but 'for there religion they desire some respit further to consider'.[45] Edward Cotton of Leigh in Surrey took 'all in the othe of protetacion, onlie all clases concerning Religion, I excepte'. In other parishes no refusers of any kind were recorded.[46]

In general, these parish returns contain only lists of names either written in by a single hand or with individual marks and signatures. Nevertheless, equivocal responses do occur with some frequency, and not just from Catholic parishioners. By the time that national subscription was being demanded in January 1642 it was clear that the Protestation was not an oath that guaranteed the survival of the ecclesiastical status quo. The explanation that the Commons had annexed to the oath stated that it did not bind the taker in any way to defend the form of government or any rites or ceremonies of the Church of England. Instead, subscribing to the Protestation seems to have been the catalyst for acts of iconoclasm against perceived 'popish innovations'. Even

---

[41] Guildhall Library MS 1196/1, f. 30–4; 4835/1.

[42] *Protestation Returns 1641/2: Lincolnshire*, ed. W. F. Webster (privately printed, 1984), p. 73.

[43] HLRO, Main Papers, Protestation Returns, Bucks, f. 72.

[44] HLRO, Main Papers, Protestation Returns, Lancs [B], Croston Parish, 24 Feb. 1641 (unfoliated).

[45] HLRO, Main Papers, Protestation Returns, Bucks, f. 34.

[46] 'The Surrey Protestation Returns 1641/2', ed. H. Carter, *Surrey Archaeological Collections*, lix (1962), 35–69, at 47.

before the addition of the Commons' explanation to the oath, the Protestation inspired some to take direct action against popery. On 30 June 1641 the Lords reviewed a petition from the parish of St Thomas Apostle to the House of Commons. The churchwarden stated that about three years ago 'rails were placed round the communion table' which gave 'great offence to many of the parishioners'. These rails 'were pulled down by some youths after they had taken the protestation'.[47] From the churchwarden's accounts it also appears that the church windows were smashed. Taking the Protestation inspired others to attack their ministers or destroy the Book of Common Prayer.[48] Sensing that such sentiments were behind the framing of the oath, many Anglican clergy-men responded negatively, or at best equivocally, to the demand to take the Protestation. The greatest example of this was the reply attached to the return from the heads of houses at the University of Oxford, discussed previously.[49] Individual fellows offered their own equivocal responses. Robert Bassell of Magdalen took the Protestation so far as 'it is not contrary to the mayntinance of the King, Royal Prerogative', and 'the Doctrine and Discipline of the Church of England by law established since the Reformation'.[50] At Cambridge no such equivocal returns are to be found.[51] However, John Twigg has noted that the Commons sent for Mark Frank, a fellow of Pembroke, on 16 May 1642 as a delinquent on account of a sermon he had preached on the previous day. No text exists of this, but in another sermon of 1641 Frank talked of 'Oaths and Protestations . . . abused, to maintain rebellion and profaneness, construed so in pulpits, and professed by their scholars in the face of God and man'.[52]

Such sentiments were not only to be found amongst the fellows and scholars of the universities. Parochial clergy were frequently recorded as having refused the Protestation. One of the most commonly cited charges levelled against clergymen brought before the Committee for Scandalous Ministers was that they had preached against or refused to administer the Parliament's covenants. Such charges need to be treated with some care. Disaffected parishioners did not instigate proceedings against the clergy. Instead, local committees would summon men from each hundred to inform against their ministers. On receipt of charges from these handpicked informants the committee would then receive evidence. The minister accused was not allowed to be present during these depositions for fear of 'countenancing' the witnesses.[53] Many of the

[47] HMC, 4th Report, p. 80.
[48] For this activity see Cressy, 'Protestation Protested', p. 263.
[49] See above, pp. 63–4.
[50] Oxfordshire and North Berkshire Protestation Returns, ed. Gibson, p. 153.
[51] HLRO, Main Papers, Protestation Returns, Cambridge (only the returns for the university survive for this county).
[52] J. Twigg, The University of Cambridge and the English Revolution: 1625–1688 (Cambridge, 1990), pp. 62–3; CJ, ii, 572, 606.
[53] C. Holmes, The Suffolk Committee for Scandalous Ministers (Suffolk Record Society, xiii, 1970), p. 16.

articles presented by petitioners to these committees seem to have been formulated by local gentry with Parliamentarian/puritan sympathies or by those who wished simply to place their chosen incumbent in the living. Accusations of 'malignancy' were made not only against those that were dyed-in-the-wool Royalists, but also against those that were merely perceived as being lukewarm in the Parliament's cause.[54]

With this caution in mind, some of the less extravagant charges still carry a ring of plausibility. The key role of ministers in administering the Parliament's oaths of loyalty allowed Royalist clergy to use their sermons to remind parishioners of the obligations placed upon their consciences by other oaths of loyalty. In April 1643 the House of Lords sequestered the living of William Ingoldsby, the minister of Watton in Hertfordshire whom we encountered earlier.[55] He was committed to the Fleet prison not only for publishing a book full of 'malignant expressions and imputations upon the proceedings of Parliament', but also for preaching that 'those that have taken the protestation and do fight against the King are foresworn'.[56] Few were quite as blunt in refusing the oath as Thomas Lever, vicar of the parish of Leamington in Warwickshire, who demanded to 'knowe what authority any proud rascally knave hath to give him a protestation'.[57] William Hollington, a royal chaplain and minister of Allchurch in Worcestershire was accused of calling the constable who delivered the Protestation to him a 'knave' 'blockhead' and 'loggerhead' and of hindering subscription to it.[58] More considered reasons for refusal were given by John Dennet, clerk of the parish of Ockford Fitzpaine in Dorset, who would only promise to defend 'the True Reformed Protestant Religion' as it was expressed in the Thirty-Nine Articles against all popery and popish innovations 'contrary to the same doctrine'.[59] In Lincolnshire the overseer of the poor, William Pittman, informed the mayor, John Beale, that Mr Dodsworth, their vicar, had refused to assist him in tendering the Protestation. He claimed that Dodsworth had 'refused to set his hand to our petition for the Bishops . . . [and] therefore he would not take the protestation'.[60] The under-minister of

---

[54] I. M. Green, 'The Persecution of "Scandalous" and "Malignant" Parish Clergy During the English Civil War', *Eng. Hist. Rev.*, xciv (1972), 507–32, at 513, 519; See also J. Sharpe, 'Scandalous and Malignant Priests in Essex: The Impact of Grassroots Puritanism', in *Politics and People in Revolutionary England*, eds. C. Jones, M. Newitt and S. Roberts (Oxford, 1986), pp. 253–75.

[55] See p. 68.

[56] HMC, *5th Report*, p. 82.

[57] HLRO, Main Papers, Protestation Returns, Warwickshire; Leamington, Hastings and townships (unfoliated).

[58] Worcestershire Record Office, Quarter Sessions Rolls, 1/1/79/17. For good measure he was accused of being a drunk, 'defamed of incontinence with his neighbours' wives', who was often accompanied 'with a dangerous and armed Papist'; see also Cressy, 'Protestation Protested', p. 276.

[59] *Dorset Protestation Returns*, p. 62.

[60] *Protestation Returns, Lincolnshire*, p. 38.

Bradford was held to have violated the Protestation by using the sign of the cross in baptism and was prevented from performing his duties by the parish's churchwardens.[61] One of the charges levelled against the Suffolk minister Robert Sugden was that he had 'taken the protestation with the reservation that the Church might be governed by Bishops, which caused some in his parish to take it with the same reservation'.[62] The Dorset minister William Oates was also accused of encouraging his parishioners to follow his example in taking the Protestation in a limited sense.[63]

Laymen too objected to the Protestation on religious grounds. In Exeter several subscribers 'took the protestation only and refused to take it according to the annexed explanation'.[64] In the parish of Whitchurch, Buckinghamshire, William Withalls refused the Protestation 'because part of the doctrine of the church of England is like to be altered as the government and the discipline and the like'.[65] Some separatists refused the Protestation on the grounds that it would bind them to defend a national church. At Wingham in Kent, one Thomas Hues 'contemptuosly refused it . . . and sayd openly in the Church-yard, that who soever swear it, the next time he came to church he was for-sworne'. Hues's religious opinions are clear from his description of the Book of Common Prayer as 'a stinkinge ragg or relique of Poperye'.[66] In the parish of Wilton, Somerset, Mathew Pococke, described as 'an anabaptist', refused either to come to church or to take the Protestation.[67]

Equivocation was not the only method of evasion used. Several chose delay as a means of escaping punishment for outright refusal. In Charlbury, Oxfordshire, John Phippes 'demurred' upon the oath 'as pretending not to understand what is meant by the true reformed Protestant Religion'.[68] Joseph Crowther of St John's College, Oxford, claiming to be doubtful 'in some passages of proposing the Protestation, and not presuming to limit the sense of it' accepted 'the Indulged licence of Deliberating'.[69] Edward Bisse of Batcombe parish in Somerset echoed Crowther in claiming that his prevarication was born out of a wish to avoid equivocating with the Protestation. His comments provide evidence of the widespread use of reservations in taking the oath, claiming that it was 'taken so many ways, some will take it one sense and some in

---

[61] Hopper, 'Readiness of the People', pp. 9–10.
[62] Holmes, *Suffolk Committees*, p. 69.
[63] *Dorset Protestation Returns*, p. 112.
[64] *The Devon Protestation Returns 1641*, ed. A. J. Howard (privately printed, 1973), pp. 313, 324.
[65] HLRO, Main Papers, Protestation Returns, Bucks, f. 72.
[66] HLRO, Main Papers, Protestation Returns, Kent, f. 76.
[67] *The Somerset Protestation Returns and Lay Subsidy Rolls 1641–2*, ed. T. L. Stoate (privately printed, 1975), p. 120.
[68] *Oxfordshire and North Berkshire Protestation Returns*, ed. Gibson, p. 35.
[69] Ibid., p. 164.

another'.[70] Others appear to have been willing to swear orally to the Protestation but not to set their name to it. Alexander Worth of Luccombe in Somerset 'made the protestation but refused to set his hand to the paper unless we could show authority from the justices'.[71]

Many others appended their subscriptions with phrases intended to limit or disoblige themselves completely from fulfilling their duties under the oath. John Dennet promised to defend the power and privileges of Parliament and lawful rights and liberties of the subject 'as farre as lawfully I may' and so far as he was at present 'or hereafter shall be informed [of them] truly so to be'.[72] Richard Lewes, clerk of Stoke Tything in Dorset, said that he 'wolde take it as farr as a good conscience wolde goe'.[73] The use of this tactic was not limited to the literate. At Grimoldby in Lincolnshire John Yardburgh would not set his mark to the Protestation unless the scribe would 'write these wordes at the end of his marke, (So farre as I may)'. As the recorder refused to allow this exposition, Yardburgh went away, 'uppon better consideration' subscribing later.[74] Some of these additions seemed to take away the obligation of the Protestation altogether. One subscriber from the University of Oxford promised only to keep his oath 'unless I shall think it expedient to alter or revoke it, in which case I reserve my freedom'.[75] It is possible that some avoided subscribing completely by getting sympathetic officials to testify that they had taken the oath. Richard Rocke, minister of Chettle in Dorset, who was described by a Parliamentarian newssheet as a 'desperate malignant priest', did not take the Protestation before the justices in the local market town with the other ministers but 'since hath taken it as it is certified by the overseers of the parish'.[76] The readiness of ministers to vouch for the loyalty of some absentees may also have covered a number of would-be non-subscribers.

The Protestation provides evidence of the use of a variety of equivocal responses by Protestants as well as Catholics. Many Anglican ministers, seeing the oath as part of the attack on episcopacy, would only take the oath with limitations. Some religious radicals refused the Protestation but on the conflicting grounds that it continued to bind swearers to defend a national church. Those with Royalist sympathies expressed misgivings about the definition of political allegiance in the Protestation. Others still equivocated with the oath to avoid committing themselves politically to either the king or Parliament. In concentrating on the use of these tactics, it must be remembered that in some counties there were few or no replies of this kind (for instance, the returns

[70] *Somerset Protestation Returns*, p. 142.
[71] Ibid., p. 27.
[72] *Dorset Protestation Returns*, p. 62.
[73] Ibid., p. 129.
[74] *Lincolnshire Protestation Returns*, p. 60.
[75] *Oxfordshire Protestation Returns*, p. 170.
[76] *Dorset Protestation Returns*, p. 112; *Walker Revised*, p. 136.

for Wiltshire contain no equivocal responses, the Middlesex returns only one).[77] A significant number preferred to use delaying tactics rather than equivocations. The vast majority of subscribers seem to have taken the Protestation without any apparent scruples at all. However, county returns are not always conclusive. 'Subscriptions' like that made by Richard Rocke and allusions to parishioners following their ministers' example in taking the Protestation with exceptions suggest that many equivocal responses may have been given and not recorded.

Vow and Covenant

With more divisive oaths of loyalty, and with greater penalties annexed for refusal, a greater number of works began to argue the merits of subscribing and the range of tactics that could or could not be employed to avoid their obligations. The Vow and Covenant of June 1643 contained no pretence that it was being made for the defence of the king's honour and person. Indeed, as some subscribers would later complain, its text seemed to be in direct conflict with earlier oaths of loyalty, including the Protestation. As will be made clear later, many refused on these grounds, out of fear of being forsworn, rather than because they were politically opposed to the content of the Vow. This itself, though, raises questions about how well the message that these Parliamentary covenants were all part of one national covenant had got across.

Royalist writers recognised the straits that many subscribers were now being put in. The author of *Observations upon the Vow and Covenant* (1643) said that if men would not take the Vow and Covenant 'the feare of being plundered, imprisoned, and utterly ruined in their estates will seize upon them'. If they did take the covenant 'the guilt of God's displeasure against rebellion, treason and perjury' would swallow them up 'and whether they take it or take it not, they themselves are taken, there is the snare.'[78] Nevertheless, using equivocations, as means through this political briar patch, was not an option permitted by Royalist writers. Those that swore to the Vow and Covenant with the phrase 'saving previous oaths and protestations' could not avoid being held to the full performance of it by other covenanters.[79] The author of *The Anti-Covenant* (1643) showed that the Vow and Covenant must be refused as it in no way met the criteria of truth, justice and righteousness required of a lawful oath.[80]

---

[77] *Wiltshire Protestation Returns 1641–2*, ed. B. Hurley (Wiltshire Family History Society, 1997); 'The Protestation Oath Rolls for Middlesex: 1641–42', ed. A. J. C. Guimraens, *Miscellanea Genealogica et Heraldica* (1921), p. 17.

[78] *Observations*, p. 11.

[79] *A Letter to a Noble Lord*, p. 4.

[80] *Anti-Covenant*, pp. 26–9.

There are far fewer surviving returns for the Vow and Covenant than for the Protestation. Returns are extant only for parishes in London, Norfolk, Essex, Kent, Sussex and Suffolk.[81] On 10 June 1643 Parliament ordered that the members of the University of Cambridge should subscribe to the oath. On 17 of the same month it was ordered to be taken in all the parishes of London and finally on 27 to be tendered to the kingdom at large.[82] As with the Protestation, the Vow and Covenant was first subscribed at the local market town by the ministers and parish officers before JPs and then taken down to be subscribed by each parish. Subscriptions were taken from June 1643 in some London parishes up to August of the same year.[83]

Again, as with the Protestation, a large number of those that equivocated or refused the Vow and Covenant were Anglican ministers. Evidence of their responses comes largely from the charges presented to local committees for dealing with 'scandalous and malignant' ministers. It is likely that charges of refusing or equivocating with these oaths of loyalty were fabricated. The Suffolk minister William Keeble was accused, amongst other things, of refusing the Protestation, the oath of association tendered in the Eastern Association and the Vow and Covenant. With the help of his well-connected brother Richard, Keeble was later able to prove to the Earl of Manchester that he had taken the above oaths and the Solemn League and Covenant. Manchester sub-sequently ordered that charges against Keeble should be dropped.[84] Refusing these oaths and covenants was one of the most frequently cited articles against ministers presented to the Suffolk committee.[85] Failure to take the Parliamentary covenants was such a common charge against Anglican clergy that John Walker admitted that many of those who contributed information to his *Sufferings* might simply have assumed that their relatives or friends were ejected on this basis.[86]

Bearing these problems with the evidence in mind, it still seems safe, given the evidence from the Protestation returns, to assume that some of the equivocal responses recorded were genuine. William Walker, vicar of Winson in Suffolk, was charged with taking the Vow and Covenant 'according to his owne invention'. When he was asked to sign it without these equivocations 'he answered in a great rage, sayeing before he would take it without limitation

[81] Gibson, *Protestation Returns*, pp. 34, 42, 49, 67; A Fletcher, *A County Community in Peace and War: Sussex 1600–1660* (London, 1975), p. 107.

[82] *CJ*, iii, 124, 132, 147.

[83] Guildhall Library MS 977/1, St Clement Eastcheap, at the back of the churchwarden's accounts, dated 17 June; 959/1 f. 381v–2, St Martin Orgar, 2 July 1643; ERO, Hadleigh T/R 138/1, 23 July 1643.

[84] Holmes, *Suffolk Committee*, pp. 97–101.

[85] Ibid., p. 21.

[86] J. Walker, *An Attempt Towards Recovering an Account of the Number and Sufferings of the Clergy of the Church of England* (London, 1714), part one, p. 107.

he would be drawn in peices with horses'.[87] Seth Chapman, rector of Hasketon in the same county, swore to the Vow and Covenant with the limitation, 'Savinge my former oaths, vowes, protestation and promises and so farr as lawfully I may'. According to the charges, Chapman's example was followed by most in the parish.[88] The one remaining Vow and Covenant return for Suffolk shows parishioners using exactly these kinds of equivocations. Here at Brantham John Constable, John Wingfield and George Corke all took the Vow and Covenant with the limitation 'so far as lawfully I may'.[89] Robert Large, another Suffolk minister, hoped to use Latin to baffle the authorities, subscribing with the clause *'ibidem quatanus de iure subscribo'* (only as far as the law allowed).[90]

As noted earlier, the Vow and Covenant was intended not only to uncover Royalists, but also to divide the zealous from the lukewarm within the Parliamentarian cause itself. It seems to have been almost too effective in this regard. The Venetian secretary Gerolamo Agostini reported on 17 July 1643 that tendering the Vow and Covenant was causing discontent in the Earl of Essex's army. The earl stated that he had given the Vow and Covenant to his officers 'and this had led to no small stir, twelve of his most trusted colonels having refused to take it'. These same colonels themselves wrote to Parliament, 'but it was only read before secret commissioners, who are in considerable doubt owing to the ambiguity of one of their expressions, in which they say they know what is becoming to good and loyal subjects'.[91] Sir Cheney Culpeper told Samuel Hartlib that there were 'many persons in this Cownty whoe wowlde nowe willingly make voluntary contribution to the Parliamente & pay all presente & future assessementes but can by noe meanes be browght to take the oathe or Couenante'. He asked whether even those that had contributed financially to the Parliamentarian cause but could not take the Vow would be deemed delinquents.[92] In Norfolk it appears that opposition to the Vow and Covenant was expected to be considerable. The deputy lieutenants ordered that one hundred 'honest men' should be raised 'for the appeasinge of any stire or tumults that may arise' on the day it was tendered.[93]

However, the returns for the Vow and Covenant also demonstrate that individuals used equivocations, not only as a means of accommodating various oaths with their religious or political beliefs, but also as a way of avoiding forswearing or perjuring themselves. It was not merely because the Vow and

---

[87] Holmes, *Suffolk Committee*, p. 58.
[88] Ibid., p. 77.
[89] Suffolk Record Office, Ipswich branch, FB 190/D1/1 PRC 527, transcript of Brantham Vow and Covenant.
[90] Holmes, *Suffolk Committee*, p. 84.
[91] CSPV, 1643, p. 297.
[92] 'Cheney Culpeper Letters', p. 175.
[93] NRO, NCR 16A/20, f. 393r, order dated 12 July 1643.

Covenant was committed to continuing the war against the king that it raised scruples with those that supported Parliament. On 31 July 1643 Agostini told the Venetian senate that despite the 'violence shown in administering the oath', the Covenant was 'refused by the majority of people, who know that it is improper and directly contrary to others taken'. For this reason many parts of London otherwise 'most devoted to the party', had asked for, and been granted exception from some points from it.[94] The small number of parishes for which returns survive, only six out of one hundred and two, makes corroborating the comments of the Venetian ambassador difficult. Only in one of these returns, that for St Stephen Coleman Street, is there an equivocal response. Here John Wells subscribed to the Vow and Covenant saving his 'alegantes to my kinge and the only Supreme majesty, and the laste prottesta-cion'.[95] In Essex many also appear to have refused the Covenant on the grounds that it was in conflict with previous oaths and protestations. On 25 July 1643 Sir Richard Everade wrote to his brother-in-law Sir Thomas Barrington, deputy lieutenant of Essex, that he 'had an intimation that many in our parts refuse the Covenant, suspected upon this ground, that they have formerly taken an oath to the contrary'.[96] There is no evidence left of refusals or equivocations with the oath on these grounds in the Essex returns themselves, largely because no lists of refusers were made. What information exists actually points to a strong Presbyterian influence in some parishes. At Prittlewell the returns for the Vow and Covenant and Solemn League and Covenant were followed by a declaration made in 1648 protesting about the proceedings of the army as being a violation of these two covenants.[97] The Vow and Covenant return for Boxted was followed with the exhortation 'Pray God yee will keep it.'[98]

The Vow and Covenant provides further evidence that Anglicans were using tactics of equivocation to limit or nullify the obligation of oaths that were in religious or political terms anathema to them. Equivocation was not the only option open to those that wished to avoid swearing to the Vow and Covenant. The diarist John Evelyn, hearing that the Covenant was to be tendered in London, went into exile.[99] As a consequence of the geographical areas in which it was tendered, the Vow and Covenant was also put before a large number of people otherwise supportive of Parliament's war against the king. There is evidence from official correspondence, and limited corroboration from the remaining returns, that supporters of the Parliament were using equivocations in taking the Covenant. Faced with an oath of loyalty in conflict with previous oaths and protestations, but not with their own political sympathies, many

---

[94] CSPV, 1643, pp. 305–6.
[95] Guildhall MS 4458/1 pt. 2, undated return placed upside down at back of the vestry book.
[96] HMC, *7th Report*, p. 556.
[97] ERO, T/R 182/1.
[98] ERO, D/P 155/1/1.
[99] *The Diary of John Evelyn*, ed. E. S. de Beer (6 vols., Oxford, 1955), ii, 81–2.

nevertheless decided to make reservations rather than flatly break previous obligations.

Solemn League and Covenant

The Vow and Covenant was only tendered from June to August 1643 and even then, it appears, only in a small number of counties. As a result of this, the small number of pamphlets written in response to the oath only dealt sparingly with the issue of subscription. Pamphlets concerning the Solemn League and Covenant, as a result of the fact that it was imposed more extensively and over a greater period of time than its predecessor, went into much greater detail on the ways in which it could be taken. The majority of Royalist writers would maintain their ban on the use of equivocations or reservations in taking the Long Parliament's oaths of loyalty. This position was not universally kept to, possibly as a consequence of the increasing pressure to subscribe exerted by the need for Royalists to compound for their estates. As we will see, though some Royalists continued to employ equivocations, these same pressures were probably leading many simply to swear and be damned.

Both the supporters and the opponents of the Covenant stressed the need to swear truthfully. The covenanting sermons of Case, Caryl and Coleman emphasised the need for sincerity in taking it.[100] Royalist pamphlets in general demanded that those tendered the oath refuse it outright. Many of them cautioned against using equivocations to ease taking the Covenant. The author of *The Iniquity of the Late Solemne League* (1644) stated that it was commonly accepted that oaths and covenants should be taken 'not according to the reserved meaning of him that takes it, but according to the known and notorious meaning and intention of them that impose or require it'.[101] *Certain Disquisitions* (1644) reminded its readers of the 'Jesuitical' pedigree of equivocations like 'as far as lawfully I may' and 'saving former oaths', and noted the irony that 'this Popery' should be reserved 'in swearing, while they swear to extirpate Popery'. The pamphlet reminded readers that oaths and covenants should be taken according to the common sense meaning of their words.[102] *New Quaeres of Conscience* (1643) argued that taking the Solemn League and Covenant was in violation of the three conditions of a lawful oath. Those that took the oath with 'private Reservations inconsistent with the Sense and

---

[100] Coleman, *Hearts Ingagement*, pp. 24–5; Caryl, *The Nature*, pp. 29–30; Case, *Quarrell of the Covenant*, pp. 3–5; see also D. Swift, *A Pious President to Both Kingdoms for a Sacred Covenant* (1643), pp. 38–9.

[101] *The Iniquity of the Late Solemne League, or Covenant Discovered* ([Oxford], 1643), pp. 2, 7–8.

[102] [J. Barwick], *Certain Disquisitions and Considerations Representing to the Conscience the Unlawfulnesse of the Oath Entitled 'A Solemne League and Covenant for Reformation'* (Oxford, 1644), pp. 26–9.

purpose of the Oath' offended against the need for truthfulness in swearing. Those that took it for 'favour of men' offended against justice. Anyone that took the oath out of 'emulation and rage, to the damage of his Brother' offended against righteousness.[103] Daniel Featley echoed Sanderson's opinion that ambiguous oaths ought not to be taken. 'Ambiguities, Equivocations, or mental reservations (especially in Leagues and Oaths)', he said, were 'abominated by all Protestants'.[104]

By declaring that the Covenant was a rash and unlawful oath, a few Royalist writers did offer some comfort to those that had, through force or fear, already sworn to it. Using the example of Herod's oath they stated that it was better to incur a lesser sin by breaking a rash oath, than commit a greater one by keeping it.[105] However, Royalist authors essentially insisted that the Covenant must be refused. They condemned the use of equivocations and reservations to evade the obligation of the oath and stated that those that took the Covenant believing that, as it was unlawful, it did not bind to performance were gravely mistaken. Instead they were to renounce their oath and 'repent the grievious sinne they have committed'.[106]

There were some important exceptions to this Royalist attack on equivocating with the Solemn League and Covenant. The author of *The Iniquity of the Late Solemne League* noted that some had thought to use 'express Reservations of their owne framing' to avoid the obligations of the Covenant. He condemned reservations which destroyed the Covenant 'in the whole', as this would be an 'open mocking, a presumptious taking of God's name in vain', but seemed to permit equivocations which limited it only in parts.[107] The pamphlet *The Plain-meaning Protestant* also acknowledged that many were in any case making private reservations when taking the Covenant. There was a prevailing opinion, which the author said 'seemed to bring reliefe to many even of the composers of it', that held it was lawful for everyone to take the Covenant in their own sense.[108] The author of the pamphlet could not allow such private interpretations. Instead he looked to the general ends of the Covenant, the reformation and defence of religion, the honour and happiness of the king and the peace and the safety of the three kingdoms, which he felt none could balk at. He felt that the authors of the Covenant had allowed some equivocation as they had themselves limited the observation of it with provisos about keeping to one's place and calling. He had, therefore, entered into the Covenant with a protestation to do only so much as would not attack the king's person and authority or be contrary to the Oaths of Allegiance and

---

[103] *New Quaeres*, pp. 7–8.
[104] Featley, *League Illegal*, pp. 21–2.
[105] *A Briefe Discourse*, p. 16; *New Quaeres*, p. 7.
[106] *The Iniquity*, p. 8.
[107] Ibid., pp. 7–8.
[108] *The Plain-meaning Protestant* (Oxford, 1644), p. 3.

Supremacy. He would support the reformation of the church only as was fitting his place as a subject. With regard to the clause demanding the extirpation of popery, the author distinguished popish superstitions from the notion of prelacy or any attack on episcopacy.[109] The author was clear that he did not disguise these equivocations but 'plainly and ingeniously' declared the way in which he took the Covenant.[110]

In some cases, we can see that these pamphlets influenced the political actions of their readers. The Royalist Sir Thomas Knyvett, who took the Solemn League and Covenant in March 1644, in a letter of 20 June that year declared that he had 'met with a booke call'd the plaine dealing [sic] protestant [which] is able to satisfye any man concerning the Cov'[enan]t'. The pamphlet had come too late to influence his own subscription, but Knyvett noted that its reading of the oath had satisfied his cousin Anthony.[111] Similarly, Francis Cheynell believed that the Oxford Reasons against the Covenant had been produced not only to voice publicly the university's opposition, but also to serve as a guide to the correct conduct of university members in refusing to subscribe to it. The heads of colleges, Cheynell said, only used the Reasons 'for the strengthening and arming of their owne party against the covenant'. Those sympathetic to the Parliamentary visitors could not get a sight of the pamphlet.[112]

Print was only one channel through which writers on both sides tried to direct the public as to whether to take or refuse the Covenant. Regular preach-ing was seen as vital to maintaining the national covenant. The word of God as given in a sermon formed the body of the covenant with the Lord, whilst the act of subscription signified merely the entering into it. Covenanting ministers used their sermons to instruct their congregation in the need for a covenant, the obligations placed upon those that took it, and the penalties that could be expected to fall on those that broke it. Sermons could be a powerful means to sway the largely illiterate members of the minister's congre-gation. A particularly striking example comes from the remarkable effect of Scottish covenanting ministers in Ulster. Undoubtedly, linking the Covenant with the offer of supplies to support the British garrisons against the Irish (the Scottish government sent £10,000 of food and equipment for the British troops along with the four ministers) helped make their message seem more appealing.[113] However, there was also a clear element of popular religious enthusiasm, like that seen in Scotland itself, in the response to the ministers'

---

[109] Ibid., pp. 4–6.
[110] Ibid., p. 7.
[111] Knyvett Letters, p. 160.
[112] [F. Cheynell], The Sworne Confederacy Between the Convocation at Oxford and the Tower of London (1647), p. 2.
[113] M. Perceval-Maxwell, 'The Adoption of the Solemn League and Covenant by the Scots in Ulster', Scotia: Interdisciplinary Journal of Scottish Studies, ii (1978), 3–18.

message.[114] Sir James Montgomery wrote to Ormonde in April 1644 that 'wheresiever the Ministers come and preach unto them the Covenant (w[hi]ch is now their cheafe subject) the comon people flock to them amazed and take it'.[115] Colonel Audley Mervyn described these Scottish ministers as 'Evangelists' who insisted that the Covenant was 'as necessary as ye sacra-ment'.[116] Later Mervyn himself took the Covenant, having been swayed by the preaching of one of these ministers. He noted that in his exposition of the Covenant the preacher was 'much more sparing then I had heard him formerly'. Mervyn encouraged his men to take it as the minister 'both in church and privately had declared that there was nothing meant in the Covenant repug-nant to the preface'. He had insisted that the Covenant only bound those that took it to 'maintain the honor and happinesse of the King, the peace and safety of the three kingdomes, and the defense of our religion'. Such 'plaine truths', the minister said, 'begged no exposition which would rather intangle than satisfie men's consciences.'[117]

However, as in the case of the Protestation, the importance given to sermons as a means to promote the taking of the Covenant also afforded Royalist clergy an opportunity to preach against it. Nicholas Coleman, rector of Preston St Mary's in Suffolk, was accused in June 1644 of refusing to take the Covenant and was said to have advised his parishioners not to take it either 'for he said their blood would be required at his hands, & said that those that took it were Traitors to ye King, & pull'd out ye Kings declaracon [sic] & read it in ye Church to ye discouragem[en]t of ye well affected people'. Coleman also disparaged those ministers that promoted the Covenant, saying of Mr Smith of Cuckfield 'who stirred up his Parishioners to take ye Coven[an]t that he would observe anything & turne as the wind or weathercock'.[118] Other ministers were not as blatant in their opposition to the Covenant as Coleman but instead attempted to water down the meaning of it in their sermons. Theodore Beale, vicar of Ash Bocking in Suffolk, was accused of insisting 'only upon Charity & forsaking Popery and drawing near to ye best reformed Churches' in his exhortation to take the Covenant. He had shown 'no reasons for ye d[e]position of Episcopacy in w[hi]ch many would gladly have been satisfied, nor for approx[i]macon p[ar]ticularly to ye Church of Scotland, nor yet to the People to resist ye Rebellion of ye Cavaleers ag[ains]t ye King & Parliam[en]t'.[119] For his sermon

---

[114] Steele, 'Politick Christian', p. 31. However, David Mullan offers evidence of the use of coercion in getting subscriptions to the Covenant, Mullan, Scottish Puritanism, pp. 290–1.

[115] Bodl. MS Carte 10, f. 207, Montgomery to Ormonde, 14 April 1644.

[116] Ibid., f. 336.

[117] HMC, Ormonde MSS, i (London, 1895), pp. 90–1; Mervyn was also encouraged to swear as a means to maintain his authority in Derry, Perceval-Maxwell, 'Solemn League and Covenant', 11, 13.

[118] Bodl. MS Walker C. 6, f. 28.

[119] Ibid., f. 27.

at the taking of the Covenant Richard Watts, vicar of Chesterton in Cambridgeshire, 'preached out of Romans 14 verse 3 & said let not him that taketh the Covenant despise him that taketh it not for We ought not Judge one another for Indifferent things'.[120] Sermons were not the only way that the spoken word was used to direct the conscience. Less frequently, casuistic 'surgeries' or conferences were held in which ministers would attempt to remove individuals' conscientious scruples. Montgomery noted that the Scottish ministers in Ulster had used conferences in an attempt to win the clergy over to the cause of the Covenant.[121]

The returns for the Solemn League and Covenant, unlike those for its predecessor, can be found outside the counties of the Eastern Association and the city of London. Lists of subscribers exist for parishes in Durham, Sussex, Cheshire, Gloucestershire, Hampshire and Huntingdonshire, as well as Essex, London, Norfolk, Suffolk and Kent.[122] The majority of returns were made between February and March 1644, following the demand for nationwide subscription, but as with the Protestation, it was taken earlier in some areas. The London parishes again were the quickest to take the Covenant with both St Olave Jewry and St Clement Eastcheap dating their lists October 1643.[123] However, not all of the London ministers were so eager to gather subscriptions to the Covenant. Information was received on 10 October 1643 that William Lance, a member of the Westminster Assembly, had dissuaded his parishioners from taking it. Another London minister, Mr Haines, was reported to have subscribed with reservations, 'having awhile refused to subscribe at all, and having at first cast away the pen'. As a consequence of this resistance, the Assembly appointed ministers to preach in place of the recalcitrant clergy. On its own this did not quell the opposition to the Covenant. At St Andrew's Undershaft, one of the ministers appointed by the Assembly, Mr Rodbrugh, claimed that queries over the lawfulness of the oath were laid on his desk before he went into the pulpit.[124] There is little evidence in England of the same popular enthusiasm for the Solemn League and Covenant seen in Scotland and Ulster, though in the parish of Baconsthorpe, Norfolk, the minister carefully preserved the subscriptions to the oath in a 'towne Booke w[i]th the

---

[120] Ibid., f. 9.

[121] Bodl. MS Carte 10, f. 350–2.

[122] Entries for relevant counties in Gibson's guide; Durham Record Office, EP/Ea 1, Easington, St Mary; EP/Ho 1, Houghton-le-Spring, St Michael and All Angel; Gloucestershire Record Office, P29 IN1/1, Avening. There is some evidence that it was taken in Bedfordshire as well, B. R. O. P 44/5/2, Shillington churchwarden's accounts, 'item spent at Potton when we took the Covenant 4s.'. It also appears to have been administered in Surrey, see below, p. 150.

[123] Guildhall Library MS 4415 f. 117–18v, Olave Jewry, 977/1, St Clement Eastcheap: entered upside down at the back of the churchwarden's accounts.

[124] J. Lightfoot, 'Journal of Westminster Assembly', The Whole Works, ed. J. R. Pitman (13 vols., London, 1822–5), xiii, 16, 18, 21.

forme of the Covenant thereto adioyned . . . kept under locke'.[125] In his recent doctoral thesis, Eliot Vernon has argued for the centrality of the Solemn League and Covenant to the concerns of lay Presbyterians (who described themselves as 'Covenant-engaged citizens') in civil war London.[126] Of course, the London Presbyterians' petitions, like that of December 1646 which called for the disbanding of the army and the restoration of central control of the militia to the city, were as often concerned with political or material problems (the weight of taxation, the threat of revolutionary tyranny) as with religious grievances.[127] However, on occasion, city Presbyterians refused to pay excise tax to exact pressure to resolve their religious grievances.[128]

Anglican ministers again feature prominently as equivocators with this oath through the charges levied against them at local committees. Daniel Whitby, rector of Theydon Mount in Essex, was accused of having refused the Covenant. He replied that he believed 'that the Parl[iament] tooke up armes for Religion Lawes and Priviledges to maintain them and I beleeve the King doth the same and I must not drive out one nayle with another'.[129] In his own vindication of himself, Whitby claimed that he had taken a fortnight to consider the Covenant and told the committee that he 'would take it as farre as it concern'd the good of the Parliament, but not the Pro and Con'. Whitby made it clear that he did not want his assent to the Covenant to be seen as giving approval to any one side.[130] On 29 December 1644 he was charged on more articles. When asked again if he would take the Covenant Whitby replied that he would 'take it passive, but not active' as it did not belong to his calling 'to root out episcopie'.[131] Andrew Lamont, vicar of Claybrooke in Leicestershire, was charged on nine articles including that he had refused the Covenant. Lamont replied that he had offered to take it in February 1645 'so far as was agreeable to the Word of God'.[132] John Walker related a wonderful anecdote, sadly unsubstantiated, concerning Thomas Pelling, rector of Trowbridge. According to Walker, Pelling was ejected from his living for refusing the Covenant but when quitting his house with his wife and family he met a Parliamentarian colonel who happened to be an old friend. Having

---

[125] HLRO, Main Papers, 24 March 1643/4, Baconsthorpe Covenant return, f. 132.

[126] E. C. Vernon, 'The Sion College Conclave and London Presbyterianism during the English Revolution' (University of Cambridge Ph.D., 1999), pp. 314, 381–2. See also *Diary of Thomas Juxon*, pp. 17n., 85, 95, 98, 108, 130, 139 & n., 156.

[127] M. Tolmie, *The Triumph of the Saints: The Separate Churches of London 1616–1649* (Cambridge, 1977), pp. 131–6: See also R. Ashton, *Counter-Revolution: The Second Civil War and its Origins, 1646–8* (New Haven, 1994), chs. 2 and 3.

[128] Ibid., p. 75.

[129] *Walker Revised*, p. 168.

[130] D. Whitby, *The Vindication of a True Protestant, and Faithfull Servant to His Church* (Oxford, 1644), p. 11.

[131] *Walker Revised*, p. 169.

[132] Ibid., p. 239.

been told of the reason for Pelling's departure, the colonel went to the man who tendered him the Covenant, got a copy from him and then gave it to the minister, telling Pelling to put it in his pocket. The colonel then informed the authorities that Pelling had 'taken' the Covenant.[133]

Those wishing to compound their estates were required to take the Solemn League and Covenant and Negative Oath or face imprisonment and the seques-tration of their estates. The severity of these penalties seems to have persuaded most of those that came before the committee for compounding not to quibble over taking either the Covenant or the oath. A few flatly refused to subscribe, like Sir John Strangeways and his son Giles, who was later a key figure in the 'church party' in the Cavalier Parliament.[134] Others like Bruno Ryves fell back on articles of surrender that exempted them from being tendered any oaths of loyalty.[135] A small number still tried to avoid having to take the oath in full. Sir Peregrine Bertie of Evedon in Lincolnshire was admitted to compound on 17 October 1645 but was committed to custody for refusing the Negative Oath. On 24 October Bertie took the oath, but with the reservation 'so far as it is agreeable to the word of God'. Having been returned to gaol Bertie appeared again on 1 November, promising to take it unreservedly. However, when he was brought before a minister to take the oath, he again used the same reservation and was committed for contempt. Bertie finally took the Negative Oath without any limitations on 18 December 1645.[136] Sir Henry Berkeley of Yarlington, Somerset seems to have used an ingenious method to attempt to avoid taking the Solemn League and Covenant. On 24 July 1646 the com-mittee ordered him to be delivered to the Sergeant-at-Arms, and kept in custody 'till report is made to Parliament of his hiring one to personate him in taking the National Covenant'.[137]

In spite of the heavy penalties for refusing it, the decision to take the Covenant clearly remained a very difficult one for some Royalists. Some time between early 1645 and early 1647, whilst under house arrest in St Martin's Fields, the Royalist John, first Viscount Scudamore, drew up a series of queries relating to the Covenant and Negative Oath. Taking the oaths apart article by article, he concluded that he would only be prepared to take the Covenant so long as it bound him to nothing against the laws of the kingdom, God, or the Oaths of Allegiance and Supremacy. Only in this sense, Scudamore said, would he take the Covenant, 'and not otherwise: protesting not to admit any contrary sense hereunto, but to make it the rule of my interpretation and action'. These rationalisations were clearly successful, as Scudamore took both

[133] Ibid., p. 379.
[134] *Calendar of the Proceedings of the Committee for Compounding etc. 1643–1660*, ed. M. A. E. Green (5 vols., London, 1890), iii, 1828.
[135] Ibid., ii, 1593.
[136] Ibid., ii, 908.
[137] Ibid., ii, 1405.

oaths in early 1647, allowing him to compound for his estate.[138] Similar lists of conscientious queries detailing scruples over the Solemn League and Covenant can be found in the Marquis of Ormonde's papers. These largely followed the same lines as other Royalist attacks on the oath, by complaining that the Covenant equivocated with the subject's allegiance to the king, attacked the monarch's spiritual supremacy, and perverted the patriarchal order of nature by demanding that sons informed on 'malignant' fathers.[139]

Letters too demonstrate that the Solemn League and Covenant weighed heavily upon individual consciences. Perhaps the most celebrated crisis of conscience of this kind belonged to Sir Ralph Verney. Verney was from a Royalist family, but had continued to attend the Westminster Parliament as an MP after the outbreak of the civil war. Verney's allegiances seem largely to have been determined by his religious outlook, viewing Charles and Laud's innovations as a threat to the Church of England. Verney even took the Vow and Covenant of June 1643, which made no reference to defending the king's person.[140] It seems that it was the prospect of a Presbyterian church held forth in the Solemn League and Covenant that split Verney from the Parliament. Many of Verney's friends and relatives, including Henry Parker, the Parliamentarian pamphleteer, attempted to convince him to make his choice one way or another. Parker reminded him that the conscience gave all private individuals a power to act. Neutrality offered no protection, rather

> all men ought to adhere to that cause which is dictated to them to bee the better and the more harmless by the light of nature and the most forcible indications of reason. No man can say that God has left him no part to act, nor no station to make good.[141]

Verney promised on Parker's advice to consider the Covenant more thoroughly, but in the end chose not to subscribe and consequently was disqualified from sitting in the Commons.[142]

Verney's prevarication over taking the Covenant may have been exceptional in its degree, but he was not alone in writing to others about his scruples over the oath. The lawyer Guybon Goddard wrote to his brother-in-law in February 1644 with news of the siege of Newcastle. He also took time to comment on their friend 'T. Sc.'s' hesitancy in taking the Solemn League and Covenant. It is clear from his letter that Goddard understood the difference between the Covenant and a mere oath of loyalty. He felt their friend had not rightly

[138] PRO C115/99 nos. 7312–7314; Ian Atherton, *Ambition and Failure in Stuart England: The Career of John, First Viscount Scudamore* (Manchester, 1999), pp. 220–2, 228.
[139] Bodl. MS Carte 8, f. 384–9.
[140] *Memoirs of the Verney Family During the Civil War*, ed. F. P. Verney (2 vols., London, 1892), ii, 160–1.
[141] Ibid., ii, 211–12.
[142] Ibid., ii, 216.

distinguished between 'a voluntary and spontaneous Oath, and a Judiciall Nationall, or as he calls it a Necessary Covenant and Vowe'. Unlike in an oath, in a covenant God was engaged as a party and the takers of it became debtors to him. In this way covenants were more effective than oaths, said Goddard, because 'such who will make no scruple or difficulty to breake promises with men will be kept to a more strict and awfull performance when they finde themselves accountable to God'. He warned that their friend, and not the imposers of the Covenant, would be the guilty party if he dared violate or profane such a 'sacred and sanctimonious ingagement'.[143] One William Warwick, replying to a query over the oath, stated that his resolution with regard to the Covenant was to refuse it even if this meant not going to church. Citing Aquinas, he stated that it was better to abstain from public worship rather than impugn the whole doctrine of the church by admitting pious frauds like the Covenant. Warwick ended by pleading with his correspondent to consider this advice carefully as he was 'a leading man' and his decision 'pro or con' would be 'a Matter of soe great importance'.[144]

Unfortunately, the evidence from subscription returns for the Solemn League and Covenant is far less revealing. There is only limited evidence from parish records of the use of equivocations. Writing to William Dillingham in March 1644 William Sancroft reported that the Covenant was 'heere Universally taken & al good people in Suff[olk]., have soe p[rofes]sedly learnt the mystery of As farre as lawfully I may: that now noth[ing]. can come amisse to them were it Mohamed's Alkuran'.[145] The returns for Suffolk do not contain any evidence of the use of these kinds of reservations. Again, returns only survive for a small number of parishes and, as with the returns for parishes in most of the rest of the country (with the exception of Norfolk), no records were kept of refusers of the oath.[146] Only one parish in London contains a record of an equivocal reply. The same John Wells of St Stephens, Coleman Street, who had made a reserved subscription to the Vow and Covenant, here gave his assent to the Solemn League and Covenant saving 'the Protestation taken before by [me] and as far as it agrees with that'.[147] (Providing evidence that limitations of this kind were occasionally accepted.) At Beccles in Norfolk John Webb would only subscribe to 'so much of this Covenant as I already

<hr>

[143] BL Add. MS 39922 A, f. 1: Goddard to J. Greene, 25 Feb. 1644.

[144] 'A Treatise concerning ye Cov.[enant] by Wi[lliam] War[wick]', Bodl. MS Rawlinson D 1347, f. 364–75.

[145] Bodl. MS Tanner 62, f. 641.

[146] Returns exist for six parishes in Suffolk; SR O., Ipswich Branch, FC 199/A5/1, Earl Soham, FC 89/A1/1, Brundish, Bury Office FL 551/4/1, Chilton, FB 51/A3/1, Cretingham, FC 193/D1/1; transcript PRC 596, Linstead Parva and Mellis, published as 'Solumne League and Covenant in Suffolk', ed. C. Morley, *East Anglian Miscellany* (1945), pp. 30–6. For Norfolk see J. T. Evans, *Seventeenth-Century Norwich Politics, Religion and Government, 1620–1690* (Oxford, 1979), pp. 145n., 146n.

[147] Guildhall MS 4458/1 pt. 2.

know, or shall hereafter know, to be agreeable to the word of God, the laws of this kingdom, or my oaths formerly taken'. As Webb was the leading parishioner it is likely that others took the Covenant using the same equivocation.[148] In the same county, a number of those that refused the Covenant later recanted and had their names added to the list of subscribers.[149]

The response to the Solemn League and Covenant appears at first more muted than that which followed the tendering of the Protestation. Though aimed at extirpating the remnants of popery from the church, the Covenant does not appear to have inspired similar acts of popular iconoclasm.[150] However, as will be shown in later chapters, the apparent failure of the Covenant to inspire the public to direct action should not lead us to conclude that it did not exercise a powerful hold over some subscribers.

The choices facing those opposed to the content of the Covenant were made harder by its incorporation into the process of compounding and by its use as a garrison oath. In general, Royalist pamphleteers continued to condemn the use of equivocations, though they made the concession that it was better that those that had already sworn to the Covenant should break their oath rather than compound their sin by keeping it. It seems likely that this stance was intended more to give the impression of unwavering loyalty than actually to inspire it. Sancroft's comments and the charges against parochial clergy suggest it is possible that many were employing reservations in taking the Solemn League and Covenant. The author of *The Plain-meaning Protestant* believed that the use of equivocations was commonplace and personally sanctioned the use of declared reservations. It also seems likely that there was some collusion between ministers and their parishioners in making a limited subscription to these covenants. Equally, Walker's anecdote concerning Thomas Pelling may not be as far-fetched as it sounds. Ian Green has noted that a number of the charges made against ministers for prevaricating with the Covenant revealed that clergy anticipated sympathetic county officials would not prosecute them for replying in an equivocal way.[151] Moreover, as the subscriptions of John Wells and John Webb demonstrate, equivocations were again being employed (and it seems accepted by parish officers) as a means to avoid breaking previous oaths.

It is clear from this survey of public responses to the imposition of the Protestation, Vow and Covenant that subscribers were frequently resorting to

---

[148] R. W. Ketton-Cremer, *Norfolk in the Civil War: A Portrait of a Society in Conflict* (London, 1969), p. 220; Jones, *Conscience and Allegiance*, p. 130.

[149] HLRO, Main Papers, 7 April 1644, Colby, Norfolk, f. 11; 15 April 1644, Heydon, Norfolk, f. 55–6.

[150] Although there are indications that soldiers may have been inspired by the Covenant to carry out acts of iconoclastic violence. See J. Spraggon, *Puritan Iconoclasm During the English Civil War* (Woodbridge, 2003), p. 188.

[151] Green, 'Persecution', p. 516.

the use of tactics of equivocation. It is also apparent that the advice offered on how to take these covenants was moving away from the rules for lawful swearing established by earlier casuists. It is harder to see how far the political and theological arguments advanced by writers on the Protestation, Vow and Covenant had been absorbed by their readership. We have numerous examples of hostile reactions to these documents, many coming from Anglican clergy but a significant number coming from laymen too. The Protestation does seem to have inspired acts of popular iconoclasm and spontaneous pro-Parliamentarian risings in Yorkshire and Essex, but the Vow and Covenant and Solemn League and Covenant seem to have acted far less effectively as catalysts to direct action. The fact that many subscribers refused the Vow and the Covenant on the grounds that they conflicted with previous oaths of loyalty (namely the Protestation) suggests that the message of Parliamentarian preachers and pamphleteers that these were all part of the same national covenant had failed to convince their intended audience.

However, it would be wrong to conclude that the public was overwhelmingly resistant to the ideas expounded by covenanting ministers. For one thing, the nature of subscription returns makes it harder to assess positive rather than negative reactions to these documents. We have the equivocal replies and recorded refusals for those that were opposed to the Parliament's covenants. However, the signatures and marks of those that signed without protest offer us ambiguous evidence. Did they add their names willingly or under duress, were they enthusiastic about what they were being asked to sign, or were they simply choosing the path of least resistance by subscribing? Without corroborating evidence it is hard to tell. What can be said is that some subscribers clearly saw the Protestation as giving them *carte blanche* to begin the work of removing idolatrous altar rails and images without Parliamentary approval. Equally, Goddard's letter demonstrates that some were aware of the difference between these covenants and earlier oaths of loyalty. Most importantly, as David Cressy has noted, the 'practical mobilisation of citizenship' involved in subscribing to these documents 'gave everyone a stake in the outcome [of the English Revolution]'.[152] As will be demonstrated in the next chapter, Diggers and Levellers would take this implicit expansion of the political nation, along with the emphasis of covenanting divines on the linkage between personal and national reformation, as offering support for their far more radical notions of citizenship.

[152] Cressy, 'Protestation Protested', p. 253.

Part II

The Solemn League and Covenant, 1644–1682

6

'A Covenant for Liberty of Conscience'

The Levellers, the Diggers and the national covenant

As we will see in Chapter 8, following the Restoration of Charles II, the Covenant became a rallying standard for the 'good old cause', as Presbyterians, Congregationalists, Baptists and Fifth Monarchists, all excluded from the national church, held meetings over the issue of liberty of conscience. These radical defences of the Solemn League and Covenant were not simply a product of the restrictive Restoration religious settlement. We've already seen how, in the early 1640s, churchmen from a variety of denominational backgrounds were supportive of the idea of national covenant. This should not disguise the fact that many Congregationalists and separatists harboured deep misgivings about the form this took in the Solemn League and Covenant (and, as we will see, some rejected it altogether). These reservations became more pronounced between 1644 and 1646 as the Solemn League and Covenant became the emblem of a Presbyterian party opposed to demands for religious toleration and bent on the suppression of 'heretical' sects. However, conservative here-siographers, like Thomas Edwards in his influential *Gangraena* (1646), often charged Independents and separatists, not with actually breaking the Solemn League and Covenant but with equivocating with its terms. Indeed, the interpretation of the Solemn League and Covenant as a document binding subscribers to enforce a rigid Presbyterian uniformity was itself a new 'reading' of a document that had been framed with deliberate ambiguity. In turn, radical churchmen like Henry Burton, John Saltmarsh and William Dell did not respond to these attacks by repudiating the Covenant (indeed, in the case of Burton and Saltmarsh they had once been staunch advocates of it) but by offering their own 'tolerationist' gloss upon it.

My purpose here is not only to offer a caveat to the view that the Solemn League and Covenant was anathema to most political/religious radicals, but also to show the importance of the idea of a national covenant to both Leveller and Digger political thought. The covenants which bound together gathered churches have long been linked with the Leveller 'Agreements of the People'. The American liberal historiography of the 1930s and 1940s, exemplified in the work of William Haller, Perry Miller and W. K. Jordan, saw these congre-gations as, in essence, mini-democracies founded on the social contract of the church covenant. In turn, the British Marxist scholars Christopher Hill and A. L. Morton adopted much of this liberal thesis. Along with many other aspects of the Whig/Marxist interpretation of the English Revolution, the whole association of puritanism with liberty, including the significance of church covenants, has been challenged by revisionist scholars. W. M. Lamont, C. H. George and J. C. Davis have instead pointed up the generally repressive impulses of the godly and the undemocratic features of their thought. The evidence presented in this chapter supports the revisionists' assertion that church covenants were not the model for 'Leveller democracy' (without necessarily concurring with their arguments concerning puritanism and liberty as a whole). It will instead be suggested that the heavily promulgated concept of a national covenant, incorporated into the New Model Army's declarations and engagements, formed an important model for the Agreements of the People. The chapter will then trace the similar reinterpretation of the Solemn League and Covenant as a social contract by the Digger leader Gerrard Winstanley. Yet these radical readings of the Covenant were a product of more than the rhetorical dexterity of Winstanley and the English Levellers. They represented a logical, if considerable, extension of the discourse of covenanting divines and Parliamentarian pamphleteers. In the case of Winstanley, his attachment to the Solemn League and Covenant was also a direct result of the mass public subscription to these oaths.

Presbyterian heresiographers often listed the refusal to swear oaths of loyalty (or conversely a complete disregard for the value of sworn statements) amongst the many errors of schismatic sects which they portrayed as mushrooming in the fertile soil of de facto toleration in mid-1640s England.[1] Thomas Edwards's *Gangraena* (1646), published in three parts, accused the sects of repeatedly attacking the Solemn League and Covenant.[2] Edwards urged Parliament and the City of London to renew their covenant with God, as Asa, Hezekiah and Josiah had done in biblical times, and called for monthly fasts and humiliations to atone for the failure to keep terms with God.[3] Ephraim Pagitt reminded his readers of the grave divine punishments that would be exacted upon England if they did not act to root out 'Errors, Heresies and Schisme' according to the Covenant 'which we have ministered and you received with great alacrity'.[4] The barrister William Prynne attacked John Lilburne's anti-Covenant works and stated that the Independents and separatists' church covenants were little more than 'meere Anti-Covenants to the National League and Covenant'.[5]

---

[1] E. Pagitt, *Heresiography: or, a Description of the Hereticks and Sectaries of these later Times* (1645), p. 24.
[2] T. Edwards, *Gangraena* (1646, 1977 Rota reprint), p. 52.
[3] Ibid., pp. 168, 171.
[4] Pagitt, *Heresiography*, epistle dedicatory.
[5] W. Prynne, *A Fresh Discovery of Some Prodigious New Wandering-Blasing Stars and Firebrands* (1645).

It was certainly the case that the passing of the Solemn League and Covenant had caused great anxiety amongst Independent and separatist churches. A petition had been drawn up by 'Independents and Brownists' against the Covenant only to be staved off by soothing overtones from Philip Nye and by the insistence of Sir Henry Vane that reformation be 'according to the word of God', as well as the example of the best reformed churches.[6] However, there had not been any explicit repudiation of the Covenant from either Independents or sectaries, as the heresiographers effectively conceded when they accused their Congregationalist opponents, not of breaking the Solemn League and Covenant, but of placing an equivocating new gloss upon it. John Vicars stated that Independent divines like John Goodwin, Henry Burton and the Leveller leader William Walwyn had made the Covenant 'an ensnaring dangerous Dilemma to our consciences' by their 'subtleties'.[7] Edwards attacked Walwyn as a

> man of an equivocating Jesuiticall spirit, being full of mental reservations and equivocations, as appears by the sense that he hath put upon the Nationall Covenant, there being hardly any Jesuite could have put a more equivocall interpretation upon the Covenant, then himself.[8]

This was recognition of the fact that those divines that Edwards and other heresiographers attacked often claimed that they were actually following the true intent of the Covenant by supporting pleas for liberty of conscience.[9] In general, Independents followed Henry Burton in arguing that they had only covenanted to defend the Scottish Presbyterian church, not have it imposed on England. In fact, Burton said, it would be against the Covenant to demand submission to a form of church government few had knowledge of as 'we promise to extirpate all Popery: whereof blind obedience is one of the main Pillars'.[10] Other opponents of Edwards also used the clauses against popery to claim that the imposition of a Presbyterian church system was against the tenor of the Covenant. John Saltmarsh argued that the Covenant could not be

---

[6] 'A Secret Negociation with Charles the First 1643–44', ed. B. M. Gardiner, *Camden Miscellany*, 8 (1883), p. 4; V. A. Rowe, *Sir Henry Vane the Younger: A Study in Political and Administrative History* (London, 1970), pp. 19, 25 suggests that Vane, a long term supporter of freedom of conscience, advocated the Covenant essentially as a means to prosecute the war against Charles I more rigorously.

[7] J. Vicars, *The Schismatick Shifted* (1646), pp. 23, 26.

[8] Edwards, *Gangraena*, pt. two, p. 26.

[9] For an exception to this stance see J. Goodwin, *Twelve Considerable Serious Cautions* (1646), p. 4.

[10] H. Burton, *The Peace Maker: or, Solid Reasons, Perswading to Peace: Grounded upon the Late Solemn Covenant* (1646), p. 2. The same point was made by John Saltmarsh, *A New Quaere* (1645), p. 3.

fulfilled until the popery of a tithe-supported church had been extirpated.[11] How, he asked, could ministers ordained by popish prelates and tithe-supported clergy claim to be upholding the Covenant?[12]

The general thrust of the Independent and sectarian reading of the Covenant was that the supreme rule for church reformation was the word of God, not the example of other reformed churches.[13] In any case, for Henry Burton the churches of New England offered a better model of church govern-ment than the Scottish kirk.[14] Saltmarsh argued that the first clause of the Covenant, which called on subscribers to bring the churches of the three kingdoms into the 'nearest conjunction', bound covenanters not to enforce uniformity but to foster religious unity. Each nation, he said, should be free to reform itself according to the word of God, as it sees fit.[15] Both Burton and Saltmarsh contended that the Covenant should not be used as the weapon of one faction or party, indeed Burton called for an 'Amnestia' on the labels of Independent and Presbyterian. Instead, covenanters should keep peace with their Christian brethren.[16] These authors also reinterpreted the clauses demanding the extirpation of heresy and schism. Heresy, Walwyn said, was not to be interpreted as any doctrines contrary to Presbyterianism. A man only became a heretic when he forsook 'an infallible and knowne truth'. In that instance, the weapons used to extirpate heresy should be gentle persuasion, not imprisonment or physical punishment.[17] Both Saltmarsh and Walwyn were clear that it was not the preserve of ecclesiastical synods like the Westminster Assembly to punish heresy or schism. Only Parliament, and in a purely restrictive sense, had any authority to regulate the individual conscience.[18] For those like Burton who saw the church as 'an organical body of living members', separation from a national church did not constitute schism.[19] If schism was interpreted in this way, said Walwyn, then the Presbyterians were themselves schismatics from the Church of England.[20]

If most of these writers did not explicitly denounce the Covenant, we might still agree with Edwards and other heresiographers in seeing them as employing

---

[11] J. Saltmarsh, The Smoke in the Temple (3rd edn., 1646), p. 36.

[12] Idem., Reasons for Unitie, Peace and Love (1646), p. 9. The fact that elements of 'popery' were either tolerated or had a being in law raised scruples for some in taking the Covenant, 'Cheney Culpeper Letters', pp. 186–8.

[13] W. Walwyn, A Word More to Mr. Thomas Edwards Minister (1646), p. 4; W. Dell, Right Reformation: or the Reformation of the Church of the New Testament (1646), p. 35; H[enry]. B[urton]., Conformities Deformitie (1646), p. 25.

[14] Burton, Peace Maker, p. 4.

[15] J. Saltmarsh, The Divine Right of Presbytery (1646), p. 10.

[16] Burton, Peace Maker, p. 7; Saltmarsh, Smoke in the Temple, pp. 1, 16.

[17] Walwyn, A Word More, pp. 6–8.

[18] Ibid., p. 4; Saltmarsh, Smoke in the Temple, p. 20.

[19] Burton, Peace Maker, p. 6.

[20] Walwyn, A Word More, p. 6.

weasel words so as effectively to render it a dead letter. However, Edwards's reading of the Solemn League and Covenant as a document binding subscribers to the adoption of Presbyterian state church was itself a partisan gloss upon the text. Edwards's *Gangraena* remains one of the most, if not the most, crucial source for our information on the radical sects of the English civil war. However, its obviously skewed perspective has led some historians, notably J. C. Davis, to question whether it can be used at all.[21] From a slightly different angle, Jonathan Scott has argued that Edwards's skill in labelling sectarian groups has imposed too static and compartmentalised a view of radical religion in 1640s England.[22] Christopher Hill, on the other hand, a historian who believed fervently in the existence of a considerable radical underground in the seventeenth century, argued that such an important source should not be discarded and that what was needed was a critical edition to test Edwards's accounts.[23]

Recently, Ann Hughes has argued that approaches to *Gangraena* which concentrate on the veracity or otherwise of Edwards's stories are, to some extent, missing the point.[24] Contextualising Edwards's accounts will only help so much. Most of the individuals featured in *Gangraena* did exist, but Edwards's interests, suggests Hughes, meant that he only ever delivered an incomplete picture. He was concerned, not with intellectual heresy, but with forms of behaviour that he saw as morally, socially or politically threatening. Moreover, the reports, letters and pamphlets which Edwards quoted from in order to give his book 'the look of truth' often presented him with a welter of information that he was barely in control of. Consequently, his readings of radical books were 'as often carelessly as deliberately distorted'.[25] It is more important, Hughes persuasively suggests, to recognise the role of *Gangraena* in 'reinforcing local communities of clergy whose networks risked fragmentation and division in the complex debates of the mid-1640s'.[26] Edwards used similar tactics of

---

[21] J. C. Davis, *Fear, Myth and History: The Ranters and the Historians* (Cambridge, 1986), pp. 126–8, at p. 126: 'Relying on Thomas Edwards for evidence of the reality of sectarian development in his time, is like relying on Horatio Bottomley or Joseph McCarthy for sound, objective depictions of the social and political realities of their day.' Contrast this with A. L. Morton's earlier judgement that *Gangraena* was a 'document of first-rate historical value', *The World of the Ranters* (London, 1970), p. 26.

[22] J. Scott, *England's Troubles: Seventeenth-Century English Political Instability in European Context* (Cambridge, 1999), pp. 238–40.

[23] C. Hill, 'Irreligion in the "Puritan" Revolution', in *Radical Religion in the English Revolution*, eds. J. F. McGregor and B. Reay (Oxford, 1984), ch. 8, at p. 206.

[24] A. Hughes, 'Approaches to Presbyterian Print Culture: Thomas Edwards's *Gangraena* as Source and Text', in *Books and Readers in Early Modern England*, eds. E. Saver and J. Anderson (Pennsylvania, 2001), pp. 97–116 (I am very grateful to Professor Hughes for letting me see a pre-publication copy of her chapter).

[25] Ibid., p. 102.

[26] Ibid., p. 109.

inversion to early modern demonologists to create a binary opposition between the godly Presbyterians on the one hand and an unholy alliance of soldiers, sectaries and Independents on the other.[27] This not only gave the misleading impression that there was a community of radicals, as has been noted by critics of Hill (an impression aided by the habit of Edwards's targets to defend others who had incurred the heresiographer's ire), but also gave an artificial cohesion to the Presbyterian camp. Recent accounts of puritanism under the early Stuarts, especially Tom Webster's, have stressed the absence of a doctrinal commitment to Presbyterianism in England pre-1641.[28] Even after fear of the sectaries had led conservatives to unite around a Presbyterian system as the best means to enforce conformity in belief and practice, they remained divided over important issues such as the role of secular authority in any religious settlement.[29]

Edwards's reading of the Covenant as a document committing England to a Presbyterian church was as much a careful literary construct as his depiction of the radical sects. The reality was that the Covenant was a far more ambiguous document than Edwards would admit. As we have seen, when the Solemn League and Covenant had been taken by MPs in St Margaret's, Westminster, the Independent Philip Nye had told the congregation, in the presence of the Scots commissioners, that the kirk would not inevitably be the model for reformation south of the border. The Scottish, he insisted, must be prepared to learn from their southern neighbours if the English reformation was found to be more in harmony with God's word. Even a Presbyterian like Thomas Case was keen to assure his parishioners that, in taking the Covenant, they were not binding themselves to the imposition of a foreign style of church government. The heavy emphasis on the rooting out of heresy and schism was a product of the debates of 1644 and 1646. It had not been evident in the initial sermons urging the taking of the Covenant, which had instead stressed its importance in uniting the people against the forces of the popish anti-Christ. Indeed, the second clause of the Covenant emphasised the need to remove popery and prelacy far more than it did heresy and schism.

We are not here merely dealing with two partisan readings of the Covenant, one restrictive and one liberal, hastily constructed to meet the needs of different sides in the wider debate about liberty of conscience of which *Gangraena* was part. In the case of two of the radical authors discussed, John Saltmarsh and Henry Burton, their comments on the Covenant in 1646 were built on earlier commitments to the idea of a national covenant. Both Saltmarsh and

---

[27] On inversion in early modern Europe see N. Z. Davies, *Society and Culture in Early Modern France* (London, 1975); S. Clark, 'Inversion, Misrule and the Meaning of Witchcraft', *Past and Present*, 87 (1980), 99–106.

[28] Webster, *Godly Clergy*, esp. pt IV.

[29] Hughes, 'Approaches', p. 109.

Burton underwent considerable shifts in their religious outlook from the beginning to the end of their careers: the former moving from Anglicanism to puritanism to mystical antinomianism; the latter moving from conformity to non-conformity to semi-separatism. J. C. Davis has rightly warned us against imposing a posthumous radicalism upon the whole of an individual's life when we are really only talking about radical 'moments'.[30] This is particularly necessary in the ideologically fluid environment of mid-1640s England, when individuals often moved from one loose-knit group to another. As we shall see, however, despite the changes in their religious beliefs, neither Burton nor Saltmarsh recanted upon their earlier commitment to an English national covenant.

Henry Burton, after graduating from St John's College, Cambridge, served as clerk of the closet to Henry, Prince of Wales. In his short life, Charles I's older brother developed an iconography and courtly literature that portrayed him as an aggressive champion of Protestantism, a youthful English Gustavus Adolphus. Burton was in tune with the tone of the prince's court, writing a treatise on the Book of Revelation for his master. However, the premature death of the prince left Burton in a court far out of touch with his own religious sensibilities. He wrote to Charles warning him of the dangerous influence of spiritual advisers like Laud and Neile, but the new king responded only by dismissing him from his service.[31]

At first Burton continued, in print at least, to profess his loyalty to both the king and the national church (though not the Laudian form of it). His interest in apocalypticism was, however, evident in his early sermons, stating in 1627 that Antichrist had 'come to his full height' and would now 'adventure his Kingdome, in one maine battle'.[32] England's 'safety and security' depended at this point on cleaving fast to God, by reviving 'our Covenant with him by our holy vowes of reformation and better obedience'.[33] He continued to attack the king's spiritual advisers and, in the first work to bring him public notoriety, *Israel's Fast* (1628), suggested the device of a 'solemn generall Covenant sealed by particular sacred oath to each member of the Three Estates in Parliament' as a means to uncover the dividing Achans 'lurking amongst you'.[34] The call was repeated in 1629, when he urged Parliament to entreat the king to set up a 'publicke weekly fast and humiliation for the renewing of our Covenant with God, never to be broken againe'. The idea of a covenant was clearly linked

---

[30] J. C. Davis, 'Radical Lives', *Political Science* 37 (1985), 166–72.
[31] H. Burton, *A Narration of the Life* (1643), pp. 2–3; R. T. Hughes, 'Henry Burton: The Making of a Puritan Revolutionary', *Journal of Church and State*, 16 (1974), 421–35.
[32] H. Burton, *The Baiting of the Pope's Bull* (1627), p. 37.
[33] Ibid., To the Reader.
[34] H[enry]. B[urton]., *Israels Fast, or a Mediation upon the Seventh Chapter of Joshua* (1628), A3 (Burton controversially included the king as one of the three estates). Burton was questioned by the Commissioners for Causes Ecclesiastical for having failed to get this book licensed, *CSPD*, 1628–9, p. 533.

to the embarrassing failure of Charles I's foreign policy. These measures, along with the ejection of Catholics from the court and stricter censorship of popish books, were needed to regain 'our English credit, now shamefully trampled under our enemies insulting foot'.[35]

Throughout Burton's sermons of the late 1620s he had emphasised the need for England to renew its covenant with God.[36] Until at least the early 1630s he still saw himself as an orthodox divine acting within the Church of England, defending it from Laudian heterodoxy. In 1631, he published a treatise dedicated to Charles I attacking antinomianism.[37] However, by October 1634 it had been reported that Burton had preached a seditious sermon at the private church in Colchester of Thomas Cotton, labelled 'a great depraver of government'.[38] By the time his sermons For God and the King were published in 1636, he was identifying himself as a puritan.[39] He continued to see England in a covenanted relationship with God and lamented the lack of solemn fasting in England.[40] It was these two sermons which led to Burton's suspension from his living of St Matthew's, Friday Street and to his famous punishment along with William Prynne and John Bastwick.[41] According to R. T. Hughes, by 1638 Burton was urging popular resistance to popish innovations.[42]

By the early 1640s Burton was openly advocating the setting up of covenanted Congregational churches alongside the existing parochial structure, most famously in his The Protestation Protested (1641). Like George Lawrence, Burton argued that the term popery in the Protestation was to be read in the broadest sense possible.[43] In a sermon before Parliament given on 20 June the same year, Burton stated that the Protestation was made not only against recent popish innovations, but also against those 'that have been in the Church of God, ever since the Apostles, . . . that are in the sight of God, Idolatrous and against scripture'. He hoped that the Protestation would not be read in a more narrow sense and made 'like a Bee without a sting'.[44] Those that had taken the Protestation did not need to wait for a 'generall Reformation over the whole Land' before making their own efforts to reform the church. Burton took the Protestation as giving carte blanche to individuals to take direct action in this respect, an opinion that the research of John Walter suggests was highly influential. Burton went so far as to accuse those who waited on the Parliament before acting to be making a mockery of their vow. For Burton, popery now

---

[35] H. Burton, Babel no Bethel (1629), Epistle Dedicatory.

[36] See also H[enry]. B[urton]., The Christians Bulwarke Against Satans Battery (1632), A3.

[37] The Law and the Gospell Reconciled (1631).

[38] CSPD, 1634–5, p. 253.

[39] For God and the King (1636), pp. 130–1.

[40] Ibid., pp. 14, 144–5.

[41] Burton, Narration of the Life, pp. 9–10; CSPD, 1636–7, pp. 198, 360.

[42] Hughes, 'Burton', p. 431.

[43] For Lawrence see above, p. 65.

[44] H. Burton, Englands bondage and Hope of Deliverance (1641), p. 30.

included 'the Liturgie, Discipline, Government, Rites and Ceremonies of the Church of England'. Given the corruption of the national church, it was not only lawful, but a sworn duty to set up covenanted congregations. Far from scrupling at the Protestation, a document which, as has already been shown, was interpreted by many as an English national covenant, Burton eagerly supported it, seeing it as a call to begin immediately the work of root and branch reform.[45] He would continue to support the idea of a national covenant, as embodied in the Solemn League and Covenant, into the mid-1640s, though he distinguished between these covenants and church covenants which were 'about our own persons, as enquiring whether wee indeed are willing to give up our selves to the Lord Jesus'.[46]

John Saltmarsh was a far younger man than Burton and in 1640 was still a conforming minister, having taken the infamous 'etcetera' oath of 1640, opposition to which, as has already been noted, was an important factor in forging links between puritan clergy.[47] It seems that it was his family connections to Sir John Hotham which converted him to the Parliamentarian cause. Either these ties of kinship were not very strong, or Hotham had done too good a job in convincing Saltmarsh of the justice of the Parliament's war. As Royalist forces advanced over Yorkshire in early 1643, Saltmarsh fled from his living in West Heslerton to Hull where Hotham was the governor. There he learnt of his kinsman's growing discontentment with Parliament and the overtures he was making to Royalists about switching sides. Saltmarsh passed this information on to Parliament who indicted Hotham for treason, for which he was later executed.[48] Saltmarsh further testified to his zeal for the Parliamentarian cause in three pamphlets of 1643 which praised the Solemn League and Covenant in both verse and prose. He described national covenants as 'Divine Engines, which the godly have found to winde up their soules from irregular wanderings and strayings'.[49] Though the Covenant had been made in heaven it would bring down on earth 'cheerfull concurrences and contributions in both Kingdoms'.[50] He even composed the poem 'A Divine Rapture' extolling its virtues.[51] These benefits, though, would only be enjoyed if the nation remained faithful to the Covenant, and to ensure that this occurred the ministry would need to make frequent inculcations, even draw up catechisms, to remind the public of their duties.[52] Keeping faith with the

---

[45] The Parliament did not warm to his reading of the Protestation and ordered the book to be burned, Bodl. MS Tanner 66, f. 109; CSPD, 1641–3, p. 24.

[46] H. Burton, A Vindication of Churches Commonly Called Independent (1644), pp. 29, 43.

[47] See above, p. 48.

[48] 'The Memoirs and Memorials of Sir Hugh Cholmley of Whitby 1600–1657', ed. J. Binns, Yorkshire Archaeological Society, 153 (1997–8), p. 129 and n.

[49] Saltmarsh, Grand Covenant, p. 10.

[50] J. Saltmarsh, A Solemn Discourse upon the Sacred Covenant (1643), p. 3.

[51] In ibid., p. 8.

[52] Saltmarsh, Grand Covenant, pp. 69–70.

terms of the Covenant included, according to Saltmarsh, pursuing the war until its end could be fulfilled.[53]

Despite this militancy, it was clear as early as 1643 that Saltmarsh did not believe that the Covenant tied subscribers to establish a particular form of church government.[54] Before any new settlement could be effected the last vestiges of popery and prelacy had to be removed, even though they remained 'rivetted into our Laws and usages'.[55] By 1644, when he had moved from his Yorkshire living to Cranbrook in Kent, Saltmarsh was still describing the Parliament's 'Protestations and Covenants' as evidence of God's mercy to England and stating that 'Associations and Covenants' were very agreeable to the work of reformation.[56] Yet, he now also talked about the imminent end of all formal worship.[57] Saltmarsh, whilst not unequivocally defending the doctrine of free grace at this stage, argued that the works of heresiographers were only fanning the flames of controversy, not helping to eradicate error. In any case, Saltmarsh insisted, individuals needed to search their Covenant more fully to see if what they were prosecuting was really heresy.[58]

Saltmarsh later explicitly voiced his belief in the doctrine of free grace, viewed as rank heresy by Calvinist heresiographers like Edwards, but he retained a firm attachment to the idea of a national covenant. In his most famous and controversial work *Smoke in the Temple* (1646) Saltmarsh would offer a reinterpretation of the concept which would prove highly influential in Leveller thought. This redefinition will be discussed in greater detail below.

American liberal historiography of the 1930s and 1940s saw the notion of covenants as central to the development of the Levellers' political ideas, which in turn were seen as an important influence on the American constitution.[59] Leveller ideas provided the bridge between the gathered churches of the 'New England Way' and the moral ideals they were seen to enshrine, and the founding fathers of the American republic and the political ideas they espoused. In this symbiotic relationship between puritanism and liberty, the church covenants that bound congregations together were seen as offering the blueprint for the overtly political Leveller Agreements. A. S. P. Woodhouse, in his influential anthology *Puritanism and Liberty*, stated that 'Congregationalism . . . by emphasizing the idea of the covenant, preserved the possibility of a free and democratic church order.' Woodhouse followed A. D. Lindsay in seeing the gathered church as the nursery of democracy. Congregationalists quickly

---

[53] J. Saltmarsh, *A Peace but no Pacification* (1643), p. 9.

[54] Saltmarsh, *Grand Covenant*, p. 22.

[55] Ibid., p. 50; J. Saltmarsh, *Dawnings of Light* (1644), 'Considerations'.

[56] Ibid., pp. 63, 68.

[57] Ibid., p. 66.

[58] Ibid., pp. 75–9.

[59] *Leveller Manifestoes of the Puritan Revolution*, ed. D. M. Wolfe (New York, 1944), p. 4.

extended their religious covenant into a social covenant, like the charter and constitution of Providence Plantation.[60] Marxist historians like A. L. Morton, who also wanted to place the Levellers within a secular intellectual tradition, this time of English popular radicalism, readily adopted the conclusions of these liberal scholars. Morton saw the Agreements as the simple translation of the concept of the church covenant to the whole nation. Under the Agreement of the People 'England was to become a gathered nation, with a covenant . . . which was to be signed by all and was to guarantee the fundamental democratic rights and liberties of all.'[61] The idea that the Agreements of the People were a development from the organisational features of Congregationalism gained further credence with the research of Murray Tolmie into the relationship between the Leveller leaders and the sects. Tolmie found close links between William Walwyn and the city Independents, John Lilburne and the Particular Baptists and Richard Overton and the General Baptists. The Levellers relied heavily upon the gathered churches to print and distribute their political pamphlets and promote and sign their petitions.[62] For Tolmie the 'Leveller organisation had a deep sectarian taproot that shaped their aspirations and their polemic in a distinct way'.[63]

The notion that church covenants formed the basis for the Leveller Agreements has fallen by the wayside as the connections between puritanism, liberty and democracy (and the extent of political and religious radicalism in the New Model Army) have been challenged.[64] C. H. George launched the first assault on the notion that the roots of modern democracy lay in seventeenth century puritanism. He accused William Haller, A. S. P. Woodhouse and Don M. Wolfe of performing 'alchemistic tricks' by transmuting 'the base stuff of puritan piety into the gold of egalitarianism, individual liberty and tolerance.[65] William Lamont followed up George's criticisms. Lamont stated

---

[60] *Puritanism and Liberty Being the Army Debates (1647–9)*, ed. A. S. P. Woodhouse (2nd edn., London, 1974), pp. 74–6; similar comments were made by W. Haller, *The Rise of Puritanism* (London, 1957), p. 180.

[61] Morton, *World of the Ranters*, p. 14.

[62] M. Tolmie, *The Triumph of the Saints: The Separate Churches of London 1616–1649* (Cambridge, 1977), esp. chs. 7 and 8.

[63] Ibid., p. 144.

[64] M. Kishlansky, *The Rise of the New Model Army* (Cambridge, 1979); *idem*, 'The Army and the Levellers: The Roads to Putney', *Historical Journal*, 22 (1979); *idem*, 'The Case of the Army Truly Stated: The Creation of the New Model Army', *Past and Present*, 81 (1978); *idem*, 'Consensus Politics and the Structure of Debate at Putney', *Journal of British Studies*, 20 (1981); *idem*, 'What Happened at Ware?', *Historical Journal*, 25 (1982). For some qualifications to his approach, see A. Woolrych, *Soldiers and Statesmen: The General Council of the Army and Its Debates, 1647–1648* (Oxford, 1987); I. Gentles, *The New Model Army in England, Ireland and Scotland 1645–53* (Oxford, 1992); A. Laurence, *Parliamentary Army Chaplains: 1642–1651* (Woodbridge, 1990).

[65] C. H. George, 'Puritanism as History and Historiography', *Past and Present*, 41 (1968), 77–104.

that during the heated debates over religious toleration between 1644 and 1646, the opposing sides were still in agreement upon the need for godly discipline to restrain behaviour that could not be brought to enter the 'strait gate and narrow way' that led to Christ's kingdom.[66] For Lamont, the main aim of English puritans was the establishing of 'godly rule' not religious toleration. Lamont specifically attacked Haller, Lindsay and Woodhouse's argument that the gathered churches were essentially democratic institutions. On the contrary, Lamont argued, the 'impulse to form Independent congregations was, at root, disciplinarian in its nature, not libertarian: to create, not asylums from tyranny, but superior vehicles for godliness'.[67] J. C. Davis has argued that demands for liberty of conscience had very little to do with a belief in the inviolable intellectual rights of individuals, and had very much more to do with granting people the freedom to submit themselves to the governance of an arbitrary and omnipotent God. Toleration was about freeing possible agents of God's divine will from human interference.[68] Similarly, though the gathered churches may have demanded corporate autonomy, 'internally they were about discipline, orthodoxy and conformity'.[69]

As with a lot of revisionist historiography, the work of Lamont, Davis and George has suffered from its own success in destroying the explanations of the origins of Leveller democracy offered by liberal historiography. Along with the sloppy association of puritanism with liberty and democracy has gone the notion that the Leveller Agreements were social contracts extrapolated from church covenants. But this still leaves us with the problem of how the civilian Levellers came up with the idea of a written constitution. The preference of most current historians has been to suggest that it was an 'inspired improvisation, designed specifically to exploit the opportunity offered by a hearing before the General Council of the Army'.[70] Davis has suggested that the idea 'may have originated in the example of the army's Solemn Engagement of June 1647 rather than in covenant theology'.[71] Both Austin Woolrych and

---

[66] W. M. Lamont, 'Pamphleteering, the Protestant Consensus and the English Revolution', in *Freedom and the English Revolution: Essays in History and Literature*, eds. R. C. Richardson and G. M. Ridden (Manchester, 1986), pp. 72–93.

[67] Ibid., p. 78.

[68] J. C. Davis, 'Religion and the Struggle for Freedom in the English Revolution', *Historical Journal*, 35 (1992), 507–31.

[69] Ibid., p. 512. For an important corrective to these revisionist interpretations see J. Coffey, *Persecution and Toleration in Protestant England, 1558–1689* (Harlow, 2000), p. 57; see also idem, 'Puritanism and Liberty Revisited: The Case for Toleration in the English Revolution', *Historical Journal*, 41 (1998), pp. 961–85.

[70] Woolrych, *Soldiers and Statesmen*, p. 215.

[71] J. C. Davis, 'The Levellers and Christianity', in *Politics, Religion and the English Civil War*, ed. B. Manning (London, 1973), pp. 225–50, at p. 240. Professor Davis has also suggested that the army's Heads of Proposals may have offered a template for the Agreements. I thank him for his comments on these matters.

Davis have noted that there was little mention of an agreement in earlier Leveller literature.[72]

Contrary to Davis, the idea of an Agreement may indeed have emerged from covenant theology, though not from the example of covenants binding together congregations. One possible source for the idea of an Agreement suggested by Davis was the concept of a national covenant, but he noted that this had only been mentioned in one tract, Richard Overton's *The Arraignment of Mr. Persecution* (1645), and that this suggestion was not followed up in subsequent pamphlets.[73] In this tract, Overton noted that the spirit of persecution was destructive of 'all National Pacifications, Leagues and Covenants'.[74] To guard against this, he recommended that the magistrate 'ought to bind all Religions, that no Religion have power over another, that all in the Generall have Toleration'. This would be secured by a 'National Covenant . . . to engage all to this publicke freedome, that as all should be sharers in it, so all should be defenders of it'.[75] Overton was a satirist of great skill, and we must be wary of taking his words at face value. There was clearly some irony in the suggestion that a weapon of persecuting Presbyterians could be converted into a shield to defend religious freedom. However, other comments in this pamphlet place it amongst the Independent and sectarian defences of the Covenant that we have already discussed, including that of his fellow Leveller, William Walwyn. Overton suggested that there had been 'a Designe of blood in the Covenant'. Presbyterians had used Jesuitical subterfuge to get Independents to take the Covenant 'under the name of Reformation' and afterwards had infused 'the trayterous bloodthirsty spirit of Persecution into it'.[76]

Viewed in the context of other tolerationist readings of the Covenant, Overton's comments appear less isolated and ironic. Significantly, the call for a national covenant to defend liberty of conscience was repeated by John Saltmarsh in his *Smoke from the Temple*. Irenic in sentiment, Saltmarsh's work detailed the strengths and weaknesses of the positions put forward by each of the religious groups involved in the debate over toleration. Each had its flaws, but Saltmarsh suggested that this 'common weaknesse . . . may be a ground of common embodying and associating against this Common Enemy, or Grand Antichrist'.[77] This 'associating' would take the form of a 'Nationall Covenant for Liberty of Conscience'. It was only for God to judge men's conscience and there was no infallible human judge of what constituted heresy or popery,

---

[72] Ibid., p. 240; Woolrych, *Soldiers and Statesmen*, p. 215.

[73] Davis, op. cit.

[74] R. Overton, *The Arraignment of Mr. Persecution* ('Europe', 1645), p. 5.

[75] Ibid., p. 30.

[76] Ibid., pp. 35–6.

[77] Saltmarsh, *Smoke in the Temple*, p. 16: His interpretation of the Covenant was attacked by John Ley, *The New Quere, and Determination upon it, by Mr Saltmarsh Lately Published* (1646), 'The Epistle'.

therefore individuals were engaged by covenant to defend liberty of conscience. The magistrate would still have the power to judge in matters which 'go out from their meer spirituall condition into a morall offence'. In such cases, however, danger must be actually and expressly happening not simply suspected or implied.[78]

Saltmarsh was not a Leveller, but he was at this point chaplain to Fairfax's regiment of horse and was viewed as one of the most influential preachers in the New Model Army.[79] It seems plausible that Saltmarsh's call for a covenant for liberty of conscience, along with other tolerationist works on the Solemn League and Covenant, influenced the army in framing its 'Solemn Engagement' of June 1647.[80] The Engagement promised that it would be followed by a declaration that would vindicate the army from desiring 'the overthrow of Magistracy, the suppression or hindering of Presbytery, the establishment of Independent government, or upholding of a generall licentiousnesse in Religion under pretence of Liberty of Conscience'. The 'Representation of the Army' which justified the Engagement explicitly compared it to the action of the Scots who 'in the first beginning of these late differences associated in covenant from the very same principles and grounds' and, as they were 'therein justified and protected by their own and this kingdom also, so we justly expect to be'.[81] They again disclaimed any intention to overthrow Presbytery but asked that

> such who upon conscientious grounds may differ from the established forms, may not for that be debarred from the common rights, liberties, or benefits belonging equally to all as men and members of the commonwealth, while they live soberly, honestly, inoffensively towards others, and peacefully and faithfully towards the state.[82]

The Case of the Armie Stated (1647), an indictment of the Parliament's and to a lesser extent the army leadership's failure to keep their 'Engagement, Representations, Declarations and Remonstrances', was more explicit, demanding that 'all statutes enforcing the taking of oaths, as in townes corporate, the oath of supremacy, and wherein either the whole oaths, or some clauses in them, are burdens, and snares to conscientious people may be repealed and nulled'.[83]

---

[78] Saltmarsh, *Smoke in the Temple*, pp. 19–20.

[79] L. F. Solt, 'John Saltmarsh: New Model Army Chaplain', *Journal of Ecclesiastical History*, 2 (1951), 69–80, at p. 69. See also Morton, *World of the Ranters*, ch. 3.

[80] The pamphlet, *Englands Freedome, Souldiers Rights* (1647), referred to the Engagement as 'that Association', a term, as we have seen, closely allied to covenanting in England, Wolfe, *Leveller Manifestos*, p. 253.

[81] In Woodhouse, p. 404.

[82] Ibid., p. 409.

[83] Wolfe, *Leveller Manifestos*, p. 216; the tract was once assumed to have been written by John Wildman. Recently, however, John Morrill and Philip Baker have made a strong

The *Case of the Armie* and the first *Agreement of the People* were at the centre of the discussions that took place at Putney church in October 1647. As William Lamont has noted, the focus of earlier historians on the question of the extension of the franchise led them to practically ignore the first half of the debates which concern the obligation of covenants and engagements. Ireton represented the debate between the grandees and the agents and civilian Levellers as one between promise keepers and promise breakers.[84] Edward Sexby, on the other hand, urged that he would be a 'covenant-breaker' if he did not speak out at the meeting, considering the solemn obligations placed upon him as an agent.[85] Ireton complained that those that sought a new agreement, either in the Leveller document or *The Case of the Armie*, had been those that had made most of the obligation of the 'Solemn Engagement'. Contrary to the suggestions of John Wildman and Robert Everard, there was a need, Ireton said, to submit to unjust engagements, otherwise the principle would 'take away the force of this [very] engagement [if] it were entered into'.[86] Cromwell was more cautious, stating that it was 'an act of duty to break an unrighteous engagement; he that keeps it does a double sin' but that circumstantial considerations could mean that it was unwise to default on an engagement at a certain time.[87] John Morrill and Phil Baker suggest that, following prayer meetings to discern the hand of God in events, the grandees and agents were able to agree on a settlement based on the proposals in *The Case of the Armie*, whilst the civilian Levellers with their Agreement were left out in the cold.[88]

This, of course, was not the end of the idea of an agreement, and as the army leadership sought for a way to settle the kingdom after the second civil war, the device grew in its appeal. It is in the Second Agreement that we can see the closest parallels (noted by contemporaries) between these Leveller documents and the idea of a national covenant for liberty of conscience. The Second Agreement would have prohibited the representatives once elected from imposing any oaths or covenants which could be used to force the conscience, though they would be permitted to set up (non-compulsory) national forms

---

case for Edward Sexby as its writer, viewing it as an army document, not a Leveller piece, J. S. Morrill and P. Baker, 'The Case of the Armie Truly Re-Stated', *Putney Debates*, ed. Mendle, pp. 103–24. 'The Heads of Proposals' drawn up in August 1647 demanded that 'the taking of the Covenant be not enforced upon any, nor any penalties imposed on the refusers, whereby men might be constrained to take it against their judgements or conscience, but all orders or ordinances tending to that purpose to be repealed.' Woodhouse, p. 424. See also W. Walwyn, *Gold Tried in the Fire, or the Burnt Petition Revived* (1647) in *The English Levellers*, ed. A. Sharp (Cambridge, 1998), p. 82.

[84] Lamont, 'Puritanism, Liberty and the Putney Debates', pp. 243–5.
[85] Woodhouse, p. 75.
[86] Ibid., p. 11.
[87] Ibid., p. 16.
[88] Morrill and Baker, 'The Case of the Armie', pp. 114–15.

of worship.[89] At the same time, subscription to the Second Agreement was a prerequisite for exercising the vote in this version of the franchise. The Agreement thereby resolved the conundrum for the Levellers, that though they in principle favoured popular government, they were aware the majority might actually reject their political programme. So the Agreement would perform the function of previous covenants, to purge and exclude political opponents. Not without reason has Ian Gentles argued that this form of the Agreement 'would have ushered in something more resembling a dictatorship of the well-affected than a golden age of democracy'.[90] The exclusive nature of this projected settlement was picked up on by the 'seeker' William Erbury when the Agreement was debated at Whitehall in January 1649. He feared that 'as it was with the Parliament in [imposing] the Covenant that which they looked for to be for agreement proved to be a great disagreement amongst the nation'.[91] Ireton assured him that the Agreement was only meant as a testimony of the army's intentions and would not be administered upon compulsion.[92] In the 'Officers Agreement' presented to Parliament on 20 January 1649 the proposal that those that refused the Agreement would be disenfranchised was indeed dropped, though elaborate instructions for recording subscriptions were retained.[93] The final version of the Agreement, published by the imprisoned Leveller leaders on 1 May 1649, also left out the proviso that only subscribers would be eligible to vote. However, it retained as part of the 'reserves' the clause preventing magistrates from imposing oaths or covenants that were a burden on people's consciences. At the same time, endeavours to destroy the Agreement by force were made a capital offence.[94]

The idea of an agreement which would secure liberty of conscience against the fickle whims of Parliament, and also an unsympathetic populace, was not plucked out of the air in 1647. The notion of a national covenant for liberty of conscience had been the essence of tolerationist glosses upon the Solemn League and Covenant produced between 1644 and 1646, including those by Richard Overton and William Walwyn. The New Model Army had taken to the remedy of a 'Solemn Engagement' consciously paralleled with the Scottish National Covenant as a means, similarly, to protect its interests against the threats of a Presbyterian-dominated Parliament and possible betrayal by its leading officers. Even after the invasion of Scotland, the failure of the Leveller Agreements and the declaration of a republic, the army retained some sympathy

[89] Wolfe, *Leveller Manifestos*, p. 300.
[90] I. Gentles, 'The Agreements of the People and their Political Contexts, 1647–1649', in *The Putney Debates*, ed. Mendle, p. 162. T. N. Corns argues that Levellers adopted the stylistic conceit of the 'assumed collective voice' to cover this tension, *Uncloistered Virtue: English Political Literature 1642–1660* (Oxford, 1992), p. 135.
[91] Woodhouse, p. 171.
[92] Ibid., p. 172.
[93] Wolfe, *Leveller Manifestos*, pp. 344–6.
[94] *English Levellers*, ed. Sharp, pp. 173, 175.

for the idea of a national covenant. In the Declaration of Musselburgh, 1 August 1650, the New Model Army defended its taking of arms against its former allies. Many of the soldiers, it said, had rejoiced 'at the Covenant, because we found in it a strain towards these ends [of reformation]' though some saw that it was 'so mixed with worldly interest that they justly feared the interest of Jesus Christ would be only pretended to'. None the less, though they did not idolise the Covenant, the army would 'ever pursue its true and lawfull ends'. In this sense, it was justified in remaining in arms, until reformation 'according to the word of God' was effected.[95]

The Levellers were not the only political radicals to make use of the concept of a national covenant. The Digger leader Gerrard Winstanley was also able to reinterpret the Parliament's covenants as embodying a social contract between magistrates and people. George Sabine noted that the Solemn League and Covenant was central to Winstanley's political philosophy. Sabine felt that Winstanley took the Covenant 'as creating nothing less than a solemn personal obligation on every subscriber to effect a real reformation in England'. In a corporate sense, the Covenant also embodied a 'contract between Parliament and the common people for prosecuting the war against the King to recover England's fundamental liberties'.[96] J. C. Davis has recently restated the importance of the Solemn League and Covenant to Winstanley's thought.[97] It has long been noted that Winstanley's works, after the Digger colony had been founded on St George's Hill on 1 April 1649, take on a more politically engaged tone. In contrast to his mystical works of 1648, which Nigel Smith notes are free of the discussion of any social or political institutions, Winstanley started to introduce concepts like the 'Norman Yoke' and references to Parliament's ordinances and declarations.[98] I am not interested here in entering into the tired debate about whether Winstanley was a mystical or political writer, or whether there was a break in his thought between a religious phase up to 1648, and a communist phase post-1649. I do want to suggest, however, that the introduction of the Solemn League and Covenant into Winstanley's pamphlets was not simply a consequence of the Digger experiment. Rather, it was the most radical by-product of public subscription to these Parliamentary covenants.

The past few years have seen great advances in our knowledge of Winstanley's life. Thanks to the research of James Alsop, we know that Winstanley took

[95] Woodhouse, p. 476.
[96] *The Works of Gerrard Winstanley*, ed. G. H. Sabine (New York, 1941), pp. 54–5.
[97] Davis, 'Political Thought', pp. 380, 387; *idem* with J. D. Alsop, 'Gerrard Winstanley', forthcoming Oxford DNB article. I am very grateful to Professor Davis for letting me see pre-publication copies of his article.
[98] N. Smith, *Literature and Revolution in England 1640–1660* (New Haven, 1994), p. 175; C. Hill, 'The Religion of Gerrard Winstanley', *Past and Present Supplement*, 5 (1978), 49.

the Solemn League and Covenant in the parish of St Olave Jewry, London on 8 October 1643.[99] As Alsop correctly states, we cannot take this as offering any firm evidence of either Winstanley's religious or political convictions. In London he had been apprenticed to Sarah Gater, a devout woman but one whose piety was inspired by Arminians like Isaak Walton, the author of *The Compleat Angler*, not the Parliament's fast sermon preachers who extolled the virtues of the Covenant. John Gurney's suggestion that the preaching of the future Fifth Monarchist minister Christopher Feake may have influenced Winstanley seems shaky to say the least.[100]

Winstanley might then, as doubtless many other Londoners did, have taken the Covenant with little or no thought other than a desire to avoid the penalties set aside for refusing it. However, a reference in one of Winstanley's later pamphlets, *A Watchword to the City of London and the Army* (1649), hints at something more. Here he states that he was present when the Surrey ministers 'took it [the Covenant] with great zeal at Kingstone',[101] and we know that on 19 February 1644 the Committee of Safety for Surrey had ordered that all local officers should subscribe to the Covenant at Kingston upon Thames the next Saturday.[102] It is not clear why Winstanley was present at the taking of the Covenant in Kingston. This would have been the occasion when the local ministers and other parish officials took the Covenant before the document was sent out to individual parishes for subscription. Winstanley would not have had to be there, nor, as he had already taken the Covenant in London, would he have had to subscribe to it.[103]

It seems possible that at this stage, Winstanley was receptive to the rhetoric of covenanting ministers. We know from the biographer of the vicar of Kingston, Edmund Staunton, that there were separatists in Surrey at this time, and Winstanley's own parish of Cobham had a tradition of religious radicalism.[104] However, there is no actual evidence of Winstanley having any contact with local separatists, like John Fielder, until 1649.[105] Winstanley himself presented his conversion to a radical theology disowning an external heaven and hell

---

[99] J. D. Alsop, 'Revolutionary Puritanism in the Parishes? The Case of St. Olave, Old Jewry', *The London Journal*, 15 (1990), 29–37, at 30–1.

[100] J. Gurney, 'Gerrard Winstanley and the Digger Movement in Walton and Cobham', *Historical Journal*, 37 (1994), 775–802, at 795; Alsop, 'Revolutionary Puritanism', p. 30; *idem*, 'Gerrard Winstanley: What Do We Know of His Life?', in *Winstanley and the Diggers 1649–1999*, ed. A. Bradstock (London, 2000), pp. 19–37, at pp. 24–5.

[101] *Works*, ed. Sabine, p. 325.

[102] *CSPD*, 1644, p. 20. The minister of Barnes was recorded as having fled rather than administer the Covenant, Jones, *Conscience and Allegiance*, p. 130 and n.

[103] In the case of individuals who had subscribed elsewhere, ministers usually either entered testimonies to this fact or presented authenticating certificates in place of their signatures on parish lists.

[104] R. Mayo, *The Life and Death of Dr. Edmund Staunton* (1673), p. 12.

[105] Gurney, 'Digger Movement in Walton and Cobham', pp. 794–6.

and denying the bodily resurrection of Christ as a rapid and ecstatic process. He described his religious outlook prior to 1648 as that of a 'blind professor and strict goer to church, as they call it, and a hearer of sermons' believing then 'as the learned clergy . . . believed'.[106] From what we know, it seems likely that Winstanley's presence in Kingston was the result of the pious puritan habit of 'sermon gadding'.

From 1649 onwards, the Solemn League and Covenant appears regularly in Winstanley's and other Digger pamphlets. In *The True Levellers Standard* (1649) Winstanley complained that the Parliament had 'made the people take a Covenant and Oaths to endeavour a Reformation, and to bring in liberty, every man in his place; and yet while a man is in pursuing of that Covenant, he is imprisoned and oppressed'. In fact, the reciprocal nature of the Covenant meant that Parliament was bound to accede to the True Levellers' demands because of their 'Covenants and Promises'.[107] In *A Declaration from the Poor Oppressed People of England* (1649) Winstanley claimed that the need to make the land a common treasury was manifested by 'the National Covenant'.[108] Writing to Fairfax the same year, he asked whether it was not 'a great breach of the Nationall Covenant, to give two sorts of people their freedom, that is Gentry and Clergy, and deny it to the rest'. Those that did not endeavour reformation according to the word of God 'and that is the pure law of right-eousnesse before the fall' (meaning common ownership of the land) were, he said, covenant breakers.[109] The same point was made in *An Appeal to the House of Commons* (1649) where he accused those that did not 'restore to us that Primitive freedom in the earth' of being 'double-hypocrites' by breaking covenant both with men and God.[110] The Covenant was even integrated into Digger songs, with the verse 'The Diggers Mirth' stating that 'A Covenant they did take/And promises they did make/All burthens to remove/ And to unite in love/ Yet we cannot see that good hour/ The taking down of kingly power.'[111]

Winstanley's reading of the Covenant was the most radical yet and it might be asked whether we can really relate Winstanley's political vision in any meaningful way with the sermons and tracts produced in support of the Solemn League in 1643–4. Winstanley himself was certain, however, that he was only following the rhetoric of covenanting divines. These divines had 'in their sermons, most vehemently prest upon the people to take [it]'. The intent of these sermons had been, as Winstanley understood it, that

---

[106] Quoted in Hill, 'Religion of Gerrard Winstanley', p. 20.
[107] *Works*, ed. Sabine, pp. 255–7.
[108] Ibid., pp. 291–2.
[109] Ibid., p. 291.
[110] Ibid., pp. 305–6.
[111] 'The Diggers Mirth or Certain Verses Composed and Fitted to Tunes' (London, 1650), in *Digger Tracts, 1649–50*, ed. A. Hopton (London, 1989), p. 21.

every one in his severall place and calling, should endeavor the peace, safety and freedom of England, and that the Parliament should assist the people, and the people the Parliament and every one that had taken it, should assist those that had taken it, while they were in pursuit thereof, as in the sixth Article of the Nationall Covenant.

The Parliament was bound, therefore, to assist the Diggers in their efforts towards these ends.[112]

The idea of a covenant or oath acting as a social contract between magistrates and people remained part of Winstanley's political thought even after the failure of the Digger communes. His pamphlet urging taking the Engagement of loyalty to the commonwealth reinterpreted this promise of loyalty as guaranteeing regular parliaments and freedom from the oppression of the Norman Yoke (which Winstanley associated with the bringing in of private ownership of land). Along with acts abolishing monarchy and declaring a republic, the Engagement restored the birthright of Englishmen to the common land and allowed the people to choose their own representatives. If the Parliament acted contrary to this Engagement, then Winstanley said, 'the people may freely plead against them; and every Towne and County, may call these [the Rump] treacherous'.[113] The idea of a sworn contract of this sort reappears in Winstanley's last and most famous work, The Law of Freedom in a Platform (1652). In the dedication to Cromwell, Winstanley repeatedly stressed the need for the Lord General to fulfil the Parliament's promises and engagements.[114] Drawing a biblical analogy with the story of Jonah's gourd, Winstanley said that the 'worm in the Earth, now gnawing at the root of your Gourd, is Discontent, because Engagements and Promises made to them by such as have power, are not kept'.[115] In his scheme for 'Commonwealth Government' there was to be an engagement between the Parliament and the people: 'Do you maintain our Laws and Liberties, and we will protect and assist you.'[116] Following liberal historiography's assumptions about the religious basis of the Leveller Agreements, Gerald Aylmer suggested that Winstanley's whole scheme of government in The Law of Freedom could be compared to 'a covenant or contract, made by the members of a gathered church or even the whole community' similar to that adopted by the New England colonists.[117] As seems clear from Winstanley's own writings, the actual models were the oaths and

[112] Works, ed. Sabine, pp. 325–6.
[113] 'Englands Spirit Unfoulded, or an Incouragement to Take the Engagement: A Newly Discovered Pamphlet by Gerrard Winstanley', ed. G. E. Aylmer, Past and Present, 40 (1968), 3–16.
[114] Works, ed. Sabine, pp. 502–3.
[115] Ibid., p. 503.
[116] Ibid., p. 561.
[117] G. E. Aylmer, 'The Religion of Gerrard Winstanley', in Radical Religion, eds. McGregor and Reay, pp. 91–121, at pp. 111–12.

covenants imposed by the Long Parliament upon the nation in the 1640s and 1650s.

It is still possible to question how sincere Winstanley's attachment to the Covenant was. The more politically engaged nature of Winstanley's later works has been attributed to the influence of the Leveller-like pamphlets produced by the Digger commune in Iver, Buckinghamshire.[118] Some authors have stressed Winstanley's skill in adopting different modes of discourse for different audiences. This has usually been part of an argument that he was using religious language, talk of visions etc., as a screen for his political message (or vice versa, that political references masked what remained essentially religious aims). The picture of Winstanley presented by some historians, as that of a skilful manipulator of genres and styles, is unconvincing. He was certainly a gifted prose writer, but not gifted in the manipulation of form and text in the way that the Levellers were. This was, after all, a man who had answered charges of blasphemy levelled against himself and William Everard with the pamphlet *Truth Lifting Up Its Head* (1649). Here Winstanley spelt out his belief that those that worshipped a God at a distance, or a God of the scriptures, worshipped their 'own imagination, which is the Devil' and that when the apostles saw Christ rising from the grave this was 'onely a declaration in vision to them'.[119] These words were hardly likely to get Everard, or him, off the hook. Equally, it is difficult to see what the rhetorical value of placing so much faith in the Covenant would be in 1649 (when, as we will see, the Rump had practically disowned it), nor of reminding Cromwell of the obligation of the Engagement in 1652 (when it had become a virtual dead letter). It seems more likely that Winstanley, having heard covenanting ministers preach up the personal and corporate obligations of the Covenant, reinterpreted these injunctions to individual effort in the cause of reformation through the filter of his own, unique, mixture of millenarianism and agrarian communism.

The foregoing is not intended to obscure the fact that the repeated tendering of oaths and covenants of loyalty in the 1640s did lead some radical groups and individuals either to a highly circumspect attitude to sworn statements or to a complete disregard for the usual solemnities observed in swearing. The Anglican John Gauden noted that it was one of the major justifications used by the Quakers in support of this blanket prohibition that they had been

> scared from all Swearing by the frequent forfeited Oaths and repeated Perjuries of those Times, in which the cruel Ambitions and disorderly Spirits of some men, like the Demoniacal in the Gospel, brake all bonds of lawful Oaths, by which they were bound to God and the King; daily imposing, as any new Partie or Interest

---

[118] Hill, 'Religion of Gerrard Winstanley', p. 23.
[119] G. Winstanley, *Truth Lifting its Head Above Scandals* (2nd edn., 1650), pp. 1, 13.

prevailed the Superfoetations of new and illegal Oaths, monstrous Vows, factious Covenants, desperate Engagements, and damnable abjurations.[120]

Quakers saw oath taking as an example of the world's continuing apostasy from Christ's covenant. William Penn described swearing as a symptom of the 'Degeneration of Man from primitive Integrity' when 'Yea and Nay were enough; for when men grew corrupt, they distrusted each other, and had recourse to extraordinary Wayes to awe one another into Truth speaking.'[121] Disputing with Gauden the lawfulness of public oaths, another Quaker, Samuel Fisher, stated that swearing could only be necessary in a country 'where sin, perfidiousness, and deceit abound and increase'.[122]

Neither were all of the civilian Levellers amenable to the idea of a national covenant. John Lilburne (who later gravitated towards Quakerism himself) voiced his opposition to nationally imposed oaths of loyalty in several of his tracts.[123] In his *Innocency and Truth Justified* (1645) Lilburne stated that he had left the New Model Army when swearing to the Solemn League and Covenant was made a requirement of all officers in 1644.[124] He argued that though the Covenant demanded the extirpation of popery, the tithe-supported church it would help establish was 'one of the greatest branches of popery that ever was established in Rome'. Presbytery itself was simply another form of prelacy.[125] Lilburne's greatest attack on oaths of loyalty in general came in his *Rash Oaths Unwarrantable* (1647). Here he used the oaths imposed by the Long Parliament as evidence of the two Houses' hypocrisy. The Parliament had declared that its actions were governed by the need to provide for the 'safety and weale' of the people. The Commons insisted that this occasionally forced the Parliament to depart from the written law. Yet at the same time, Lilburne noted, the two houses had imposed 'illegal, devilish, impossible to be kept contradictory Oaths, and covenants' which, 'without any provisos, cautions, limitations, or declared exceptions and reservations', tied the people

---

[120] J. Gauden, *A Discourse Concerning Publick Oathes, and the Lawfulness of Swearing in Judicial Proceedings* (1662), p. 9.

[121] [W. Penn], *A Treatise of Oaths Containing Several Weighty Reasons Why the People Call'd Quakers Refuse to Swear* (n. pl., 1675), p. 9.

[122] S. Fisher, *Episkopos Aposkopos, The Bishop Busied Beside the Businesse* (n. pl., 1662), p. 32; on Quaker attitudes to swearing see C. W. Horle, *The Quakers and the English Legal System 1660–1688* (Pennsylvania, 1988), p. 4.

[123] B. Reay, *The Quakers and the English Revolution* (London, 1985), pp. 19–20.

[124] J. Lilburne, *Innocency and Truth Justified; First Against the Unjust Asperation of W. Prinn* (n. pl., 1645), p. 46; Sir Oliver Luke reported that there was widespread opposition in the Commons to imposing the Covenant on New Model Army officers, 'The Letter Books of Sir Samuel Luke', ed. H. G. Tibbutt, *Bedfordshire Historical Society*, 42 (1963), 435, 438–9. Samuel Luke felt that the imposition of this ordinance would not cause problems provided 'they [the officers] may be their own interpreters' Ibid., p. 140).

[125] J. Lilburne, *Englands Birth-Right Justified Against All Arbitrary Usurpation, Whether Royall or Parliamentary* (1646), pp. 13–14.

to maintain the law of the land. The oaths themselves were not in agreement. Concurring with Royalist writers, Lilburne stated that it was 'impossible for any man breathing' to take the Solemn League and Covenant and not break the Oaths of Allegiance and Supremacy. The Negative Oath (which the Parliament required of Royalist soldiers seeking quarter) would make all that surrendered perjurers, being 'point blank' against the Oath of Allegiance. Finally Lilburne quoted Christ's prohibition of swearing in Matthew 5: 33–7, confirmed in James 5: 12, to show that there was no justification for promissory oaths either public or private from the New Testament.[126]

However, this ban on oath taking and swearing was less complete than it appeared at first sight. Elements of Lilburne's own position also seem to have more in common with the traditional puritan scruples over oaths than the blanket prohibitions of swearing made by the Quakers. In particular, his complaint against the Oath of Supremacy, that its wording seemed to place the monarch above God, was reminiscent of those made by some Elizabethan puritans.[127] It was noticeable too that Lilburne did not make a blanket prohibition of swearing in *Rash Oaths*. He stated that Christ 'that hath said Thou shalt not kill, hath also said, thou shalt not *in that manner* [my emphasis] swear'. Lilburne admitted the lawfulness of assertory oaths (that is, oaths concerning matters that have already come to pass) 'for confirmation of that truth which a man delivers for the ending of all strife'.[128] In a later pamphlet, Lilburne agreed to take the Engagement provided that he might be allowed to declare 'before all the people the grounds of my doing so'.[129] Finally, though he may have had grave misgivings over the lawfulness of making sworn statements, Lilburne had no doubt about the reality of the divine punishments that would accompany the breach of oaths and covenants. Along with the Presbyterians Willliam Prynne and John Vicars, Lilburne used the example of the covenant between Vladislaus and Amurath as a warning to those who would swear fast and loose.[130]

Independents and Leveller writers, rather than repudiate the Solemn League and Covenant once it became an emblem of conservative Presbyterians, chose instead to offer their own glosses upon it. These tolerationist readings of the Covenant, including those by the Levellers William Walwyn and Richard Overton, in turn, informed the creation of the army's 'Solemn Engagement'

---

[126] J. Lilburne, *Rash Oaths Unwarrantable; and the Breaking of Them as Inexcusable* (1647), pp. 9, 14, 16–18.

[127] Lilburne, *Rash Oaths*, pp. 14–15; M. Adams, 'Peter Chamberlen's Case of Conscience', *Huntington Library Quarterly*, liii (1990), 281–311, at 287.

[128] Lilburne, *Rash Oaths*, pp. 17–18.

[129] J. Lilburne, *The Engagement Vindicated and Explained or the Reasons upon Which Lieutenant Colonel John Lilburne Tooke the Engagement* (1650).

[130] Lilburne, *Rash Oaths*, p. 11.

and the 'Agreements of the People'. These would have established in concrete terms the 'National Covenant for Liberty of Conscience' advocated in John Saltmarsh's *Smoke in the Temple*. Gerrard Winstanley also intermingled the concept of a national covenant with his own political and theological ideas as a result, it has been argued, of exposure to the rhetoric of covenanting divines earlier in his life. In the case of both Winstanley and the Levellers, they took the emphasis in covenanting sermons on the involvement of the individual subscribers as an invitation to active political agency. The mixed-government ideas that were often combined with the theological arguments helped instil the notion too that this was a secular as well as a religious contract. In these Leveller and Digger writings we can see the full implications of Parliament's 'mass mobilisation of citizenship' being realised. In their different ways, the Levellers and Diggers saw these documents as not only involving spiritual obligations, but also bestowing extensive political and economic rights upon subscribers.

7

The Covenant, the execution of Charles I and the English republic

From 1646 to 1647, the Covenant came to be clearly identified with a conservative political and religious programme that urged a negotiated peace with the king, the disbandment of the New Model Army, the suppression of religious sects and the enforcement of a Presbyterian church settlement. The 'tolerationist' readings made of the Covenant by some Independents were severely tested. The end of the first civil war saw an increasing emphasis not only amongst Presbyterian ministers but also the self-titled 'covenant-engaged' citizens of the city of London upon the obligations of the Solemn League and Covenant. This reflected genuine enthusiasm for Presbyterianism in some parishes, and the influence of Scottish divines, via Sion College and the Westminster Assembly, with changes in the parochial organisation occurring before the formal establishment of the new church.[1] However, as Valerie Pearl demonstrated, other important elements in stirring up popular support for the Presbyterian movement were largely secular in origin: namely, fear of the army, (especially fear of property destruction and the consequences of billeting of the army on the city) and the burden of taxes.[2] A petitioning campaign by the High Presbyterian party in the city, in co-ordination with 'Peace Party' MPs and peers such as Denzil Holles and the Earl of Essex, tapped into this body of support. Religious grievances were given a prominent place in these petitions, including demands for an altogether stricter church, the outlawing of separatist congregations, punishment for heresy and exclusion from office not only of those who refused the Covenant but all who were disaffected to its ends. The petition produced by Common Council on 29 December 1646 complained that there were 'some officers, and many common soldiers of the Army, who either have never taken the covenant, or are disaffected to the Church government'.[3] On 8 February, the Lords bowed to city pressure and

---

[1] V. Pearl, 'London's Counter-Revolution', in *The Interregnum*, ed. G. E. Aylmer (1978), ch. 1, pp. 32–4.
[2] Ibid., pp. 37–9.
[3] *To the Right Honourable the Lords and Commons Assembled in the High Court of Parliament* (1646).

voted that anyone refusing the Covenant should be barred from both civil and military posts.[4]

The political pressure exerted by city Presbyterians and conservatives in Parliament culminated in Holles's plan for a counter-revolutionary coup in the summer of 1647. As part of this scheme, Holles wanted not only to disband the New Model Army, linked as it was with political Independents and religious radicals, but also to create an alternative fighting force made up of 'reformadoes' (former Parliamentary and Royalist soldiers now in London), 'safe' units of the New Model and the trained bands of London. As part of this project Independents such as Fowke and Pennington were removed from the city Militia Committee and replaced with men closely linked to the Presbyterians. Money to cover the army's pay arrears was redirected to funding the reformadoes. The plot was brought out into the open by Cornet Joyce's seizure of the king for the army, and the army's subsequent move on London. The political hierarchy of the Presbyterian party went on the back foot, eleven members of Parliament were charged with conspiracy and the acceptance of bribes, including Denzil Holles and Sir John Clotworthy, and the London militia was wrested out of the hands of the Presbyterians. These actions prompted large number of Londoners to sign the so-called Solemn Engagement of the city by which they swore to bring the king to London to treat with Parliament, to restore him to his rights and to implement the Covenant. The Engagement was denounced by Parliament, but two days later on 26 July both houses were invaded by a counter-revolutionary mob which forced Parliament to repeal acts passed that month, restore the eleven members and invite the king back to London. A day of humiliation was observed at the Guildhall in which Simeon Ashe, Edmund Calamy and Cornelius Burges preached. These actions prompted the army to occupy London, ostensibly to restore order to the capital and protect the integrity of Parliament. The Presbyterian dominated Parliament, however, remained less than grateful, it taking three attempts in August for a motion from the Lords vindicating the actions of Fairfax and the army to pass the lower house.[5]

In 1648 a mass petitioning movement of ministers reaffirmed their faith in the Solemn League and Covenant, and their loyalty to the clause promising to defend the king's person and authority, prompted by the issuing of a testimony from the London Presbyterian ministers in December 1647.[6] These petitions often complained of the interpretations of the Covenant made by

---

[4] Pearl, 'Counter-Revolution', p. 44.

[5] R. Ashton, *The English Civil War, Conservatism and Revolution 1603–1649* (1978), pp. 300–2; see also *idem, Counter-Revolution: The Second Civil War and its Origins, 1646–8* (New Haven, 1994), chs. 8 and 9.

[6] *A Testimony to the Truth of Jesus Christ, and to Our Solemne League and Covenant . . . Subscribed by the Ministers of Christ Within the Province of London* (1648). Ministers in Essex, Gloucestershire, Shropshire, Lancashire, Staffordshire, Northamptonshire and Devon made similar testimonies.

Independent ministers. A supporting petition from the 'citizens and inhabitants of London' stated that they took the Covenant in the 'plain, literall, grammatical sense of it' 'abominating all other glosses upon it'.[7]

The decisive break came as Charles, with Scottish forces, waged war against the Parliament in July 1648. For the republican MP Henry Marten, the Scottish invasion represented a fundamental breach of the two nations' mutual covenant. He argued that the Covenant had never been intended to bind England and Scotland indefinitely 'but like an Almanack of the last yeer . . . shews us rather what we have done, then what we be now to do'.[8] Presbyterians responded with a number of tracts denouncing the apostasy of many politicians in apparently breaking their covenants. John Vicars, the Presbyterian school-master and poet, was especially preoccupied with the execution of divine judgement, usually fatal and often grisly, against covenant breakers. His *A Caveat for Covenant-contemners and Covenant-breakers* (1648) reproduced the text of the Solemn League and Covenant with bordering marginalia of 'Scripture Terrours and Threatenings to Covenant Breakers and Despisers'. This was accompanied with a historical example of punishment for breach of covenant, the case of King Vladislaus of Hungary. Vladislaus was decapitated in battle and his head set on a pike for breaking his holy covenant with the Turkish leader Amurath. Evidently there were divine punishments even for breaking covenants with the forces of Antichrist.[9]

As Eliot Vernon has demonstrated, following the Parliament's victory in the second civil war Presbyterian writers used the Covenant to argue that the army was unjustified in pressing for the king to be brought to justice. In fact, the Presbyterian opposition to the trial of the king was far more overt and vocal than that mounted by Royalists, being expressed in three open letters: the *Serious and Faithful Representation*, the *Apologeticall Declaration* and the *Vindication of the Ministers of the Gospel*.[10] The authors of the lay Presbyterian document the *Apologeticall Declaration*, printed on 24 January 1649, stated that having sworn to defend the king's person, now under threat from an illegal trial, they were forced to plead against it to discharge their consciences, to 'wash our hands and clear our innocence in the sight of God'.[11] Thomas Watson, minister of St Stephen, Walbrook, announced to the post-purge Commons on 27 December that 'We act against God, when we act against his

---

[7] *The Hearty concurrence of the citizens and inhabitants of the city of London, with the ministers of the province thereof . . . to our solemn league and covenant* (Edinburgh, 1648), p. 6.
[8] H. Marten, *The Independency of England Endeavored to be Maintained* (1648), p. 11. For similar accusations see *The Scots Apostacy Displayed in a Treacherous Invasion of the English* (1648), p. 1.
[9] This seems to have been a popular example, see above, p. 155.
[10] E. Vernon, 'The Quarrel of the Covenant: The London Presbyterians and the Regicide', in *The Regicides and the Execution of Charles I*, ed. J. Peacey (Basingstoke, 2001), ch. 9.
[11] *An Apologeticall Declaration of the Conscientious Presbyterians of the Province of London* (1649), pp. 6–7, 9.

Covenant' adding that 'Breach of Covenant is no better than perjury, and if we breake the Oath, look that God should make good the curse.' Other Presbyterian ministers admitted that the king had committed 'many and very great ... wofull miscarriages' so that he was 'cast down from his Excellency into a horrid pit of misery'. Yet this did not absolve men from obedience to the Solemn League and Covenant: it was a righteous oath made with God, not the king, and to break it would 'provoke the wrath of the Lord'.[12] The threat of divine punishment for breach of covenant was a recurring theme of Presbyterian pamphlets: 'For what greater sinne can there be, then for a Nation to breake their Vow and Covenant with their God? and Nationall sinnes, always have Nationall punishments attending them.'[13] Some Presbyterian authors went to the extent of backtracking on the earlier use of theories of limited monarchy and mixed-government to support taking the Covenant. Mary Pope urged that the king was only accountable to God and indeed effectively undid the Parliament's case of the last six years by arguing it was they and not Charles who had been the original aggressors.[14]

After Pride's Purge and the execution of the king, the Rump itself declared that the obligation of the Covenant, at least as it extended to Scotland, had been annulled. The MPs stated that they could conceive that there was little reason for the Scots 'to object the breaking thereof [the Solemn League and Covenant] unto us, being wholly broken, and all Treaties with it, by that National Invasion'.[15] John Canne, the radical divine who had written in defence of Charles's trial and execution, urged the Parliament to repeal the oath. The Covenant, he argued, would only act as a bone of contention between rival factions:

Every side justifies it self, and chargeth the other with a breach: And without doubt the contention about this Covenant will continue, yea I fear rise higher, and break out into greater flame if the right way be not wisely taken: for so long as the lawfulnesse of the Oath is not questioned, but rather a pleading for keeping it, the differences can never be reconciled or taken up.[16]

Though the Rump Parliament did not formally repeal the Covenant, a fact that would later assume great significance, the Commonwealth felt it necessary

---

[12] Vernon, 'Quarrel', p. 214.

[13] *The New Allegiance or the Subjects Duty to their King upon their Protestation, Oath and Covenant* (1648), p. 1.

[14] [Mary Pope], *Heare, Heare, Hear, a Word or Message from Heaven, to All Covenant Breakers (Whom God Hates)* (1648), pp. 2, 6–7. Also published as *Behold Here is a Word; or an Answer to the Late Remonstrance of the Army* (Jan 24th 1648[9]).

[15] *A Declaration of the Parliament of England, in Answer to the Late Letters Sent to Them from the Commissioners of Scotland* (1648 [22 Feb. 1649]), p. 22.

[16] J. Canne, *The Snare is Broken. Wherein is Proved by Scripture, Law and Reason, that the Nationall Covenant and Oath was Unlawfully Given and Taken* (1649), 'To the right honourable, the Commons.'

to produce a new test of loyalty to the republican regime. The Council of State had discussed framing an engagement of loyalty to the Commonwealth as early as March 1649.[17] On 11 October 1649 it was finally decided that all members must subscribe to an Engagement in which they would 'declare and promise' to be 'true and faithful to the Commonwealth of England, as the same is now established without a King, or House of Lords'.[18] Some attempt at leniency was made, with the deponent only required to make a declaration, not a sworn statement, of his loyalty. In addition, the oath had originally required the subscriber to swear to the Commonwealth, as it was now established 'against a King and Lords'. This was changed in the revised version to the less politically charged 'without a King and Lords'. The Parliament was aware that some would view the Engagement as contrary to oaths and covenants they had previously taken. On 24 October 1649 a committee was appointed 'to take into consideration all former Engagements made from the Beginning of this Parliament'. The committee was to inform the Parliament 'what is fit to be done therein; to take away Misconstructions that are put upon them, and to undeceive the people therein'. Nevertheless, in drafting the act for nationwide subscription to the Engagement (finally passed in January 1650) a motion was voted down that requested a declaration be published, 'to satisfy the People, That the Engagement is not against the former Protestation and Covenant'. A proviso was also struck out which would have given immunity 'to such Persons that have constantly adhered to the Parliament . . . who shall not take and subscribe the said Engagement', provided they gave a promise of good behaviour before 1 March 1650.[19] The Rump had made clear, at least in this instance, that promises of passive obedience would not be deemed adequate. Those who refused the Engagement, irrespective of any protestations of past loyalty, would be denied the protection of the law.[20]

Discussions of the controversy over the imposing of an Engagement of loyalty to the Commonwealth largely focus on the arguments made for and against allegiance to de facto powers centred on the Pauline injunction

---

[17] S. Barber, 'The Engagement of Loyalty to the Council of State and the Establishment of the Commonwealth Government', *Historical Research*, cl (1990), 44–58. The oath of the Lord Mayor of London, JPs and sheriff was changed to bind the swearer to obey the Commonwealth, *The Parliamentary or Constitutional History of England from the Earliest Times to the Restoration of King Charles II* (24 vols., London, 1768), xx, 96–8. *CJ*, vi, 135, 136, 140, 142.

[18] Ibid., vi, 306.

[19] Ibid., vi, 337, 339.

[20] B. Worden, *The Rump Parliament* (Cambridge, 1974), pp. 226–32; *Acts and Ordinances*, ii, 325–7. Nonetheless, some Presbyterians made exactly these kinds of declarations, promising good behaviour under the new regime but refusing to subscribe to the Engagement for fear of breaking previous oaths and covenants. Petitions were sent to the Rump from heads of houses at both Oxford and Cambridge, and from Presbyterian ministers in London; Bodl. MS Wood F35, f. 358; Bodl. MS Tanner 66, f. 40–2.

to obedience given in Romans 13: 1–2. Quentin Skinner saw this debate as the English context for the writing of Hobbes's *Leviathan*. Margaret Judson suggested that these pamphlets, especially the works of Anthony Ascham, represented a new, more secularised, kind of political thought.[21] The controversy over *de facto* powers was not, though, as Glenn Burgess has shown, the sole or perhaps even the dominant theme in this debate.[22] For many Anglicans and Presbyterians the issue of whether they continued to be bound by previous oaths and covenants, and were thereby forsworn if they took the Engagement, was of greatest importance. Anglicans feared that by taking the Engagement they would be breaking the Oaths of Allegiance and Supremacy, which bound them to give allegiance, not only to the king, but also to his rightful heirs and successors. Presbyterians balked at taking a declaration of loyalty to the Commonwealth that seemed in contradiction to the third clause of the Solemn League and Covenant. There was, then, a significant element of the debate that was concerned not with *de facto* powers but with the obligations of oaths and covenants upon the conscience.

The greatest opposition to the Engagement came from Presbyterians who felt that to promise to be true and faithful to the Commonwealth would be a breach of the Solemn League and Covenant, in particular the clause promising to defend the king's person and authority. By forswearing themselves in taking an Engagement prejudicial to a former covenant they would be guilty of perjury. One Presbyterian author insisted that the Solemn League and Covenant was perpetual 'so that nothing but death, which dissolveth the knot between our Bodies and our Souls, can dissolve this Covenant'.[23] Edward Gee reminded the Parliament that subjects were under both 'the morall tye of subjects duty; and the Religious bond of sworne Covenants, so even if the Engagement was lawful not withstanding it is unlawfull to us and we are bound out from it.'[24] One writer described the 'Engagers' as 'the new Independent Jesuits of our Age', as for them 'no Oathes, Obligations, Divine or Civill by the Lawes of God and Man are bynding'.[25] William Prynne spared no effort in denouncing former advocates of the Covenant such as John Dury and Joseph Caryl who now

---

[21] M. A. Judson, *From Tradition to Political Reality* (Ohio, 1980); Q. Skinner, 'History and Ideology in the English Revolution', *Historical Journal*, viii (1965), 151–78; idem, 'The Ideological Context of Hobbes's Political Thought', *Historical Journal*, ix (1966), 286–317; idem, 'Conquest and Consent: Thomas Hobbes and the Engagement Controversy', in *The Interregnum*, ed. G. E. Aylmer (London, 1972), pp. 79–98; J. M. Wallace, 'The Engagement Controversy 1649–52: An Annotated List of Pamphlets', *Bulletin of the New York Public Library*, lxviii (1969), 385–465; idem, *Destiny His Choice: The Loyalism of Andrew Marvell* (Cambridge, 1968), pp. 9–69.

[22] G. Burgess, 'Usurpation, Obligation and Obedience in the Thought of the Engagement Controversy', *Historical Journal*, xxix (1986), 515–37.

[23] *A Pack of Old Puritans Maintaining the Unlawfulness and Inexpediency of Subscribing the New Engagement* (1650), p. 23.

[24] [E. Gee], *A Plea for Non-Scribers* (1650), p. 35.

[25] *Vox Veritatis* (n. pl., 1650), A2.

worked as promoters of the new regime. Prynne described Dury as a 'divine of many editions' who had first dallied with bishops, then with Presbyterians and had now finally turned to Independency.[26]

As in the debate over the trial and execution of the king, Presbyterians were keen to play up the divine punishments that would befall covenant breakers. Prynne used Thomas Beard's *The Theatre of God's Judgements* (1597) and Richard Knolles's *The Generall Historie of the Turkes* (1603) to outline the harsh punishments that God reserved for covenant breakers.[27] John Vicars's posthumously published *Dagon Demolished* (1660) offered *Twenty Admirable Examples of God's Severe Justice and Displeasure Against the Subscribers of the Late Engagement.* Vicars detailed the unpleasant ends of those who had broken their covenant to defend the king's person and authority by taking the promise of loyalty to the English Commonwealth. He recounted the fate of Sir Henry Holcroft, once a great 'Professour of Religion', who, by taking the Engagement of loyalty to the Commonwealth, became an 'Independent apostate'. For these sins Holcroft was afflicted with a 'sore disease, much and often bleeding at his nose and mouth . . . and strongly vomiting up even of gobbets of blood' from which he shortly died.[28]

Beyond lambasting their opponents as turncoats, perjurers and king killers, some Presbyterian authors, in particular Edward Gee, developed a sophisticated ideology of political obedience to justify denying recognition of the Rump's authority. Gee was quick to make a distinction between usurped powers and legitimate authority. This could partly be discerned from the way that power was exercised as an 'unjust power in regard of measure, or the Stretching of Power beyond its due bounds, or the abuse of it is generally denied to be of God by way of warrant'. God himself had denied such powers to be of his ordination: 'They have set up kings, but not by me, they have made Princes and I knew it not' (Hosea 8: 4). Lawful power was founded upon 'the wills of those over whom it is sent'. Some act of public consent, whether by direct election or via some ancient contract between ruler and ruled, was vital to the exercise of legitimate authority. Usurpation was built only upon the will and power of those that held the reigns of government.[29] Several Presbyterian authors insisted on this basis that Romans 13 applied only to power with a legal title to rule. This was the case with the English monarchy which had had its powers confirmed by many oaths, vows and protestations. The Pauline injunction

---

[26] [W. Prynne], *The Time-Serving Proteus and Ambidexter Divine, Uncased to the World* (n. pl., 1650), title page. According to George Thomason the broadside *Be it Known and Declared to the World* (1649), which listed the Presbyterian divines that had taken the Engagement, was 'posted upon divers Church doors in London'.

[27] William Prynne, *Summary Reasons Against the New Oath and Engagement and an Admonition to All Such as Have Already Subscribed it* (1649), p. 13. [Also published as *The Arraignment, Conviction and Condemnation of the Westminister Juncto's Engagement.*]

[28] J. Vicars, *Dagon Demolished* (1660), p. 18.

[29] E. Gee, *An Exercitation Concerning Usurped Powers* (London, 1650), pp. 1, 4.

therefore applied in reverse, forbidding subjects to recognise usurping powers on pain of damnation.[30]

In denying arguments drawn from the possession of power or from usurpation by force, Presbyterian opponents of the Engagement also refuted the claims of providence to confer a lawful title. The distinction was made between the permission of the rule of evil by God as a means to correct sin and the divine authorisation of lawful power. Gee stated that a 'passive submission under what is a divine castigation, while we find no redresse is expedient; but an embracement of them . . . active obedience to them, and maintenance or support of them . . . cannot upon this ground be infered as necessary.' Henry Hall argued that providence could only be followed when it concurred with other divine precepts:

> So that it is manifest, that following of Providence is so far from being a Christians duty, that many times it is a desperate sin: and therefore it was that holy David when he might have cut off Sauls head, and when Providence had cast him into his hands, he durst not walk by acts of Providence, but by divine precepts, which commanded him to do no murther.[31]

Contrary to the position of pro-Covenant writers in the 1640s, Edward Gee and other Presbyterian authors opposed to the Engagement returned to a strict, non-reciprocal interpretation of the duty of allegiance. Of course, many Presbyterians did not believe that Charles had violated the Covenant to the extent that he should lose his life, as demonstrated in Mary Pope's pamphlet discussed above. Presbyterian opponents of the Engagement argued that the king's invasion of his subjects' rights had not freed subjects from their obligations. The Solemn League and Covenant had been set up when it was claimed that the king was violating his trust but the clause in defence of the king's person and authority made it clear that Charles had not forfeited his right to his subjects' obedience.[32] The author of A Pack of Old Puritans (1650) employed the same argument with reference to the Oath of Allegiance, claiming, in contrast with earlier Parliamentarian propaganda, that the obedience promised in the oath was unconditional.[33] Like many of the Royalist critics of the Solemn League and Covenant, Henry Hall suggested that the Engagement was full of ambiguities and snares for the conscientious man. It was 'politiquely gilded like a poysoned Pill, with as much subtilty and craft to induce people to take it as

---

[30] Pack of Old Puritans, p. 14; Arguments and Reasons to Prove the Inconvenience and Unlawfulness of Taking the New Engagement: Modestly Propounded to All Persons Concerned (n. pl., n. d.), p. 2.

[31] An Exercitation, p. 63; [H. Hall], Digitus Testium, or a Dreadful Alarm to the Whole Kingdom (1650), p. 26. But see below on Richard Baxter's claims to be the original author of this tract.

[32] Gee, An Exercitation, pp. 12, 56.

[33] Pack of Old Puritans, p. 20.

may be, for they call it an Engagement, not an Oath, for then they supposed people would scruple it.' From the two lines of the declaration, Hall had been able to produce twenty-two queries needing satisfaction.[34] Both Gee and Henry Hall allowed that subjects might co-operate with the usurping power in paying taxes and having recourse to their courts but they were not to swear loyalty to the Rump.[35]

In order to win over their main opponents, Presbyterians who continued to adhere to the Solemn League and Covenant, the supporters of the Rump used two basic arguments: that all or most of the duties contained in the Covenant had ceased to be obliging; or that the promise of loyalty to the Commonwealth could be reconciled with previous oaths and covenants. Against the claim that the Solemn League and Covenant prevented subjects from taking the Engagement on pain of committing perjury, a number of pro-government writers argued that subscribers were no longer bound to the terms of the Covenant. Henry Parker described the Covenant as being 'too rude a lump'. In line with earlier Royalist writers, he argued that the parts of the Covenant were contradictory and ill framed.[36] Some of the government's supporters reminded those who pleaded the obligations of the Covenant that allegiance to the king had been made conditional in that document. The author of A Logical Demonstration (1650) stated that subjects were obliged to preserve the king's person and authority 'Conjunctim, with Religion, and the Kingdoms Liberties; not separatim, and as a Common Enemy to these'.[37] Another pro-government writer insisted that there was more warrant to take the Engagement on the basis of the qualified obedience to the king given in the Covenant than there had been from the Oath of Allegiance to take up arms against Charles. For, he said, 'when our dissenting friends, came to perswade the people to helpe the Parliament against the King, they could make little of that Oath [of Allegiance], yea, could goe quite against the letter of it.'[38] John Rocket argued that by his divine providence God had blocked 'up our waies' to fulfilling previous oaths and covenants. This was clearly the case where God 'stood in the way against the political ends of the Covenant, literally expressed in it'.[39]

An alternative and less confrontational tactic was to state that the Engagement was compatible with the Solemn League and Covenant. Supporters of the republic argued that the various articles of the Covenant had to be weighed

---

[34] [Hall], Digitus Testium, p. 19.

[35] Gee, An Exercitation, pp. 22–3; [Hall], Digitus Testium, p. 26.

[36] H. Parker, Scotland's Holy War . . . as Also an Answer to a Paper Entitled, Some Considerations in Relation to the Act of 2. Jan 1649. for Subscribing the Engagement (1650), pp. 6–7, 34; A. Ascham, Of the Confusions and Revolutions of Governments (1649), p. 91.

[37] A Logical Demonstration of the Lawfulness of Subscribing the New Engagement (1650), p. 98.

[38] Englands Apology for its Late Change: or a Sober Perswasive (1651), p. 34. N. W., A Discourse Concerning the Engagement: or, the Northern Subscribers Plea (1650), p. 17.

[39] [J. Rocket], The Christian Subject (1651), p. 122.

according to their importance, creating what John Sanderson has described as a 'hierarchy of obligations'.[40] The latter argument was supported by the idea that oaths and covenants could be kept whilst making new and apparently conflicting promises of loyalty as long as their 'primary intention' was being fulfilled. Thomas Paget stated that the 'main and chief scope and end of the oaths of Supremacy and Allegiance formerly; and of the Protestation and Covenant lately, and likewise of the Engagement at the present' was 'the just safety and preservation of the Commonwealth of England'. Paget suggested that those who refused the Engagement on the basis of the Covenant should ask themselves whether the safety of the king was really to be placed above the cause of reformation and the safety of the people.[41] John Dury also insisted that all the specific articles of the Covenant must be made subordinate to the primary intention of all law, the public good. According to Dury, if 'the change of circumstances alter the whole care of your business' the oath 'is made *ipso facto* void'. Dury stated that the key to understanding the primary intention of an oath or covenant lay in the first intention of those that framed it, not any subsequent gloss that was attached to it. So, in the case of the Oath of Allegiance, the intention was to defend the king and the kingdom against popish oppressors and conspirators, not to defend the king and his papist cohorts against the kingdom.[42] Some authors reminded the Presbyterians of the religious content of the Covenant. One pamphleteer insisted that subjects 'distinguish between the letter of the covenant, and the intent of it'. The ends of the Covenant were the safety of the covenanters and the preservation of religion, which, it was argued, the Engagement itself was in no way opposite to.[43] A few Presbyterians actually pledged allegiance to the Commonwealth in this sense. Ralph Josselin wrote that he 'subscribed the engagement as I considered it stood with the Covenant'.[44]

Dury was also the leading advocate of the doctrine that all promissory oaths had to be taken with certain 'tacite conditions'. Oaths of loyalty were to be taken with the understanding that they would only be kept so long as they continued to benefit the cause of religion and public safety. As a result, some oaths whose matter was lawful could be rendered void as circumstances made the consequences of keeping them prejudicial to the public good.[45]

---

[40] J. Sanderson, *'But the People's Creatures': The Philosophical Basis of the English Civil War* (Manchester, 1989), p. 157.

[41] Paget, *A Religious Scrutiny . . . Together with a Faithfull and Conscientious Account for Subscribing the Engagement* (1650), pp. 21, 32.

[42] J. Dury, *Considerations Concerning the Present Engagement, Whether it May be Lawfully Entered into; Yea or No?* (1649), pp. 9–10; [J. Dury], *A Disingag'd Survey of the Engagement in Relation to Publike Obligations* (1650), p. 3.

[43] *Certain Particulars Further Tending to Satisfie the Tender Consciences of Such as are Required to Take the Engagement* (1651), pp. 3–4.

[44] *Diary of Ralph Josselin*, p. 186.

[45] [Dury], *A Disingag'd Survey*, pp. 4, 8.

Marchamont Nedham listed these 'tacite conditions' comprehensively. In all 'promissory State-Oaths', Nedham said, 'there lurk severall tacit Conditions, inseperable from the nature of all Oaths and Engagements.' The words of the oath were to be interpreted in a 'fair and equitable construction', not wrung by the imposers into a persecuting new sense. The swearer himself, in the absence of other guidance, was to use a 'prudentiall latitude' in ascertaining the oath's meaning. The second tacit condition was that oaths could only oblige so far as God permitted or as far as things stood. Neither was the subscriber to swear to anything without 'this Reservation, as far as lawfully he may'. Finally, all promissory oaths were at the mercy of divine providence as to their performance. If such an alteration should happen 'that neither the same persons nor things are in being which I swore to maintaine my Oath is at an end and the obligation ceaseth'.[46] Dury stated likewise that in 'things *de futuro*, and of a contingent nature, we may not draw conclusions absolute and peremptory, but with subordination to the Divine Majesty, many times contrary to our expectations, by an over-ruling power, wisdome and goodnesse interposing.' Dury said that a number of the clauses of the Covenant had clearly been voided by events, the union between England and Scotland had been annulled by their declaration of war and the king had, by his actions, forfeited his right to allegiance. Yet so long as subjects remembered that the Covenant should be pursued according to our callings, there was no reason that the remaining articles of it could not be fulfilled.[47]

The idea that promissory oaths might contain 'tacit conditions' did not represent a fundamental challenge to the accepted rules concerning lawful swearing. In fact, the whole notion of 'tacit conditions' was taken from Robert Sanderson's *De Juramento*. As Sanderson was the foremost English Protestant authority on oaths and the conscience in the seventeenth century, pro-Engagement authors freely advertised their borrowings to give their arguments the stamp of authority.[48] The section in question formed just two pages of Sanderson's lengthy treatise, which in general was very strict on the lax interpretation of oaths. He did, nevertheless, state in section ten of the second lecture that all promissory oaths must be taken with four tacit conditions: 'if

---

[46] M. Nedham, *The Case of the Commonwealth of England Stated* (1650), pp. 25–31.

[47] [J. Dury], *A Second Parcel of Objections Against the Taking of the Engagement Answered* (1650), pp. 26–34. See also [A. Ascham], *The Bounds and Bonds of Publique Obedience* (1649), pp. 40–2; *idem*, *A Discourse* (1648), p. 81; S. Eaton, *The Oath of Allegiance and the National Covenant Proved to be Non-obliging* (1650), pp. 1–2, 36.

[48] Sanderson was a close associate of Laud and a favoured chaplain of Charles I, I. Walton, *The Compleat Angler: the Lives of Donne, Wotton, Hooker, Herbert and Sanderson*, ed. G. Keynes (London, 1929), p. 480; but was also adopted by moderate puritans as a shining example of a good Calvinist bishop, F. D., *Reason and Judgement: or, Special Remarques of the Life of . . . Dr. Sanderson* (1663); and was highly respected by European theologians, H. R. McAdoo, *The Structure of Caroline Moral Theology* (London, 1949), p. 72.

God permit'; 'as farre as is lawfull'; saving the decision of a superior power; and so long as the matter of the oath remained the same.[49]

The final tactic of pro-Engagement authors was simply to offer the easiest terms possible for subscription. Here they were well out of step with the normal prohibition on the use of limitations in swearing. The supporters of the Solemn League and Covenant had at least continued to maintain the pretence of requiring sincere and whole-hearted subscriptions. Those that promoted the Engagement, on the other hand, appear to have positively encouraged subscribers to swear equivocally. In print, at least, Anglican opponents of the Commonwealth continued to condemn the use of limitations and reservations in taking oaths. Yet in individual cases of conscience raised by the Engagement, they permitted subscribing to the declaration of loyalty with declared equivocations.[50] As we will see, many Presbyterians also subscribed to the Engagement with reservations. However, there was no guarantee, despite the advice of pro-Engagement authors, that the Rump would accept equivocal promises of loyalty.

As he was receiving payment from the Rump it may be said that John Dury was producing an officially sanctioned view of the way in which the Engagement could be subscribed.[51] In his very first contribution to the controversy, Dury stated that he had taken the Solemn League and Covenant according to his own reserved sense of it. He reproduced a transcript of this reading as 'The Vow which J. D. hath made', implicitly endorsing making these equivocations.[52] In a later pamphlet Dury claimed that subscribers were no more obliged to the imposers' sense than the imposers themselves had made clear in the wording of the oath, or to that sense assented to by the takers if they had made their own declarations. He stated that this was the way that he had taken both the Covenant and the Engagement, suggesting that he had taken the promise of loyalty to the Commonwealth with similar reservations.[53] In another of his pamphlets, Dury offered just such an equivocal gloss on the Engagement, rendering it compatible with the ends of the Covenant.[54] Several other Presbyterian apologists for the republican regime used the same tactic. The author of *Certain Particulars* (1651) interpreted the words of the Engagement in the broadest sense possible. 'Commonwealth' only meant 'the publicke Affairs and welfare of the place where his [the subscriber's] lot is cast to inhabite'. The phrase 'as it is now established' indicated that subscribers were not required to approve of the events that had produced a free

---

[49] Sanderson, *De Juramento*, pp. 54–6.

[50] On this see my, 'Oaths, Casuistry and Equivocation: Anglican Responses to the Engagement Controversy', *Historical Journal*, 44 (2001), 59–77.

[51] S. Barber, *Regicide and Republicanism: Politics and Ethics in the English Revolution, 1646–1659* (Edinburgh, 1998), p. 189.

[52] Dury, *A Case of Conscience Resolv'd*, pp. 23–38.

[53] [Dury], *A Second Parcel of Objections*, p. 26.

[54] [Dury], *Considerations Concerning the Present Engagement* (1649), p. 5.

state; neither did the Engagement prescribe a republic as the settled form of government in the future.[55]

As we have seen, in printed pamphlets Presbyterian opponents of the Commonwealth insisted that, though passive obedience might be offered to the republican government, the Engagement itself could not be taken. However, there is clear evidence that individuals were following the lead of the Rump's spokesmen and offering limited subscriptions to the Engagement. The Engagement was supposed to be imposed nationwide from January 1650 onwards. Returns exist for Wigan, Blackburn, Bury, Heywood, Middleton, Preston, Manchester and Salford in Lancashire, the parish of Rye in East Sussex and for parts of Gloucestershire.[56] One Somerset JP, John Preston, used a double-sided postcard-sized piece of paper when taking subscriptions to the declaration. On one side were the two lines of the Engagement, on the other were 'the reasons of urging the Engagement'.[57] In a letter dated 10 May 1650 the Royalist Colonel Keane said that the Parliament's officers and commissioners were 'pressing the engagement generally westward'. Keane claimed that the declaration 'was refused by most, and resolved to be broken by those that took it'.[58] It also seems that the Engagement was taken as a means to qualify for legal proceedings. In Kent both men and women were required to make the declaration of loyalty in the course of their trials. Thomas Taylor and Elizabeth Cleeve, each charged with murder, had their sentences commuted to manslaughter and were then pardoned after subscribing to the Engagement. Robert Olliver of the same county seems to have taken the Engagement to qualify himself to pursue an action against two JPs, William James and Martin Pike, whom he had accused of forcibly entering his house.[59]

Although this evidence demonstrates that in some parishes the Engagement was tendered to the general public, it seems that the Commonwealth was mainly interested in using the declaration to test the political loyalties of the clergy and those that were employed on government business. A summons issued by Luke Robinson and Isaac Newton in North Yorkshire on 16 January 1650 for persons to take the Engagement did not expect any to appear 'but

---

[55] *Certain Particulars*, pp. 2–3.
[56] BL Add. Roll 7180, 'Engagement to be faithful to the Commonwealth taken at Wigan'; Lancashire Record Office DDB 42/3, Engagement return for Salford hundred (my thanks to Alex Craven of the University of Manchester for providing me with this reference taken from his doctoral work on county government in Lancashire under the Commonwealth and for letting me see his chapter on the administration of the Engagement in the county); Fletcher, *County Community*, pp. 296–7; F. A. Inderwick, 'The Rye Engagement', *Sussex Archaeological Collections*, xxxix (1894), 16–27; G. R. O. D1571 F116.
[57] Barber, *Regicide and Republicanism*, p. 181.
[58] *CSPD*, 1650, p. 154.
[59] *Calendar of Assize Records-Kent Indictments 1649–1659*, ed. J. S. Cockburn (London, 1989), pp. 98–9, 102–3, 139. Alex Craven also suggests that the Engagement was incorporated into the sequestration process.

such as have augmentations from the parliament or derive there [sic] authority from it'.[60] In his letters to his father, Viscount L'Isle confirmed the impression that the government was essentially interested in gaining subscriptions from public officials. He told the Earl of Leicester that there was 'no probability that any man of note or estate' could 'live in England without subscribing' but those persons who were not in office would not 'be necessetated to declare this point till ther want the courts of justice'.[61] It is likely that mass subscription to the Engagement was only required in areas where zealously republican officials, like John Pyne of Curry Mallet in Somerset, were in control. In November 1649 Pyne wrote that he was very glad there were 'resolutions taken to proceed vigorously with the engagement', which he thought would 'make a notable discovery and indeed rout amongst all professions and callings whatsoever', and that for his own part he had already sworn in 'all constables and tithingmen according unto the engagement'.[62] At Fugglestone in Wiltshire in May 1650, one of the churchwardens took away the key to the church from the clerk as he went to ring the bell in the afternoon, 'saying that neither Mr Pinkney, the vicar, nor Mr Fawconer, the curate, should come into the church until they had taken the Engagement'.[63]

As has already been shown, by focusing tendering the Engagement on the most literate and articulate sections of the population, the Commonwealth provoked a great war of words over subscribing to the declaration of loyalty. The key opponents of the Engagement were Presbyterian ministers, though, as with Walker's sufferers who refused the Covenant, the degree of opposition was almost certainly exaggerated by later hagiographers of nonconformity. In fact there were many earlier advocates of the Covenant who went on to take and/or promote the Engagement of loyalty to the Commonwealth, including Joseph Caryl, John Dury and Stephen Marshall. Many other Presbyterians were allowed to make equivocal subscriptions to the Engagement. William Jenkin's submission to the government, made from prison after the failure of Christopher Love's Presbyterian plot in 1651, was published as pro-Rump propaganda. However, contrary to Blair Worden's description of it as a 'cringing confession', upon closer inspection, Jenkin's acceptance of the purged Parliament's right to rule was less than whole-hearted.[64] Jenkin based his submission on the providential favour he felt had been granted to the Parliament in its victories over Charles II. He also stated that the title of the possessor of power was accounted better than that of the next pretender who is out of possession. Yet in ascribing such importance to providence, Jenkin suggested that these were events that God had permitted but not ordained. It

---

[60] Barber, *Regicide and Republicanism*, p. 181.
[61] HMC, *De L' Isle MSS*, *vi* (London, 1966), p. 472.
[62] HMC, *Leyborne-Popham MSS* (London, 1899), p. 51. For Pyne see *DNB*.
[63] HMC, *Various Collections*, *i* (London, 1901), p. 123.
[64] Worden, *Rump Parliament*, p. 248.

was not the case, Jenkin argued, 'that these Providences shewes God approving of all the meanes and wayes used in and for the alteration of the Government'.[65] Similarly equivocal 'submissions' were made with equal success by Jenkin's co-conspirators Thomas Case, Ralph Robinson, Arthur Jackson, Roger Drake, Thomas Watson, Colonel Jackson, Colonel Joseph Vaughan and Captain Hugh Massey, though, as the Earl of Leicester noted in his journal, they were as guilty of treason as the ring leader Christopher Love who was executed.[66]

There is evidence too that sympathetic magistrates were accepting equivocal subscriptions from Presbyterian ministers in the localities. In May 1650 the Council of State resolved to write to Wroth Rogers, governor of Hereford, and other justices of the peace there asking them to examine the 'expositions made by some ministers in that county of the engagement, with which they have taken it'. The Council of State ordered the justices to tender the declaration to them again and see if they would take it without any limitations. If they persisted in making these equivocations they would be brought to answer before the Council. The Council also demanded to hear the replies of 'the justices of the peace before whom the engagement was so taken, and demand of them by what warrant they did it'.[67]

However, as we shall see, in spite of the limited kind of allegiance demanded by spokesmen for the Rump, and the acceptance of equivocal subscriptions by some magistrates, the Engagement seems none the less to have presented a considerable case of conscience for English Presbyterians. In part this demonstrates that many continued to feel bound to the terms of the Solemn League and Covenant. Yet the scale of the debate over the Engagement was also a product of uncertainty as to what kinds of subscriptions would be accepted. Evidence from the universities of Oxford and Cambridge shows that there was no clear line as to whether limited subscriptions to the Engagement would be taken. Instead, the success or failure of tactics of equivocation often depended on whether an individual could call on influential figures to intercede on his behalf.

The Engagement was tendered to the fellows and students at Oxford on 12 November 1649.[68] It caused particular difficulties for the Presbyterian members of the university, especially those transplanted from Cambridge, most of whom had earlier sworn by the Covenant to defend the king's person. It was partly for this reason, and because the Earl of Manchester's visitation had imposed a more distinctly Presbyterian character on her sister university than at Oxford, that the number of ejections for refusing the Engagement was so high at

---

[65] W. Jenkin, *Three Conscientious Queries from Mr. Will. Jenken: Being the Grounds of His Late Petition and Submission to the Present Power* (1651), pp. 1–2.

[66] Ibid., p. 7; HMC, *De L'Isle MSS, vi,* p. 608.

[67] *CSPD,* 1650, p. 150.

[68] *Register of the Visitors of the University of Oxford from A.D. 1647 to A.D. 1658,* ed. M. Burrows (Camden Soc., n.s., 29, 1881), p. 274.

Cambridge. When the declaration was tendered in December 1649 only John Bond of Trinity Hall of the heads of houses took it without reservations.[69] The attempt to gain more subscriptions dragged on into the next year. William Sancroft noted a meeting at the Bear tavern in September 1650 where the 'business was to angle for proselytes, and any that would subscribe might be received'.[70] Later that same year Samuel Dillingham wrote to Sancroft that 'the study of most' was to seek ways of equivocating with the Engagement. He could not see how such reservations could be lawful unless 'happily it be deemed that the weakness of the authority urging take from the solemnity of the Engagement, and that a man may give cross answer to a saucy companion who has nothing to do with him'.[71] Some fellows seem to have kept their places with only the promise of passive obedience. Richard Love avoided subscription up to the middle of November 1650. Though he was prepared only to state that he would live peaceably and quietly under the new regime, he nevertheless kept his place at Corpus Christi. Despite the fact that equivocal subscriptions were occasionally accepted and that Cromwell had promised to offer protection to non-subscribers, Twigg estimates that forty-nine fellows lost their places as a result of the purge of 1649–50.[72]

The numbers ejected at Oxford for refusing the Engagement were far fewer but there was still considerable opposition to taking the declaration of loyalty. Convocation produced a petition against the Engagement. The petitioners claimed the benefit of the articles for the surrender of Oxford agreed in 1646, one of which promised an exemption from all oaths and engagements. The petitioners promised, nevertheless, that they would 'live quietly and peaceably in their places and callings under the present Government'. The speaker of the House of Commons replied abruptly that had ' "true and faithful" been in any other language happily the most of you had not understood it, but', he thought, 'you could have understood English.'[73] Samuel Dillingham concluded that the Parliament intended 'to interpret that phrase positively, which will make a greater slaughter still'.[74] Guarantees of passive obedience, as given in the Oxford petition, were deemed inadequate. Edward Reynolds lost the vice-chancellorship and Edward Pococke his canonry at Christ Church (though he retained his post as professor of Hebrew through the intervention of John Wilkins and Gerard Langbaine). Baldwin Acland, finding this test of loyalty too much to swallow, was also ejected. Simon Ford, a protégé of Reynolds, lost his place for preaching against the government in St Mary's church.[75]

[69] Twigg, *University of Cambridge*, pp. 156–7.
[70] *Memorials of the Great Civil War in England from 1646 to 1652*, ed. H. Cary (2 vols., London, 1842), ii, 232.
[71] Ibid., ii, 240, 243.
[72] Twigg, *University of Cambridge*, pp. 159–62.
[73] Bodl. MS Wood F35, f. 358.
[74] *Memorials*, ed. Cary, ii, 240.
[75] *Register of the Visitors*, p. 274n., L. Twells, *The Lives of Dr. Edward Pocock* (2 vols., London, 1819),i, 130; Bodl. MS Wood F41, f. 236v, S. Ford to A. Wood 28 February 1682; B. Worden,

In spite of this, there was evidence, as at Cambridge, that the visitors were prepared to accept declarations of loyalty and submissions that were highly equivocal. The case of Dr Conant, vice-chancellor of Oxford from 1657 to 1660, offers a vivid illustration of such a response. When asked by the Parliamentary visitors whether he would subscribe to the Engagement, Conant replied that he would, so long as 'he must not be understood to approve of what hath been done unto or under the present government' and 'that if God shall remarkably call me to submit to any other power I may be at liberty to obey that call, not withstanding the present Engagement.'[76] Conant could hardly have offered a more hollow promise of obedience. However, there was no clear guide under the Rump as to which responses would be deemed acceptable and which would not. As a bare minimum, the republic seems to have demanded either subscription to the Engagement (in whatever sense), or at least an acknowledgement of the Parliament's right to rule. This would not necessarily keep individuals in their places. Even the help of influential friends was at times inadequate.[77] In attempting to broaden its base of support, some of the Rump's supporters gave the impression that it was permissible to use equivocations and these would be accepted as subscriptions, but in practice this was not always the case.

Casuistic advice poured through a whole variety of channels in an attempt to extricate Presbyterian consciences from this political briar patch. The amount of printed advice on the point of the Engagement was considerable (seventy plus titles) but not everyone found it helpful. The Cheshire minister Adam Martindale recalled that the tendering of the Engagement had 'occasioned many little pamphlets pro and con', but he found these 'little to my satisfaction'. Too much, he said, of these works 'was spent in the charge of usurpation upon the governours by one partie, and wording it off by another'. This meant little to Martindale 'who was satisfied of the usurpation, but doubted whether, notwithstanding that, the engagement was lawful'.[78] Others though were influenced by these tracts. Richard Baxter stated that he had been persuaded to refuse the Engagement by the arguments put forward in *The Humble Proposals of Sundry Learned and Pious Divines* (which he mistakenly attributed to the moderate Presbyterian Richard Vines).[79] Books were also exchanged as a means of helping friends in dilemmas of conscience. In March

'Cromwellian Oxford', *The History of the University of Oxford IV*, ed. Tyacke (Oxford, 1997), pp. 733–73, esp. pp. 736–7, 751–2; *CJ*, vi, 549, Reynolds was reported as having taken the Engagement 'in terms' but this did not save him from losing the deanery of Christ Church as well as the vice-chancellorship.

[76] *Register of the Visitors*, pp. xlvii–xlviii. Conant, though identified as an arch-Presbyterian, did not take the Covenant.

[77] Bodl. MS Selden supra 108, f. 147; Bodl. MS Selden supra 109, f. 323.

[78] *The Life of Adam Martindale*, ed. R. Parkinson (Chetham Society, 4, 1845), p. 92.

[79] *Calendar of the Correspondence of Richard Baxter*, eds. N. H. Keeble and G. Nuttall (2 vols., Oxford, 1991), i, 59.

1650 William Lowe thanked Colonel Edward Harley for the (sadly unidentified) book that he had sent him. Lowe stated that he could not 'but approve of it, finding nothing in it that forbids us to endeavour the common good of the people of England, or to live quietly in our callings under this present Government'.[80]

Aside from the considerable amount of printed material produced, the Engagement also prompted a great amount of letter writing. One anonymous correspondent (probably writing between 1650 and 1651) complained that he could not 'forget our vows to god in the day of our distress and those many engagements that lie upon us'. These previous obligations precluded him 'from entertaining any dispute about change of government in this kingdom'. The writer's hope was that his correspondent might satisfy him that the Engagement could be taken without violating earlier oaths and covenants.[81] Richard Baxter, renowned as a Protestant casuist, received letters from the Presbyterian minister Richard Vines who was lost in conscientious difficulties over the Engagement.[82]

Manuscript material often found its way into print. Baxter recalled how, when he had first heard of the Engagement, 'being in Company with some Gentlemen of Worcestershire, I presently wrote down above twenty Queries against it'. One of the gentlemen present took a copy of these queries 'and shortly after, I met with them verbatim in a Book of Mr. Henry Hall's as his own.'[83] Other manuscript treatises were drawn up as justifications of a personal course of action. The Parliamentarian administrator William Jessop, a client of Robert Rich, earl of Warwick, and Robert Devereux, earl of Essex, recorded his scruples over taking the Engagement.[84] Jessop excused himself from breaking the third article of the Covenant promising to preserve the king's person, as Charles was now dead 'and so my obligation to him is ceased'. Equally, as the constitution of the Parliament had changed, the Covenant could not be taken to oblige Jessop to defend it as it was constituted when he first took the oath. The present powers offered him protection and in return he owed them the duty of obedience.[85] Significantly, he took this promise to be true and faithful to the Commonwealth as 'a merely not opposing them and so amounts to no more then a conformity w[hi]ch I intend however to give them'.[86] In addition, Jessop kept the reservation that when swearing to any government his allegiance was still under an implicit condition 'that my concernment as a Christian or an Englishman be not neglected by those that

---

[80] HMC, *Portland MSS, iii* (London, 1894), p. 172.

[81] HMC, *Ormonde MSS, New Series, i* (London, 1902), pp. 144–6.

[82] *Baxter Correspondence*, i, 58–9.

[83] *Rel. Bax.*, part one, p. 64.

[84] G. E. Aylmer, *The State's Servants: The Civil Service of the English Republic 1649–1660* (London, 1973), pp. 234–8; BL Add. MS 46190 (Jessop Papers vol. iii), f. 190–3.

[85] Ibid., f. 190.

[86] Ibid., f. 191.

manage it'.[87] It is unlikely that the government would have accepted such a qualified promise of obedience. Instead, Jessop probably sought to use his queries to satisfy himself that he had not committed the sin of perjury by breaking his Covenant. Despite these doubts, Jessop acted as a committed and energetic servant of both the Commonwealth and the Protectorate.

The spoken word could be just as, if not more, effective than the written or printed in guiding consciences. In 1650 those Presbyterian ministers who had previously used their rhetorical talents to promote the Covenant turned their skills to stirring up opposition to the Engagement. In March 1650, Richard Bradshaw, mayor of Chester, wrote to John Bradshaw, president of the Council of State. He had hoped to send the president Engagement returns for the city, but so far had only been able to collect the signatures of a few excise officers. Bradshaw believed that this delay had been caused by the

> deterring arguments from pulpits whence the rigid Presbyterians shake the minds of men, setting the engagement directly in opposition to the covenant, charging covenant-breaking and perjury upon all that have subscribed, and labouring to render them odious to the people.

The mayor believed that to attempt to gag or imprison these ministers would only increase sympathy for these 'crafty incendiaries'. The only way to effectively curb their influence was to have 'two or three able ministers sent down to these northern parts, to clear the equity of subscribing, as consistent with the real ends of the covenant'.[88] This kind of trouble was clearly not confined to Chester. In November 1650 the Council of State noted that it had demanded the removal of 'some ministers who, by refusing to subscribe the engagement, and disowning the present government, are an ill example to others'. This order had been ineffective as ministers had simply continued to preach outside the garrisons and a new order had to be passed for removing these seditious clergymen to a safe distance from garrison towns.[89] On 23 November 1650 depositions were made accusing Constance Jessop, a Presbyterian minister in Bristol, of preaching against the present government. Jessop was to be sent copies of the depositions 'so that he may give his answer in writing, in which he is to express himself touching his owning the Parliament and present Government to be a lawful authority . . . and also concerning his willingness to take the engagement'. On 14 December it was recorded that Jessop was to be allowed to preach again, having taken the Engagement and recognised the present government, provided that he did not return to Bristol and remained 'well-affected to the government in his sermons'.[90] However, on 7 January 1651

---

[87] Ibid., f. 193.
[88] *CSPD*, 1650, p. 20.
[89] Ibid., 1650, p. 427.
[90] Ibid., 1650, pp. 440, 470.

it was ordered that Jessop should be examined again as to 'miscarriages' of his party in Bristol. On 24 of the same month the minister was ordered not to come within ten miles of the city.[91]

Conferences were used again during the Engagement controversy. Adam Martindale went to a meeting of ministers at Warrington to discuss the lawfulness of taking the declaration (attended by some of those troublesome divines, including Edward Gee and Richard Hollingworth, that Richard Bradshaw had complained to the Council of State about). Martindale was no more convinced by the arguments of these ministers than he had been by the early Engagement pamphlets but he gradually began to be swayed by lower readings of the declaration as merely a promise of good behaviour offered in *The Northern Subscribers Plea* (1650). However, having been led by this tract into taking the Engagement, Martindale subsequently found that the publication of Edward Gee's *A Plea for Non-scribers* (1650) (in part based on the debate at Warrington) raised further 'doubts and scruples' in his mind as to the lawfulness of his actions and he later confessed in the pulpit that he should never have taken the Engagement.[92] Conferences also appear to have been held in London on the same subject. A pamphlet printed in 1650 reproduced the memoranda of a conference between 'brethren that scrupled at the Engagement; and others who were satisfied with it' held on 15 and 22 February and 1 March 1650.[93] John Wallace suggested that Edward Reynolds's call for a 'solemn debate' on the Engagement in his *The Humble Proposals of Sundry Learned and Pious Divines* (1649) may have instigated these discussions.[94]

Some Presbyterians clearly were convinced that they were no longer obliged by the Covenant (or they were at least persuaded that it was not politically wise to keep it). Yet with regards to the most celebrated strand of pro-Engagement theory, it is highly debatable how effective de facto arguments were in resolving conflicting claims for obedience. Following the victories of Cromwell's forces in September of 1650 and 1651, justifications from divine providence and the possession of power probably carried more currency. Yet, until arms had decisively settled the issue, subjects were left with the dilemma of whether the Rump did constitute the powers in possession. In the 'Review and Conclusion to Leviathan' Hobbes stated that 'the point of time, wherein a man becomes subject to a Conqueror' was that point 'wherein having liberty to submit to him, he consenteth either by express words, or by other sufficient sign, to be his Subject.' So having taken the Engagement, the individual would

---

[91] Ibid., 1651, pp. 5, 22.
[92] *The Life of Martindale*, pp. 92–100. Martindale was not the only Presbyterian minister to experience second thoughts after subscribing to the Engagement, see *The Autobiography of Henry Newcome, M. A.*, ed. R. Parkinson (2 vols., Chetham Society, 26–7, 1852), i, 24–5.
[93] *Memorandums of the Conferences Held Between the Brethren that Scrupled at the Engagement; and Others Who Were Satisfied* (1650).
[94] Wallace, 'Engagement Controversy', 395.

become subject to the Rump. However, Hobbes's remarks did not resolve the issue of how the subject might know when the 'conquest' had been achieved. It remained up to the subject's private judgement to decide when the transfer of power had occurred.[95] As a consequence of the existence of this political grey area, all sides attempted to resolve the troubled consciences of individual subscribers. As Martindale shrewdly put it, the real question was not whether the Rump constituted a legitimate political authority, few even of its own spokesmen were prepared to argue this, but rather whether it was morally safe to take the Engagement.

By 1653 the Engagement was in any case rendered a dead letter with the removal of the legal penalties for refusing it.[96] In the same year an act was drafted against customary oaths. They would have been dispensed with altogether in the case of becoming a member of one of the universities, joining a corporation or society, or in giving fealty to the owner of land rented by a tenant, the only exception being that individuals would still have taken oaths of office if occupying a place of public employment.[97] However, rather than do away with them entirely, the Protectorate actually saw a return to a more traditional use of oaths of loyalty, with the Lord Protector taking a coronation style oath to uphold the Protestant religion and govern according to the law. Similarly, privy councillors and MPs were required to take an oath of loyalty to the Protector.[98] Ann Forster has noted the irony that in 1656 the Protectorate appointed an oath of abjuration to be taken by all Roman Catholics which borrowed directly from the Jacobean Oath of Allegiance the phrase condemning the 'Damnable Doctrine and Position, That Princes Rulers, or Governors, which be Excommunicated or Deprived by the Pope, may, by virtue of such Excommunication or Deprivation, be killed, murthered, or deposed from their Rule or Government'. This came from the same men who had seven years earlier tried and executed their king.[99] A similar anti-Catholic oath passed in August 1643 was notable for the way in which it had strenuously avoided the issue of resistance.[100]

However, if oaths of loyalty continued to be imposed in the 1650s, it is also the case that the repeated tendering of often conflicting oaths was leading to public dissatisfaction. The Protectorate continued to demand oaths of loyalty from its officers and troops. According to the Venetian secretary, these demands were not met with great enthusiasm. On 24 January 1655 he wrote to the doge and senate stating that some of Cromwell's leading officers had refused

---

[95] T. Hobbes, *Leviathan*, ed. R. Tuck (Cambridge, 1991), p. 484; A. Fukuda, *Sovereignty and the Sword: Harrington, Hobbes, and Mixed Government in the English Civil Wars* (Oxford, 1997), pp. 64–7.

[96] *CJ*, vii, 283, 336, 346.

[97] *CSPD*, 1653, p. 338; *CJ*, vii, 110.

[98] *CJ*, vii, 571–2.

[99] A. M. C. Forster, 'The Oath Tendered', *Recusant History*, xiv (1977), 86–97.

[100] Kenyon, *Stuart Constitution*, p. 460.

the oath of allegiance. 'Some of them', he claimed, 'said openly that after ten oaths had been imposed for the requisite administration and never observed, it was useless to swear any more and they would not do so.'[101]

The controversies over the trial and execution of the king and the imposition of the Engagement revealed the extent to which many English Presbyterians continued to see themselves as bound to the Solemn League and Covenant. It was without doubt safer to plead a tender conscience on the point of breaking previous covenants than to explicitly state one's support for monarchy. In the late 1640s and 1650s, many Presbyterians preferred to stress the importance of the personal, religious obligations of the Covenant, rather than point up its defence of the kingly office. As we will see, post-Restoration apologists for the Covenant continued this trend. Unlike the Cavalier Parliament, however, most of the Rump's supporters did not repudiate the Covenant as a whole. They resorted instead to arguing either that the Covenant was a temporary arrangement which was now past its political sell-by date or that it was compatible with the Engagement. The 'Engagers' discussion of the 'tacit' conditions in all oaths was not in itself an attack on the rules established by Protestant casuists for lawful swearing. However, their tactic of encouraging limited subscriptions to the Engagement furthered the process begun in the 1640s of relaxing the prohibitions against using equivocations when swearing. These tactics in turn sowed confusion amongst subscribers who often found that these limited subscriptions to the Engagement were not considered satisfactory. In inviting the use of these tactics, the Rump's supporters also devalued the political worth of the whole exercise. There was not much to be gained from promises of obedience as empty as John Conant's. Partly as a result of the experience of the Engagement, the Protectorate would turn its back on any attempt to legitimise its rule through a publicly subscribed oath or declaration. The late 1640s and early 1650s also saw the ambitions of the English covenanters in retreat. Now the Solemn League and Covenant was seen as a bulwark against the forces of revolution, not as the vehicle for carrying Parliament's and England's reformation forward.

[101] CSPV, 1653–4, pp. 172, 175.

8

Covenants, oaths and the Restoration settlement

Despite the efforts made by supporters of the Engagement to show that the Solemn League and Covenant was no longer in effect, debate over its continued obligation was sustained in the 1660s, not only through the combined political and religious aims still invested in it by some Presbyterians, but also because the Covenant became a central component of proposals for the comprehension or toleration of dissenters. However, whereas in the 1650s writers had urged that the Covenant was no longer obliging so as to include Presbyterians in the political settlement, in the 1660s declarations against the Covenant were inserted into legislation designed to exclude nonconformists from public office. The decision as to whether to take or refuse the declaration represented a major case of conscience for Presbyterians, the difficulties of which led some to resort to tactics of equivocation. The problems these declarations posed dissenters (and indeed, the success with which some evaded their strictures) encouraged their Anglican opponents to press for new nationwide oaths of loyalty. As we will see, these oaths, which bound swearers not to attempt any alteration in the government of church and state, were intended not only to purge non-conformists from public office, but also to tempt them into making politically damaging defences of the right of resistance. However, these abortive attempts to petrify the constitution did not curtail the continued resort to radical oaths of association, with their barely disguised threat of armed force. When proposals were made for a new oath of association to secure the Protestant succession during the Exclusion Crisis, these were attacked as attempts to revive the Solemn League and Covenant. Though undoubtedly this invective was part of the Tory attempt to link Restoration dissent with civil war puritanism, there was, as we shall see, a grain of truth to these accusations.

Following Monck's decision to readmit the secluded members in February 1660, the strong Presbyterian character of the restored Long Parliament was revealed in the members' decision to reimpose the Solemn League and Covenant. It was ordered that the Covenant should be read in every church in the land and a copy of it was posted in the Commons itself.[1] The Convention Parliament that replaced it also contained a significant Presbyterian party. During

---

[1] CJ, vii, 862, 872.

discussions over the re-establishment of episcopacy, the issue of how this could agree with the Covenant was raised with both Colonel John Birch and Sir Gilbert Gerrard urging resolution on this question. The committee managed to refer judgement to the king and adjourned itself until October of that year.[2] The resurrection of the Covenant was part of the conservative reaction against the 'Indian summer' of political and religious radicalism which had followed the downfall of Richard Cromwell's Protectorate.[3] No longer a vehicle for apocalyptic beliefs and notions of universal reformation, the Covenant was reintroduced as a device to suppress sectaries, stifle republicanism and secure monarchy. The prominent role of the Presbyterian party in securing Charles II's restoration, and the declaration of Breda, in which the king promised to give relief to 'tender consciences', seemed to offer hope for both their political and religious ambitions. Clarendon noted retrospectively that at this time the Presbyterians had tried to ingratiate themselves with the king 'by loud and passionate inveighing against that monstrous parricide'. They declared they had been the chief party by which the king had been restored to his throne 'and that the very covenant had at last done him good and expedited his return', as their ministers had pressed upon the consciences of the swearers the importance of the clause defending the king's person.[4] Presbyterian broadsides urged the Solemn League and Covenant as a loyal document that would thwart the remaining Rumpers' republican designs.[5]

The mood of optimism quickly disintegrated in the face of the sustained onslaught upon both political and religious dissent made by the 'church party' in the Cavalier Parliament. The declarations inserted into the Corporation Act of 1661 and the Act of Uniformity of 1662 required subscribers to state that the Solemn League and Covenant was an 'unlawful oath' which was 'imposed upon the subjects of this realm against the known laws and liberties of the kingdom'. In addition, those swearing were also to declare that they believed it was 'not lawful upon any pretence whatsoever to take up arms against the King' and that they abhorred 'the traiterous position of taking arms by his authority'. The declaration in the Act of Uniformity was extended to oblige the swearer to promise not 'to endeavour any change or alteration of government either in Church or State'.[6] In Parliament, those sympathetic to

---

[2] 'Seymour Bowman's Diary of the Convention Parliament', Bodl. MS Dep. f. 9, f. 82–6.

[3] B. Reay, 'The Quakers, 1659 and the Restoration of the Monarchy', *History*, 63 (1978), 193–213; A. Woolrych, 'Last Quests for Settlement, 1659–60', in *The Interregnum: The Quest for Settlement, 1656–1660*, ed. G. E. Aylmer (1972), ch. 8.

[4] E. Hyde, *The History of the Rebellion and Civil Wars in England, Also His Life Written by Himself, in Which is Included a Continuation of His History of the Grand Rebellion* (Oxford, 1853), p. 996.

[5] *A Phanatique League and Covenant* (n. pl., 1659[60]); W. Collinne, *The Spirit of the Phanatiques Dissected and the Solemne League and Covenant Solemnly Discussed in 30 Queries* (1660).

[6] Kenyon, *Stuart Constitution*, pp. 377, 381; CJ, viii, 410–11.

the Presbyterians' cause had to temper their remarks in support of the Covenant in such a hostile political climate. In May 1661, Robert Milward wrote to Sir Robert Leveson that the Presbyterians were now 'so inconsiderable in the House that the more prudent men of that party are silent'.[7] Sir John Holland, speaking on the Act of Uniformity, urged the removal of the clause abjuring the Covenant. However, he insisted that this was not motivated by any love for the covenanters, remembering how 'Rigid some of those that desire this Indulgence were in the prosecution of the Covenant'. Instead Holland claimed that removing the clause would accommodate a considerable interest within the church.[8]

The attack on the Covenant did not stop there. On 21 May 1661 both houses resolved that the common hangman should, on the following day, publicly burn the Solemn League and Covenant.[9] Subsequently, according to Sir Henry Townshend, the Lords and Commons issued a declaration stating that anyone who by word or deed defended the Covenant would be regarded as enemy of the king and the kingdom.[10] Burnings of the Covenant became incorporated into celebrations of Charles's birthday. At Linlithgow in Scotland, the Solemn League and Covenant was placed into a four-pillared wooden arch in the market place, along with other ordinances from the years of rebellion. At the drinking of the king's health, the arch was set alight to reveal beneath it a loyal inscription to Charles II. Townshend reported similar festivities taking place in Edinburgh. During the Exclusion Crisis, burnings of the Covenant became part of the Tory counter-processions organised in the wake of Whig pope-burning processions.[11]

There was considerable opposition inside and outside of Parliament to both the declarations abjuring the Covenant and the public burning of it. During the debates over the motion to burn the Covenant, one MP urged that it instead should be incorporated into the Act of Oblivion and Indemnity. There still remained a significant body of MPs who were sympathetic to Presbyterianism; 103 members voted against the motion to burn the Solemn League and Covenant.[12] (However, this vote represented the high-water mark

---

[7] HMC, 5th Report, p. 207.

[8] C. Robbins, 'Five Speeches, 1661–3, by Sir John Holland, MP', BIHR, xxviii (1955), 189–202, 196.

[9] CJ, viii, 254, 256; LJ, xi, 260.

[10] The Diary of Henry Townshend of Elmley Lovett, 1640–63, ed. J. W. Willis Bund (2 vols., Worcs. Hist. Soc., 1915–1920), i, 76.

[11] Historical Fragments, Relative to Scottish Affairs, from 1635 to 1664 (Edinburgh, 1833), pp. 100–3, a reprint of A Dismal Account of the Burning of our Solemne League and Covenant ([Edinburgh], 1661 or 1662); Townshend, Diary, i, 92; T. Harris, London Crowds in the Reign of Charles II (Cambridge, 1987), pp. 59, 168, 169; The Parallel: or the New Specious Association an Old Rebellious Covenant (1682).

[12] CJ, viii, 256; The Funeral of the Good Old Cause (1661); A Reply to the Funeral of the Good Old Cause (n. pl., 1661).

of Presbyterian opposition in the Cavalier Parliament.) In spite of the stigmatising of these documents as manifestos of sedition, a number of attempts were made to reimpose the Covenant. In September 1660 the committee of Common Council voted a petition for reinstating the Solemn League and Covenant only for this to be thrown out at Common Council itself.[13] An attempt was made in Parliament in April 1662 to renew the Covenant (though this seems to have had the opposite effect of provoking the Commons into voting that all records relating to it should also be burnt).[14]

From the mid-1640s onwards, the Solemn League and Covenant had become increasingly identified with a rather rigid Presbyterianism. The destruction of it perversely allowed it to become an emblem of the 'good old cause' for a variety of religious dissenters. Giles Calvert, a Baptist and the printer of many Leveller works in the 1640s, reissued Edmund Calamy's 1645 sermon on covenant breaking with the text of the Solemn League and Covenant as *The Phenix of the Solemn League and Covenant* in 1661. The frontispiece pictured the Covenant, like the mythical bird, rising from its ashes.[15] Calvert was not the only radical now prepared to defend it. *The Valley of Achor* (1660) ascribed by a conservative critic to John Rhye, a former Leveller and agitator, combined a vindication of the regicide court with support for the Solemn League and Covenant.[16] At his execution, Sir Henry Vane read out a speech justifying the 'good old cause' 'wherein he was engaged and for which suffred, from the Remonstrance of the Howse of Commons, [and] the Sollemne League and Covenant'.[17] Other advocates of the Covenant tried to remind Charles II that he had himself sworn to it at his coronation at Scone in 1651. Henry Townshend recorded a ballad of the time which urged God to 'save our Sovereign from presumptious sins/Let him remember, Lord; in mercy grant/ That solemnly he sware the Covenant.' The Presbyterian pamphleteer William Wickins reminded MPs, ministers and the general populace that 'thousands' of them still stood engaged to the obligations of the Covenant.[18]

A large proportion of these Presbyterian authors claimed that the Covenant was still in force as a religious obligation. Zachary Crofton, an Irish Presbyterian and the most outspoken of the pro-Covenant writers of the 1660s, argued

---

[13] HMC, *5th Report*, p. 156.

[14] CSPV, 1662, p. 133.

[15] *Biographical Dictionary of British Radicals in the Seventeenth Century*, eds. R. L. Greaves and R. Zaller (3 vols., Brighton, 1982), i, 119–20; [G. Calvert], *A Phenix, or the Solemn League and Covenant* (Edinburgh [really London], 'printed in the year of Covenant breaking' [1661]); CSPD, 1661–2, pp. 23, 50, 87.

[16] R. L. Greaves, *Deliver Us From Evil: The Radical Underground in Britain, 1660–3* (Oxford, 1986), p. 211.

[17] E. Ludlow, *A Voyce from the Watch Tower: Part Five: 1660–1662*, ed. A. B. Worden (Camden Society, Fourth Series, 21, 1978), p. 313.

[18] Townshend, *Diary*, i, 71; W. Wickins, *The Kingdoms Remembrancer, or the Protestation, Vow and Covenant, Solemne League and Covenant, Animadverted* (1660).

that it remained in force because 'in respect of its obligation, [the Covenant] is Publique and Nationall, as well as Private and Personall.' Therefore the Covenant was not limited in lifespan to the existence of those that had taken it 'but abideth fixed in things and capacities, which continue and abide under all mutation of persons, and so passe upon all persons whatsoever . . . who shall succeed into those things, places or capacities'. According to Crofton, even those who did not swear to it were bound to the Covenant and would be punished for breaking it for many hundreds of years to come.[19] This view of the oath as a perpetual obligation was supported by the sixth article of the Solemn League and Covenant itself by which the swearers promised to continue in it 'all the days of our lives'.[20] It was also pointed out by another pro-Covenant author that whilst the Protestation had been sworn to with a personal 'I, A. B.' the Solemn League and Covenant was taken by corporate bodies.[21]

The Covenant remained in effect not only because it was nationally imposed but also because it was a religious bond. Richard Baxter argued that the Covenant was essentially an embodiment of fundamental Christian duties. This, he said, did not make it a superfluous vow any more than the sacraments of baptism and the Lord's Supper were unnecessary.[22] Some Presbyterians argued that, as a covenant made with the lord, with God involved as an active party, no human authority could void its obligation. *The Covenanters Plea* (1661) explained that the Covenant could not be dispensed with by an act of Parliament or a declaration from the king because it was a vow to God as well as an oath or covenant between men.[23] The Presbyterian divine John Corbet stated the Covenant was 'not meerly a League between men' but 'a Vow to God of several things directly respecting him'. Consequently he said, 'God being a Party in an Oath or Vow of Duties directly respecting him, and antecedently required by his Law, no humane Authority can nullifie the obligation thereof.'[24] Anglican authors were aware that the conception of the Covenant as a perpetual obligation was one of the primary obstacles for Presbyterians in taking these declarations. John Gauden noted that some viewed the Covenant as a 'religious obligation, either newly made or renewed upon the soul of any

---

[19] Z. Crofton, *Analepsis Aneleplithe. The Fastning of St. Peters Fetters by Seven Links, or Propositions, or, the Efficacy and Extent of the Solemn League and Covenant Asserted and Vindicated* (1660), pp. 133–4; Crofton gained considerable notoriety in the 1660s. He was satirised in Francis Kirkman's *The Presbyterian Lash* (1661) in which a hot-headed Presbyterian minister, Notcroffe, is accused of administering 'dorsal discipline' to his maid.

[20] Kenyon, *Stuart Constitution*, p. 265.

[21] *A Short Surveigh of the Grand Case of the Present Ministry* (n. pl., 1663), pp. 45–6.

[22] R. Baxter, *The English Nonconformity, as Under King Charles II and King James II* (1689), pp. 125–9. See also *idem, The Nonconformists Plea for Peace: or an Account of their Judgement* (London, 1679), pp. 211–16.

[23] T. Timoricus, *The Covenanters Plea Against Absolvers* (1661), pp. 69–71.

[24] J. Corbet, *The Remains of the Reverend and Learned* (1684), pp. 167–8.

that willingly and freely took it', and that thereby some thought 'themselves eternally obliged to fulfill the letter of it, or that sense they had of it'.[25]

Presbyterians also argued that the ends of the Covenant could still be pursued lawfully in spite of the Act of Uniformity because it bound subscribers only to setting up of the kind of 'primitive episcopacy' advocated earlier by James Ussher, late archbishop of Armagh, not the removal of all church hierarchy. Although they had covenanted to extirpate prelacy absolutely, it was 'the abuse, not the thing; the adjuncts, not the subject; the defects and excesses, not its Fabrick' which were covenanted against.[26] Richard Baxter stated to Clarendon that, in considering the king's offer of bishoprics to them, he, Calamy, and Reynolds had agreed that the Covenant was no bar to accepting episcopal office.[27]

As in the Engagement Controversy, a number of Presbyterian authors backtracked on the Solemn League and Covenant's apparent commitment to limited monarchy. One defender of the Covenant denied that the clause relating to the king's person could be interpreted equivocally. However, the author argued the clause might be read as meaning as far as religion bound the subject, which from St Paul would require us to submit to the earthly magistrate in all things.[28] Zachary Crofton reminded the nation of the loyalty of the covenanters. The limitation that Royalists conceived the Covenant placed upon allegiance to the king was not borne out by the practice of the covenanters, which had, he said, been to defend the king's person. Crofton pointed to the efforts of the Presbyterians in opposing the 'late sinful Engagement', citing in particular the works of Edward Gee.[29]

However, these protestations of loyalty, and the emphasis on the religious character of the Covenant, concealed the extent to which some Presbyterians continued to employ familiar arguments from Parliamentarian political thought. Many of the Restoration defences of the Covenant used theories of mixed-government, popular sovereignty and lawful resistance to back their claims. Thomas Tomkins, later chaplain to Gilbert Sheldon, noted that Crofton used Prynne's *The Soveraigne Power of Parliaments* as a source in his vindication of the Covenant.[30] The authors of *A Short Surveigh of the Grand*

[25] J. Gauden, *Analysis: or the Loosing of St. Peter's Bands; Setting Forth the True Sense and Solution of the Covenant* (1660), pp. 14–15; CSPD, 1661–2, p. 62.
[26] Timoricus, *Covenanters Plea*, pp. 15–16; *A Declaration of the Presbiterians; Concerning His Maiesties Royal Person, and the Government of the Church of England. with Several Propositions Touching the Solemn League and Covenant* (1660), p. 2; *A Discourse Concerning the Solemne League and Covenant Proving it to be Obligatory* (n. pl., 1661), p. 12.
[27] *Baxter Correspondence*, ii, 8.
[28] *A Discourse Concerning the Solemne League and Covenant*, p. 6.
[29] Crofton, *The Fastning of St. Peters Fetters*, p. 103.
[30] T. Tomkins, *Short Strictures or Animadversions on So Much of Mr Croftons [Fastning St.Peters Fetters] as Concern the Reasons of the University of Oxford Concerning the Covenant* (1661), p. 5.

Case of the Present Ministry (1663) refused to agree with the second declaration forbidding the taking up of arms against the king. They insisted that a distinction between the monarch's private and public person was wholly necessary, particularly in the instance of a regency or protectorate.[31] Zachary Crofton relied heavily on the use of theories of co-ordinate powers to justify the continued obligation of the Covenant, a fact noted by one of his Anglican critics, Robert Cressner.[32] The Protestation, Crofton argued, proved that the Parliament had a co-ordinate power to make legislation without the royal consent.[33] Another pro-Covenant author revived the biblical precedents of covenants made with God without the magistrate's consent.[34]

Tomkins later insisted that the tendering of the declarations abjuring the Covenant had been a necessary response to the storm that had been provoked by removing it.[35] The supporters of the declarations claimed that the Covenant was 'not dead, as was alleged', but still retained 'great vigour; was still the idol to which the Presbyterians sacrificed'.[36] The element of fear motivating the opponents of the Covenant cannot be discounted. The bill for security of the king's person passed in May 1661 actually prohibited the making of all political or religious covenants.[37] In the early years of the Restoration, news of plots, real or imagined, against the monarchy abounded and even Presbyterians as prominent and respectable as Richard Baxter were implicated.[38] These fears were sustained throughout the 1670s by the reality of Covenanter rebellion in Scotland.[39]

Although some Restoration defences of the Covenant did make use of Parliamentarian arguments from the 1640s, it was not the threat of Presbyterian insurrection that really prolonged the debate over the oath. The opposition to the burning of the Covenant was not raised primarily in defence of a theory of resistance. It is better understood as part of the wider opposition to the exclusiveness of the Restoration settlement and the political and religious purges that sought to guarantee Cavalier–Anglican hegemony. The dispute

---

[31] *A Short Surveigh*, pp. 21–2.

[32] R. Cressner, *Anti-Baal Berith Justified* (London, 1662), p. 54.

[33] Z. Crofton, *Berith Anti-Baal, or Zach. Croftons Appearance Before the Prelate Justice of Peace* (1661), p. 39.

[34] *The Anatomy of Dr. Gauden's Idolised Non-sense and Blasphemy, in His Pretended Analysis, or Setting Forth the True Sense of the Covenant* (1660), pp. 15–17.

[35] [T. Tomkins], *The Modern Pleas for Comprehension Toleration and the Taking Away of the Obligation to the Renouncing of the Covenant, Considered and Discussed* (1675), p. 37.

[36] Hyde, *Continuation*, p. 1079.

[37] HMC, *5th Report*, p. 160; SR, v, 304–5.

[38] R. Hutton, *The Restoration: A Political and Religious History of England and Wales, 1658–1667* (Oxford, 1985), p. 165; CSPD, 1661–2, p. 143; HMC, *Finch MSS*, i (London, 1913), pp. 136–7; HMC, *Hastings MSS*, iv (London, 1947), p. 134.

[39] D. L. Smith, *A History of the Modern British Isles, 1603–1707: The Double Crown* (Oxford, 1998), pp. 253–5.

over the Covenant was actually sustained by the crown's desire for a policy of accommodation both with Protestant dissenters and Catholics. However, the frequency of debates on the obligation of the Covenant should not be read as meaning that the issue was necessarily of vital importance to nonconformists. Indeed, many dissenters appear to have been more troubled with the 'assent and consent' clause of the Act of Uniformity than with the requirement to renounce the Covenant.[40] (Although it is difficult to separate these issues as some writers alleged that they could not 'assent and consent' to the liturgy of the Church of England as the Covenant bound them to uphold the Directory of Worship.)[41] David Appleby has found that the farewell sermons of ministers ejected on Bartholomew's Day, 24 August 1662, contain no explicit references to the Covenant, though some do make allusions to the covenants of biblical Israel which have obvious political resonances.[42]

Moreover, although many works were produced after the Restoration in defence of the Solemn League and Covenant, there appears to have been little discussion of whether godly ministers should take or refuse the declarations abjuring it in the Act of Uniformity and Corporation Act. John Corbet noted that it was a popular argument that the declaration renouncing the obligation of the Covenant could be taken 'in a restrained sense, *viz*. That there lies no obligation from this Covenant, by Seditious, Factious, Turbulent and Tumultuous ways, to disturb the publick peace and Government now Established in Church and State.'[43] Corbet himself rejected the use of these limitations but it seems that some dissenters did employ them.[44] Some ministers seem to have used the tactic of reading their declarations out in church using the exact form of words in the statute – and thereby failing to replace the usual 'A. B.' with their names.[45] In spite of this, later historians of nonconformity claimed that the requirement to renounce the Covenant was a major stumbling block to conforming for many dissenters.[46] In a few cases, ejected

---

[40] *Short Surveigh*, p. 9.

[41] [T., P.,] *Jerub-Baal Redivivus* (1663), pp. 43–6; see also *idem*, *Jerub-baal or the Pleader Impleaded* (1662) (a reply to Zachary Crofton's call for Presbyterians to maintain communion with the Church of England in *Reformation not Separation*). Andrew Hopper has recently discovered that some godly ministers claimed that those that had taken the 1641 Protestation would be committing perjury if they attended Anglican services, 'The Farnley Wood Plot and the Memory of the Civil War in Yorkshire', *Historical Journal*, 45 (2002), 281–303, at 288.

[42] D. Appleby, 'For God or Caesar: The Dilemmas of Restoration Nonconformists', unpublished conference paper, delivered at the 'Conscience and the Early Modern World: 1500–1800' conference, Sheffield, July 2002. My thanks to David for letting me see a pre-circulation copy of this.

[43] Corbet, *Remains*, p. 170.

[44] Bodl. MS Rawl 373, f. 70–1.

[45] D. Appleby, 'For God or Caesar', citing C. Stanford, 'The Farewell Sunday', *St. Bartholomew's Bicentenary Papers*, VII (London, 1862), pp. 8–9.

[46] R. Baxter, *The English Nonconformity*, pp. 125–9; E. Calamy, *An Abridgement of Mr. Baxter's History of His Life and Times* (1702), pp. 538–42.

ministers had refused to conform specifically because of the declarations against the Covenant. Joseph Alleine's wife had fully expected her husband to conform but 'when he saw those clauses of Assent, and Consent, and Renouncing the Covenant, he was fully satisfied . . . seeing his way so plain for quitting the publeck Station that he held.'[47]

However, it is clear that the Covenant was artificially sustained as a live political issue by its use as a device to forestall debate on more sensitive matters (such as the imposition of penal legislation on Roman Catholics). The continued desire of Charles II for some policy of accommodation with Catholic and Protestant dissenters kept the debate alive. Charles's preference was for a policy of royal indulgence but the 'church party' in Parliament regarded this exercise of prerogative with jealousy. Instead, the two houses discussed proposals for a policy of 'comprehension', incorporating groups of Protestant dissenters into the church, which renewed discussions over removing the clause abjuring the Covenant.[48] Dropping the requirement to renounce the oath was a feature of a number of comprehension bills drafted in 1667.[49] One bill, drawn up by Matthew Hale, baron of the Exchequer, suggested removing all the current declarations required of ministers and replacing them with a new oath. This would require them only to *approve* 'the doctrine of Worship and Government established in the Church of England as concerning all things necessary to salvation' and to promise not to endeavour to bring in 'any doctrine contrary to that which is soe established'. This was followed by a promise to keep the peace and continue in communion with the Church of England.[50] None of these comprehension proposals could receive a proper hearing in the Commons. Instead the house requested on 4 March 1668 that the king put all penal laws against nonconformists into execution.[51] On 11 March during a debate on one of the proposals, Sir John Berkenhead, the former Royalist propagandist, urged the house to ignore the pleas of tender consciences. He reminded them how the Presbyterians had forced the Covenant upon the nation and would not admit any to a spiritual living that did not take it.[52]

The apparent centrality of the Covenant to debates over toleration or comprehension is deceptive, as is made clear by a discussion of the oath that took place in 1672. As a means to placate Charles for having opposed his declaration of indulgence of that year, Parliament discussed a 'Bill for granting

---

[47] [T. Alleine], *The Life and Death of Mr. Joseph Alleine* (1672), pp. 52–3; Calamy, *A Continuation of the Account*, ii, 754.

[48] J. Spurr, 'The Church of England, Comprehension and the Toleration Act of 1689', *English Historical Review*, civ (1989), 927–46.

[49] Contained in Bodl. B. 14. 15. Linc.

[50] Ibid., f. 9.

[51] Ibid., f. 8.

[52] *The Diary of John Milward, September 17th, 1666 to May 8th, 1668*, ed. Caroline Robbins (Cambridge, 1938), p. 220.

ease to his Majesty's Protestant Dissenting subjects'. These debates were moved to a grand committee of the house and focused heavily upon the obligation of the Solemn League and Covenant. Representatives of the court such as Henry Coventry, the Secretary of State, argued that the removal of the clause against the Covenant was too high a price to pay for broadening the church. If, he stated, 'we are to increase our garrison', he 'would not do it with those that have the plague'. The speaker, Heneage Finch, argued that the removal of the clause would honour the Covenant. He urged members to consider rather 'the Honour of this House; how often you have burnt it, and how many thousands are perjured by it'. On the whole, the defenders of the proviso that would have removed the obligation to renounce the Covenant did not attempt to vindicate the oath. Sir William Coventry urged that keeping this clause in the Act of Uniformity would only perpetuate the memory of a document that was best forgotten. Sir Thomas Meres, the Whig MP for Lincoln, stated that he was only interested in the union of Protestant subjects against common enemies and not in defending the Covenant. Sir Philip Warwick proposed a proviso which would still refer to the Solemn League and Covenant as a 'detestable oath' but would involve only those that had taken the oath swearing against its obligations and not any statement as to the obligation on others. John Birch, one of the leading spokesmen for the Presbyterians in the Commons, was the most outspoken defender of the Covenant, reminding the house of the efforts of the covenanters in restoring the king and their opposition to the execution of Charles I in 1649. The proposals were sent up to the Lords, but the bill was abandoned following the royal prorogation of Parliament on 20 October 1673.[53]

The debate on the Covenant that occurred in 1672 was lengthy but misleading. There can be little doubt that representatives of the court, including Henry Coventry and Sir Robert Carr, prompted a discussion of the Solemn League and Covenant as a means to delay moves to impose putative measures against Roman Catholics. There can be no other way of explaining the actions of the hard-line Anglican Giles Strangeways, who urged that the proviso for the covenanters be accepted so that the committee could get on with the more pressing matter of discussing measures against the papists.[54] The Covenant was being used as a political tool with which to frustrate the court's opponents. For some, in any case, the Covenant appeared to be somewhat of an irrelevancy. One contributor to the debates described it as a thing now only of interest to 'a few old gentlemen'.[55]

Similar partisan motivations can also be detected in the increasing resort after the Restoration to 'no alteration' oaths as a means to secure the

[53] Cobbett, *Parl. Deb.*, iv, 518–42; *Debates 1667–1694, Collected by the Hon. A. Grey* (10 vols., London, 1769), ii, 100–81; *CJ*, ix, 261.
[54] *Grey Debates*, ii, 101–2.
[55] Cobbett, *Parl. Deb.*, iv, 542.

constitution from change. These oaths tapped into fears about the country's security and so helped increase government support whilst forcing political opponents into a potentially damaging discussion of the right of resistance. The first concerted attempt at this was made in the Oxford session of the Cavalier Parliament in 1665. The oath, which later became a part of the Five Mile Act, followed the wording of the declaration against resistance in the Act of Uniformity except for the addition of the sentence, 'And that I will not at any time endeavour any Alteration of Government either in Church or State.' George Morley, bishop of Winchester, argued that, in refusing the declarations in the Act of Uniformity, Presbyterians mainly balked at denying the right of resistance:

> I have asked them can you read the Booke of Common Prayer? Yes. Can you use the Ceremonies? Yes. Why do you not then subscribe to the assent & consent since it is only to the use of it? I can: Can you subscribe that which Concerns the Covenant? Noe. Here they stick. They will not say they will renounce the last War, and they will forestall another. The Oath now in hand is not to Parliament Men & it may bee explained to Satisfaction.[56]

The oath was eventually defeated but only by the opportune introduction of Peregrine Bertie as a new member of the house. His vote, and those of his introducers, the Earl of Lindsay and Sir Thomas Osbourne, buried the bill.[57]

It is clear that some Presbyterians viewed the 'Oxford Oath' as effectively demanding the repudiation of the Covenant. Supporters of the test, including Archbishop Sheldon, tried to argue that the oath did not attempt to frustrate the legislative role of Parliament. The test, he claimed, was intended only to secure the fundamentals of government. 'What the Government is in England is well knowne,' said Sheldon, 'It is Monarchy in the State and Episcopacy in the Church, and the thing promised in the Oath is not to alter the Government in either.'[58] The one Presbyterian to write in support of the oath, John Tickell, suggested that 'considering the Principles and Practises of the late times' it would act as greater security than the Oaths of Allegiance and Supremacy. The test could, he argued, have been framed far less prudently by including a declaration renouncing the Covenant. Instead, it had been ordered in this way so that the 'sober and peaceable' could be distinguished from those that would return to their old persuasions.[59] Like other Restoration apologists for the Covenant, Tickell claimed that no one who had sworn to the Covenant could now suppose himself to be bound by it to alter the government in church and

---

[56] C. Robbins, 'The Oxford Session of the Long Parliament of Charles II, 9–31 October, 1665', *BIHR*, xxi (1948), 214–24, at 223–4.
[57] Ibid., 220.
[58] Ibid., 222.
[59] J. Tickell, *A Sober Enquiry About the New Oath Enjoyned on Nonconformists According to Act of Parliament* (1665), p. 2.

state 'since such endeavours would be against the Laws of the Land, to which we owe obedience; against the terms of the Covenant itself, and the Exhortation to it, is lawfully, and in place and calling, etc.'.[60] Some Presbyterians clearly found Tickell's arguments unconvincing. One anonymous critic asked, 'Wither the Apostles and Primitive Christtians had ever the like case, living under a Christtian state; wth Oaths & Covenants clashing one wth another?'[61] It was also evident that as applied to nonconforming ministers, hostile judges occasionally saw the oath as a repudiation of the Covenant. Baxter reported the appearance of twenty nonconforming ministers before Lord Chief Justice Keyling under advice that making the oath would only proscribe unlawful endeavours to alter the government. Keyling stated, however, that he was glad to see that so many nonconformists had chosen to renounce the Covenant.[62]

It seems clear that the 'Oxford Oath' was designed to make a further purge of dissenters and their political supporters within Parliament whilst exploiting the fears of Anglican gentry to increase the support for the 'church party'. Sheldon and Finch claimed that the oath was only an emergency measure aimed at uniting a country threatened by war abroad and plague at home.[63] Given the atmosphere of Anglican triumphalism in which the oath was passed, the claim seems dubious.[64] More probable is Baxter's opinion that the oath was designed as a snare to entrap those that took it and make those that refused it public pariahs. It would have been hard for non-subscribers to avoid being labelled as disloyal. The oath pushed dissenters into discussing extremely sensitive topics, including the right of resistance. Baxter claimed that when the oath was first imposed he had busied himself in producing a tract protesting the dissenters' political loyalty only to be dissuaded from the task by Lazarus Seaman.[65] The test divided nonconformists into subscribers and non-subscribers, with those that took the oath often being denounced as turncoats or Covenant renouncers. Baxter said that congregations reviled the London ministers who subscribed.[66] Similar divisions amongst non-conformists in Devon were noted with glee by the then bishop of Exeter, Seth Ward, who told Sheldon that he hoped to use these splits to increase the interest of the church in the county.[67]

---

[60] Ibid., p. 6.
[61] Bodl. MS Rawlinson D 1350, f. 324–7, at f. 327.
[62] Rel. Bax., part three, pp. 13–14.
[63] Tickell, A Sober Inquiry, pp. 1–2.
[64] On the background to the Oxford Parliament see R. A. Beddard, 'Restoration Oxford and the Remaking of the Protestant Establishment', The History of the University of Oxford IV: Seventeenth Century Oxford, ed. Tyacke, pp. 803–63.
[65] Rel. Bax., part three, p. 13.
[66] Ibid., part three, p. 14.
[67] Bodl. Add. MS C. 305, f. 168–71; The Nonconformist's Memorial, ed. S. Palmer (2 vols., London, 1778), i, 363, records that John Howe and eleven other Devon ministers took the oath but with reservations.

Certainly the 'Oxford Oath' succeeded in sowing division amongst non-conformist casuists asked to resolve queries over subscribing to it. What advice there was on taking the declarations against the Solemn League and Covenant had prohibited the making of limited subscriptions. In the case of the 'Oxford Oath', Presbyterian authors seem to have been split over whether or not tactics of equivocation could be used. Corbet felt that it could be read as only requiring the subscriber to abjure unlawful or seditious attempts to alter the government of church and state.[68] In making such a reading Corbet stated the need for caution so as not to use words otherwise than 'in their ordinary significations'. Even to force upon words 'a sense in it self Rational enough which is Alien from their ordinary signification', was, Corbet said, 'indeed Irrational'.[69] As the lawmakers had not declared their sense of the oath, Corbet argued that the oath could be taken in the most equitable sense that the words would bear. In this way it was 'most Rational to conceive that the Word endeavour' was 'to be taken in a restrained sense'. It could not be imagined that the framers of the oath 'intended to bind only one sort of men, called Nonconformists, from, lawful endeavours of the publick good' while others were left free.[70] Corbet finished his treatise on the 'Oxford Oath' by giving his limited reading of the oath, stating that he presented it not as the only way in which he would take the oath but declaring his sense of it in the hope of receiving further satisfaction.[71]

John Tickell followed the same line in his influential pamphlet on the oath. Tickell noted that the oath was 'somewhat ambiguous' but he judged that, if there was no public exposition of it, the subject was to understand it according to the 'common usage' of the words and by comparing it with other laws. However, the subject must not take the oath according to 'private suppositions' of the imposers' intentions.[72] Hoping to show that the oath was not in conflict with the Solemn League and Covenant, Tickell followed Corbet in arguing that it only bound the subscriber to refrain from all unlawful or seditious attempts to alter the government of church or state.[73] However, there was no consensus among Presbyterians as to whether it was lawful to use limitations in this case. Richard Baxter rejected the limited readings of the 'Oxford Oath' made by Tickell and Corbet. To Baxter the intent of the legislators was clear. It could not, he said, be the sense of the imposers that we were still allowed lawful endeavours because the oath applied to the government of both church and state. No one, Baxter argued, would say that there were lawful

[68] J. Corbet, *An Enquiry into the Oath Required of Nonconformists by an Act Made at Oxford* (1682), p. 8.

[69] Ibid., pp. 2–3.

[70] Ibid., pp. 9–13.

[71] Ibid., pp. 16–17.

[72] Tickell, *A Sober Inquiry*, p. 2.

[73] Ibid., pp. 4–6.

means to depose the king or change the constitution, so the oath must apply unconditionally.[74]

Divisions amongst casuists like Corbet and Baxter seem only to have increased the difficulties experienced by nonconformists in taking this oath. In seeking advice on whether it was lawful in this case to swear with limitations, Richard Baxter and other Presbyterians turned to judges for their reading of the oath. Baxter sent his queries on the oath, and a gloss on it that limited it to prohibiting unlawful endeavours to alter the church and state, to John Fountaine, sergeant-at-law and Sir John Maynard.[75] Fountaine replied that the 'fair and plain sense' of the oath was no more than that 'Subjects ought not to take up Arms against their Lawful King, or such as are lawfully Commissionated by him; and for private persons to be unquiet in the place where they live, to the disturbance of the government in Church or State.'[76] Despite the legal judgments in support of a limited reading of the oath, Baxter was not satisfied that he could subscribe, believing that the intention of the imposers had been to demand unconditionally that the takers would make no alteration to church or state. He informed John Humfrey, who intended to take the oath with just this kind of equivocation, that, if the imposers had not now made the sense of the words plain, they would soon enough once Humfrey had sworn to it.[77] Thomas Manton also refused to be drawn in by any legal indulgence.[78]

However, other ministers were convinced by legal advice that they could take the oath. The Lord Keeper, Orlando Bridgeman, informed the leading Presbyterian divine, William Bates, that the oath only prohibited seditious endeavours to alter the government of the church. Bates wanted this interpretation confirmed and, despite Keyling's outburst, limited subscriptions were given and accepted in open court from twenty ministers along with Bates.[79] We have evidence of several other instances where limited subscriptions from ministers were accepted in open court. Some ministers in Exeter refused to take the oath 'being not fully satisfied about the sence' and fearing what they would 'be guilty of if wee sweare in a sense of our owne agst or besides the true intent and meaneing of or legislators', but they stated that they were 'fully resolved never to take Armes agst the kings Person, Crowne, Diginity or Authority'.[80] Other ministers took the oath, but only after having made the following declaration, accepted by the magistrates:

That ye Oath hath no other meaning or End than to secure ye Person of ye Kings Ma ty. & his Authority; Wether in his Person or Commissioners, & ye govermt in

---

[74] *Rel. Bax.*, part three, pp. 11–13.

[75] Ibid., part three, pp. 7–9.

[76] Ibid., part three, p. 9.

[77] Ibid., part three, pp. 11–13; *Baxter Correspondence*, ii, 68–9.

[78] W. Harris, *Some Memoirs of the Life and Character of Dr. Thomas Manton* (1725), p. 36.

[79] *Rel. Bax.*, part three, pp. 13–14.

[80] Bodl. MS Rawlinson D 1320, f. 328.

church or state from being shaken or subverted, by any impeaceable or seditious Endeavours. out of our place & calling: I am aboundantly satisfied to tender my selfe to this Honorable court for ye takeing of itt.

Some of the ministers who used this declaration also added the phrase 'so far as ye laws of man are agreeable to ye word of god'.[81] William Ollyver, parson of Launceston in Somerset refused to swear not to endeavour to alter the government of church and state but declared that it was not lawful to 'take up armes against ye King upon anny pretence whatsoever'.[82] Henry Newcome reported that the Oxford Oath provoked very serious discussion amongst ministers in Yorkshire and London 'both by word and writing' but that the disagreements between Keyling and Bridgeman about the meaning of the oath cleared up the way for ministers as it made 'the sense clearly unclear, and so is a sufficient ground to waive the oath, till it be agreed what is the sense'.[83]

'No alteration' oaths were revived with the introduction of the Earl of Danby's test into the Lords on 19 April 1675. (It was an irony noted at the time that Danby's vote had helped to stop the extension of the Oxford Oath in 1665.)[84] Andrew Marvell listed the tests of 1665 and 1675 as key components of the design 'to change the Lawfull Government of England into an Absolute Tyranny, and to convert the established Protestant Religion into down-right Popery'.[85] However, it is hard to see these tests as part of a plot to set up an absolutist state. The preservation of the church and state from change does not appear to have been a significant motivating factor in producing these oaths. However, discussions over the Covenant and these tests were clearly part of a political plan. In 1675, Danby's test formed one component of a programme designed at cementing a Tory/Anglican alliance in support of the king. As well as uniting parts of the political nation, 'no alteration tests' were aimed at stigmatising the supporters of dissent and barring them from public employment. Oaths of loyalty were increasingly used after the Restoration, not as nationwide tests of allegiance, but as tools of exclusion, designed to purge political and religious opponents from office. In the 1660s and 1670s it was the dominant Anglican–Tory alliance that resorted to these tests, but in the 1680s, and, as will be demonstrated later, the 1690s Whigs would prove equally willing to use similar devices once they held the reins of power.

[81] Ibid., f. 329.
[82] Ibid., f. 330.
[83] Newcome, *Autobiography*, i, 154–5.
[84] On the 1675 test see K. H. D. Haley, *The First Earl of Shaftesbury* (Oxford, 1967), pp. 373–80; *Rel. Bax.*, part three, pp. 167–71; T. Harris, *Politics Under the Later Stuarts: Party Conflict in a Divided Society 1660–1715* (London, 1993), pp. 57–8, 73, 74; *CSPV, 1673–5*, pp. 397–8, 406,409–10; Cobbett, *Parl. Deb.*, iv, appendix v; Bodl. MS Rawlinson D 924, f. 297–300; HMC, *7th Report* (London, 1879), p. 492; *CSPD, 1675–6*, pp. 107, 112, 116, 129,136, 140.
[85] A. Marvell, *An Account of the Growth of Popery and Arbitrary Government in England* (Amsterdam, 1677), p. 3.

Significantly, it was again the issue of how to limit the powers of a popish successor to the throne which revived proposals for nationally subscribed oaths of loyalty. As in the 1640s, it was the renewed threat from popery which saw oaths of association restored as a means to secure the Protestant state. Equally, there remained a connection, at least in the eyes of the opponents of exclusion, between Protestant associations and the idea of a national covenant. Tory propagandists were quick to portray proposals for new oaths of association in the 1680s as really being the Solemn League and Covenant in sheep's clothing. The discovery of an association to resist the Duke of York in the Earl of Shaftesbury's papers, following his arrest for treason in 1681, led one author to write that it was 'the Scotch Covenant in a New Edition'.[86] John Knightley described the ignoramus jury which acquitted Shaftesbury as a 'band of covenanting associators'. He claimed that the branding of the oath as an association was precisely to make it more acceptable. 'Association', he said, 'will be easily swallowed, when League might stick a little in the Throat.'[87] Tory clerics John Knights, Nathaniel Bisbie and Edward Pelling preached sermons denouncing the association as a new covenant.[88] The pamphlet *The Two Associations* (1682) simply reprinted the Vow and Covenant side by side with Shaftesbury's association. Visual propaganda too employed the Covenant as an emblem of sedition; Stephen College's print *The Committee*, featuring a copy of it, hung above the heads of a cabal of plotting dissenters (Figure 8.1).

It was fairly common practice for Tory propagandists to portray their Whig opponents and dissenting allies as adherents to the 'good old cause' of the 1640s. As we have already seen, the Covenant was often exploited as a means to link Restoration dissent with civil war puritanism. Equally, the comparison of historical documents for political gain was unexceptional.[89] However, there still seems to be a grain of truth to these Tory accusations. Certainly, when the first few proposals were made for an oath of association in October 1678 and April 1679, this was just one of a raft of measures suggested for securing the nation from the dangers posed by a popish successor. None the less, Mark Knights has argued that the intent of these proposals was 'that the subjects' right to resist such a king, if he should invade religion or property should be acknowledged in the form of an "association of protestants" based upon Elizabethan precedent'. (In fact, members sought even earlier precedents,

[86] *Massinello: or, a Satyr Against the Association, and the Guildhall Riot* (1682), p. 7.
[87] [J. Knightley], *The Parallel: or, the New Specious Association an Old Rebellious Covenant* (1682), pp. 1, 7. See also *The True Loyalist: Wherein is Discovered, First, the Falsehood and Deceipt of the Solemn League and Covenant* (London, 1683).
[88] J. Knights, *The Samaritan Rebels Perjured by a Covenant and Association* (1682); N. Bisbie, *Prosecution no Persecution, or the Difference Between Suffering for Disobedience and Faction, and Suffering for Righteousness* (1682); idem, *The Modern Pharisees* (1683); E. Pelling, *A Sermon Preached at St. Mary le Bow, Nov. 27 1682* (1683).
[89] See Scott, *England's Troubles*, pp. 439–43.

Figure 8.1 The Committee or Popery in Masquerade (1680).
(By permission of the British Library (BMC 1080).)

Colonel Edward Cooke referring to an act of association made in Edward III's time.)[90] A long debate in the House of Commons on 7 December 1678 included an association in provisions that would enable Protestants to 'withstand and defend themselves against any Papist whatsoever that should come with commission and bear arms in any military employment'.[91] By December 1680 the idea of an association was radicalised further by linking it with proposals for the exclusion of James II. It was now suggested that no one should bear office in the government without taking such an oath. It is clear that by this stage the political demands of the crisis rendered an association like that imposed in 1584 unsatisfactory. In a debate of a Grand Committee of the house on 15 December, Sir William Jones stated that the Elizabethan Association was now an inadequate model, as it was important that the association 'take effect during the King's lifetime, so that if the Papists should be in arms to bring in their religion, we may have a law on our sides to defend ourselves'.[92] He reminded the members that Charles II's privy councillors were not cut from the same cloth as Burghley and Walsingham. These proposals were now also linked to the idea of an interregnum with the suggestion that Parliament would continue sitting in the event of the king's death.[93]

Further links back to earlier oaths and covenants are apparent in the texts of these draft associations. The Protestant association bill proposed on 23 November 1680 shares far more similarities with the Solemn League and Covenant than with the Elizabethan Association. As with the Covenant, the association was to be read and pasted up in churches. It was to be taken not only by the gentry and nobility but all males over the age of 18. Upon the king's death the people within the association were to arm themselves until the Parliament should be recalled. Those that took the association were also to subscribe to the test acts as proof of their Protestantism. The militia was to be placed in the control of the heads of the association who were also to have the power of martial law during the time between the king's death and the recall of Parliament.[94] Pamphleteers emphasised the necessity of this association 'not only for the right ordering of a Protestant League and Association within . . . these three kingdoms, but to further and promote the same amongst all Protestant Princes and Countries'.[95] Even Tory critics of the association found in Shaftesbury's papers had to admit that it was little different in sub-

---

[90] HMC, *Ormonde MSS*, n. s. v. (1908), p. 502. (This is probably a reference to the petition of 1376 which urged Edward to recognise Richard of Bordeaux, not John of Gaunt, as his heir, see *English Historical Documents 1327–1485*, ed. A. R. Myers (London, 1969), p. 122.)
[91] Knights, *Politics and Opinion*, p. 33.
[92] Grey, *Debates*, viii, pp. 167–8; *The History of the Association* (1682), p. 5; see also HMC, *Finch MSS*, ii (1922), p. 95.
[93] *LJ*, xiii, p. 684; HMC, *Ormonde MSS* n. s. v., p. 502.
[94] HMC, *House of Lords MSS, 1678–88* (London, 1887), pp. 210–11.
[95] *The Instrument: or Writing of Association: that the True Protestants of England Entred into in the Reign of Queen Elizabeth* (1679), p. 12.

stance from the bill that had already been discussed in Parliament.[96] The radical potential of these proposals extended to suggestions that whilst Parliament was not in session, an extra-Parliamentary association should be formed 'to preserve the King's person, Protestant Religion and Government'.[97]

There was an element of truth to the claims of Tory propagandists that the projected association in defence of Charles II was really a reconstituted version of the Solemn League and Covenant. They were both documents which saw England as in the centre of an international conflict between the forces of Protestantism and the allies of Antichrist. The protestations of allegiance to the reigning monarch in both the Covenant and the Exclusionist association are equivocal to say the least. We can gain an idea of what the impact of these schemes would have been if they had been put into effect by looking forward to the Revolution of 1688. Despite the taint of sedition attached to them during the Exclusion Crisis, Englishmen of a variety of political persuasions were again to be found subscribing an oath of association in December of that year. Historians have essentially seen the bond of association to the Prince of Orange signed at Exeter as a means of avoiding explicitly stating that William's supporters were resisting the king. J. P. Kenyon pointed to it as evidence of the lack of ideological conviction in 1688, whilst W. A. Speck discussed it as a pragmatic measure designed to give the heterogeneous group of supporters William had attracted some cohesion.[98] However, although it was proposed by the Tory Sir Edward Seymour (who would later refuse the 1696 Williamite Association), it was in fact an astoundingly bold political statement. We should recall at this point that even the associations drawn up in the 1640s were made ostensibly for the defence of the king's person. Here, though, was an association made by English subjects to a foreign head of state whilst the actual sovereign was still alive. As in previous associations, the takers promised that they would pursue not only those that attempted to kill or injure William, 'but all their Adherents, and all that we find in Arms against us'. Even a successful assassination attempt would not divert them 'from prosecuting this cause . . . but that it shall engage us to carry it on with all the vigour that so barbarous a Practice shall deserve'.[99] Nowhere in this association is there mention of the subject's duty of allegiance to James II and it seems probable that the king was meant to be included in the clause discussing the punishments to be handed out to the adherents of papists in arms. Like earlier associations this oath was also tendered to the public as William made his progress east. The Assembly of Commoners also subscribed the association, with, according to Roger Morrice, fewer than twenty of two hundred and twenty members refusing it.

---

[96] *A Second Return to the Letter of a Noble Peer, Concerning the Addresses* (1682?), p. 1.
[97] *The Instrument*, p. 4; Knights, *Politics and Opinion*, p. 238.
[98] J. P. Kenyon, *Revolution Principles* (Cambridge, 1977), p. 6; W. A. Speck, *Reluctant Revolutionaries: Englishmen and the Revolution of 1688* (Oxford, 1988), pp. 230–2.
[99] *CJ*, x, p. 6.

It was even rumoured that no one would be allowed to hold public office without taking the Exeter Association.[100] As John Guy has noted, in December 1688 it almost seemed as if the schemes of the 1580s and 1680s for an interim republic, secured by an oath of association, had been made a reality as ad hoc assemblies of peers and commoners bound themselves to defend William and the Protestant religion.[101]

Whilst it is clear that the Solemn League and Covenant remained a politically live document in the Restoration period, it is harder to assess how significant an obstacle the Covenant was in preventing Presbyterians from conforming to the Restoration church. It was, of course, very dangerous to claim still to be bound to the terms of the Solemn League and Covenant. Many may have preferred to cite less contentious reasons for their nonconformity, such as objections to the Anglican liturgy and ceremonies. However, as we have already seen, liturgical objections could not easily be separated from the matter of the Covenant. Some ministers did, though, explicitly list the demand to renounce the Covenant as a key reason for refusing to take the declarations included in the Act of Uniformity. The issue of the Covenant appears to have presented Presbyterians with a case of conscience of remarkable longevity, revealing the ways in which some dissenters did believe that they were bound to its terms in perpetuity. In 1677 advice was still being offered to dissenters over whether it was sinful to attend the services of those who had broken their Covenant in order to keep their livings.[102] William Faulkner's *Libertas Ecclesiastica* (1673), a work intended to answer dissenters' scruples about conforming to the Church of England, included in all its editions (the last of which was published in 1683) a section proving that the Covenant was non-obliging.[103] Writing some time between 1707 and his death in 1710, the Newcastle nonconformist Ambrose Barnes wrote that the

> Solemn League and Covenant, for the substance of it, was certainly a sacred bond between the two nations, tending to the establishment of Protestant religion in them both. It was the oath of god which we can never discharge ourselves of, til God forego his part, which to be sure he never will . . . Whatever be the frame of

---

[100] R. A. Beddard, 'The Unexpected Whig Revolution of 1688', *The Revolutions of 1688*, ed. Beddard (Oxford, 1991), pp. 11–102, at pp. 40, 45, 52. See BL Add. MS 28252, f. 53, 'List of members that refused the association to the Prince of Orange'.
[101] Guy, *Reign of Elizabeth*, p. 15.
[102] P. Nye, *A Case of Great and Present Use, Whether We May Lawfully Hear the Now Conforming Ministers, Who are Re-Ordained and Have Renounced the Covenant* (1677) [published posthumously]. See also *Calendar of the Correspondence of Richard Baxter*, eds. N. H. Keeble and G. Nuttall (2 vols., Oxford, 1991), ii, 49–52.
[103] W. Faulkner, *Libertas Ecclesiastica* (1677 edn.), pp. 66–84. J. Troughton, *An Apology for the Non-Conformists* (1681), p. 59.

civil government amongst us, tis a further reformation that can alone discharge us from the obligations of that covenant.[104]

Although the requirement to abjure the Covenant as part of the Act of Uniformity lapsed after 25 March 1682, there was no time limit on the same declaration in the Corporation Act and civic officers were still being asked to renounce it into the eighteenth century.[105]

Yet we would be taking the later hagiographers of nonconformity too much at their word if we were to assume that Presbyterians in the post-Restoration period only viewed the Covenant as carrying religious obligations. The motivations behind Anglican attacks on the Covenant are obvious but within all the bitter invective were a few words of truth. Advocates of the Solemn League and Covenant like Zachary Crofton did make use of Parliamentarian political theory and they did refuse to abjure the right of resistance. Many continued to view the Covenant as a commitment to limited monarchy and the theory of co-ordinate powers. The inability of Restoration spokesmen for the Covenant to divorce their religious arguments from a radical political philosophy provided their opponents with an opportunity to press for new, nationwide tests which would expose their constitutional heterodoxy. As it turned out, neither the 1665 or 1675 'no alteration' oaths were ever imposed on the public at large. However, the idea of a nationally subscribed oath as a 'limitation' measure was revived during the 1680s but quickly became linked to plans not merely to curb the powers of a popish successor but actually to exclude James from the throne. Again the idea of a Protestant association was coupled, as it had been in the past, with proposals for an interim government in event of the king's death and security measures to protect against foreign invasion and domestic insurrection. In 1688 such schemes were put into effect, as James II 'vacated' the throne, only for the reins of power to be taken up by assemblies of lords and commoners. As will be demonstrated in the Epilogue below, sworn associations would be used again to defend the Protestant succession, although, as we will see, these measures were successfully detached from their contentious past.

---

[104] *Memoirs of the Life of Ambrose Barnes*, ed. W. H. D. Longstaffe (Surtees Soc., 50, 1866), p. 267. I am dating the writing of this from Barnes's references to the union with Scotland.
[105] Kenyon, *Stuart Constitution*, p. 356 n. NRO, NCR 13c/3 contains rolls of declarations against the Covenant from 1678 to 1718.

Epilogue

'For the Preservation of Our Happy Constitution in Church and State': Protestant associations in the eighteenth century

Tory propagandists alleged that the oaths of association proposed and tendered in the 1680s had close similarities with the Long Parliament's oaths of loyalty and, as we have seen, they did indeed share some features with the Solemn League and Covenant. This final chapter looks at the continued importance of Protestant associations in the eighteenth century, in particular the Association to William III in 1696 and the anti-Jacobite associations of 1715 and 1745. Although these associations evidently built upon the frequent practice of tendering oaths of allegiance to the adult male population in the sixteenth and seventeenth centuries, and specifically upon the practice of forming defensive Protestant associations, we will see that this earlier history of oath making was barely acknowledged post-1700. The reasons for this are varied: the cooling of millenarian and apocalyptic expectations post-Restoration; the Tory/Jacobite tactic of linking Whiggery and dissent with civil war radicalism; and the desire of the Whig leadership themselves to distance their party from the republican aspirations of 'Commonwealthsmen'. Combined they contributed to obscure the extent to which many in early modern England, as in Scotland, had invested into the idea that it was a covenanted nation.

With the flight of James II and the end, for the time being, of the possibility of the crisis being militarily resolved, William was left needing to build a broadly based political coalition. In spite of the previous flirtation with an association to the Prince of Orange, the new oath of allegiance to William and Mary passed in 1689, unlike those to previous monarchs, made no reference to their being 'rightful and lawful' sovereigns.[1] The tendering of the new oaths none the less

---

[1] J. C. Findon, 'The Non-Jurors and the Church of England 1689–1716' (Oxford Univ. D.Phil. thesis, 1978), pp. 6–14; E. N. Williams, *The Eighteenth Century Constitution 1688–1815* (Cambridge, 1960), pp. 29–30; H. Horwitz, *Revolution Politicks: The Career of Daniel Finch, 2nd Earl of Nottingham, 1647–1730* (Cambridge, 1968), p. 82; idem, *Parliament, Policy and Politics in the Reign of William III* (Manchester, 1977), pp. 21–2, 24–5, 26.

sparked a considerable controversy which was largely dominated by arguments about giving allegiance to the king in possession of the throne.[2] For the Whig party, the presence of so many Tory statesmen in government whose allegiance to the king was equivocal at best offered them the opportunity to press for more stringent oaths of loyalty, as a means to exclude their political opponents from office. Bills for an oath of abjuration disclaiming James's right to the throne were introduced in 1690 and 1693, but failed in Tory dominated Parliaments.[3]

A more stringent test of loyalty was finally passed in 1696 as news of an assassination plot against William led the Commons to agree to a sworn 'association' in defence of the king. According to this, the subscribers were to 'heartily, sincerely, solemnly profess, testify and declare, That his present Majesty, King William, is rightful and lawful King of these Realms'. They promised to assist each other in revenging the king's death should any assassination plot prove successful.[4] Unlike the oaths of allegiance passed in 1689, which were only imposed on the clergy and those in public office, the association was tendered to the public at large.[5] In wording and form the oath harked back to the 1584 Association, and contemporaries noted the Elizabethan parallel.[6] In this instance, however, the anxiety caused by the assassination plot was relatively minimal and it was even rumoured that the whole conspiracy had been fabricated to serve the government's purposes.[7]

Dennis Rubini concurs with John Kenyon in seeing the 1696 Association as a means for court Whigs to cut off a ministerial challenge from de factoist Tories and, by imposing the oath nationally, cripple the country opposition in England as a whole. Certainly, a large number of Tory MPs and peers had considerable problems in swearing to William as a *de jure* monarch. Sir Edward Seymour and Heneage Finch complained that the words rightful and lawful 'imported one, who was king by descent, and so could not belong to the present king'. In the Lords, Edward Hyde, earl of Rochester, successfully moved that the wording of the Association, as taken by the peers, should be changed so

[2] M. Goldie, 'The Revolution of 1689 and the Structure of Political Argument', *Bulletin of Research in the Humanities*, lxxxiii (1980), 473–564.
[3] Kenyon, *Revolution Principles*, pp. 31–2; Horowitz, *Parliament, Policy and Politics*, p. 56; Cobbett, *Parl. Deb.*, v, 595, 602.
[4] *CJ*, xi, 470.
[5] D. Cressy, 'Literacy in 17th Century England, More Evidence', *Journal of Interdisciplinary History*, viii (1977), 141–50, at 144; J. S. W. Gibson, *The Hearth Tax, Other Later Stuart Tax Lists and the Association Oath Rolls* (Federation of Family History Society Publications, 1985).
[6] *The Parliamentary Diary of Sir Richard Cocks*, ed. D. Hayton (Oxford, 1996), p. 36.
[7] 'Association Oath Rolls for Wiltshire', ed. *LJ* Acton Pile, *Wiltshire Notes and Queries*, vi (1908–10), 197–201, at 198. On the plot see J. Garrett, *The Triumphs of Providence: The Assassination Plot, 1696* (Cambridge, 1980).

that it would acknowledge only that William had a 'right by law' to the throne.[8] Overall, one hundred and thirteen MPs and more than twenty peers refused to take the oath, though at this stage there were no penalties for failing to subscribe.[9]

In the localities, the Association was used to oust the 'disaffected' from public office.[10] Occasionally, whole towns which were deemed politically suspect were left off the Association returns. In Radnor, Wales, Sir Rowland Gwyn would only allow 'friends' to sign the Association, as a means to help him form a new county committee in opposition to the clients of Sir Robert Harley.[11] In a number of returns, the inhabitants promised in future only to elect MPs that had subscribed the Association and/or were deemed loyal to the present government. The address from Brackley in Northamptonshire swore 'never to send up' members that had refused the oath.[12] On the Isle of Wight subscribers went even further offering, as a mark of their 'undoubted loyalty and most dutifull affection' to William III, to 'endeavour to expose such unfitt representatives to serve in Parliam[en]t as shall refuse to signe the Association'.[13] Before the 1698 election there were actually rumours that those who refused to sign the Association would be barred from sitting in Parliament, although the court seems not to have implemented this proposal.[14] In the 1699/1700 session of Parliament, bills were introduced which would have disabled MPs and members of corporations that refused the oath from holding office.[15]

Aside from being used as an instrument to exclude the country opposition from both central and local government, the Association was also intended to bolster William's title. The death of Queen Mary in 1694 had deprived the king of the argument, which had been popular with Williamite Tories, that he had an hereditary right by proxy to the throne. The notion that the failure of Fenwick's plot demonstrated 'God's signal providence' towards William, strengthened the claims of earlier court propaganda that the king was the nation's divinely appointed deliverer from popery. In fact, given the lack of court-sponsored pamphlets (in contrast to 1689) promoting the Association,

[8] Cobbett, *Parl. Deb.*, v, 992: HMC, *Kenyon MSS* (1894), p. 406; HMC, *Hastings MSS*, ii (1930), p. 259; *An Impartial Account of the Horrid and Detestable Conspiracy to Assassinate His Sacred Majesty King William* (1696), p. 17; D. Rubini, *Court and Country 1688–1702* (London, 1967), p. 64.

[9] Cressy, 'Binding the Nation', p. 228.

[10] Cressy, 'Binding', p. 230 states that 86 JPs and 104 deputy lieutenants lost their posts for failing to subscribe or failing to do so quickly enough.

[11] Rubini, *Court and Country*, p. 66.

[12] PRO C213/191. Similar promises were made by subscribers in Nottinghamshire and Shropshire, PRO C213/204, 218.

[13] PRO C213/256.

[14] Rubini, *Court and Country*, p. 65.

[15] *Diary of Sir Richard Cocks*, p. 7; LJ, xvi, pp. 557, 559, 561, 578.

it is fair to say that the oath returns themselves were the regime's propaganda. Hundreds of printed copies of the text of the Association were made on vellum or parchment, ready to be signed. The returns for some counties were vast; David Cressy estimates that those for Suffolk contain over 70,000 signatures.[16] Loyal addresses provided the public with an opportunity to demonstrate their fidelity to the king. The officers of the Shropshire militia hoped that 'the gratious providence that hath sav'd you, from so many imminent dangers ever watch over you and preserve you long the impregnable bulwark of our Religion, Lives, Liberties and Properties.'[17] Many of these addresses referred to William as the saviour of the Protestant religion, not only in Britain, but also in Europe as a whole. The signatories to the Lichfield Association described William as 'the defender of our fayth, the deliverer of our Church and Nation, the Preserver of the Reformed Religion and Libertyes of Europe'.[18] Others commented on the threat of invasion from France. The subscribers for Malmesbury wrote that, by their 'Villanous and detestable conspiracy', Louis XIV and James II had hoped they might 'with more ease and felicity Invade this Kingdom, subvert its Government, plunder its Cities, alter its laws and religion and make it the miserable seat of Warr and Desolution'.[19] The Oxfordshire watchmaker, John Harris, clearly felt signing the Association alone was an inadequate expression of loyalty and added to his subscription that he did 'ack[n]o[w]ledg[e] and o[w]ne my sovran Lord King William to be Rightfull and Lawfull King of England'.[20] In some areas, subscription to the Association was accompanied by great pomp and ceremony. Edward Canby wrote to John Roades in April 1696 with news of subscription at Doncaster where for 'the honour of my Lord and the credit of our lordship, we marched in with 200 horse. . . . It made a great noise in the town so that the streets were filled and windows decked with fair ladies.'[21]

The 1696 Association represented a considerable coup for William and the court Whigs, both in terms of its value as propaganda for the regime and its effectiveness as a political purgative. However, the sheer volume of returns alone cannot be taken to indicate that the whole nation was united in its loyalty to William III. Rubini suggests that many subscribed out of fear or self-interest, arguing that a large proportion of the 28,000 who took the Association in Lancaster did so to prevent the abrogation of the privileges of the duchy. The Whig leaders of the county told weavers in Norwich that the more zeal they showed for the king, the more support there would be from the court for a bill prohibiting the import of Indian silks.[22]

---

[16] Cressy, 'Binding the Nation', p. 231.
[17] PRO C213/213.
[18] PRO C213/263B.
[19] PRO C213/201.
[20] PRO C213/208.
[21] HMC, *Various MSS*, viii (1913), p. 81.
[22] Rubini, *Court and Country*, p. 66.

Loyal declarations, whilst presenting the public with an opportunity to declare their support for the government, also allowed the public to make professions of allegiance on different terms from those offered in the Association itself. The oath was taken in Britain's colonies and by British merchants in Europe, and their declarations reflected the different political relationship with the monarchy. The address from Montserrat made no mention of William being rightful and lawful king but only hoped that his survival would allow the colonists to continue to go about their business freely and 'eate our Breade with more safety'. William Wilkinson and his son appended a declaration to their subscriptions to the Bermuda roll that they would be 'willingly subject to' William's 'just and Lawfull Commands' and suffer his unlawful ones (hardly a ringing endorsement of the king's title).[23] Within England the tone of the declarations ranged from the unctuously toadying to that produced by the inhabitants of Bere Regis in Dorset which marked a return to the language of the 1640s. Suggesting, as John Pym had done, that the Association be used as a shibboleth to test the faith of Protestants, they called on William to become an 'Angel of God' and 'discern between ye good and ye wicked, that yor searching and trying may not be over, till a compliant purge be made'.[24] The borough of Arundel drafted a loyal address which made no mention of James II or his claims to the throne but only the threat of French invasion.[25] In Malmesbury, the declaration referred to William as 'lawfull and rightfull' king. This may have only been an accidental inversion of the phrase in the Association itself, but it could also be taken as meaning that William only had a 'right by law' to the throne.[26] The address produced by the officers and sailors of Trinity House, Newcastle upon Tyne, made no reference to the king's legal, providential or hereditary right to the throne and described William only as the 'deliverer of these nations' whom they promised to assist 'against the force and power of France'. There were far more signatures to this loyal declaration than to the text of the Association itself, though the subscribers to the oath claimed they were signing for the rest of Trinity House.[27]

Aside from the ambiguous wording of some of the humble addresses to the king, the Association returns also contain a significant number of refusers or equivocators with the test. Perhaps the most striking feature of these county subscriptions, in comparison with earlier oaths of loyalty, is the almost total absence of any record of Catholics refusing the oath. Only a mere handful are registered as declining the Association.[28] Mike Braddick's research on the

---

[23] *The Association Oath Rolls of the British Plantations*, ed. W. Gandy (London, 1922), pp. 60, 67.

[24] P[ublic] R[ecord] O[ffice, Kew] C213/104; For toadying see the Windsor roll, PRO C213/7.

[25] PRO C213/282.

[26] PRO C213/301.

[27] PRO C213/196.

[28] For Catholic refusers see PRO C213/264 pt. 21; C213/2 f. 1v.

administration of the Association has revealed that deputy lieutenants were very familiar with the make-up of local Catholic populations by 1696.[29] Those Catholics judged to be a danger to the state were easily located and placed in custody.[30] The Buckinghamshire militia harried their recusant population with such zeal that Robert Throckmorton, a prominent local Catholic who had asked to stay at home with his sick wife, she 'havving binn lately lyke to Dye', and had offered profuse expressions of loyalty to the king, was nonetheless placed in custody in London.[31]

Quakers, on the other hand, regularly appear as refusers of or equivocators with the Association. Friends are recorded as declining to take the oath in Brainford in Norfolk, Hoston in Middlesex, Mundon Magna in Herefordshire, Whitechurch near Southampton, Hilsham and Holipstow in Suffolk, and Hawkeshead, in Lancashire.[32] Other Quakers chose to subscribe but with the limitation that they could not promise to revenge for themselves or anyone else. Robert Gerces of Winington in Lancashire stated that he was 'willing to be a trew subject but not to take up any carnall weapon'.[33] Suffolk Quakers followed the declaration adopted by the London members of the sect on 28 March 1696 which stated that the setting up of 'Kings and Governments' belonged to 'God's peculiar Prerogative' and that they had no part in it but to 'pray for the King and for the safety of the Nation'. Treacherous designs, they said, were the works of 'the Devil and Darkness'. They blessed God and were 'heartily Thankful to the King and Government, for the Liberty and Priviledges we Enjoy under them by law'.[34] Mary Geiter has argued that the Quaker declarations were part of a political bargain, in return for which the government would promote the passing of the Affirmation Bill, allowing Friends to avoid having to swear.[35] If so, the court ought to have felt somewhat short-changed. Stripped of its hyperbole, this declaration represents little more than a promise of passive obedience. Given some Friends' previous co-operation with James II's religious policies, and the fact that the Quaker leader William Penn was

---

[29] M. J. Braddick, *State Formation in Early Modern England* (Cambridge, 2000), pp. 327–30.

[30] Ibid., p. 329.

[31] Ibid., pp. 328, 330. Steve Pincus, in his forthcoming book on the Revolution of 1688–9 has found MS sources indicating great interest amongst Catholics to associate, including lobbying foreign diplomats to beg Secretary Somers to allow them to present separate Catholic lists.

[32] C213/181 pt. 5; / 121 f. 90, 105; / 251; /264 pt. 8; /152; *Lancashire Association*, ed. Gandy, p. 85.

[33] *Lancashire Association*, ed. Gandy, p. 63; for similar declarations see the Westhorpe Suffolk return, PRO C213/264 pt. 17 and returns for Godalming and Godalming hamlet in Surrey PRO C213/269.

[34] PRO C213/170b; for similar returns see C213/264 pt. 1.

[35] Geiter, 'Affirmation, Assassination and Association'; *idem*, 'William Penn and Jacobitism: A Smoking Gun?', *Historical Research*, LXXIII, 181 (2000), 213–19.

probably a Jacobite conspirator and had been implicated in the plot, this was less than reassuring.[36]

By far the most equivocal response to the demand for a show of allegiance to the king came from the Anglican clergy. Parochial ministers figure regularly in county returns as either refusing or placing limitations on the Association. In Bedfordshire several ministers refused to take the oath, whilst Edward Gibson, vicar of Hawnes in the same county, would only subscribe 'as far as by ye laws of God and those of this Realm doe oblige or allow'.[37] These individual returns might be deemed relatively insignificant were it not for the fact that, with the exception of Beacon in the diocese of St Davids,[38] none of the deans and chapters actually put their names to the text of the Commons' Association. What they signed instead were two variant forms of a loyal address to the king, which significantly diluted the meaning of the original oath. The first 'Canterbury version' of this address acknowledged the 'gracious providence of God' in saving William and described him as 'Rightfull and lawfull Soveraigne Lord and King'. However, though they vowed to 'stand by and assist each other to the utmost of our power' in defending the king's person and government from the attempts of King James and William's other enemies, the promise to revenge or even punish would-be assassins and their adherents was absent from this address, which was not only taken by the clergy in the diocese of Canterbury, but in Shropshire, Rochester, Worcester, Bath and Wells and Lincoln as well.[39] On the Strafford and Buckingham returns, the text of the original address had clearly been scratched out where it referred to the king's title, and the words 'rightfull and lawfull' inserted instead.[40] It is likely that the initial wording of these two addresses followed that subscribed at York. This was identical to the Canterbury version except that it only described the king as having a 'Right by Law to the Crowne'.[41] Humphrey Prideaux advised the Norwich clergy to take the Association in this more moderate form as the 'ready subscribing of it will be ye surest way to prevent an harder form being imposed on us'. In spite of its leniency he expected only a 'lame return' from the archdeaconry.[42] The York address was followed by all the remaining

[36] Geiter, 'Affirmation, Assassination and Association', pp. 277, 281; see also M. Goldie, 'James II and the Dissenters' Revenge: The Commission of Enquiry 1688', *Historical Research*, LXVI (1993), 53–88. An equally anodyne address was produced by the London Baptists C213/170A.

[37] C213/2, f. 3v, 4v, 7v, 9. Equivocal returns also exist for Kent clergy C213/129. See also C213/152 pt. 4 for the subscription of Robert Ivory, vicar of Hoston parish, Middlesex: 'In ye sense I understand this association, and as farr as it concerns me, I subscribe it.'

[38] C213/420.

[39] C213/402; /417[same roll as Stafford clergy]/419/430/431/448/452.

[40] C213/417; /454.

[41] C213/404.

[42] *Letters of Humphrey Prideaux, sometime Dean of Norwich to John Ellis, sometime Under-secretary of State, 1674–1722*, ed. E. M. Thompson (Camden new series, 15, 1875), p. 170.

deaneries and archdeaconries that delivered returns with the exception of Exeter cathedral where the bishops, dean and chapters acknowledged that William was invested 'with a legall Right and Title'. In Exeter it was even alleged that clergymen were encouraging locals to refuse the oath by putting 'scruples into peoples heads' about the words 'rightful and lawful' and 'revenge'.[43]

It is perhaps understandable that the clergy would have had problems with swearing to personally revenge the death of the king, but the omission of the word was a consequence of more than just clerical scruples, as returns from some laymen demonstrate. In Norwich, the original association of the corporation used the term 'punish' instead of 'revenge'.[44] Humphrey Prideaux's letters suggested an alternative reason for this unease at the idea of 'revenging' William's death. He was concerned that those carrying out any post-assassination vengeance 'would draw their swords and cut the throats of all the Jacobites' and that Jacobite might be interpreted by these vigilantes to mean all 'whom the rabble shall think fit to plunder and abuse'.[45] Tory clerics (and perhaps Tory politicians) who scrupled at acknowledging that William had anything other than a legal claim to the throne would, Prideaux suspected, be amongst the first of those that would suffer reprisals. It seems that some objections were raised to the clergy subscribing in this equivocal way, but the government did not, in the end, demand that they take the Commons' Association.[46]

If the intention of the Association was, in part, to set William's title on a firmer footing, it clearly failed in the case of the Anglican clergy. Given the pre-history of the Non-Juring schism and the controversy over the new oaths of allegiance in 1689, this was, to some degree, to be expected. What was more surprising was that the few published defences of the Association which were produced employed radical contract theory, rather than the 'divine right of providence', to support William's title.[47] The author of *The Necessity of Altering the Present Oath of Allegiance* (1696) (possibly the Whig polemicist William Atwood) stated that the king was the subject's 'liege lord' and that 'Allegiance at Common Law, binds to the Defence of the Kingdom as well as the King'. James had broken the political contract with the people and had consequently forfeited the right to demand their obedience. To those that

---

[43] HMC, *Fitzherbert MSS* (1893), pp. 38–9.

[44] NRO, NCR 16 d/8, fols 200v–1. In the end, two association oath rolls were produced for the city, with another headed by the Mayor Nicholas Bickerdike following the Association's original wording, NRO, NCR 13d/1. I thank Mark Knights for pointing me to these references.

[45] Rubini, *Court and Country*, p. 66.

[46] *Prideaux–Ellis Correspondence*, p. 174.

[47] On this concept see G. M. Straka, *The Anglican Reaction to the Revolution of 1688* (Madison, 1962); *idem*, 'The Final Phase of Divine Right Theory in England 1688–1702', *Eng. Hist. Rev.*, lxxvii (1962), 638–58.

objected to such proposals on the grounds of the dangerous precedent of radical oaths of loyalty during the civil war, the author bluntly stated that 'few if any of 'em, have been against the King till he, by the Constitution of the Monarchy, ceased to be King.' Getting into his stride the writer argued that if Cromwell had lived a while longer, the Restoration of Charles II would have been 'morally impossible'. He noted that many delayed taking the Association, shamefully keeping off 'from the Cause of God and their Country; thinking it a commendable piece of wisdom to attend the events of providence.'[48] The Presbyterian John Humfrey claimed that the Association actually bound William to rule according to law for 'if William be Lawful King, King by Law then he must be Rightfull King.'[49] He hoped these arguments would convince not only the doubtful to take the oath, but would also remind William to rule within the law.[50] One anonymous author attacked divines who preached against the right of resistance following the 1696 assassination attempt and the passing of the Association.[51] William Atwood used the Association to argue that historically English kings were not made monarchs by the death of their predecessors but by a Parliamentary settlement of the crown upon them. Atwood claimed that James I had only come to the throne by the express vote of Parliament, as the 1584 Association had abjured the right of Mary Queen of Scots and her progeny, and it was a 'piece of flattery' for the act of recognition to describe him as king by 'inherent birthright'.[52]

Both the draft associations produced during the succession crisis of 1677–83 and the 1696 Association in defence of William were developed to counter the threat, political, religious and economic, posed by Louis XIV's France. Far more than in earlier associations, the dominant fear was of the growth of French influence and the possibility of invasion. This was reflected at a popular level too, as many of the loyal declarations to William spoke of him protecting England from the French 'Interest'.[53] Equally, these associations demonstrate the expansion of the political nation after 1660. The scale of the Williamite Association rolls dwarfs those gathered under Elizabeth to the extent that it

[48] W.[illiam] A.[twood]?, *The Necessity of Altering the Present Oath of Allegiance* (1696), pp. 2–3.

[49] [J. Humfrey], *The Free State of the People of England Maintained* (1702), p. 9.

[50] Ibid., p. 10.

[51] S. P., *A Letter Written in the Year 1697 to Dr. Lancaster* (1710), p. 3. This was written in response to William Lancaster's sermon of 30 January 1697, *A Sermon Preached Before the Hon. House of Commons* (1697). The publication of the reply was probably timed to coincide with the Sacheverell trial, in which Lancaster [now Vice-Chancellor of Oxford] was involved on the defence side, see *The History of the University of Oxford, Vol. 5*, eds. L. S. Sutherland and L. G. Mitchell (Oxford, 1986), pp. 84–5.

[52] W. Atwood, *Reflections upon a Treasonable Opinion, Industriously Promoted, Against Signing the National Association* (1696), pp. 55–7.

[53] PRO C213/32, Chester, Non-Conformist Ministers.

seems some of the rolls were never even opened.[54] Mike Braddick's work, discussed earlier, reminds us just how much more capable local government now was to administer such an association. Servants and journeymen took it as well as deputy lieutenants and judges.[55] The 1696 returns also reveal a nation that was more and more defined in corporate and commercial terms. In many rolls, the occupations of subscribers were recorded next to their names.[56] In Newcastle, signatories to the Association were divided into groups by profession with columns for bricklayers, barber-surgeons, tanners, coopers and freemasons.[57] In St Michael's parish in Suffolk, the marital status of subscribers was recorded as well as their occupations.[58] Separate lists were produced for dissenting clergy, Anglican ministers, judges and county officers and servants of the crown. The returns make very clear the way that not only the political nation, but also the state itself had expanded by the end of the seventeenth century. In spite of these differences there remains some resonance with earlier associations. Pamphleteers continued to stress the limitations these oaths placed upon the king, obliging him to follow the rule of law. As in the 1640s, these associations were sometimes seen as part of a European effort to resist the forces of Counter-Reformation Catholicism. However, by the 1680s the apocalyptic element to this struggle had diminished significantly, as had the focus upon the threat from domestic popery.[59] Some ministers preaching in support of the Association continued to make allusions between it and the idea of a national covenant.[60] However, it was now largely secular contract theory, rather than the notion of a religious covenant binding king and people to God, which most threatened the notion of giving unconditional allegiance to the king.

Protestant associations continued to play an important part in eighteenth century British history. Two serious Jacobite rebellions in 1715 and 1745 posed a serious threat to the Hanoverian regime. In the case of both insurrections, associations were formed to bind British subjects to the present government.[61]

---

[54] *Lancashire Association Oath Rolls, 1696*, ed. W. Gandy (Soc. Genealogists repr., 1985), p. xvii. The Elizabethan rolls are in PRO SP 12/174.

[55] C213/264 pt. 2; /269 Caterham return.

[56] C213/244.

[57] C213/194.

[58] C213/264 pt. 10.

[59] See V. Alsop, *God in the Mount: a sermon upon the wonderful deliverance of his majesty from Assassination* (1696), at p. 31 where his horror is directed at the fact that the conspirators were Protestants. My thanks to Steve Pincus for this reference.

[60] Ibid., p. 25. 'Let's examine whether we are a people in Covenant with God. I know special care has been taken that these Nations should not be God's people in Covenant: Men are afraid of an Association but it will do them no harm if God be not the bond of it, and his honours and interest the great end of it.'

[61] Oaths of allegiance to Queen Anne and to George I, after the Jacobite Atterbury plot of 1722, were also produced which were modelled on the 1696 Association. See NRO, NCR 13 d/4.

Yet, as with previous loyal associations, the response to these documents represented more a show of support for the state, than a demonstration of allegiance to the person of the monarch. The notion that the state that was being defended was a Protestant one remained important and there were significant preaching efforts made to promote the Association to George II in 1745. However, both the providential and apocalyptic overtones present in the 1640s and, to a lesser extent, the 1690s were absent from the ministers' vocabulary in 1745. Far more than in earlier associations, subscribers were expressing their approval for a form of government and the secular benefits that it provided.

The Jacobite rebellion of 1715 led to the circulation of a draft loyal association in Scotland. This referred to the 'laudable practice in former times of imminent danger' but made no explicit references to either Elizabethan or Williamite precedents. Unlike earlier associations, this committed subscribers to raising money for an armed volunteer force. The association was signed at Edinburgh on 1 August 1715.[62] However, it appears that there were problems with forming these associations as the 'Act Asserting His Majestys Royal Prerogative in Making of Leagues' had made it illegal to arm people in Scotland, leading to the idea of county associations being dropped.[63] A far more serious rebellion in 1745 produced a much more extensive scheme of county associations. These seem to have started in Ulster with an association formed in Belfast in August of that year.[64] The suggestion of forming local associations in England was made by the Duke of Newcastle at a private dinner on 3 September.[65] On the 6 September Lord Irwin floated the idea of an association to leading Yorkshire Whigs at Wakefield races. A more formal gathering in Yorkshire to discuss the matter was held at Sir John Ramsden's house on the 11th. This led to the nobility, gentry and clergy of York taking an association to defend George II on the 24th, at York Castle.[66] By this the subscribers acknowledged George to be 'the only rightful and lawful king of these realms' and promised to 'stand by and assist each other in the support and defence of his Majesty's sacred person and government'. They vowed to 'withstand, defend and pursue, as well by force of arms as by all other means, the said Popish Pretender and Traitors' and not to separate themselves from the association

---

[62] P. Rae, *The History of Rebellion, Raised Against his Majesty King George I* (1746), pp. 175, 178–9, 243; PRO SP 54/7/14, 'Correspondence of Archbishop Herring and Lord Hardwicke During the Rebellion of 1745', ed. R. Garnett, *English Historical Review*, 19 (1904), 528–50, at 540.

[63] PRO SP 54/7/33. Although a volunteer force of 400 men was raised in Edinburgh, Rae, *History of the Rebellion*, p. 180; PRO SP 54/7/7/B.

[64] R. C. Jarvis, *Collected Papers on the Jacobite Risings* (2 vols., 1971–2, Manchester), i, 234.

[65] W. A. Speck, *The Butcher: The Duke of Cumberland and the Suppression of the '45* (Oxford, 1981), p. 55, PRO SP 36/67 f. 146.

[66] Speck, op. cit.

'for any respect of persons or causes, or for fear or reward'.[67] Many other counties would later follow this version of the association, though there was no universally agreed text.

Unlike in 1715, the efforts to raise county associations in 1745 were sponsored and directed by the government. The poor state of the militia in 1745 (for which the Jacobite code was 'small beer') offers some explanation for this change of heart. At the time of the rebellion the Earl of Derby calculated that there were only twenty or so rifles in the whole of Lancashire.[68] The administration as well as the ordinance for the militia had also become badly neglected. There were no lord lieutenants in Scotland and in many English counties the post had also been left vacant as a result of factional squabbles.[69] Most importantly, until George II returned from Europe and assented to a bill from Parliament, there was no legal mechanism for imposing taxes to pay and equip troops.[70]

However, though some areas did raise volunteer regiments, their military value was questionable. The 'Derbyshire Blues' retreated at the news that the Highland army was advancing in their direction, fleeing first to Nottingham and then to Mansfield.[71] The first military engagement of the 'Liverpool Blues' was a daring attack on a gaggle of geese, mistaken for Jacobite raiders.[72] Instead, the main purpose of these county associations was to give the impression to foreign powers that the nation was united behind the Hanoverian dynasty. As Lord Chancellor Hardwicke told Thomas Herring, archbishop of York, it was 'material to convince Foreign Powers . . . that the appearances in England are very different from those in Scotland, and that they will be mistaken if they take their measures from the latter.'[73]

Historians are divided as to the usefulness of the 1745 associations, in terms both of their military and propaganda value. F. J. McLynn argues that they were of little worth. Apart from the weakness of the volunteer units in comparison with the Jacobite troops, McLynn suggests that, behind the 'smokescreen of

---

[67] C. Wyvill, *Political Papers, Chiefly Respecting the Reformation of the Parliament of Great Britain* (5 vols., York, 1794–1804), i, ix.

[68] R. J. T. Williamson, *History of the Old County Regiment of Lancashire Militia* (London, 1888), p. 30.

[69] Colley, *Britons*, p. 81.

[70] C. Collyer, 'Yorkshire and the "Forty-Five"', *Yorkshire Archaeological Journal*, 38 (1952), 71–95, at 73. F. J. McLynn, *The Jacobite Army in England: 1745 The Final Campaign* (Edinburgh, 1983), p. 4. It was a legal requirement that the king should pay counties a month's subsistence and pay for the militia before it was raised. This couldn't be done until Parliament had passed the necessary statute, which could not be effected until George II had come back from Europe.

[71] F. J. McLynn, 'Nottingham and the Jacobite Rising of 1745', *Transactions of the Thoroton Society* 83 (1979), 63–70, at 67.

[72] Williamson, *Old County Regiment*, p. 63.

[73] 'Herring/Hardwicke Correspondence', p. 542.

verbiage' produced by the loyal associations, England was fundamentally apathetic towards the outcome of the dynastic struggle.[74] Eveline Cruickshanks contends that many of those that subscribed did so out of fear of reprisals, rather than affection for George II. Even so, in Oxfordshire the Tories refused to take the association whilst in Shropshire none of the Tory gentlemen appeared at the county meeting or signed the loyal declaration.[75] For Linda Colley, however, the 1745 associations represent a significant display of support for the Hanoverian regime. She quotes the mayor of Exeter who explained that their loyal address had reached London blotted and crumpled as it had been 'impossible to restrain the impetuous and eager zeal of our citizens. Every one pressing forward to give the earliest marks of his duty and loyalty.'[76] Colley believes that this show of support was often motivated by commercial considerations, and she points out that it was in large trading ports like Liverpool and Bristol that significant subscriptions were raised and volunteer companies put together.[77]

The 1745 associations do demonstrate considerable support for the Hanoverian regime, if not great personal loyalty to the monarchs themselves. There were some refusers, notably the Oxfordshire Tories, but as Colley points out this was a result, not of latent Jacobitism but of constitutional misgivings concerning the association.[78] Some Whigs voiced similar concerns, Lady Isabella Finch claiming that 'success would turn them [the volunteer companies] on any side, and all the desperate people who have either ruined their affairs or never had estates . . . would be for confusion.'[79] Even in some southern counties significant subscriptions were raised. In Surrey £30,290 was collected for forming a volunteer company.[80] Quakers too contributed to these associations, though in the form of clothing for the soldiers or money for their supplies rather than through purchasing weapons.[81] However, the county associations demonstrate less a show of allegiance to George II, and more an

---

[74] F. J. McLynn, 'Hull and the Forty-Five', *Yorkshire Archaeological Journal*, 52 (1980), 135–43.

[75] E. Cruickshanks, *Political Untouchables: The Tories and the '45* (London, 1979), pp. 84–5.

[76] Colley, Britons, pp. 81–4.

[77] For examples see Speck, *Butcher*, p. 58; PRO SP 36/67 f. 170. Tellingly, Colley places her comments on the 1745 associations in her chapter on 'Profits', not 'Protestantism'.

[78] *An Authentick Copy of the Association Entered into by Part of the Nobility, Gentlemen and Clergy of the County of Oxford* (1745), the names of refusers are on the reverse of this broadsheet.

[79] Quoted in Collyer, 'Yorkshire', p. 77n.

[80] *A list of the Subscribers, and the Several Sums of Money Subscribed for Carrying the Association of the County of Surrey into Execution* (1745). To show that these sums were actually collected, see MS note on Bodleian copy, 'The Yeare after Viz. 1745,6. There was return'd 14 p[er]cent to the subscribers.'

[81] 'Herring/Hardwicke Correspondence', p. 735; Williamson, *Old County Regiment*, p. 40.

endorsement of Parliamentary government, the commercial society it had fostered, and, to a lesser degree, Protestantism. Added to these positive attributes was the element of fear, overwhelmingly the fear of French invasion, an important motivating factor in promoting Protestant associations from the 1680s onwards.

Religion seems to have been a factor of only limited importance in gaining subscriptions despite the major preaching effort that accompanied the move to raise county associations. Again, as with the associations themselves, this proselytising was prompted by the government. Lord Chancellor Hardwicke asked Herring as early as August 31 whether it was not 'time for the Pulpits to sound the Trumpet against Popery and the Pretender?' He even advised as to the content of these sermons, urging that ministers represent 'the Pretender as coming (as the truth is) under a dependence upon French support: I say, stating this point, together with Popery, in a strong light, has always the most popular effect.'[82] The bishops were instructed to send out circular letters to their clergy, demanding that they exhort their parishioners to show the necessary zeal towards the government.[83] This central direction was reflected in the relative uniformity of message in sermons on the rebellion.[84] Many of the preachers stated that the anti-Jacobite cause was God's cause. Zachary Suger used the biblical comparison of Senecherib's invasion of Judah, and his defeat at the hands of Hezekiah (a popular comparison for pro-Hanoverian divines) to show that the associators were 'the champions of heaven'.[85] John Hill, chaplain to Herring, stated that the 'cause for which we strive is the Cause of God'.[86] Equally, these preachers were quick to descant on the dangers of popery, a word, according to Suger, 'that implies everything that is shocking and detestable'. A successful Jacobite invasion would doubtless lead to the replacing of a faith based on reason, Anglicanism, with one grounded in superstition and mental slavery.[87] Attacks on popery from the pulpit were only part of a wider effort, which saw the publication of a large amount of

---

[82] 'Herring/Hardwicke Correspondence', pp. 532, 535.

[83] PRO SP 36/67 f. 166. The Bishop of London thought that the Archbishop of Canterbury's letter was inadequate in this respect with too little direction on preaching. Compare their texts, *The Gentleman's Magazine For September* (1745), p. 482.

[84] See F. Deconinck-Brossard, 'The Churches and the "45"', in *The Church and War* (Studies in Church History, 20, 1983), pp. 253–63.

[85] Ibid., p. 253; Z. Suger, *The Preservation of Judah from the Insults and Invasions of the Idolatrous Assyrians* (York, 1745), pp. 2, 14.

[86] J. S. Hill, *False Zeal and Christian Zeal Distinguish'd, or, the Essentials of Popery Described* (York, 1745), p. 29.

[87] Suger, *Preservation of Judah*, pp. 19–20. The theme of the 'irrationality' of popery was picked up by other divines, see R. Hargreaves, *Unanimity, and a Patriot-Spirit Recommended in Two Sermons* (York, 1745), p. 47; I. Maddox, *The Lord Bishop of Worcester's Letter to the Clergy of his Diocese, and His Lordships Speech upon the Presenting an Association* (London, 1745), p. 7.

anti-Catholic material in the aftermath of the rebellion, including reprints of works from the Popish Plot.[88]

However, these ministers spent just as much, if not more time in their sermons extolling the secular benefits of George II's government. The Archbishop of Canterbury's letter urged his clergy to show 'utmost zeal', not for the king himself, but 'for the preservation of our happy constitution in church and state'. The Bishop of London advised his clergy to state that Charles Edward Stuart would impose arbitrary government as well as the popish religion, for which there was no better evidence than the reign of his grandfather, James II. The Bishop of Winchester suggested that his clergy remind their parishioners that George II had ruled within the law.[89] The preachers themselves relayed the same constitutional message.[90] More than being a threat to the English constitution, Zachary Suger made clear that the Jacobite invasion was a threat to an English way of life:

> where the People have Laws and Rights, and Sacred Justice to guard their Properties and Person from Violence and Oppression; where whate'er king Heaven bestows upon them is their own and must not be violated; where within his own Territories every Man sits upon his little Throne, and needs not be molested; where he may enjoy himself in uninterrupted Tranquility, under his own Vine and under his own Fig-Tree, and there is none to make him afraid.[91]

Ministers stressed the economic damage the invasion would do, the Bishop of Chester managing to link heavy taxation with the doctrine of transubstantiation.[92]

The texts of the loyal associations themselves reflected the importance of these constitutional and commercial considerations. Many of these associations followed the wording adopted by the Archbishop of Canterbury, pledging to defend, not George II, but the 'present most happy Establishment'.[93] The association of the admiral, captain and officers of the fleet at Portsmouth spoke of their 'peculiar Happiness to be born under a Constitution the best calculated in the World for the Dignity and Welfare of Mankind'.[94] The association of the city of Westminster attested to their 'just zeal for the best of Governments, administered under the best of princes'.[95] The association formed in Devon

[88] C. Haydon, *Anti-Catholicism in Eighteenth-Century England, c. 1714–80* (Manchester, 1993), pp. 138–9.

[89] *Gentlemans Magazine*, p. 483.

[90] Hargreaves, *Unanimity*, pp. 10–11; J. Free, *The Bloody Methods of Propagating the Popish Religion* (London, 1746), pp. 14–15.

[91] Suger, *Preservation of Judah*, pp. 15–16.

[92] Deconinck-Brossard, 'Churches and the "45"', p. 257.

[93] See *London Gazette*, no. 8472.

[94] Ibid., no. 8481.

[95] Ibid., no. 8477.

employed financial inducements – of a kind – to encourage subscriptions. Tenants would not be charged heriots (a form of death duty on land) if they were killed in the service of the association and their families and other interested parties would be able to renew their lease without fine.[96] Only a few of these associations gave notice that George II was 'rightful and lawful' king of England.[97]

The anti-Jacobite associations seem fundamentally different in character from those that had preceded them. It may well be, as Colin Haydon asserts, that in 1745 hatred of popery was 'synonymous with loyalty to the Hanoverians'.[98] Yet, this was a form of anti-popery that was significantly different in character from that which had been such an important catalyst to the formation of associations in the seventeenth century. As Lord Chancellor Hardwicke recognised, it was a prejudice that could only rouse the public to action when yoked together with hatred and/or fear of the French. The rhetoric of religious war used by pro-Hanoverian preachers seems empty in comparison with their fulsome eulogies on the benefits of a commercial society, private property and constitutional monarchy. These were not full-blooded nationalist associations, though many sermons were jingoistic in tone, as the terms of subscription often stated that soldiers would not fight outside their county.[99] However, they did display the increasing vested interest of large sections of society in defending the Hanoverian state.

What is remarkable about these eighteenth century associations is the absence of any discussion of their historical predecessors. There is one important exception to this historical amnesia. James Burgh, author of the highly influential *Political Disquisitions* (three volumes, 1774–5), explicitly linked his proposals for a 'Grand National Association for Restoring the Constitution' to the precedents provided by the Elizabethan and Williamite Associations (and, revealingly, the Solemn League and Covenant).[100] Burgh's ideas, along with those of John Jebb and John Cartwright, were an important influence on Charles Wyvill's reformist association movement of 1779–80. There are overtones of the associations of the 1640s and 1680s in Jebb's suggestion that a central representative body formed from the county organisations could

---

[96] Ibid., no. 8480.
[97] Ibid., no. 8476 (Sussex) and no. 8480 (Devon).
[98] Haydon, *Anti-Catholicism*, p. 160.
[99] London Gazette, no. 8477; Williamson, *Old County Regiment*, pp. 36–9.
[100] J. Burgh, *Political Disquisitions*, vol. III (1775), pp. 428–34; however, Burgh's association was now targeted at those very eighteenth century concerns, political corruption and luxury. On this see also his *Britains Remembrancer: or the Danger Not Over* (1746), p. 40; elsewhere Burgh made clear that he did not see the persecution of Catholics as benefiting the security of the state, *Crito, or Essays on Various Subjects*, vol. I (1766), xii; on Burgh see C. H. Hay, *James Burgh: Spokesman for Reform in Hanoverian England* (Washington, 1979). My thanks to Mark Goldie for pointing me towards Burgh's writings.

become an anti-Parliament, superseding the now corrupt institution at Westminster.[101] The pamphlets produced in support of Wyvill's associations often used the Convention under William III as an example of just such a national assembly.[102] Yet, as Sir Herbert Butterfield noted, though these writers used seventeenth century historiography, the works of Prynne, Nathaniel Bacon and Sir Edward Coke, to support their arguments, they did not employ the actual incidents of previous Protestant associations as precedents for their actions.[103] When Wyvill produced his collected political papers, he began them with the text of the Yorkshire association of 1745 but included no other historical examples.

In general, in contrast to the case in 1641 or even in 1696, no attempt was made to tie these documents into part of an English tradition of Protestant associations. One explanation for this, as already discussed, was the decline in the apocalyptic expectations invested in these associations, itself a reflection of wider changes in the religious climate. A further reason was that Jacobite propaganda routinely linked the Revolution with the civil war and mainstream Whiggery with religious 'fanaticks' and republican radicals.[104] As one Jacobite ballad put it: 'The Baptist, and the Saint/ The Schismatick, and Swearer/ Have ta'n the Covenant/ That Jemmy comes not here Sr.'[105] As Blair Worden has demonstrated, partly in response to these Jacobite accusations, and also to distinguish themselves from eighteenth century 'Commonwealthsmen', Whig historians stripped the civil war of its atmosphere of apocalyptic, millenarian expectation, retelling the 1640s as a dress rehearsal for the Revolution but one which ended in the tragedy of the regicide, not the triumph of a peaceful 'abdication'.[106] Overall, there was little political advantage for Whigs in tracing back the lineage of eighteenth century associations. England's covenant with God had been forgotten.

---

[101] Sir H. Butterfield, George III, Lord North and the People, 1779–80 (London, 1949), p. 192.
[102] Ibid., p. 257; Copy of a Letter from the Right Honourable Lord Corysfort to the Huntingdonshire Committee (1780), p. 5; The Associators Vindicated; and the Protestants Answered (London, 1780), p. 13.
[103] Butterfield, George III, p. 345.
[104] P. Monod, Jacobitism and the English People 1688–1788 (Cambridge, 1989), pp. 49–54.
[105] Ibid., pp. 50–1.
[106] B. Worden, Roundhead Reputations: The English Civil War and the Passions of Posterity (London, 2002).

Conclusion

A belief in the idea of a national covenant was not peculiar to England. A mere glance at the history of Scotland, Northern Ireland, North America or Western Europe demonstrates the importance of the concept in these contexts too.[1] Colin Kidd has recently argued that covenanter ideas formed an important part of some Scottish Presbyterians' opposition to the Revolution settlement (but support for a British union, at least of the ecclesiological kind implicit in the Solemn League and Covenant).[2] J. C. D. Clark has suggested that covenanting ideas, imported from Scotland, may have fostered disaffection with Hanoverian rule in the American colonies, exemplified in its most extreme, Cameronian form in the pamphlet *The Renewal of the Covenants* (Philadelphia, 1743, 1748).[3] When Samuel Adams and other members of the Boston Committee of Correspondence learnt that the Boston Port Act forbade trade with the town until the East India Company had been compensated for the tea they had lost, they responded with an agreement not to consume British goods, which they titled the Solemn League and Covenant.[4] The idea of a national covenant remains a potent one today. Donald H. Akenson has shown the centrality of the concept to the outlook of Afrikaners, Israelis and the Ulster Scots.[5] A quick search on the internet under 'Solemn League and Covenant' will bring up the websites of numerous Northern Irish, American and Canadian Presbyterian churches that continue to view a document first formulated in the context of a bitter civil war as a founding statement of their

---

[1] Luther's opposition to the idea of Protestant associations was in part a reaction to the combination of secular defensive leagues and evangelical covenants by the radical preacher Thomas Muntzer, see T. Scott, 'The Volksreformation of Thomas Muntzer in Allsted and Muhlhausen', *Journal of Ecclesiastical History*, xxxiv (1983), 194–213, at 199.

[2] C. Kidd, 'Conditional Britons: The Scots Covenanting Tradition and the Eighteenth-century British State', *English Historical Review*, cxvii (2002), 1147–76.

[3] J. C. D. Clark, *The Language of Liberty 1660–1832: Political Discourse and Social Dynamics in the Anglo-American World* (Cambridge, 1994), pp. 264–5.

[4] R. D. Brown, *Revolutionary Politics in Massachusetts: The Boston Committee of Correspondence and the Towns, 1772–1774* (Cambridge, Mass., 1970), pp. 178–200.

[5] D. H. Akenson, *God's Peoples: Covenant and Land in South Africa, Israel and Ulster* (Ithaca, NY, 1992); Colin Kidd points out that Ian Paisley's mother was a Cameronian Presbyterian, 'Conditional Britons', 1175–6.

faith. The website of Loughbrickland Presbyterian Church in County Down, Northern Ireland states that:

> We must maintain the biblical goals of the Solemn League and Covenant in church and state. We must use all our powers, including the use, or non-use, of the elective franchise only in a manner compatible with these goals, however far off the attainment of them may seem. We must recognise that the Solemn League and Covenant was the means of passing down to us the excellent Westminster Confession of Faith and Catechisms that we have. We must still desire the three kingdoms to be in a union under Christ as King over church and state.[6]

However, we can compare the lively scholarly interest in the significance of covenanting in Scotland with the relative lack of work on the concept of a national covenant in England. The identification of the Solemn League and Covenant with a rigid, intolerant Presbyterianism of the Thomas Edwards variety explains in part the lack of interest shown by historians of the civil war period in the idea of a national covenant. Groups that can be roughly characterised as 'conservative' in their political and religious outlook, Royalists and Presbyterians, have received much less attention than the numerically far smaller 'radicals'. However, this book has demonstrated that there is some irony in this skewed focus, given the use of the idea of a national covenant by advocates of religious toleration, Leveller writers and the Digger Gerrard Winstanley. For these individuals, the Long Parliament's covenants seemed to offer a model for both religious and political settlement. In the case of both Leveller and Digger writing, they were also seen as contracts obliging the Parliament to remember its commitment to defend the rights and liberties of the subject. In this way, the book supports the work of David Wootton which has demonstrated the radical potential of Parliamentarian writing from the early years of the civil war. So the Parliament's war against the king not only provided the opportunity for the expression of radical ideas, through the breakdown of censorship and the abolition of church courts, but also the base materials, in this case pro-covenant propaganda, from which radical thought was constructed.

This book also suggests that a qualitative adjustment is necessary as regards how we characterise the mainstream of Parliamentarian resistance thought. The arguments of Parliamentarian writers, especially in the first year of the civil war, have tended to be described as conservative, defensive and over-whelmingly secular in the case they presented for resisting the king's forces. This overlooks an important strand of Parliamentarian thought that empha-sised instead the right of resisting secular authority on the grounds that the monarch and his followers tolerated, or worse, positively supported idolatrous worship. They emphasised how in the last resort, the need to purge the land

---

[6] http://www.loughbrickland.org/Articles.shtml

of idolatry overrode social and political norms of behaviour. Moreover, as England was a covenanted nation with a covenanted monarch, that monarch could be held accountable for his failings, and his subjects absolved of their allegiance to him, should he not fulfil his contracted duties.

This presentation of Parliamentarian thought as largely secular in content has partly been a result of the materials that historians have chosen to designate as works of 'resistance theory': relatively lengthy, legalistic works like Hunton's *A Treatise of Monarchy* and Prynne's *Soveraigne Power of Parliaments*. We can even see this distinction operating within texts themselves. Jeremiah Burrough's *Brief Answer* to Henry Ferne is really an appendix to his sermon *The Glorious Name of God*, but has usually been detached from it and treated as a separate work. This reflects in broader terms implicit categories historians have imposed concerning which works constitute 'serious' political discourse in early modern England and which do not. For a long time political historians dismissed court rumour and scandal as insignificant froth and salacious tittle-tattle. Through the work of Alastair Bellany, Adam Fox and Richard Cust we are beginning to recognise the role that rumour and scandal played in affecting perceptions of the Stuart monarchy over the whole of the seventeenth century.[7] Likewise, the content of fast sermons, short religious pamphlets and broadsheets, and soldiers' bibles, had an equally significant impact on how subjects saw their duty of allegiance towards the king. In particular, I have suggested that subscription returns to oaths of loyalty, sources that are usually treated only as data to be 'crunched' by demographers, genealogists and historians of literacy, can also be viewed as political texts.[8]

In writing this book, I have been influenced by the recent excellent work by Bellany, Fox, Cust and others on communicative practices in early modern England. Like them, I have urged that the analysis of oath subscription returns and the attendant literature in print and manuscript on oath taking suggest that the 'political nation' in early modern England was far more broadly based than previously thought. Women as well as men frequently signed oaths of loyalty. In doing so, pamphlets and sermons assured them that they were taking part in a process of both personal and national reformation that had secular as well as religious ramifications. To be sure, some of these arguments seem to have either been rejected by or passed right over the heads of their intended audience. Yet, in one notable case at least, that of Gerrard Winstanley, the experience of subscribing to these covenants appears to have convinced him

[7] R. Cust, 'News and politics in early 17th Century England', *Past and Present*, 112 (1986), 60–90; A. Fox, 'Rumour, News and Popular Political Opinion in Elizabethan and Early Stuart England', *Historical Journal*, 40 (1997), 597–620; idem, *Oral and Literate Culture in Early Modern England* (Oxford, 2001); A. Bellany, *The Politics of Court Scandal in Early Modern England: News Culture and the Overbury Affair 1603–1666* (Cambridge, 2002).
[8] This point is made in more detail in my article, 'Protestation, Vow, Covenant and Engagement, swearing allegiance in the English Civil War', *Historical Research*, 75 (2002), 408–24.

that he had entered into a political contract with the Parliament, albeit on terms that those in Westminster would barely have recognised. Besides Winstanley, many others, including laymen like Ambrose Barnes as well as clerical figures, continued to feel bound by the obligations of the covenant long after the Cavalier Parliament had declared it null and void.

However, I must add a final caveat concerning current work on the 'news culture' of early modern England. Since the publication in 1989 of an English translation of Jürgen Habermas's *Structural Transformation of the Public Sphere*, historians have spent a great deal of effort in trying to verify Habermas's claim that a 'public sphere that functioned in the political realm arose first in Great Britain'.[9] So far historians have made claims for the existence of a public sphere in the late Elizabethan period, in the 1620s, during the civil war and around the time of the Exclusion Crisis.[10]

English historians are often keen to state that in using the term 'public sphere' they are not rigidly applying the model established by Habermas. To use Dena Goodman's neat description the Habermasian public sphere was composed of 'literate men and women, who, through their participation in burgeoning discursive institutions of print and sociability, transformed the social and political landscape of eighteenth-century Europe while empowering themselves as autonomous individuals'.[11] Many historians, on the other hand, treat Habermas's model as an 'ideal type' which can be amended according to the particular historical context in which they are working. Peter Lake

---

[9] J. Habermas, *The Structural Transformation of the Public Sphere*, trans. T. Burger (Cambridge, 1989), p. 57.

[10] For examples see D. Zaret, 'Petitions and the "Invention" of Public Opinion in the English Revolution', *American Journal of Sociology*, 101 (1996), 1497–555; idem, *The Origins of Democratic Culture: Printing, Petitions, and the Public Sphere in Early Modern England* (Princeton, NJ, 2000); A. Halasz, *The Market Place of Print: Pamphlets and the Public Sphere in Early Modern England* (Cambridge, 1997); P. Lake and M. Questier, 'Puritans, Papists and the "Public Sphere" in Early Modern England: The Edmund Campion Affair in Context', *Journal of Modern History*, 72 (2000), 587–628; and see now their *The Anti-Christ's Lewd Hat: Protestants, Papists and Players in Post-Reformation England* (Yale, 2002); S. Pincus, '"Coffee Politicians Does Create": Coffeehouses and Restoration Political Culture', *Journal of Modern History*, 67 (1995), 807–35; D. Freist, 'The King's Crown is the Whore of Babylon: Politics, Gender and Communication in Mid-Seventeenth Century England', *Gender and History*, 7 (1995), 457–81; idem, *Governed by Opinion: Politics, Religion and the Dynamics of Communication in Stuart London, 1637–1645* (London, 1997); N. Mears, 'Counsel, Public Debate and Queenship', *Historical Journal*, 44 (2001), 629–50. This is a mere sampling of the ever-expanding list of books and articles on the subject. For further bibliographic references see H. Mah, 'Phantasies of the Public Sphere: Rethinking the Habermas of Historians', *Journal of Modern History*, 27 (2000), 153–82. For good surveys of the subject see J. Van Horn Melton, *The Rise of the Public in Enlightenment Europe* (Cambridge, 2001); T. C. W. Blanning, *The Culture of Power and the Power of Culture* (Oxford, 2002); *Habermas and the Public Sphere*, ed. C. Calhoun (Cambridge, Mass., 1992).

[11] D. Goodman, 'The Public and the Nation', *Eighteenth Century Studies*, 29, 1 (1995), 1–4, at 1.

and Michael Questier use the term public sphere instead to denote only 'the spaces (both conceptual and practical) created by the particular politico-religious circumstances of Elizabeth's reign for "public" debate and discourse on a number of topics central to the future and purpose of the regime'.[12] Unlike the Habermasian public sphere this was not theoretically open to all, nor inherently oppositional, nor freed from secrecy norms. Looking at the civil war period, David Zaret has argued for an examination of the emergence of a public sphere through 'an empirical study of communicative practices in popular politics'.[13] He contends that mass publication of petitions during the 1640s 'simultaneously constituted and invoked public opinion'[14] as the framers of petitions 'produced texts for an anonymous audience of readers, a public presumed not only to be capable of rational thought but also to possess moral competency for resolving rival political claims'.[15]

Leaving aside the question of its historical specificity, broader reservations should be raised about the concept of a public sphere. The term seemingly encourages us to elevate the examination of the spaces and media available for political discussion above the analysis of the actual ideas expressed in the public domain. Habermas has himself acknowledged that in 'constructing public opinion as a rhetorical device' there is a danger that we may be left with 'an overculturalized view of history, where the hard facts of institutions or economic imperatives and of social and political struggles are then too easily assimilated into fights over symbolic meanings'.[16] Moreover, for all this focus on communicative practices, investigations of the public sphere tend to gloss over questions concerning how these ideas were understood and received. This feeds into the problem of causation. The search for the emergence of a public sphere in early modern England is rarely accompanied with any justification of why proving the existence of such a thing will be of any significance. As critics of Habermas have pointed out, there is no reason why the content of debate within the public sphere should necessarily threaten the political status quo. Indeed, the ideas expressed in this space could be completely anodyne.

Here I have resisted the temptation to offer my own modified definition of the public sphere, preferring to employ the term 'political nation' instead. My own feelings about the concept are closer to Andy Wood's sceptical comments. He has argued that if a public sphere did emerge in the late seventeenth century 'this represented a public recognition of the broad basis of the early modern polity, rather than a fundamental readjustment of the social basis of government.' Those involved 'were not so much attempting to define a socially

---

[12] Lake and Questier, 'Puritans, Papists and the "Public Sphere"', 590.
[13] Zaret, 'Petitions and the "Invention" of Public Opinion', 1541.
[14] Ibid., 1517.
[15] Ibid., 1532.
[16] J. Habermas, 'Concluding Remarks' in *Habermas and the Public Sphere*, ed. Calhoun, p. 465.

capacious public sphere within which their differing ideologies could be rationally debated, so much as finding new ways of conducting long-established religious and ideological conflicts.'[17] The tendering of oaths of allegiance to the general public requiring them to assert or deny certain religious and/or political positions was just one such new strategy for pursuing older polemical agendas. To some extent, oath taking was a socially inclusive activity. Considerably more people subscribed to the Commons' Protestation of 1641 than could vote in Parliamentary elections. Yet oaths like the Protestation were also designed to purge and exclude portions of society from the body politic (in the civil war 'malignants', 'delinquents' and 'the popishly affected').

To conclude, the dangers of an 'overculturalised' interpretation of history can be seen in recent work on eighteenth century England. The 'associational culture' that has been identified by Peter Clark and others can certainly be linked with eighteenth century conceptions of sociability, but, as has been demonstrated in the last chapter of this book, it can also be traced back to a seventeenth century practice of forging Protestant associations against the threat of the popish Antichrist.[18] Certainly, by the eighteenth century, the apocalyptic, even the anti-popish elements of these associations had become more muted but the potential for them to become vehicles for such aspirations and prejudices remained. I am not attempting here to reaffirm an argument akin to J.C.D. Clark's that England remained a confessional state in the eighteenth century.[19] Rather I would assert that a phenomenon that has been seen as fostering greater inclusiveness and openness in eighteenth century England paradoxically rests on a tradition that once employed associations as, in Pym's words 'shibboleths', devices to discriminate and exclude. The associational culture of the eighteenth century included Lord George Gordon as well as James Burgh and Charles Wyvill.

---

[17] A. Wood, *Riot, Rebellion and Popular Politics in Early Modern England* (London, 2002), p. 186.

[18] P. Clark, *British Clubs and Societies 1580–1800: The Origins of an Associational World* (Oxford, 2000); R.J. Morris, 'Clubs, Societies and Associations', in *The Cambridge Social History of Britain, Vol. 3 of Social Agencies and Institutions*, ed. F. M. L. Thompson (Cambridge, 1990); *The Middling Sort of People: Culture, Society and Politics in England, 1550–1800*, eds. J. Barry and C. Brooks (London, 1994). Clark is more cautious than others in relating the growth of voluntary associations to the emergence of an eighteenth century 'public sphere'.

[19] J.C.D. Clark, *English Society, 1688–1832* (Cambridge, 1985).

Select bibliography

For reasons of space, entries for early modern printed books and pamphlets, and for modern anthologies, editions of diaries, etc. have been omitted as the footnotes provide a running bibliography in this case.

MANUSCRIPT SOURCES

Bedfordshire Record Office

P 44/5/2 Shillington Churchwarden's Accounts.

Bodleian Library

Add. MS C. 305, f. 168–71. Letters of Seth Ward, Bishop of Exeter to Archbishop Sheldon concerning the Oxford Oath.
B. 14. 15. Linc. documents relating to 1667 proposals for comprehension.
MS Carte 7–10.
MS Clarendon 31, f. 30–30v, 'Texts of Scripture Applied by the Rebel Preachers in their Discourses'.
MS Clarendon 73, f. 2–3, 6, 378, oaths of privy councillors, lord justices, dukes earls, lords and knights.
MS Clarendon 92, f. 202, oath of lord lieutenants.
MS Dep., f. 9 'Seymour Bowman's Diary of the Convention Parliament'.
MS Jones 17, f. 247–9, 'Queries Propounded by Sundry of ye Clergy of ye Dioces of London Touching ye Oath Enioyned by Late Synod Canon 6'.
MS Rawlinson 373, f. 70–1, queries concerning the declaration against the Solemn League and Covenant.
MS Rawlinson D 924, f. 297–300, Lords debates on Danby's Test.
MS Rawlinson D 1041, f. 127–32, J. Humfrey's queries concerning the assent and consent clause of the Act of Uniformity.
MS Rawlinson D 1347, f. 364–75, 'A Treatise Concerning ye Cov.[enant] by Wi[lliam] War[wick]'.
MS Rawlinson D 1350, f. 324–8, 'A Modest Answer to ye Sober Enquiry About ye New Oath'.

MS Rawlinson D 1494, f. 79–88, 'To the Authors of the late Act of Conform[ity] An appeale to theyr own Consciences conce[rning] the Solemn League and Covenant'.

MS Sancroft 78, f. 15–19, Annotations by Sancroft on some of Bishop Wren's papers.

MS Selden supra 108, f. 147, G. Langbaine to J. Selden, 14 November 1648.

MS Selden 109, f. 323, same to same, 29 October 1650.

MS Tanner 56, f. 257, letter to William Sancroft signed T. S. on the writer's leaving Cambridge for refusing the Engagement: 9 December 1649.

MS Tanner 62, f. 641, W. Sancroft to S. Dillingham, March 1644.

MS Tanner 65, f. 42–3, 139, 199, queries of clergy relating to, etc., oath.

MS Tanner 66, f. 40–2, petitions of London clergy and University of Cambridge against the Engagement.

MS Tanner 66, f. 109 Order of the Commons to burn Henry Burton's *Protestation Protested* (1641).

MS Tanner 104, f. 263–4, queries on the assent and consent clause of the Act of Uniformity.

MS Tanner 114, f. 98, subscriptions to 1642 oath of association.

MS Tanner 284, f. 42–7, subscriptions to 1642 oath of association.

MS Walker C. 6, transcripts made by J. Nalson of ministers subscribing to the Engagement.

MS Wood F35, papers relating to the Parliamentary visitation of the University of Oxford.

MS Wood F41, f. 236v, S. Ford to A. Wood, 28 February 1682.

British Library

Add. MS 25277, f. 101–102v.

Add. MS 28252, f. 53, 'List of members that refused the association to the Prince of Orange'.

Add. MS 38823, f. 13–16.

Add. MS 39922 A, f. 1, G. Goddard to J. Greene, 25 Febuary 1644.

Add. MS 46190 (Jessop Papers vol. 3), f. 190–3.

Add. MS 48099 (Yelverton MS 108), f. 6–21.

Add. Roll 7180, 'Engagement to be faithful to the Commonwealth taken at Wigan'.

Eg. MS 2877, f. 90–90v, Commonplace Book of Gilbert Frevile, Bishop of Middleham, Co. Durham, 'A peticon pferred to Qi Elizabeth for association in religion, about the end of her highnes raign'.

Lansdowne MS 98, f. 14–18.

Lansdowne MS 113, f. 156–8.

Durham Record Office

EP/Ea 1, Easington St Mary Solemn League and Covenant return.
EP/Ho 1, Houghton-le-Spring, St Michael and All Angel Covenant return.

Essex Record Office

D/P 155/1/1, Boxted Vow and Covenant return.
T/R 138/1, Hadleigh Solemn League and Covenant return.
T/R 182/1, Prittlewell Vow and Covenant and Solemn League and Covenant returns.

Gloucester Record Office

D1571 F116, Gloucestershire Engagement subscriptions.
P29 IN1/1, Avening Solemn League and Covenant return.

Guildhall Library

MS 959/1, f. 400v–1, St Martin Orgar Protestation return; f. 381v–2, Vow and Covenant return.
MS 977/1, St Clement Eastcheap Vow and Covenant and Solemn League and Covenant returns.
MS 1196/1, f. 30–4, St Catherine Kree Protestation return.
MS 1303/1, St Benet Fink Vow and Covenant return.
MS 2597, f. 58v–9, St Mary Magdalen, Milk Street, Protestation return; f. 66v–7, Vow and Covenant return; f. 70–2, Solemn League and Covenant return.
MS 3579, f. 339–41, St Matthew, Friday Street, Protestation return.
MS 4384/2, f. 12v, St Bartholomew by the Exchange, Solemn League and Covenant return.
MS 4415, f. 117–18v, St Olave Jewry Solemn League and Covenant return.
MS 4458/1 pt. 2, St Stephen, Coleman Street, Vow and Covenant and Solemn League and Covenant returns.
MS 4835/1, Holy Trinity the Less Protestation return.
MS 5019/1, f. 71–3v, St Pancras, Soper Lane, Protestation return.

House of Lords Record Office

Historical Collections 114; Braye MS 21, f. 18v.
Main Papers, Protestation returns, Bucks, Cambridgeshire, Lancs (B), Kent, Middlesex, Warwickshire.

Main Papers, 13 March 1643/4 – 3 May 1644 (Norfolk Covenant returns).
Original Journals, House of Lords, 27, f. 158–61, 215–16.
Original Journals, 55, f. 400, 389–90, 406, 422.

Lancashire Record Office

DDB 42/3 Engagement return for Salford hundred.

Norfolk Record Office

NCR 16A/20, f. 393r, order concerning the administration of the Vow and
    Covenant, dated 12 July 1643.
NCR 13c/3, declarations against the Covenant from 1678 to 1718.
NCR 16 d/8, f. 200v–1, Norwich Association.
NCR 13d/1, 'Bickerdike Association'.
NCR 13 d/4, oaths to Queen Anne and George I.

Oxford University Archives

Gerard Langbaine's Collections vol. 3, WPψ 26/1, Langbaine's Annotations
    on the Protestation.

Public Record Office, Kew

C115/99 nos. 7312–7314, John, first Viscount Scudamore's queries on the
    Covenant.
C213/1–476, 1696 Association oath rolls.
SP 12/174, Elizabethan association rolls.
SP 54/7, State Papers Scotland Series II.
SP 36/67, State Papers Domestic, George II.

Sheffield University Library

Hartlib Papers, electronic version, Disc I 29/9/1A, 67/19/1A–2B.

Suffolk Record Office

Bury Office, FL 551/4/1, Chilton Solemn League and Covenant return.
Ipswich branch, FB 190/D1/1 transcript PRC 527, Brantham Vow and
    Covenant return.

Ipswich branch, FB 51/A3/1, Cretingham Solemn League and Covenant return.
Ipswich branch, FC 89/A1/1, Brundish Solemn League and Covenant return.
Ipswich branch, FC 199/A5/1, Earl Soham Solemn League and Covenant return.
Ipswich branch, FC 193/D1/1 transcript PRC 596, Linstead Parva Solemn League and Covenant return.

Worcestershire Record Office

Quarter Sessions Rolls, 1/1/79/17.

PRINTED SOURCES

Printed oath returns

The Association Oath Rolls of the British Plantations, ed. W. Gandy (London, 1922).
'Association Oath Rolls for Wiltshire', ed. L. J. Acton Pile, *Wiltshire Notes and Queries*, vi (1908–10), 197–201.
The Devon Protestation Returns 1641, ed. A. J. Howard (privately printed, 1973).
Dorset Protestation Returns Preserved in the House of Lords, 1641 to 1642, eds. E. A. and G. S. Fry (Dorset Record Society, xxiv, 1911).
Durham Protestations or the Returns made to the House of Commons in 1641/2, ed. H. M. Wood (Surtees Society, cxxxv, 1922).
Inderwick, F. A., 'The Rye Engagement', *Sussex Archaeological Collections*, xxxix (1894), 16–27.
Lancashire Association Oath Rolls, 1696, ed. W. Gandy (Soc. Genealogists repr., 1985).
Oxfordshire and North Berkshire Protestation Returns and Tax Assessments: 1641–42, ed. J. S. W. Gibson (Oxfordshire Record Society, lix, 1994).
'The Protestation Oath Rolls for Middlesex: 1641–42', ed. A. J. C. Guimraens, *Miscellanea Genealogica et Heraldica* (1921).
'The Protestation of 1641. A Harbinger of the Covenant: Halifax Signatories', ed. C. T. Clay, *Halifax Antiquarian Society Transactions*, xvi (1919), 105–15.
'The Protestation Returns for Huntingdonshire', ed. G. Proby, *Transactions of the Cambridgeshire and Huntingdonshire Archaeological Society*, v (1937), 289–368.
Protestation Returns 1641/2: Lincolnshire, ed. W. F. Webster (privately printed, 1984).
'The Solemn League and Covenant in Wirral', *Wirral N & Q*, i (1892), 58.
'Solumne League and Covenant in Suffolk', ed. C. Morley, *East Anglian Miscellany* (1945), pp. 30–6.

The Somerset Protestation Returns and Lay Subsidy Rolls 1641–2, ed. T. L. Stoate (privately printed, 1975).
'The Surrey Protestation Returns 1641/2', ed. H. Carter, *Surrey Archaeological Collections*, lix (1962), 35–69.
West Sussex Protestation Returns 1641–2, ed. R. G. Rice (Sussex Record Society, v, 1906).
Wiltshire Protestation Returns 1641–2, ed. B. Hurley (Wiltshire Family History Society, 1997).

SECONDARY WORKS

Adams, M., 'Peter Chamberlen's Case of Conscience', *Huntington Library Quarterly*, liii (1990), 281–311.
Adamson, J. S. A., 'The Baronial Context of the English Civil War', *T. R. H. S.*, 40 (1990), pp. 93–120.
Akenson, D. H., *God's Peoples: Covenant and Land in South Africa, Israel and Ulster* (Ithaca, NY, 1992).
Alford, S., *The Early Elizabethan Polity: William Cecil and the British Succession Crisis, 1558–1569* (Cambridge, 1998).
—— 'Politics and Political History in the Tudor Century', *The Historical Journal*, 42 (1999), 535–49.
Alsop, J. D., 'Revolutionary Puritanism in the Parishes? The Case of St. Olave, Old Jewry', *The London Journal*, 15 (1990), 29–37, at 30–1.
—— 'Gerrard Winstanley: What Do We Know of His Life?', in *Winstanley and the Diggers 1649–1999*, ed. A. Bradstock (London, 2000), pp. 19–37.
Amussen, S. D. and M. A. Kishlansky, eds., *Political Culture and Cultural Politics in Early Modern England: Essays Presented to David Underdown* (Manchester, 1995).
Anderson, B., *Imagined Communities: Reflections on the Origin and Spread of Nationalism* (London, 1983).
Ashton, R., *The English Civil War, Conservatism and Revolution 1603–1649* (1978).
—— *Counter-Revolution: The Second Civil War and its Origins, 1646–8* (New Haven, 1994).
Atherton, I., *Ambition and Failure in Stuart England: The Career of John, First Viscount Scudamore* (Manchester, 1999).
Aylmer, G. E., *The State's Servants: The Civil Service of the English Republic 1649–1660* (London, 1973).
—— 'The Religion of Gerrard Winstanley', in *Radical Religion in the English Revolution*, eds. J. F. McGregor and B. Reay (London, 1984), pp. 91–121.
Bainton, R., 'Congregationalism and the Puritan Revolution: From the Just War to the Crusade', in his *Studies on the Reformation* (London, 1964), pp. 248–75.
Baker, J. W., *Heinrich Bullinger and the Covenant: The Other Reformed Tradition* (Ohio, 1980).

Barber, S., 'The Engagement of Loyalty to the Council of State and the Establishment of the Commonwealth Government', *Historical Research*, cl (1990), 44–58.

—— *Regicide and Republicanism: Politics and Ethics in the English Revolution, 1646–1659* (Edinburgh, 1998).

Bartle, H., 'The Story of Public Fast Days in England', *Anglican Theological Review*, 37 (1955), 190–200.

Baskerville, S., 'Blood Guilt in the English Revolution', *The Seventeenth Century*, 8 (1993), 181–202.

Beddard, R. A., 'The Unexpected Whig Revolution of 1688', *The Revolutions of 1688*, ed. Beddard (Oxford, 1991), pp. 11–102.

—— 'Restoration Oxford and the Remaking of the Protestant Establishment' in *The History of the University of Oxford IV*, ed. Tyacke, pp. 803–63.

Black, E. C., *The Association: British Extraparliamentary Political Organisation 1769–1793* (Cambridge, Mass., 1963).

Black, J., 'Pikes and Protestations: Scottish Texts in England, 1639–40', *Publishing History*, XLII (1997), 1–19.

Blanning, T. C. W., *The Culture of Power and the Power of Culture* (Oxford, 2002).

Bossy, J., *The English Catholic Community, 1570–1850* (London, 1975).

—— 'Leagues and Associations in Sixteenth-Century French Catholicism', *Voluntary Religion*, ed. W. J. Shiels (Studies in Church History, 23, 1986), pp. 171–89.

Bowler, G., '"An Axe or an Acte"? The Parliament of 1572 and Resistance Theory in Early Elizabethan England', *Canadian Journal of History*, 19 (1984), 349–61.

Bozeman, T. D., 'Federal Theology and the "National Covenant": An Elizabethan Presbyterian Case Study', *Church History*, 61 (1992), 394–407.

Braddick, M. J., *State Formation in Early Modern England* (Cambridge, 2000).

Bremer, F. J., *Shaping New Englands: Puritan Clergymen in Seventeenth Century England and New England* (New York, 1994).

—— *Congregational Communion: Clerical Friendship in the Anglo-American Puritan Community, 1610–1692* (Boston, 1994).

Brown, R. D., *Revolutionary Politics in Massachusetts: The Boston Committee of Correspondence and the Towns, 1772–1774* (Cambridge, Mass., 1970).

Burgess, G., 'Usurpation, Obligation and Obedience in the Thought of the Engagement Controversy', *Historical Journal*, xxix (1986), 515–37.

—— *The Politics of the Ancient Constitution* (London, 1992).

—— 'Contexts for the Writing and Publication of Hobbes' Leviathan', *History of Political Thought*, xi (1990), 675–702.

—— *Absolute Monarchy and the Stuart Constitution* (London, 1996).

—— 'Was the Civil War a War of Religion?', *Huntington Library Quarterly*, lxi (2000), 173–203.

Burrell, S. A., 'The Covenant Idea as a Revolutionary Symbol, 1596–1637', *Church History*, xxvii (1958), 338–50.

—— 'The Apocalyptic Vision of the Early Covenanters', *Scottish Historical Review*, xliii (1964), 1–24.

Bush, M., *The Pilgrimage of Grace* (Manchester, 1996).

Butterfield, Sir H., *George III, Lord North and the People, 1779–80* (London, 1949).

Calhoun, C., ed., *Habermas and the Public Sphere* (MIT, 1992).

Chanter, J. F., *The Life and Times of Martin Blake B. D.* (Edinburgh, 1909).

Clark, J. C. D., *The Language of Liberty 1660–1832: Political Discourse and Social Dynamics in the Anglo-American World* (Cambridge, 1994).

Clark, P., *British Clubs and Societies 1580–1800: The Origins of an Associational World* (Oxford, 2000).

Clark, S., 'Inversion, Misrule and the Meaning of Witchcraft', *Past and Present*, 87 (1980), 99–106.

Clarke, A., 'Barnston Notes 1641–9', *Essex Review*, xxv (1916), 55–70.

Claydon, T., *William III and the Godly Revolution* (Cambridge, 1996).

Coffey, J., *Politics, Religion and the British Revolutions: The Mind of Samuel Rutherford* (Cambridge, 1997).

—— 'Puritanism and Liberty Revisited: The Case for Toleration in the English Revolution', *Historical Journal*, 41 (1998), 961–85.

—— *Persecution and Toleration in Protestant England, 1558–1689* (Harlow, 2000).

Cogswell, T., *The Blessed Revolution: English Politics and the Coming of War, 1621–4* (Cambridge, 1989).

Colley, L., *Britons: Forging the Nation 1707–1837* (New Haven, 1992)

Collinson, P., 'A Mirror of Elizabethan Puritanism: The Life and Letters of "Godly Master Dering"', *Friends of Dr Williams Library Seventeenth Lecture* (1963).

——*The Elizabethan Puritan Movement* (3rd edn., Oxford, 1990).

—— 'The Monarchial Republic of Queen Elizabeth I', *Bulletin of the John Rylands Library*, lxix (1986–7), 394–424.

—— 'The Elizabethan Exclusion Crisis and the Elizabethan Polity', *Proceedings of the British Academy*, lxxxiv (1994), 51–93.

—— 'Biblical Rhetoric: The English Nation and National Sentiment in the Prophetic Mode', in *Religion and Culture in Renaissance England*, eds. C. McEachern and D. Shuger (Cambridge, 1997), ch. 2.

Collyer, C., 'Yorkshire and the "Forty-Five"', *Yorkshire Archaeological Journal*, 38 (1952), 71–95.

Corns, T. N., *Uncloistered Virtue: English Political Literature 1642–1660* (Oxford, 1992).

Cowan, E. J., 'The Solemn League and Covenant', in *Scotland and England: 1286–1815*, ed. R. A. Mason (Edinburgh, 1987), pp. 182–203.

—— 'The Making of the National Covenant', in *Scottish National Covenant*, ed. Morrill, pp. 68–90.

Crawford, P., *Denzil Holles 1598–1680: A Study of His Political Career* (London, 1979).

Cressy, D., 'Literacy in 17th Century England, More Evidence', *Journal of Interdisciplinary History*, viii (1977), 141–50.

—— *Literacy and the Social Order: Reading and Writing in Tudor and Stuart England* (Cambridge, 1980).

—— 'Vow, Covenant and Protestation: Sources for the History of Population and Literacy in the Seventeenth Century', *Local Historian*, xiv (1980), 134–41.

—— 'Binding the Nation: The Bonds of Association, 1584 and 1696', in *Tudor Rule and Revolution: Essays for G. R. Elton from His American Friends*, eds. D. J. Guth and J. W. McKenna (Cambridge, 1982), pp. 217–37.

—— 'The Protestation Protested, 1641 and 1642', *The Historical Journal*, 45 (2002), pp. 251–79.

Cruickshanks, E., *Political Untouchables: The Tories and the '45* (London, 1979).

Cust, R. and Hughes, A., eds., *Conflict in Early Stuart England: Studies in Religion and Politics 1603–1642* (Harlow, 1989).

Danner, D. G., 'Christopher Goodman and the English Protestant Tradition of Civil Disobedience', *Sixteenth Century Journal*, 8 (1977), 61–73.

—— 'The Contribution of the Geneva Bible of 1560 to the English Protestant Tradition', *Sixteenth Century Journal*, 12 (1981), 5–19.

Davies, A., *The Quakers in English Society* (Oxford, 2000).

Davies, J., *The Caroline Captivity of the Church: Charles I and the Remoulding of Anglicanism* (Oxford, 1992).

Davies, N. Z., *Society and Culture in Early Modern France* (London, 1975).

Davis, J. C., 'The Levellers and Christianity', in *Politics, Religion and the English Civil War*, ed. B. Manning (London, 1973), pp. 225–50.

—— 'Radical Lives', *Political Science*, 37 (1985), 166–72.

—— *Fear, Myth and History: The Ranters and the Historians* (Cambridge, 1986).

—— 'Religion and the Struggle for Freedom in the English Revolution', *The Historical Journal*, 35 (1992), 507–31.

—— 'Political Thought During the English Revolution', in *A Companion to Stuart Britain*, ed. B. Coward (Oxford, 2003), ch. 19.

Dawson, J. E. A., 'Revolutionary Conclusions: The Case of the Marian Exiles', *History of Political Thought*, 11 (1990), 257–72.

—— 'The Apocalyptic Thinking of the Marian Exiles', in *Studies in Church History, Subsidia 10*, ed. M. Wilks (Oxford, 1994).

—— 'Anglo-Scottish Protestant Culture and Integration in Sixteenth-Century Britain', in *Conquest and Union: Forging a Multi-National British State*, eds. S. Ellis and S. Barber (London, 1995).

Deconinck-Brossard, F., 'The Churches and the "45"', in *The Church and War*, (Studies in Church History, 20, 1983), pp. 253–63.

Donagan, B., 'Codes and Conduct in the English Civil War', *Past and Present*, 188 (1988), 65–95.

——'Casuistry and Allegiance in the English Civil War', in *Writing and Political Engagement in Seventeenth-Century England*, eds. D. Hirst and R. Strier (Cambridge, 1999), ch. 5.

Donald, P., 'New Light on the Anglo-Scottish Contacts of 1640', *Historical Research*, lxii (1989), 221–9.

—— *An Uncounselled King: Charles I and the Scottish Troubles, 1637–41* (Cambridge, 1990).

Durston, C., '"For the Better Humiliation of the People": Public Days of Fasting and Thanksgiving During the English Revolution', *The Seventeenth Century*, 7 (1992), 129–49.

Durston, C. and Eales, J., eds., *The Culture of English Puritanism 1560–1700* (1996).

Eales, J., *Puritans and Roundheads: The Harleys of Brampton Bryan and the Outbreak of the English Civil War* (Cambridge, 1990).

Elvin, C. R. S., 'Some Notes on the Solemn League and Covenant in England', *Papers and Proceedings of the Hampshire Field Club*, viii (1919), 271–6.

Epstein, W., 'The Committee for Examination of Parliamentary Justice: 1642–47', *Journal of Legal History*, 7 (1986), 3–22.

Evans, J. T., *Seventeenth-Century Norwich Politics, Religion and Government, 1620–1690* (Oxford, 1979).

Everitt, A., *The Community of Kent and the Great Rebellion 1640–60* (Leicester, 1973).

Falla, T. J. and Rowe, M. M., 'The Population of Two Exeter Parishes in 1641–2', *Devon and Cornwall N & Q*, xxxv (1983), 89–95.

Fanshawe, R. E., 'An Intruded Minister at Dengie', *Essex Review*, xxxii (1923), 34–5.

Ferrell, L. A. and McCullough, P., eds., *The English Sermon Revised: Religion, Literature and History 1600–1750*. (Manchester, 2000).

Fletcher, A., *A County Community in Peace and War: Sussex 1600–1660* (London, 1975).

Ford, J. D., 'Conformity in Conscience: The Structure of the Perth Articles Debate in Scotland, 1618–38', *Journal of Ecclesiastical History*, 46 (1995), pp. 256–77.

—— 'The Lawful Bonds of Scottish Society: The Five Articles of Perth, the Negative Confession and the National Covenant', *Historical Journal*, 37 (1994), 45–64.

Foster, S., *Notes from the Caroline Underground: Alexander Leighton, the Puritan Triumvirate, and the Laudian Reaction to Nonconformity* (Connecticut, 1978).

Fox, A., *Oral and Literate Culture in England, 1500–1800* (Oxford, 2001).

Freist, D., 'The King's Crown is the Whore of Babylon: Politics, Gender and Communication in Mid-Seventeenth Century England', *Gender and History*, 7 (1995), 457–81.

—— *Governed by Opinion: Politics, Religion and the Dynamics of Communication in Stuart London, 1637–1645* (London, 1997).

Gardiner, S. R., *The Fall of the Monarchy of Charles I, 1637–1649* (2 vols., London, 1882).

—— *The History of the Great Civil War* (4 vols., London, 1987).

Garrett, C. H., *The Marian Exiles 1553–1559* (Cambridge, 1938).

Garrett, J., *The Triumphs of Providence: The Assassination Plot, 1696* (Cambridge, 1980).

Geiter, M. K., 'Affirmation, Assassination and Association: The Quakers, Parliament and the Court in 1696', *Parliamentary History*, xvi (1997), 277–88.

—— 'William Penn and Jacobitism: A Smoking Gun?', *Historical Research*, LXXIII, 181 (2000), 213–19.

Gentles, I., *The New Model Army in England, Ireland and Scotland 1645–53* (Oxford, 1992).

George, C. H., 'Puritanism as History and Historiography', *Past and Present*, 41 (1968), 77–104.

George, T., 'War and Peace in the Puritan Tradition', *Church History*, 53 (1984), 492–503.

Gibson, J. S. W., *The Hearth Tax, Other Later Stuart Tax Lists and the Association Oath Rolls* (Federation of Family History Society Publications, 1985).

Gibson, J. and Dell, A., eds., *The Protestation Returns 1641–42 and Other Contemporary Listings* (Birmingham, 1995).

Goldie, M., 'The Revolution of 1689 and the Structure of Political Argument', *Bulletin of Research in the Humanities*, lxxxiii (1980), 473–564.

—— 'James II and the Dissenters' Revenge: The Commission of Enquiry 1688', *Historical Research*, LXVI (1993), 53–88.

Goodman, D., 'The Public and the Nation', *Eighteenth Century Studies*, 29, 1 (1995), 1–4.

Gough, J. W., *The Social Contract, a Critical Study of its Development* (2nd edn., Oxford, 1957).

Greaves, R. L., 'The Origins and Early Development of English Covenant Thought', *The Historian*, xxxi (1968), 21–36.

—— 'John Knox and the Covenant Tradition', *Journal of Ecclesiastical History*, xxiv (1973), 23–32.

—— 'The Nature and Intellectual Milieu of the Political Principles in the Geneva Bible Marginalia', *Journal of Church and State*, 22 (1980), 233–51.

—— 'Concepts of Political Obedience in England: Conflicting Perspectives', *Journal of British Studies*, 22 (1982), 23–34.

—— *Deliver Us From Evil: The Radical Underground in Britain, 1660–3* (Oxford, 1986), p. 211.

Greaves, R. L. and Zaller, R., eds., *Biographical Dictionary of British Radicals in the Seventeenth Century* (3 vols., Brighton, 1982).

Green, I. M., 'The Persecution of "Scandalous" and "Malignant" Parish Clergy During the English Civil War', *English Historical Review*, xciv (1972), 507–32.

—— *The Christian's ABC: Catechisms and Catechising in England c. 1530–1740* (Oxford, 1996).

Greenberg, J. K., 'The Confessor's Laws and the Radical Face of the Ancient Constitution', *English Historical Review*, civ (1989), 611–37.

—— *The Radical Face of the English Constitution: St. Edward's 'Laws' in Early Modern Political Thought* (Cambridge, 2001).

Grell, O. P., Israel, J. I. and Tyacke, N., eds., *From Persecution to Toleration, The Glorious Revolution and Religion in England* (Oxford, 1991).

Gurney, J., 'Gerrard Winstanley and the Digger Movement in Walton and Cobham', *Historical Journal*, 37 (1994), 775–802.

Guy, J., ed., *The Reign of Elizabeth I: Court and Culture in the Last Decade* (Cambridge, 1995).

Habermas, J., *The Structural Transformation of the Public Sphere*, trans. T. Burger (Cambridge, 1989).

Halasz, A., *The Market Place of Print: Pamphlets and the Public Sphere in Early Modern England* (Cambridge, 1997).

Hale, J. R., *Renaissance War Studies* (London, 1983).

Haley, K. H. D., *The First Earl of Shaftesbury* (Oxford, 1968).

Hall, D. D., 'John Cotton's Letter to Samuel Skelton', *William and Mary Quarterly*, 22 (1965), 478–85.

Haller, W., *Liberty and Reformation in the Puritan Revolution* (New York, 1955).

—— *The Rise of Puritanism* (London, 1957).

Harris, T., *London Crowds in the Reign of Charles II* (Cambridge, 1987).

—— *Politics Under the Later Stuarts: Party Conflict in a Divided Society 1660–1715* (London, 1993).

Hay, C., *James Burgh, Spokesman for Reform in Hanoverian England* (Washington, 1979).

Haydon, C., *Anti-Catholicism in Eighteenth-Century England, c. 1714–80* (Manchester, 1993).

Hibbard, C., *Charles I and the Popish Plot* (Chapel Hill, 1983).

Hill, C., *Society and Puritanism in Pre-Revolutionary England* (London, 1964).

—— *Puritanism and Revolution* (Panther edn., London, 1968).

—— 'The Religion of Gerrard Winstanley', *Past and Present Supplement*, 5 (1978).

—— 'Irreligion in the "Puritan" Revolution', in *Radical Religion in the English Revolution*, eds. J. F. McGregor and B. Reay (Oxford, 1984), ch. 8.

—— *The English Bible and the Seventeenth-Century Revolution* (London, 1993).

Hillerbrand, H. J., ed. *The Oxford Encyclopaedia of the Reformation* (4 vols., Oxford, 1996).

Hindle, S., 'Dearth, Fasting and Alms: The Campaign for General Hospitality in Late Elizabethan England', *Past and Present*, 172 (2001), 44–86.

Holifield, E. B., *The Covenant Sealed: The Development of Puritan Sacramental Theology in Old and New England, 1570–1720* (New Haven, 1974).

Holmes, C., *The Eastern Association in the English Civil War* (Cambridge, 1974).

Hopper, A. J., '"The Readiness of the People": The Formation and Emergence of the Army of the Fairfaxes, 1642–3', *Borthwick Papers*, 92 (1997).

—— 'The Farnley Wood Plot and the Memory of the Civil War in Yorkshire', *Historical Journal*, 45 (2002), 281–303.

Horle, C. W., *The Quakers and the English Legal System 1660–1688* (Pennsylvania, 1988).

Horwitz, H., *Revolution Politicks: The Career of Daniel Finch, 2nd Earl of Nottingham, 1647–1730* (Cambridge, 1968).

—— *Parliament, Policy and Politics in the Reign of William III* (Manchester, 1977).

Hughes, A., *The Causes of the English Civil War* (London, 1991).

—— 'Approaches to Presbyterian Print Culture: Thomas Edwards's *Gangraena* as Source and Text', in *Books and Readers in Early Modern England*, eds. E. Saver and J. Anderson (Pennsylvania, 2001), pp. 97–116.

Hughes, R. T., 'Henry Burton: The Making of a Puritan Revolutionary', *Journal of Church and State*, 16 (1974), 421–35.

Hutton, R., *The Restoration: A Political and Religious History of England and Wales, 1658–1667* (Oxford, 1985).

Ingram, M., *Church Courts, Sex and Marriage in England, 1570–1640* (Cambridge, 1987).

—— 'Reformation of Manners in Early Modern England', in *The Experience of Authority in Early Modern England*, eds. P. Griffiths, A. Fox and S. Hindle (London, 1996), pp. 47–89.

Jones, D. M., *Conscience and Allegiance in Seventeenth Century England: The Political Significance of Oaths and Engagements* (Woodbridge, 1999).

Jonsen, A. R. and Toulmin, S., *The Abuse of Casuistry: A History of Moral Reasoning* (Berkeley, 1988).

Judson, M. A., *From Tradition to Political Reality* (Ohio, 1980).

Kelley, D. R., *The Beginnings of Ideology* (Cambridge, 1981).

—— 'Elizabethan Political Thought', in *The Varieties of British Political Thought*, ed. J. G. A. Pocock (Cambridge, 1993), ch. 2.

Kelly, K. T., *Conscience, Dictator or Guide? A Study in Seventeenth Century English Protestant Moral Theology* (London, 1967).

Kenyon, J. P., *Robert Spencer, Earl of Sutherland* (London, 1958).

—— *Revolution Principles: The Politics of Party 1689–1720* (Cambridge, 1977).

Ketton-Cremer, R. W., *Norfolk in the Civil War: A Portrait of a Society in Conflict* (London, 1969).

Kidd, C., 'Conditional Britons: The Scots Covenanting Tradition and the Eighteenth-century British State', *English Historical Review*, cxvii (2002), 1147–76.

Kishlansky, M., 'The Case of the Army Truly Stated: The Creation of the New Model Army', *Past and Present*, 81 (1978), 51–74.

—— *The Rise of the New Model Army* (Cambridge, 1979).

—— 'The Army and the Levellers: The Roads to Putney', *Historical Journal*, 22 (1979), 795–824.

—— 'Consensus Politics and the Structure of Debate at Putney', *Journal of British Studies* 20 (1981), 50–69.

—— 'What Happened at Ware?', *Historical Journal*, 25 (1982), 827–39.

Kitching, C. J., 'Prayers Fit for the Time: Fasting and Prayer in Response to

National Crises in the Reign of Elizabeth I', in *Monks, Hermits and the Ascetic Tradition*, ed. W. J. Shiels (Ecclesiastical History Society, 1985), pp. 241–51.

Knights, M., *Politics and Opinion in Crisis, 1678–1681* (Cambridge, 1994).

Kyle, R., 'John Knox and the Purification of Religion: The Intellectual Aspects of his Crusade Against Idolatry', *Archiv für Reformationsgeschichte*, 77 (1986), 265–80.

Lake, P. and Questier, M., 'Puritans, Papists and the "Public Sphere" in Early Modern England: The Edmund Campion Affair in Context', *Journal of Modern History*, 72 (2000), 587–628.

—— *The Anti-Christ's Lewd Hat: Protestants, Papists and Players in Post-Reformation England* (New Haven, 2002).

Lamont, W., *Marginal Prynne 1600–1669* (London, 1963).

—— 'Pamphleteering, the Protestant Consensus and the English Revolution', in *Freedom and the English Revolution: Essays in History and Literature*, eds. R. C. Richardson and G. M. Ridden (Manchester, 1986), pp. 72–93.

Lapidge, M., Blair, J., Keynes, S. and Scragg, D., eds., *The Blackwell Encyclopaedia of Anglo-Saxon England* (Oxford, 1999).

Laurence, A., *Parliamentary Army Chaplains: 1642–1651* (Woodbridge, 1990).

Leites, E., ed., *Conscience and Casuistry in Early Modern Europe* (Cambridge, 1988).

Lidington, D. R., 'Parliament and the Enforcement of Penal Statutes', *Parliamentary History*, 8 (1989), 309–28.

—— 'Mesne Process in Penal Actions at the Elizabethan Exchequer', *Journal of Legal History*, 5 (1984), 33–8.

Lindley, K., *Popular Politics and Religion in Civil War London* (Aldershot, 1997).

Lowe, B., 'Religious Wars and the "Common Peace": Anglican Anti-War Sentiment in Elizabethan England', *Albion*, 28 (1996), 415–35.

Lunn, D., *The English Benedictines, 1540–1688* (London, 1980).

McAdoo, H. R., *The Structure of Caroline Moral Theology* (London, 1949).

McCann, T. J., 'Midhurst Catholics and the Protestation Returns of 1642', *Recusant History*, xvi (1983), 319–23.

Macdonald, W. M., *The Making of an English Revolutionary: The Early Parliamentary Career of John Pym* (London, 1982).

McGiffert, M., 'American Puritan Studies in the 1960s', *William and Mary Quarterly* 3rd series, xxvii (1970), 36–67.

—— 'The Problem of the Covenant in Puritan Thought: Peter Bulkeley's Gospel-Covenant', *The New England Historical and Genealogical Register*, cxxx (1976), 107–29.

—— 'Covenant, Crown and Commons in Elizabethan Puritanism', *Journal of British Studies*, xx (1980), 32–52.

—— 'Grace and Works: The Rise and Division of Covenant Divinity in Elizabethan Puritanism', *Harvard Theological Review*, lxxv (1982), 463–502.

—— 'From Moses to Adam: The Making of the Covenant of Works', *The Sixteenth Century Journal*, xix (1988), 131–55.

MacInnes, A. L., *Charles I and the Making of the Covenanting Movement 1625–1641* (Edinburgh, 1991).

McLynn, F. J.,'Nottingham and the Jacobite Rising of 1745', *Transactions of the Thoroton Society* 83 (1979), 63–70.

—— 'Hull and the Forty-Five', *Yorkshire Archaeological Journal*, 52 (1980), 135–43.

—— *The Jacobite Army in England: 1745 The Final Campaign* (Edinburgh, 1983).

Maguire, M. H., 'The Attack of the Common Lawyers on the Oath *Ex Officio* as Administered in the Ecclesiastical Courts in England', in *Essays in History and Political Theory in Honor of C. H. McIlwain* (Cambridge, Mass., 1936), pp. 199–230.

Mah, H., 'Phantasies of the Public Sphere: Rethinking the Habermas of Historians', *Journal of Modern History*, 27 (2000), 153–82

Maitland, F. W., *The Constitutional History of England* (Cambridge, 1909).

Mason, R. A., 'Usable Pasts: History and Identity in Reformation Scotland', *Scottish Historical Review*, 76 (1997), 54–68.

—— ed., John Knox and the British Reformations (Aldershot, 1998).

Matthews, A. G., *Calamy Revised: Being a Revision of Edmund Calamy's Account of the Ministers and Others Ejected and Silenced 1660–2* (Oxford, 1934).

—— *Walker Revised: Being a Revision of John Walker's Sufferings of the Clergy During the Grand Rebellion* (reprint, Oxford, 1988).

Mears, N., 'Counsel, Public Debate and Queenship', *Historical Journal*, 44 (2001), 629–50.

Mendle, M., *Henry Parker and the English Civil War: The Political Thought of the Public's Privado* (Cambridge, 1995).

—— ed., *The Putney Debates of 1647* (Cambridge, 2001).

Miller, P., *The New England Mind: Part One the Seventeenth Century* (Cambridge, Mass., 1954 edn.).

—— 'The Marrow of Puritan Divinity', in his *Errand into the Wilderness* (New York, 1956), ch. 3.

Milton, A., *Catholic and Reformed: The Roman and Protestant Churches in English Protestant Thought: 1600–1640* (Cambridge, 1995).

Milward, P., *Religious Controversies of the Elizabethan Age* (London, 1977).

Monod, P., *Jacobitism and the English People 1688–1788* (Cambridge, 1989).

Morgan, N., *Lancashire Quakers and the Establishment 1760–1830* (Halifax, 1993).

Morrill, J. S., ed., *The Scottish National Covenant in its British Context* (Edinburgh, 1990).

—— 'The National Covenant in its British Context', in *Scottish National Covenant*, ed. Morrill, pp. 1–31.

—— *The Nature of the English Revolution* (Harlow, 1993).

Morton, A. L., *The World of the Ranters: Religious Radicalism in the English Revolution* (London, 1970).

Mullan, D. G., '"Uniformity in Religion": The Solemn League and Covenant (1643) and the Presbyterian Vision', in *Later Calvinism: International Perspectives*, ed. W. F. Graham (Kirksville, Mo., 1994), pp. 249–66.

—— *Scottish Puritanism, 1590–1638* (Oxford, 2000).

Neile, Sir J., *Elizabeth I and Her Parliaments 1584–1601* (London, 1957).

Orr, S., *Alexander Henderson, Churchman and Statesman* (London, 1919).

Peardon, B., 'The Politics of Polemic: John Ponet's *Short Treatise of Politike Power* and Contemporary Circumstance, 1553–1556', *Journal of British Studies*, 22 (1982), 35–50.

Perceval, R. W. and Hayter, P. D. G., 'The Oath of Allegiance', *The Table: The Journal of the Society of Clerks-at-the-Table in Commonwealth Parliaments*, xxxiii (1964), 85–90.

Perceval-Maxwell, M., 'The Adoption of the Solemn League and Covenant by the Scots in Ulster', *Scotia: Interdisciplinary Journal of Scottish Studies*, ii (1978), 3–18.

Pincus, S., '"Coffee Politicians Does Create": Coffeehouses and Restoration Political Culture', *Journal of Modern History*, 67 (1995), 807–35.

Pocock, J. G. A., *Politics, Language and Time: Essays on Political Thought and History* (London, 1971).

Procter, F. and Frere, W. H., *A New History of the Book of Common Prayer* (London, 1914).

Protestantism and the National Church in Sixteenth-Century England, eds. P. Lake and Maria Dowling (London, 1987).

Questier, M. C., 'Loyalty, Religion and State Power in Early Modern England: English Romanism and the Jacobean Oath of Allegiance', *Historical Journal*, xl (1997), 311–29.

Reay, B., 'The Quakers, 1659 and the Restoration of the Monarchy', *History*, 63 (1978), 193–213.

—— *The Quakers and the English Revolution* (London, 1985).

Redworth, G., 'Bishop Ponet, John Stow, and Wyatt's Rebellion of 1554', *Bodleian Library Record*, 16 (1999), 508–12.

Reid, W. S., 'John Knox's Theology of Political Government', *The Sixteenth Century Journal*, 19 (1988), 529–40.

Robbins, C., 'The Oxford Session of the Long Parliament of Charles II, 9–31 October, 1665', *Bulletin of the Institute of Historical Research*, xxi (1948), 214–24.

—— 'Five Speeches, 1661–3, by Sir John Holland, MP', *Bulletin of the Institute of Historical Research*, xxviii (1955), 189–202.

—— 'Selden's Pills: State Oaths in England, 1558–1714', *Huntington Library Quarterly*, xxxv (1972), 303–21.

Rose, C., *England in the 1690s: Revolution, Religion and War* (Oxford, 1999).

Rose, E., *Cases of Conscience: Alternatives Open to Recusants and Puritans Under Elizabeth I and James I* (Cambridge, 1975).

Rowe, V. A., *Sir Henry Vane the Younger: A Study in Political and Administrative History* (London, 1970).

Roy, I., 'The English Civil War and English Society', in *War and Society*, eds. B. Bond and I Roy (London, 1975).

—— and Reinhart, D., 'Oxford and the Civil Wars', in *The History of the University of Oxford IV*, ed. Tyacke, pp. 687–733.

Rubini, D., *Court and Country 1688–1702* (London, 1967).

Russell, C., *The Crisis of Parliaments: English History 1509–1660* (Oxford, 1971).

—— *The Causes of the English Civil War* (Oxford, 1991).

—— *The Fall of the British Monarchies, 1637–1642* (Oxford, 1991).

Sanderson, J., *'But the People's Creatures': The Philosophical Basis of the English Civil War* (Manchester, 1989).

—— 'Conrad Russell's Ideas', *History of Political Thought*, 14 (1993), 85–102.

—— *The Engagement Re-engaged: Political Thought in Post-regicide England* (Strathclyde Papers on Government and Politics, cvii, 1996).

Schochet, G. J., 'Sir Robert Filmer: Some New Bibliographical Discoveries', *The Library*, xxvi (1971), 135–60.

Schramm, P. E., *A History of the English Coronation*, trans. L. G. W. Legg (Oxford, 1937).

Scott, J., *England's Troubles: Seventeenth Century English Political Instability in European Context* (Cambridge, 1999).

Scott, T., 'The Volksreformation of Thomas Muntzer in Allsted and Muhlhausen', *Journal of Ecclesiastical History*, xxxiv (1983), 194–213.

Seaver, P. S., *Wallington's World: A Puritan Artisan in Seventeenth Century London* (London, 1985).

Seaward, P., *The Cavalier Parliament and the Reconstruction of the Old Regime, 1661–1667* (Cambridge, 1989).

Sharpe, K., ed., *Faction and Parliament* (Oxford, 1978).

Sharpe, J., 'Scandalous and Malignant Priest in Essex: The Impact of Grassroots Puritanism', in *Politics and People in Revolutionary England*, eds. C. Jones, M. Newitt and S. Roberts (Oxford, 1986), pp. 253–75.

Skinner, Q., 'History and Ideology in the English Revolution', *Historical Journal*, viii (1965), 151–78.

—— 'The Ideological Context of Hobbes's Political Thought', *Historical Journal*, ix (1966), 286–317.

—— 'Conquest and Consent: Thomas Hobbes and the Engagement Controversy', in *The Interregnum*, ed. G. E. Aylmer (London, 1972), pp. 79–98.

Smart, I. M., 'The Political Ideas of the Scottish Covenanters: 1638–88', *History of Political Thought*, i (1980), 167–93.

Smith, D. L., *A History of the Modern British Isles 1603–1707: The Double Crown* (Oxford, 1998).

Smith, N., *Literature and Revolution in England 1640–1660* (New Haven, 1994).

Solt, L. F., 'John Saltmarsh: New Model Army Chaplain', *Journal of Ecclesiastical History*, 2 (1951), 69–80.

Sommerville, J. P., 'The New Art of Lying: Equivocation, Mental Reservation and Casuistry', *Conscience and Casuistry*, ed. Leites, pp. 159–85.

Speck, W. A., *The Butcher: The Duke of Cumberland and the Suppression of the '45* (Oxford, 1981).

—— *Reluctant Revolutionaries: Englishmen and the Revolution of 1688* (Oxford, 1988).

Spraggon, J., *Puritan Iconoclasm During the English Civil War* (Woodbridge, 2003).

Spurr, J., 'The Church of England, Comprehension and the Toleration Act of 1689', *English Historical Review*, civ (1989), 927–46.

——'Perjury, Profanity and Politics', *The Seventeenth Century*, viii (1993), 29–50.

—— 'A Profane History of Early Modern Oaths', *TRHS*, 11 (2001), pp. 37–63.

Steele, M., '"The Politick Christian": The Theological Background to the National Covenant', in *Scottish National Covenant*, ed. Morrill, pp. 31–68.

Stevenson, D., *The Scottish Revolution 1637–44: The Triumph of the Covenanters* (Newton Abbot, 1973).

Straka, G. M., *Anglican Reaction to the Revolution of 1688* (Madison, 1962).

—— 'The Final Phase of Divine Right Theory in England 1688–1702', *English Historical Review*, lxxvii (1962), 638–58.

Sutherland, L. S. and Mitchell, L. G., eds., *The History of the University of Oxford V* (Oxford, 1986).

Tatham, G. B., *The Puritans in Power: A Study in the History of the English Church from 1640–1660* (Cambridge, 1913).

Tolmie, M., *The Triumph of the Saints: The Separate Churches of London 1616–1649* (Cambridge, 1977).

Tomlinson, H., ed., *Before the English Civil War* (Basingstoke, 1983).

Twigg, T., *The University of Cambridge and the English Revolution: 1625–1688* (Cambridge, 1990).

Tyacke, N., ed., *The History of the University of Oxford IV: Seventeenth Century Oxford* (Oxford, 1997).

Tyler, J. E., *Oaths: Their Origins, Nature and History* (London, 1834).

Underdown, D., *Fire from Heaven* (London, 1993).

Urwick, W., *Historical Sketches of Nonconformity in the County Palatine of Chester* (London, 1864).

Vallance, E., '"An Holy and Sacramentall Paction": Federal Theology and the Solemn League and Covenant in England', *English Historical Review*, cxvi (2001), 50–75.

—— 'Oaths, Casuistry and Equivocation: Anglican Responses to the Engagement Controversy', *Historical Journal*, 44 (2001), 59–77.

—— 'Loyal or Rebellious? Protestant Associations in England, 1584–1696', *The Seventeenth Century*, 17 (2002), 1–24.

—— 'Protestation, Vow, Covenant and Engagement: Swearing Allegiance in the English Civil War', *Historical Research*, 75 (2002), 408–24.

—— '"The Kingdome's Case": The Use of Casuistry as a Political Language 1640–1692', *Albion*, 34 (2003), 557–83.

—— 'Preaching to the Converted: Religious Justifications for the English Civil War', *Huntington Library Quarterly*, 65 (2002), 395–421.

—— 'The Decline of Conscience as a Political Guide: William Higden's *View of the English Constitution* (1709)', in *Contexts of Conscience in Early Modern Europe, 1500–1700*, eds. H. Braun and E. Vallance (Basingstoke, 2003), ch.6.

Van Horn Melton, J., *The Rise of the Public in Enlightenment Europe* (Cambridge, 2001).

Varley, F. J., *Cambridge During the Civil War 1642–1646* (Cambridge, 1935).

Vernon, E. C., 'The Quarrel of the Covenant: the London Presbyterians and the Regicide', in *The Regicides and the Execution of Charles I*, ed. J. Peacey (2001), ch. 9.

Waduba, S., 'Equivocation and Recantation During the English Reformation: The "Subtle Shadows" of Dr. Edward Crome', *Journal of Ecclesiastical History*, 44 (1993), 224–42.

Wallace, J. M., *Destiny His Choice: The Loyalism of Andrew Marvell* (Cambridge, 1968).

—— 'The Engagement Controversy 1649–52: An Annotated List of Pamphlets', *Bulletin of the New York Public Library*, lxviii (1969), 385–465.

Walsham, A., *Providence in Early Modern England* (Oxford, 1999).

Walter, J., *Understanding Popular Violence in the English Revolution* (Cambridge, 1999).

—— 'Confessional Politics in Pre-Civil War Essex: Prayer Books, Profanations, and Petitions', *The Historical Journal*, 44 (2001), 677–701.

Walzer, M., *The Revolution of the Saints: A Study in the Origins of Radical Politics* (London, 1966).

—— ed., *Regicide and Revolution: Speeches at the Trial of Louis XVI* (2nd edn., New York, 1992).

Webster, T., *Godly Clergy in Early Stuart England* (Cambridge, 1997).

Weir, D. A., *The Origins of the Federal Theology in Sixteenth-Century Reformation Thought* (Oxford, 1990).

Weston, C. C. and Greenberg, J. K., *Subjects and Sovereigns: The Grand Controversy over Legal Sovereignty in Stuart England* (Cambridge, 1981).

Williamson, A. H., *Scottish National Consciousness in the Age of James VI: The Apocalypse, the Union and the Shaping of Scotland's Public Culture* (Edinburgh, 1979).

Williamson, R. J. T., *History of the Old County Regiment of Lancashire Militia* (London, 1888).

Wilson, J. H., *Pulpit in Parliament: Puritanism During the English Civil Wars, 1640–1648* (Princeton, 1969).

Wood, A., *Riot, Rebellion and Popular Politics in Early Modern England* (London, 2002).

Wood, E. M. and Wood, N., *A Trumpet of Sedition: Political Theory and the Rise of Capitalism, 1509–1688* (London, 1997).

Woolrych, A., 'Last Quests for Settlement, 1659–60', in *The Interregnum: The Quest for Settlement, 1656–1660*, ed. G. E. Aylmer (Basingstoke, 1972), ch. 8.

—— *Soldiers and Statesmen: The General Council of the Army and its Debates, 1647–1648* (Oxford, 1987).

Wootton, D., 'From Rebellion to Revolution: The Crisis of the Winter of 1642/3 and the Origins of Civil War Radicalism', *English Historical Review*, cv (1990), 654–69.

Worden, B., *The Rump Parliament* (Cambridge, 1974).

—— 'Cromwellian Oxford', in *The History of the University of Oxford IV*, ed. Tyacke, pp. 733–73.

—— *Roundhead Reputations: The English Civil War and the Passions of Posterity* (London, 2002).

Wormald, P., 'The Venerable Bede and the "Church of the English"', in *The English Religious Tradition and the Genius of Anglicanism*, ed. G. Rowell (Wantage, 1992).

——, J. Gillingham and C. Richmond, 'Elton and the English: A Discussion', *TRHS*, 7 (1997), 317–36.

Zabrowski, M. K., 'The Corruption of Politics and the Dignity of Human Nature: The Critical and Conservative Radicalism of James Burgh', *Enlightenment and Dissent*, 10 (1991), 78–104.

Zagorin, P., *Ways of Lying: Dissimulation, Persecution and Conformity in Early Modern Europe* (London, 1990).

Zaret, D. R., *The Heavenly Contract: Ideology and Organisation in Pre-Revolutionary Puritanism* (Chicago, 1985).

—— 'Petitions and the "Invention" of Public Opinion in the English Revolution', *American Journal of Sociology*, 101 (1996), 1497–555.

—— *The Origins of Democratic Culture: Printing, Petitions, and the Public Sphere in Early Modern England* (Princeton, NJ, 2000).

Unpublished theses and articles

Appleby, D., 'For God or Caesar: The Dilemmas of Restoration Nonconformists', unpublished conference paper, delivered at the 'Conscience and the Early Modern World: 1500–1800' conference, Sheffield, July 2002.

Bowler, G., 'English Protestants and Resistance Writings' (University of London Ph.D., 1981).

Bozeman, T.D., 'Covenant Theology and "National Covenant": A Study in Elizabethan Presbyterian Thought' (unpublished conference paper).

Davis, J. C., with Alsop, J. D., 'Gerrard Winstanley', *Oxford Dictionary of National Biography* (forthcoming Oxford, 2004).

Findon, J. C., 'The Non-Jurors and the Church of England 1689–1716' (Oxford University D. Phil. thesis, 1978).

Jones, D.M., 'Authority and Allegiance in Seventeenth Century England: The Political Significance of Oaths and Engagements' (University of London Ph.D., 1984).

Kim, J. L., 'The Debate on the Relations Between the Churches of Scotland and England During the British Revolution (1633–1647)' (Cambridge University Ph.D., 1997).

Steele, M., 'Covenanting Political Propaganda, 1638–89' (Glasgow University Ph.D., 1995).

Vallance, E., 'State Oaths and Political Casuistry in England: 1640–1702' (Oxford University D. Phil., 2000).

Vernon, E. C., 'The Sion College Conclave and London Presbyterianism during the English Revolution' (Cambridge University Ph.D., 1999).

Wells, V. T., 'The Origins of Covenanting Thought and Resistance: c. 1580–1638' (Stirling University Ph.D., 1997).

Zaret, D. R., 'An Analysis of the Development and Content of the Covenant Theology of Pre-Revolutionary Puritanism' (Oxford University D. Phil., 1977).

Index

Abbots Aston, Buckinghamshire, 110
Aberdeen, 46
Acland, Baldwin, 172
'Act Asserting His Majestys Royal
    Prerogative in Making of
    Leagues', 210
Act of Oblivion and Indemnity (1660),
    181
Act of Uniformity (1662), 100, 180,
    181, 184, 188, 189, 198, 199
    'assent and consent' clause, 186, 187
Adams, Samuel, 217
Adamson, John, 54, 77
Adolphus, Gustavus, 139
Affirmation Bill (1697), 205
Afrikaners, 217
Agostini, Gerolamo, Venetian
    Secretary, 117, 118
Akenson, Donald H., 217
Alford, Francis, 23
Alford, Stephen, 13, 22
Allchurch, Worcestershire, 112
allegiance, 1, 102, 114
    as a natural duty, 61, 63
    St Paul and St Peter on, 61
    to Charles I, made equivocal in SLC,
    72
Alleine, Joseph, 187
Allen, William, 104
Almann, Jacques, 10
Alsop, J. D., 150
altars, 65, 129
Ames, William, 18, 41, 84, 106
Amsterdam, 42
anabaptists, 113
Anderson, Benedict, 4

Annotations upon the Late Protestation
    (1642), 67
Antichrist, 41, 86, 94, 97, 98, 138, 139,
    145, 197, 222
Anti-confederacie, The (1644), 72
Anti-covenant, The (1643), 115
antinomianism, 139, 140
apocalypse, 40, 98, 99, 139, 180, 200,
    209, 216, 222
Appelby, David, 186
Appellant Controversy, 25
Aquinas, St Thomas, 127
Armada, Spanish (1588), 16, 38
Armine, Sir William, 92
Arminianism, 43, 150
Arnold, Robert, 64
Arundel, Sussex, 204
Ascham, Anthony, 162
Ash Bocking, Suffolk, 122
Ashe, Simeon, 158
Assembly of Commoners (1688), 197
Assembly of Divines, see Westminster
    Assembly
Atwood, William, 207, 208
Augustine, on lying, 103
Austine, Robert, 74
Axholme, Isle of, Lincolnshire, 110
Aylmer, Gerald, 152
Aylmer, John, 4, 16
Aylstone, Leicestershire, 109

Bachiler, Samuel, 41, 48
Bacon, Nathaniel, 216
Baconsthorpe, 123
Baker, Phil, 147
bands of manrent, 10, 22, 44, 46

Baptists, 133, 143, 182
barber-surgeons, 209
Barnes, Ambrose, 198, 220
Barnes, Thomas, 41
Barnstaple, 52
Bastwick, John, 140
Bates, William, 192
Bath and Wells, 206
Baxter, Richard, 173, 174, 183, 184, 190, 191–2
Beacon, 206
Beadle, John, 109
Beale, John, 112
Beale, Theodore, 122
Beard, Thomas, 163
Beccles, Norfolk, 127
Becon, Thomas, 31
Bede, the Venerable 4
Bedfordshire, 206
Belfast, 210
Bellany, Alaister, 219
Benn, William, 96
Bere Regis, Dorset, 204
Berkeley, Sir Henry, 125
Berkenhead, Sir John, 187
Bermuda, 204
Bernard, Richard, 41, 42
Bertie, Sir Peregrine, 125, 189
Beza, Theodore, 10
Bible
  books of
    Deuteronomy, 6, 15
    Ecclesiastes, 68
    Hosea, 163
    James, 155
    Jeremiah, 86
    Joshua, 70
    Judges, 52
    Leviticus, 35, 42
    Matthew, 155
    Revelations, 25, 139
    Romans, 123, 161, 163
    New Testament, 94, 155
    Old Testament, 94
  editions of
    Bishops 1568, 13
    Geneva version, 12–13, 14, 48

'Bill for granting ease to his Majesty's Protestant Dissenting subjects' (1672), 187–8
Bill for the Security of the King's Person (1661), 185
Birch, Col. John, 180, 188
Bisbie, Nathaniel, 194
Bishops, petition for removal from House of Lords, 113
Bisse, Edward, 113
Bitteswell, Leicestershire, 109
Black Acts (1584), 46
Blackburn, Lancashire, 169
Blackwell, George, 25
Blake, Martin, 107
blasphemy, 153
'Blessed Revolution' of 1624, 43
Boleyn, Anne, 20
Bond, John, 172
Book of Common Prayer, 37, 113, 189
  Protestation inspiration for destruction of, 11
Boston Committee of Correspondence, 217
Boston Port Act, 217
Bowler, Gerald, 14, 16
Bowles, Edward, 55
Boxted, Essex, 118
Bozeman, T. D., 6
  'Deuteronomic punishment', 31, 32
  on idea of a national covenant, 30–2
Brabazon, Wallop, 108
Brackley, Northamptonshire, 202
Braddick, Mike, 204, 208
Bradford, Yorkshire, 113
Bradford, John, 8
Bradshaw, John, 174
Bradshaw, Richard, 174, 176
Bradshaw, William, 25
Brainford, Norfolk, 205
Brampton, Herefordshire, 109
Brantham, Suffolk, 117
Breda, Declaration of (1660), 180
bricklayers, 209
Bridge, William, 78–9, 85
Bridgeman, Orlando, Lord Keeper, 192, 193

Briefe Discourse, A (1643), 71
Brinsley, John, 35, 36, 39–40, 92
Bristol, 57, 175–6, 212
Brooke, Lord, 47, 86
Buchanan, George, 75
Buckingham, 206
Buckingham, George Villiers, Duke of, 43
Buckinghamshire, 110, 113, 153, 205, 206
Bulkeley, Richard, 92
Burgess, Cornelius, 44, 59, 66, 90, 158
Burgess, Glenn, 63, 162
Burgh, James, 215, 222
Burroughes, Jeremiah, 66–8, 78–9
    The Glorious Name of God, the Lord of Hosts (1643), 67–8, 219
Burton, Henry, 65, 66, 93, 133, 135–6, 138, 139
    on the coronation oath as national covenant, 80
    For God and the King (1636), 140
    on idea of a national covenant, 139–41
    Israel's Fast (1628), 139
    The Protestation Protested (1641), 140
Bury, Lancashire, 169
Bury St Edmunds, 86
Butterfield, Sir Herbert, 216

Caesar, Gaius Julius, 42
Calamy, Edmund, 44, 99–100, 158, 182, 184
Calvert, Giles, 182
Calvinism, 29, 33
Calvin's Case (1608), 61, 63, 72, 74, 79
Cambridgeshire, 123
Cambridge, University of, 71, 116
    Corpus Christi, 172
    Pembroke College, 111
    Response to Protestation (1641), 111
    St John's College, 139
    Tendering of the Engagement (1650), 171–3
    Trinity Hall, 172
Cameronian Covenanters, 217
Canby, Edward, 203

Canne, John, 160
canons, 1640, 51, 64, 107
Canterbury, diocese of, 206
Carleton, George, 34
Carmichael, James, 46
Carr, Sir Robert, 188
Cartwright, John, 215
Cartwright, Thomas, 31, 32
Caryl, Joseph, 89, 95, 96, 119, 162, 170
Case, Thomas, 73, 87, 89, 90, 92, 93, 95, 98, 119, 138, 171
    The Quarrel of the Covenant (1644), 89
Case of the Armie Truly Stated (1647), 146–7
casuistry, 2, 104
    casuistic advice on Engagement (1649), 173–6
    casuistic conferences, 123, 176
    Catholic, 102–5
casuists, 18, 63, 102, 103, 105, 106, 174, 178, 192
catechisms, soldiers', 88
Catholics, 26–7, 102, 103, 114, 140, 177, 187, 188
    subscription to the 1696 Association, 204–5
    subscription to the Protestation, 110
    targets for crowd violence, 65
Cecil, William, Lord Burghley, 13, 16, 21, 22, 24–5, 196
Certain Disquisitions (1644), 119
Certain Particulars (1651), 168
Chalgrove Field, 57
Chapman, Seth, 117
Charlbury, Oxfordshire, 113
Charles I, 5, 22, 35, 38, 43, 48, 53, 54, 67, 70, 73, 74, 86, 126, 139, 140, 159, 160, 165, 174
    coronation oath, 76
    as a covenanted monarch, 63, 65, 67
    personal rule, 44
    trial and execution of, 81, 159–60, 164, 178, 188
Charles II, 133, 170, 180, 181, 182, 187, 196, 197, 208
    coronation at Scone (1651), 182

Cheshire, 108, 123, 173, 175
Chester, 175
Chesterton, Cambridgeshire, 123
Chettle, Dorset, 114
Cheynell, Francis, 121
Cholmely, Sir Hugh, 68
Church of England, 111, 136, 186,
    198
  and the Protestation 1641, 52, 64
  thirty-nine articles, 65–6, 72, 112
Church of Ireland, 59
Church of Scotland, 58
civil war, English, 1, 89, 102, 106, 108,
    179, 194, 207, 218, 220
  presented as a holy war, 98
  radicalism, 137–8, 200
  second, 147
  as a seed-bed of liberal/democratic
    ideas, 62
  Whig/Marxist interpretation of, 134,
    143
Clark, J. C. D., 217
Clark, Peter, 222
Clarke, Samuel, 70
Claybrooke, Leicestershire, 124
Cleeve, Elizabeth, 169
clergy, Anglican parochial
  equivocate with the Association
    (1696), 206–7
  equivocate with Engagement (1650),
    168
  as refusers of Protestation, 111–13
  as refusers of the Solemn League and
    Covenant, 122–4
  as refusers of the Vow and Covenant,
    116–17
Clotworthy, Sir John, 158
Cobham, Lord, 24
Cobham, Surrey, 150
Coke, Sir Edward, 61, 74, 79, 216
Colchester, 140
Coleman, Nicholas, 122
Coleman, Thomas, 93, 94, 98, 119
College, Stephen, 194
Colley, Linda, 4, 212
Collinson, Patrick, 4, 15, 21, 23, 32,
    33

committee for compounding, 125
Committee for Scandalous Ministers,
    111, 116
  Suffolk committee for, 116
Committee, or Popery in Masquerade,
    The (1680), 194–5
Commons, House of, 172
  committee to examine the King's
    oath, 75–7
  debate on an oath of association
    1680, 196–7
  debate on declaration of indulgence
    (1672), 187–8
  debate on the Protestation, 86
  petition to concerning Protestation,
    111
Commonwealth, English, see Rump
    Parliament
'Commonwealthsmen', 200, 216
comprehension of dissenters into
    Church of England, 187
  see also toleration
Conant, John, 173, 178
Conde, Prince of, 22
Confederacy of Kilkenny, 95
Congregational way, 85
Congregationalists, 100, 133, 143
Connecticut, 30
conscience, cases of, 59
  civil war presented as, 62
Constable, John, 117
contract law, 82
Convention under William III, 215
Cooke, Colonel Edward, 196
coopers, 209
Corbet, John, 183, 184, 191
Corke, George, 117
Cornwall, 109
Corporation Act (1661), 100, 180,
    186, 199
Cotton, Edward, 110
Cotton, John, 80, 85, 92
Cotton, Thomas, 140
Council of State, 160–1, 171, 175,
    176
Counter-Reformation, 94, 209
county committees, 69

covenants
  biblical
    Abraham's, 31, 67
    Adam's, 28
    Asa's, 11, 134
    Ezra's, 94
    Hezekiah's, 35, 134
    Josiah's, 35, 134
    Nehemiah's, 94
  church covenants, 82, 85, 140
    as mini-democracies, 133–4, 142–3
    Winstanley's *Law of Freedom*
      influenced by, 152–3
  covenant-breaking, 99
  covenant-engaged citizens, 124, 157
  covenant of grace, 6, 28–9, 30, 83–4,
    88
  covenant of works, 29
    and relationship with idea of a
      national covenant, 30
  covenant theology 28, 82, 145
  covenanted monarch, 14, 63, 74,
    219
  distinguished from oaths, 84
  distinguished from testaments, 28
  social covenants, 29, 82
  see also national covenant
Covenanters Catechisme, The (1644), 73,
  85
Covenanters Plea, The (1661), 183
Coventry, Henry, 188
Coventry, Sir William, 188
Coverdale, Myles, 31
Cranbrook, Kent, 142
Cranmer, Thomas, 7, 37
Cressner, Robert, 185
Cressy, David, 21, 90, 129, 203
Croft, Sir William, 108
Crofton, Zachary, 182–3n, 184, 185,
  199
Crome, Edward, 106
Cromwell, Oliver, 147, 152, 153, 172,
  176, 177, 207
Cromwell, Richard, 180
Cromwell, Thomas, 20
Croston, Lancashire, 110
Crowther, Joseph, 113

Cruickshanks, Eveline, 211
Culpeper, Sir Cheney, 57, 117
Curry Mallett, Somerset, 170
Cust, Richard, 219

Danner, Dan G., 12
Dannet, Thomas, 15, 16
Davenport, John, 45
Davidson, John, 46
Davis, J. C., 80, 134, 137, 139, 144–5,
  149
Dawson, Jane, 8, 14, 45, 48
de facto powers, 161–2, 176
Dell, William, 133
demonologists, 138
Denbighshire, 109
Dengie, in Essex, 108
Denison, Stephen, 34
Dennet, John, 112, 114
Derby, Earl of, 211
'Derbyshire Blues', 211
Dering, Edward, 14–15, 30, 48
Devon, 109, 113, 190, 192, 197, 206,
  212, 214
D'Ewes, Sir Symonds, 76
Digges, Thomas, 15, 24, 25
Diggers, the, 129, ch. 6 *passim*, 218
  and the national covenant, 149–53
  songs, 151
Dillingham, William, 127, 172
Directory of Worship (1645), 186
divine punishment, 15, 31, 36, 48, 85,
  99, 115, 155
  for covenant breaking, 89, 134,
    159–60, 163
Dodsworth, Mr, Lincolnshire vicar,
  112–13
Donald, Peter, 86
Doncaster, Yorkshire, 203
Dorchester, Dorset, 96
Dorset, 64, 96, 112, 113, 114, 204
Douai, 104
Drake, Roger, 171
drinking, 88
Durham, 123
Dury, John, 45, 90, 162–3, 166–7, 168,
  170

Dutch, 110
Dutch Republic, 78, 85, 92, 94

East India Company, 217
Eastern Association, 55, 116, 123
Edinburgh, 46, 181, 210
Edward II, 75
Edward III, 196
Edward VI, 6–7
Edwards, Thomas, 66, 133, 134, 142, 218
    Gangraena (1646), 133, 134, 137–8
elect, the, 31, 40, 83–4
    see also reprobate; saving remnant
elect nation, 4, 93
Elizabeth I, 12, 94, 104
    accession day celebrations, 38
    as a covenanted monarch, 39, 67
    prayers for her sickness, 39
Ellesmere, Lord Chancellor, 62
Ellis, John, 88
Engagement of loyalty to the
        Commonwealth (1649), 84, 100, 152, 153, 155, 161–78, 184
    compatible with the Covenant, 165–9
    in conflict with third clause of the Covenant, 162–5
    pamphlet controversy over, 161–9
    rendered a dead letter, 177
    subscription to 169–77
    used to qualify for legal proceedings, 169
episcopacy, primitive, 59
equivocation, 26, 102, 103–7, 129, 178
    Independents accused of, 135, 157
    permitted in swearing by Royalist writers, 120–1, 128
    permitted in taking the Engagement (1650), 168–9
    prohibited in swearing by Royalist writers, 115, 119–20, 128
    used when taking the Association (1696), 203–7
    used when taking the declaration against the Covenant, 186
    used when taking the 'Oxford Oath', 191–3
    used when taking the Protestation, 113–15
    verbal equivocation, 105–6
    see also mental reservation
Erbury, William, 148
Essex, 108, 109, 116, 118, 123, 124, 129, 140
Essex, Robert Devereux, earl of, 157
    covenant to, 53
    Vow and Covenant causes discontent in army, 117
Evedon, Lincolnshire, 125
Evelyn, John, 118
Everade, Sir Richard, 118
Everard, Robert, 147
Everard, William, 153
Exclusion Crisis, 60, 179, 181, 194–7, 220
Exeter, Devon, 109, 113, 192, 197, 206, 212
Exeter Association, 197–8

Fairfax, Thomas Lord, 146, 151, 158
fasting 1, 6, 31, 37, 48, 134, 140
    fast sermons, 32, 44, 88, 150, 219
    public fasts, 38, 88, 139
    relationship with the idea of a national covenant, 39
Faulkner, William, 198
Fawconer, Mr, curate of Fugglestone, Wiltshire, 170
Feake, Christopher, 150
Featley, Daniel, 71, 120
federal theology, 6, 28–32, 59, 102
    and the English national covenant, ch. 4 *passim*
    and the Scottish national covenant, 45
    see also covenant theology
Felton, John, 43
feminine rule, 11
Fenner, Dudley, 14n, 30, 48
Fenwick's plot, 1696, 202
Ferne, Henry, *The Resolving of Conscience* (1642), 67–8, 219

Fielder, John, 151
Fielding, Basil, earl of Denbigh, 88
Fiennes, Nathaniel, 86
Fifth Monarchists, 133, 150
Finch, Heneage, 188, 190, 201
Finch, Lady Isabella, 212
Fisher, Edward, 68
Fisher, Samuel, 154
Five Mile Act, 1665, 189
Fleet prison, 43, 112
Flemish, 110
Forbes, John, 46
Ford, Simon, 172
Forster, Ann, 177
forswearing, 118, 162
  see also perjury
Fountaine, John, 192
Fowke, John, 158
Fox, Adam, 219
franchise, elective, 148
Frank, Mark, 111
Frankfurt, 7
free grace, 142
freemasons, 209
French Holy League, 38, 95
Frontinus, Sextus Julius, 42
Fugglestone, Wiltshire, 170

Garnet, Henry, 103
Garrett, Christina, 11
Gataker, Thomas, 37, 59
Gater, Sarah, 150
Gauden, John, 153, 154, 183
Gee, Edward, 162, 163, 164, 165, 176, 184
  A Plea for Non-scribers (1650), 176
Geiter, Mary, 205
General Assembly, Scottish, 46, 84
Geneva, 7
Gentles, Ian, 148
George II, 210, 211, 212, 213, 214, 215
Gerces, Robert, 205
Geree, John, 64, 65, 66, 87, 94, 96
Germany, 42
Gerrard, Sir Gilbert, 180
Gibson, Edward, 206
Gilby, Anthony, 8, 12

George, C. H., 134, 143, 144
George, Timothy, 40, 41
Gloucestershire, 109, 123, 169
Goddard, Guybon, 126–7, 129
'Good old cause', 133, 182, 194
Goodman, Christopher, 8, 12, 14, 15, 16, 29, 45, 48, 70
  How Superior Powers Ought to be Obeyed (1558), 8–10
Goodman, Dena, 220
Goodwin, John, 135
Gordon, Lord George, 222
Gouge, William, 41, 42
'Grand National Association for Restoring the Constitution', 215
Green, Ian, 128
Grimoldby, Lincolnshire, 114
Guildhall, the, 158
Gunpowder Plot, 26, 38, 102, 103, 105
Gurney, John, 150
Guy, John, 15, 198
Gwyn, Sir Roland, 202

Habermas, Jürgen, 220–1
Hadleigh, in Essex, 108
Haines, Mr, London minister, 123
Hale, J. R., 40, 41, 42
Hale, Matthew, baron of the Exchequer, 187
Hales, Sir James, 24
Hall, Henry, 164–5, 174
Hall, Joseph, 44
Haller, William, 133, 143, 144
Hampden's Case, 77
Hampshire, 108, 109, 123, 205
Hardwicke, Lord Chancellor, 211, 213, 215
Harley, Col. Edward, 174
Harley, Lady Brilliana, 88
Harley, Sir Robert, 86, 108,
Harley, Sir Robert, first Earl of Oxford, 202
Harleys, of Brampton Bryan, 38, 109
Harmony of our Oaths (1643), 69
Harris, John, 203
Hartlib, Samuel, 47, 57, 58, 117
Hasketon, Suffolk, 117

Hawkshead, Lancashire, 205
Hawnes, Bedfordshire, 206
Haydon, Colin, 215
Heidelburg Catechism, 46
Henderson, Alexander, 66
Henrietta Maria, 43, 70
Henry, Prince of Wales, 139
Henry VIII, 20, 77, 106
Hereford, 171
Herefordshire, 109, 171, 205
heresy, 92, 133, 136, 138, 142, 157
  heresiographers, 133, 134, 135, 136,
    142
Herle, Charles, 64, 78
Herring, Theodore, 35
Herring, Thomas, archbishop of York,
  211, 213
Hertfordshire, 108
  Watton, 68, 112
Heywood, Lancashire, 169
High Commission, court of, 44
Hill, Christopher, 1, 2, 82, 134, 137,
  138
Hill, John, 213
Hilsham, Suffolk, 205
Hobbes, Thomas, 162
  Leviathan (1651), 162, 176–7
Holcroft, Sir Henry, 163
Holipstow, Suffolk, 205
Holland, Sir John, 181
Holles, Denzil, 52, 56, 95, 157, 158
Hollington, William, 112
Hollingworth, Richard, 176
Holmes, Clive, 55
Holy Trinity the Less, parish of,
  London, 110
holy war, 41, 63, 75
homilies, church, 38, 61, 63, 72
Hooker, Thomas, 38
Hoston, Middlesex, 205
Hotham, Sir John, 141
Howie, Robert, 46, 84
Hues, Thomas, 113
Hughes, Ann, 137
Hughes, R. T., 140
Huguenot, 79
Hull, 141

Humfrey, John, 192, 208
hundred, organisation of oath returns
  by, 109
Huntingdonshire, 123
Hunton, Philip, A Treatise of Monarchy
  (1643), 219
Hutton, Justice, 77
Hyde, Edward, earl of Clarendon, 86,
  180, 184
Hyde, Edward, earl of Rochester, 201

iconoclasm, 63, 129
  Protestation and, 65, 111, 140
  Solemn League and Covenant and,
    128
idolatry, 8–9, 11, 12, 15, 59, 63, 94, 97,
  140, 218–19
  idolatrous nations, 34
impersonation, as means to evade
    swearing Solemn League and
    Covenant, 125
Independents, 58, 71, 93, 133, 134,
  138, 145, 163
  in the House of Commons, 85,
    158
  links to Levellers, 143
  petition against the Covenant, 135
  reading of the Covenant, 135–6,
    155
Indian silks, 203
Ingoldsby, William, 68, 112
Iniquity of the Late Solemne League, The
  (1644), 119, 120
inversion, 138
Ireton, Henry, 147
Irwin, Lord, 210
Israel and 'Israelite paradigm', 4, 70, 93,
  99, 186
  as applied in Scotland, 47
  Goodman's views on, 8
  use in Jacobean sermons, 33–40
  see also Judah; McGiffert, Michael
Israelis, 217
Iver, Buckinghamshire, 153

Jackson, Arthur, 171
Jackson, Col., 171

Jackson, Thomas, 34, 36
Jacobites, 5, 200, 206, 207
  the 15, 209–10
  the 45, 209, 210–15
James VI and I, 6, 24, 26, 27, 38, 40, 75, 76, 94, 208
James VII and II, 22, 194, 197, 200, 203, 204, 205, 206, 214
  as Duke of York, 194
James, William, 110, 169
Jebb, John, 215
Jefferay, Richard, 34
Jenkin or Jenkins, William, 170–1
jeremiads, 6, 32
Jessop, Constance, 175–6
Jessop, William, 174–5
Jesuits, 25, 26, 72, 103, 104, 105, 119, 135, 145, 162
Jewel, John, 40
Johnston of Wariston, Sir Archibald, 45, 46, 66
Jones, David Martin, 2
Jones, Sir William, 196
Jordan, W. K., 133
Josselin, Ralph, 166
Joyce, Cornet, 158
Judah, 6, 14, 35, 86, 94, 96, 213
Judson, Margaret, 162
just war, 41–2

Keane, Colonel, 169
Keeble, William, 116
Kent, 113, 116, 123, 142, 169, 206
Kentish Rebellion (1643), 57
Kenyon, J. P., 197, 201
Keyling, Lord Chief Justice, 190, 192, 193
Kidd, Colin, 217
Kiffin, William, 88
Kim, J. L., 98
King's Confession (1581), 46
King's Covenant, 47
Kingston-upon-Thames, Surrey, 150, 151
kirk, Scottish, 84, 92, 136
Knewstub, John, 31, 32
Knightley, John, 194

Knights, John, 194
Knights, Mark, 194
Knolles, Richard, 163
Knox, John, 8, 14, 16, 29, 45, 48
  and idea of a covenant between England and Scotland, 13–14
  and idea of a national covenant, 10–11
Knyvett, Sir Thomas, 121
Koch, Johannes (Cocceus, 1603–69), 83

Lake, Peter, 41, 220
Lamont, Andrew, 124
Lamont, W. M., 134, 143, 147
Lancashire, 23, 110, 169, 176, 203, 205, 211
Lancaster, 203
Lance, William, 123
Landsdowne, 57
Langbaine, Gerard, 64, 172
Large, Robert, 117
Late Covenant Asserted, The (1643), 70
Latimer, Hugh, 6–7, 14
Laud, William, 36, 76, 79n, 90, 126, 139, 140
Launceston, Somerset, 193
Lawrence, George, 65
Leamington, Warwickshire, 112
leet, courts of, 61
Leicester, Earl of, 170, 171
Leicestershire, 109, 124
Leigh, Surrey, 110
Leighton, Alexander, 41, 48, 63
  on national covenant, 43
  Sions Plea (1629), 43, 44
  Speculum Belli Sacri (1624), 42
Leintwardine, Herefordshire, 109
Lenthall, William, Speaker of House of Commons, 108
Letter to a Noble Lord, A (1643), 69
Leuchers, Fife, 66
Levellers, the, 5, 129, 153, ch. 6 passim, 182, 218
  Agreements of the People, 5, 133, 134, 142–9, 152
Lever, Thomas, 112
Leveson, Sir Robert, 181

Lewes, Richard, 114
Ley, John, 51, 64
liberty of conscience, *see* toleration
Lichfield, Staffordshire, 203
Lilburne, John, 134, 143, 154–5
   Innocency and Truth Justified (1645),
     154
   Rash Oaths Unwarrantable (1647),
     154–5
Lincoln, 92, 188, 206
Lincolnshire, 110, 112, 114, 125, 188
Lindley, Keith, 65
Lindsay, Earl of, 189
Lindsey, A. D., 142, 144
Linlithgow, Scotland, 181
L'Isle, Viscount, 170
literacy, 83
Liverpool, 212
'Liverpool Blues', 211
Logical Demonstration, A (1650), 165
London, 52, 56, 87, 111, 116, 125, 134,
    140, 150, 157–9, 176, 193, 205,
    212
   common council, 157, 182
   militia committee, 158
   subscription to Protestation in, 109,
     110
   subscription to Solemn League and
     Covenant in, 123, 127
   subscription to Vow and Covenant
     in, 116, 118
Long Sutton, in Hampshire, 108
Lord High Constable, 77–8
Lords, House of
   debate on association to William III,
     201–2
   debate on the Protestation, 53
   debate on the Vow and Covenant, 56
   subscription to the Vow and
     Covenant, 57
Lords of the Congregation, 13
Lord's Supper, 83, 87, 183
Loughbrickland, County Down, 218
Louis XIII, 70
Louis XIV, 203, 208
Love, Christopher, 170–1
Love, Richard, 172

Lowe, Ben, 40
Lowe, Roger, 88
Lowe, William, 174
Luccombe, Somerset, 114
Luther, 94, 99

McGiffert, Michael, 2, 6, 66
   on the idea of a national covenant, 30
   on the idea of an 'Israelite paradigm',
    33
McLynn, F. J., 211
Major, or Mair, John, 10
malignants or malignancy, 97, 111, 114,
   222
Malmesbury, Wiltshire, 203, 204
Manchester, Edward Montagu, earl of,
    55, 56, 116
   visitation of University of Cambridge,
    171
Manchester, Lancashire, 169
Mansfield, 211
Manton, Thomas, 192
Marshall, Stephen, 44, 98, 170
Marten, Henry, 159
Martindale, Adam, 173, 176, 177
Marvell, Andrew, 193
Mary I, 5, 6, 7, 48, 70
Mary II, 202
Mary, Queen of Scots, 15, 21, 23, 24
Mason, Henry, 104, 105
Massachusetts, 30, 92
Massachusetts, Bay Company, 90, 92
Massey, Col. Hugh, 171
Maynard, Sir John, 192
Melcomb Bingham, Dorset, 64
Melville, Andrew, 46
mental reservation, 26, 102, 103–7
Meres, Sir Thomas, 188
Meroz, curse of, 37 and n, 40
Mervyn, Colonel Audley, 122
Middlesex, 115, 205
Middleton, 169
militia, 211
Millenary Petition (1603), 106
Miller, Perry, 1, 6, 31, 66, 133
   on the idea of a national covenant,
    29–30

Milward, Robert, 181
mixed-government or
    mixed-constitution, 59, 74, 75,
    78, 100, 156
Mocket, Thomas, 74, 86, 87, 90, 94, 99
monarchical republic, 15
monarchomachi, 75
Monck, General George, 179
Montagu, William, 53
Montgomery, Sir James, 122, 123
Montserrat, 204
Morley, George, bishop of Winchester,
    189
Morrice, Roger, 197
Morrill, John, 77, 147
Morrissey, Mary, 33, 40
Morton, A. L., 134, 143
Morton, Thomas, bishop of Durham,
    103, 105
    Exact Discoverie of Romish Doctrine
    (1605), 105
Mullan, David, 44–5
Mundon Magna, Herefordshire, 205
Musselburgh, Declaration of (1650),
    149

national covenant, concept of, 1, 7
    baptism as equivalent of entrance into
        a national covenant, 17, 32, 36,
        83, 84, 87, 88, 183
    and idea of covenant between
        England and Scotland, 45, 57–8,
        93, 94
    and idea of covenanted union of
        Protestant states, 37
    importance of renewing, 87–8
    incorporation of confession of faith
        into, 57, 90
    as inspiring national reformation, 83,
        88
    as inspiring personal reformation, 83,
        88
    and the Long Parliament, pt 1
        passim
        as commitments to war effort
            against king, 98
    Protestation, Vow and Covenant and

Solemn League and Covenant as
    embodying, 52, 59, 83
role of human agency in making, 86
as a sign that the world was in its last
    days, 98
use of visual signs in taking, 84, 85,
    89–91
nationalism, 4, 215
*Necessity of Altering the Present Oath of
    Allegiance* (1696), 207
Nedham, Marchamount, 167
Negative Confession (1581), 45, 84, 87
Neile, Richard, archbishop of York, 139
New England, 31, 83, 84–5, 90, 92, 100,
    101, 136, 142, 153
New Model Army, 134, 143, 146,
    148–9, 154, 157, 158
New Quaeres of Conscience (1643), 119
Newcastle, 126, 198, 204, 209
Newcastle, Duke of, 210
Newcome, Henry, 193
Newton, Isaac, 169
Nineteen Propositions, The (1642), 77
non-jurors, 207
Norfolk, 116, 117, 123, 127, 203, 205,
    206
Norfolk, Duke of, 15
Norman Conquest, 17
'Norman Yoke', 149, 152
North America, 217
Northamptonshire, 202
Northern Ireland, 217–18
Northern Subscribers Plea, The (1650),
    176
Norwich, 203, 206, 207
Nottingham, 211
Nye, Phillip, 85, 87, 92, 98, 135, 138

Oates, William, 113
oaths, 1, 17–22, 62, 102, 163, 166, 174,
    190
    see also Protestation; Vow and
        Covenant; Solemn League and
        Covenant; Engagement of loyalty
        to the Commonwealth (1649)
    of abjuration (1656), 177
    of abjuration (1690 and 1693), 201

act against customary oaths (1653),
177
of allegiance (1606), 26, 27, 47, 68,
69, 70, 72, 74, 121, 155, 162,
164, 165, 166, 177, 189
of allegiance to William and Mary
(1689), 200–1, 207
assertory oaths, 155
of association, 1, 3, 6, 17, 22–3, 25–7,
53–6, 116, 179, 194–8, epilogue
passim
association in defence of Elizabeth I,
21, 23, 27, 61, 87, 196, 201, 208,
215
association in defence of William III,
200, 201–9, 215
'Canterbury version' of, 206
'York version' of, 206
subscription to, 201–7
baronial oath of fealty, 54
compurgation, 19
coronation, 19, 54, 75–80, 82
distinguished from covenants, 84
etcetera oath, 47, 64, 107, 141
Herod's, 120
Lord Protector's, 177
of loyalty, 2, 102, 109, 115, 118,
126, 166, 177, 193–4, 200, 207,
219
'Median and Persian', 64
negative oath, 59, 125, 155
'no alteration' oaths, 179, 188–94,
199
of office, 19
Oxford Oath (1665), 189–93
penalties for breaking, 99
primary intention of, 166
promissory, 155, 167
public subscription to, 3–5
removal of, 146, 147–8
sacred oath and covenant (1643), 57,
70
and Scottish National Covenant, 46
as shibboleths, 24
of succession (1534), 20
of supremacy (1543), 20
of supremacy (1559), 20, 25, 64, 68,

69, 70, 74, 121, 155, 162, 166,
189
tacit conditions to, 166–8, 178
Tudors and Stuarts' reliance on, 61
*Observations upon the Late Instructions
for the Taking [of] the Vow
and Covenant* (1643), 69,
115

Ockford Fitzpaine, Dorset, 112
Olliver, Robert, 169
Ollyver, William, 193
Ormonde, James Butler, earl of, 122,
126
Osbourne, Sir Thomas, earl of Danby,
189, 193
Overton, Richard, 143, 148, 156
The Arraignment of Mr Persecution
(1645), 145
Oxford Covenant (1643), 95
Oxford, University of, 71, 114
Christ Church, 172
Convocation, 172
Magdalen College, 111
Queen's College, 64
Reasons against the Covenant (1647),
121
response of heads of houses to
Protestation (1641), 63, 111
St John's College, 113
St Mary's Church, 172
tendering of the Engagement (1649),
171–3
Oxfordshire, 113, 203, 212

Pack of Old Puritans, A (1650), 164
Paget, Thomas, 166
Pagitt, Ephraim, 134
Palmer, Herbert, 67, 97, 98
papacy, 94
papists, 94, 96, 105, 196
Parker, Henry, 62, 64, 77, 126, 165
Parliament, 5
Cavalier Parliament, 100, 108, 125,
178–94, 220
'Church Party', 187, 190
Oxford session, 189–90
Convention Parliament, 179

Long Parliament, the, 5, 6
  alliance with Scottish covenanters
    secured, 58
  arbitrary power of, 69
  'Peace Party' within, 157
  political programme of tied to
    Solemn League, 93
  restored in 1660, 179
  supremacy of, 74
  'War Party' within, 55
  power to regulate the conscience,
    136
  Rump Parliament, 100, 153, 160, 173,
    176, 177, 178
    drafting of Engagement of loyalty,
      161
    spokesmen for on the Engagement,
      165–9, 173
Parliamentarian, 55, 56, 96
Parliamentary sovereignty, 74
Parsons, or Persons, Robert, 104
passive obedience, 161, 169
Paulet, John, marquis of Winchester,
  53
Peard, George, 52, 86
Pearl, Valerie, 157
Pelling, Edward, 194
Pelling, Thomas, 124–5, 128
Pembroke, earl of, 56
penal legislation, 105
Penn, William, 154, 205
Pennington, Isaac, 158
Percy, Algernon, earl of
  Northumberland, 56
perjury, 17, 99, 115, 118, 155, 159, 162,
  163, 165
Perkins, William, 84, 106
petitioning, 44, 221
Philip II of Spain, 7
Phippes, John, 113
Pike, Martin, 169
Pilgrimage of Grace (1536), 20
Pilkington, 40
Pinkney, Mr, vicar of Fugglestone,
  Wiltshire, 170
Pittman, William, 112
Plain English (1643), 55

Plain-meaning Protestant, The (1644),
  120–1, 128
Pococke, Edward, 172
Pococke, Mathew, 113
political nation, the, 3, 221–2
Ponet, John, 7
  A Short Treatise of Politike Power
    (1556), 7, 78
Pope, Mary, 160, 164
popery, 52, 140, 142, 209, 213, 215
  extirpation of ordered by the Solemn
    League and Covenant, 58, 119,
    121, 128, 135–6, 138
  popish councillors, 54
  popish innovations in the church,
    111, 140
  popish plot referred to in the
    Protestation, 95
  Popish Plot, the (1678), 213
Portsmouth, 214
prayers, special, 37–8
predestination, 29
prelacy, 43, 52, 90, 92, 121, 138, 142,
  184
Presbyterians, 64, 70, 71, 73, 94, 100,
  118, 133, 136, 138, 145, 155,
  178, 189, 218
  American, 217
  Canadian, 217
  Elizabethan, 3, 30, 31
  English, 138
  English, opposition to trial of Charles
    I, 81, 159–60, 180
  English, refusal to take the
    Engagement 1650, 84, 162–5,
    170–6
  Irish, 182
  lay Presbyterians in civil war London,
    124, 157–9
  London ministers, 158
  Northern Irish, 217
  in Parliament, 57
  Presbyterian Plot (1651), 170–1
  Scottish, 45, 46, 92, 135, 217
Preston, John, puritan minister, 35, 37
Preston, John, Somerset JP, 169
Preston, Lancashire, 169

Preston St Mary's, Suffolk, 122
Pride's Purge, 160
Prideaux, Humphrey, 206–7
Prittlewell, Essex, 118
Protectorate, the Cromwellian,
    177–8
Protestant associations, 5 (*see also* oaths,
    of association), 209–16
Protestation (1641), 2, 27, 58, 67, 68,
    69, 70, 79, 80, 82, 83, 85, 86, 88,
    89, 93, 94, 95, 98, 100, 102, 107,
    115, 116, 122, 123, 128, 129,
    141, 166, 183, 185, 222
  see also equivocation; iconoclasm;
    national covenant; Royalists
  compared to the 1584 association, 52,
    61, 87, 95
  compared to the Solemn League and
    Covenant, 72
  failure to make confession of national
    sins, 88
  implications for political allegiance,
    63–8
  passage through Parliament, 51–3
  as a shibboleth, 52–3
  subscription to, 53, 63, 107, 108–15
  taken by women, 110, 219
  worn as an emblem, 90, 91
providence, 14, 86, 99, 164, 165, 167,
    170–1, 176, 202, 208
  see also divine punishment
Providence Plantation, 143
Prynne, William, 44, 62, 77, 78, 134,
    140, 155, 162–3, 216
  The Soveraigne Power of Parliaments
    (1643), 74, 79, 81, 184, 219
public sphere, 220–1
puritanism, revolutionary, 63
Putney debates, 147
Pym, John, 27, 52, 54, 55, 56, 87, 96,
    204, 222
Pyne, John, 179

Quakers, 153–4, 155, 212
  and 1696 Association, 205–6
*Queries of Some Tender Conscienced
    Christians* (1642), 64

Questier, Michael, 26, 221

Radnor, Wales, 202
recusants, recusancy, 23, 109
'reformadoes', 158
Reformation, 111, 138
  'according to the word of God', 58,
    71, 90, 92, 135, 136, 151
  in the commonwealth, 90–3
  Edwardian, 8, 10, 48
  Elizabethan, 17
  English, as representing the nation's
    entrance into covenant with
    God, 80
  national, 59, 83, 86, 92
  personal, 59, 83, 86, 97
  root and branch, 141
  universal, 180
Reformation of Religion by Josiah, The
    (1590), 34
regicide, 100, 216
Renewal of the Covenants, The (1743,
    1748), 217
repentance, 88
reprobate, 31, 40
resistance theory
  Elizabethan, 12
  of the Genevan exiles, 7–12
  Lutheran, 9
  Parliamentarian, ch. 3 *passim*, 184–5,
    199, 218–19
    parallels with Scottish covenanter
      thought, 70
  private law theory, 59, 62, 67, 74
Restoration, the, 5, 108, 133, ch. 8
    passim, 208
Revolution, Glorious, 216–17
Reynolds, Edward, 172, 184
  *Humble proposals of Sundry Learned
    and Pious Divines* (1649), 173,
    176
Rhye, John, 182
Rich, Robert, earl of Warwick, 174
Richard II, 77
Ridolfi plot (1572), 15
Rivers, Earl, 53
Roades, John, 203

Robinson, John, 73
Robinson, Luke, 169
Robinson, Ralph, 171
Robinson, Thomas, 65
Rochellais, 70
Rochester, Kent, 206
Rocke, Richard, 114, 115
Rocket, John, 165
Rodbrugh, Mr, member of Westminster
	Assembly, 123
Rogers, Daniel, 38
Rogers, Nehemiah, 35
Rogers, Wroth, 171
Rollock, Robert, 44, 45, 46, 84
'rough wooing, The', 14
Royal Assent, 76–7
Royalists, 54, 55, 59, 63, 71, 81, 89, 96,
	97, 102, 112, 114, 115, 141, 155,
	159, 165, 169, 218
	advice on lawful swearing, 107,
		115–16
	response to the Protestation, 64, 68,
		109
	response to Solemn League and
		Covenant, 71–3, 108, 119–21,
		125–7
	response to the Vow and Covenant,
		69, 115–16
Rubini, Dennis, 201, 203
Russell, Conrad, 66, 86
Rutherford, Samuel, 66, 75
	Lex Rex (1644), 75
Rutland, 109
Rye, Sussex, 169
Ryves, Bruno, 125

Sa, Emmanuel, 105
Sabine, George, 149
sacrilege, 100
St Andrews Undershaft, London, 123
St Catherine Cree, London, 110
St Clement Eastcheap, London, 123
St David's, diocese, 206
St George's Hill, Surrey, 149
St Margaret's, Westminster, 138
St Martin's Fields, London, 125
St Mary's, Suffolk, 209

St Matthew's, Friday Street, London,
	140
St Olave Jewry, London, 123, 150
St Paul's Cross sermons, 32, 33
St Stephen, Walbrook, London, 159
St Stephens, Coleman Street, parish of,
	London, 118, 127
St Thomas Apostle, parish of, London,
	111
Salford, Lancashire, 169
Saltmarsh, John, 92, 93, 133, 135–6,
	138
	and the national covenant, 141–2
	Smoke in the Temple (1646), 142,
		145–6, 156
Sampson, Thomas, 12
Sancroft, William, 127, 128, 172
sanctification, 84
Sanderson, John, 166
Sanderson, Robert, 18, 19, 71, 73, 106,
	120
	De Juramento (1655), 167–8
Sandys, Edwin, 7, 40
saving remnant, idea of, 8, 32, 35, 38,
	40
Saye and Sele, Lord, 47, 56, 86
Scarborough, Yorkshire, 68
schism, 136, 138
Scotland, 53, 66, 83, 84, 86, 123, 149,
	181, 182, 210, 211, 217
Scott, Jonathan, 137
Scott, Sir Thomas, MP (1535–94), 24
Scott, Thomas, minister (1580–1626),
	37
Scottish national covenant (1638), 2,
	44–9, 66, 67, 69, 73, 74, 82, 83,
	84, 87
	Scottish covenanters on political
		allegiance, 66, 82
	viewed as a model for an English
		covenant, 55, 95, 146, 148–9
Scudamore, John, Viscount, 125–6
Seaman, Lazarus, 190
Seaver, Paul, 88
sectary, 72
separatists, 133, 134, 135, 157
	refuse Protestation, 113

sermon gadding, 151
Sexby, Edward, 147
Seymour, Jane, 20
Seymour, Sir Edward, 197, 201
Shaftesbury, Anthony Ashley Cooper,
    earl of, 194, 196
Shakespeare, Joy, 8
Shawe, John, 74, 98
Sheldon, Gilbert, archbishop of
    Canterbury, 184, 189, 190
Ship Money, 93
Short Confession (1580), 45
Short Surveigh of the Grand Case of the
    Present Ministry (1663), 184–5
Shropshire, 203, 206, 212
Sion College, 51, 157
Skinner, Quentin, 161
Smith, Mr, of Cuckfield, 122
Smith, Nigel, 149
Smith, Thomas, 16
Solemn Engagement of the Army
    (1647), 144, 145, 147, 148
Solemn Engagement of the City (1647),
    158
Solemn League and Covenant (1643),
    2, 5, 14, 27, 29, 51, 79, 80, 81,
    82, 83, 84, 85, 86, 88, 89, 98,
    100, 101, 102, 108, 118, 129, pt
    II passim, 200, 215, 217, 218
and allegiance to the king, 58, 70–4
attempt to renew 1662, 182
benefits of union of England and
    Scotland, 93, 94
burning of ordered by the Cavalier
    Parliament, 181
centrality to lay Presbyterians in
    London, 124, 157–9
as committing subscribers to a
    Presbyterian church settlement,
    126, ch. 6 passim, 157–9
confession of national sins, 88
declarations against in Corporation
    and Uniformity Acts, 179, 180,
    199
declared annulled as regards Scotland
    (1649), 160
differentiated from an oath, 126–7
as an emblem of sedition, 194
as embodying basic Christian duties,
    101, 120, 122, 183–4
engraved editions of, 90
as a garrison oath, 128
inspiring national reformation, 90–3
mass-petitioning in support of, 158
part of the compounding process, 71,
    119, 125
passage through Parliament, 57–60
as a perpetual obligation, 183
preparations before subscribing to, 89
referred to as an association, 58, 87
sacramental aspects, 122
sermonising and, 121–3
as a shibboleth, 96
subscription to, 119–28
taken by New Model Army officers,
    154
unify Europe against Catholic threat,
    95
an unlawful oath, 71, 119, 180
used to discover malignants, 97
see also equivocation; national
    covenant; Royalists
Somerset, 113, 114, 125, 169, 170,
    175–6, 193, 212
Souldiers Catechisme, The (1644), 97
Southwell, Robert, 103
Spanish Match, 43
Speck, W. A., 197
Spurr, John, 2
Stafford, 206
Staffordshire, 203, 206
Star Chamber, 43
Statute of Provisors of Benefices, Ed. III,
    75–6
Staunton, Edmund, 150
Steele, Margaret, 44, 46, 84
Stoke Tything, Dorset, 114
Strafford, Thomas Wentworth, earl of,
    51
Strangeways, Giles, 125, 188
Strangeways, Sir John, 125
Stuart, Charles Edward, 214
succession, royal, 3, 5, 16, 22, 179,
    194–6

Suffolk, 65, 70, 99, 113, 116, 117, 122, 123, 209
  oath of association tendered there, 55
  oath of association (1696) tendered there, 203, 205
  subscription to Solemn League and Covenant, 127
Sugden, Robert, 113
Suger, Zachary, 213, 214
superstition, 94
Surrey, 110, 149, 212
  subscription to Solemn League and Covenant, 150
Sussex, 116, 123, 169, 204
swearing, 88
  rules for lawful swearing, 102–6
  use of limitations in, 102
  see also oaths

Taylor, Thomas, 169
Test Acts, 196
Theydon Mount, Essex, 124
Thirty Years War (1618–48), 6, 36
Thompson, Hugh, 96
Throckmorton, Robert, 205
Throckmorton plot, 21
Tickell, John, 189–90, 191
toleration, 43, 134, 186
  liberty of conscience, 58, 133, ch. 6 *passim*
Tolmie, Murray, 143
Tomkins, Thomas, 184, 185
Tories, 179, 193, 194, 196, 197, 200, 201, 202, 207, 212
Touchet, James, earl of Castlehaven, 53
Townshend, Sir Henry, 181, 182
treason, 79, 141, 171
Tresham, Francis, 103
Trinity House, 204
Trowbridge, Wiltshire, 124
Twigg, John, 111, 172
Two Associations, The (1682), 194
Tyndale, William, 31
tyranny, 72, 80
  revolutionary, 124

Ulster, 210
  Scots, 217
  Solemn League and Covenant tendered in, 121–2, 123
Un-deceiver, The (1643), 86
Ursinius, Zacharius, 28
Ussher, James, archbishop of Armagh, 184
usurpation, 163, 165, 173
Uxbridge, 59

Vane, Sir Henry, 58, 92, 135, 182
Vaughn, Col. Joseph, 171
Vegetius, 42
Venetian secretary, 55, 56, 117, 118, 177
Vermuyden, Cornelius, 110
Verney, Sir Ralph, 126
Vernon, Eliot, 124, 159
Vicars, John, 99, 135, 155, 159
  A Caveat for Covenant-contemners and Covenant-breakers (1648), 159
  Dagon Demolished (1660), 163
Vindicae Contra Tyrannos (1579), 9, 62, 70, 79, 82
Vines, Richard, 96, 173, 174
Vladislaus, King, covenant with Amurath, 155, 159
Vow and Covenant (1643), 2, 27, 51, 58, 59, 67, 79, 80, 81, 82, 83, 85, 88, 89, 93, 96, 98, 100, 102, 107, 108, 126, 128, 129
  confession of national sins, 88
  as covenant of grace, 86
  implications for political allegiance, 69–70
  passage through Parliament, 56–7
  referred to as an association, 87
  seen as in conflict with earlier oaths, 118, 129
  subscription to, 115–19
  see also equivocation; national covenant; Royalists

Wakefield, Yorkshire, 210
Wales, 109, 202, 206
Walker, John, 116, 124, 128, 170

Walker, William, 116
Wallace, John, 176
Wallington, Nehemiah, 88, 89, 90, 99
Walsham, Alexandra, 4, 32, 33
Walsingham, Sir Francis, 21, 196
Walter, John, 65, 140
Walton, Isaak, 150
Walwyn, William, 135, 136, 143, 145,
    148, 156
Walzer, Michael, 1, 63
wapentake, 109
Ward, Richard, 73
Ward, Seth, bishop of Exeter, 190
Warmstry, Thomas, 51
Warrington, Lancashire, 176
Warwick, Sir Philip, 188
Warwick, William, 127
Warwickshire, 112
Watson, Thomas, 159, 171
Watts, Richard, 123
weavers, 203
Webb, John, 127–9
Webster, Tom, 47, 106, 138
Weir, David, 28
Wells, John, 118, 127, 128
Wells, V. T., 45, 48
West Heslerton, Yorkshire, 141
Westminster Assembly, 59, 90, 95,
    123, 157
Westminster Confession of Faith,
    28
Whigs, 5, 193, 194, 200, 201, 203,
    207, 212, 216
  radical, 5
Whitby, Daniel, 124
Whitchurch, Buckinghamshire, 110,
    113
White, John, 'Patriarch of Dorchester',
    38, 90, 96
Whitechurch, near Southampton, 205
Whitehall debates (1649), 148
Whitgift's three articles, 106
Whittingham, William, 12
Wickins, William, 182
Wigan, Lancashire, 23, 169
Wight, Isle of, 202
Wigmore, Herefordshire, 109

Wildman, John, 147
Wilkins, John, 172
Wilkinson, William, 204
William I of Orange, 21
William III, 197, 198, 200, 202, 203,
    206, 208, 215
  as Prince of Orange, 197
Williams, Griffith, bishop of Ossory, 65
Williamson, Arthur, 45, 46, 80
Wilson, J. H., 99
Wilton, Somerset, 113
Wiltshire, 115, 124, 170, 203
Wingfield, John, 117
Wingham, Kent, 113
Winington, Lancashire, 205
Winson, Suffolk, 116
Winstanley, Gerrard, 5, 134, 156, 218,
    219–20
  An Appeal to the House of Commons
    (1649), 151
  A Declaration from the Poor
    Oppressed People of England
    (1649), 151
  on the Engagement of loyalty to the
    Commonwealth, 152
  and idea of a national covenant,
    149–53
  The Law of Freedom in a Platform
    (1652), 5, 152–3
  The True Levellers Standard (1649),
    151
  Truth Lifting up its Head (1649), 153
  A Watchword to the City of London
    and the Army (1649), 150
Withalls, William, 113
Wolfe, D. M., 143
Wood, Andy, 221
Woodchurch, Cheshire, 108
Woodhouse, A. S. P., 142, 143, 144
Woodward, Hezekiah, 87–8, 89, 93, 96,
    97, 98
  The King's Chronicle (1643), 97
Woolrych, Austin, 144
Wootton, David, 79, 218
Worcester, 206
Worcestershire, 112, 174, 206
Worden, Blair, 170, 216

Worth, Alexander, 114
Wray, Sir John, 86
Wyatt's Rebellion (1554), 7, 10
Wyvill, Charles, 215–16, 222

Yardburgh, John, 114

Yarlington, Somerset, 125
York, 206, 210
Yorkshire, 109, 113, 129, 141, 169, 193, 203, 206, 210, 216

Zaret, David, 1, 221